THE COLLISION OF POLITICAL
AND LEGAL TIME

THE COLLISION OF POLITICAL AND LEGAL TIME

Foreign Affairs and the Supreme Court's Transformation of Executive Authority

Kimberley L. Fletcher

TEMPLE UNIVERSITY PRESS
Philadelphia • *Rome* • *Tokyo*

TEMPLE UNIVERSITY PRESS
Philadelphia, Pennsylvania 19122
www.temple.edu/tempress

Copyright © 2018 by Temple University—Of The Commonwealth System
    of Higher Education
All rights reserved
Published 2018

Library of Congress Cataloging-in-Publication Data

Names: Fletcher, Kimberley Liané, author.
Title: The collision of political and legal time : foreign affairs and the
    Supreme Court's transformation of executive authority / Kimberley L.
    Fletcher.
Description: Philadelphia, Pennsylvania : Temple University Press, 2018. |
    Includes bibliographical references and index.
Identifiers: LCCN 2017051560 (print) | LCCN 2017052131 (ebook)
    | ISBN 9781439914939 (E-book) | ISBN 9781439914915 (hardback)
    | ISBN 9781439914922 (paper)
Subjects: LCSH: Political questions and judicial power—United
    States—History. | United States. Supreme Court—History. | Executive
    power—United States—History. | Presidents—United States—Decision
    making—History. | United States—Foreign relations—Decision
    making—History. | BISAC: POLITICAL SCIENCE / Government / Executive
    Branch. | POLITICAL SCIENCE / International Relations / General. | LAW /
    Constitutional.
Classification: LCC KF8742 (ebook) | LCC KF8742 .F59 2018 (print) | DDC
    342.73/0412—dc23
LC record available at https://lccn.loc.gov/2017051560

For my family

For your unwavering support, your strength,

and your love

and for reminding me to always

dream the impossible

CONTENTS

ACKNOWLEDGMENTS

This book, which began as my doctoral dissertation, has evolved far beyond the original version. I am indebted to many people for their help in moving me past that first effort. I am particularly grateful to the reviewers commissioned by Temple University Press. They uncovered areas that needed more extensive analysis and offered valuable suggestions on how to go about it. Their judicious, detailed, in-depth reviews of the manuscript have made the final product much stronger than it would have been without them.

The product of not only my interest in the areas of foreign policy making, American political development, judicial decision making, and executive politics, which dates back to my undergraduate studies, this book also owes its existence to many people who helped shape the project as it developed. Portions of Chapter 1 were originally published as Kimberley Fletcher, "Truman's Rhetoric Entrenches Unilateral Authority and Fashions a Trend for Future Executive Use," *Presidential Studies Quarterly* 47, no. 4 (December 2017): 720–751.

This book is a tribute to those from whom I have learned so much along the way. It gives me the greatest pleasure to acknowledge the intellectual stimulation that Julie Novkov has generously provided over the years. She has become a good friend, and I have gained much from her insights, her intellectual curiosity, and her attention to detail. I cannot thank her enough for her unmatched support as a mentor. Novkov sharpened and deepened my curiosity about and understanding of the constitutional relationships between the Court and the president.

I am also extraordinarily lucky to have been mentored by Bruce Miroff. Miroff's input on American politics and the American presidency, which added to the depth of my analysis, has always been incisive and thought provoking. Over the years, I have come to rely on his invaluable comments and questions on various projects as I redrafted my own analyses. I am also fortunate to have had many opportunities to learn from the intellectual integrity and devotion to excellence of Susan Burgess and Mark Graber. I greatly appreciate their continued support and belief in my endeavors.

In addition, I am indebted to the members of the Political Science Department at San Diego State University, who have provided a warm and collegial intellectual environment in which to research, write, and teach. I owe special thanks to Latha Varadarajan and Ronnee Schreiber, whose friendship, encouragement, and mentorship throughout the research and writing process have given me strength when I needed it most. I could not have completed this book without the 2016 research support provided by the San Diego State University Grants Program.

I am delighted to have the opportunity to publish with Temple University Press. At each stage of production, the staff demonstrated a remarkable level of professionalism and competence. Words cannot express my gratitude to my editor, Aaron M. Javsicas, for his enthusiasm and for his faith in this project. Special thanks go to the design team at Temple University Press for creating the awesome front cover. I also appreciate the careful copyediting of Heather Wilcox and Joan S. P. Vidal, as well as Susan Thomas's excellent indexing.

This book would not have come to fruition without the unwavering support and encouragement of my parents, Stephen and Audrey Fletcher; my sisters and brother-in-law, Philippa Fletcher and Shannon and Eric Liedtke; and my nephews and niece, Jaread and Joschua Fletcher and Isaac, Amirah, and Grayson Liedtke. They have stood by me, expanded my horizons, and reminded me to stay young and laugh often. To them I owe my deepest thanks.

I dedicate this book in memory of three people I have lost along the way—my grandmothers, Magdalen Grindley and Jane Williamson McVean, and my grandfather George H. Fletcher.

THE COLLISION OF POLITICAL
AND LEGAL TIME

1

THE COURT'S CONSTITUTIVE ROLE

Shifting the Balance of Power

In 2011, President Barack Obama was met with acute disapproval from both sides of the political aisle when he sidestepped the congressional deliberative process and commanded military action against Libya without first procuring authorization. Obama insisted that the Constitution conferred on him, and him alone, the widest latitude—unbounded power—to manage the nation's foreign affairs. President Bill Clinton repeatedly claimed this power to bomb other nations unilaterally. And President George W. Bush maintained that his actions were unreviewable during the war on terror. When Congress attempts to force the president to cooperate with the legislative branch—citing the War Powers Resolution of 1973 and the Intelligence Oversight Act of 1980—the White House works hard to break the legal shackles that statutorily inhibit presidential war making. In fact, by the end of the Clinton administration, it was not clear what war powers if any, remained with Congress. And Donald Trump will walk in the same long shadow cast by past presidents who have claimed executive prerogatives, which are no longer emergency measures—these are now constitutionally and legally recognized presidential powers.[1]

The conventional view attributes this assertion of power to an aggrandizement of authority by the president, the acquiescence of Congress, and the state's capacity to act under exigent circumstances. Moreover, scholars[2] note that the Supreme Court has simply sanctioned this accumulation of power[3] and regard it as passive and constrained.[4] The courts are thus the least visible in international affairs.[5]

Whether Congress is outmaneuvered, bullied, or ignoring the assertion from a long line of executives claiming presidential prerogatives in foreign policy making, this unitary role has become commonplace.[6] What changed? Is it merely congressional acquiescence? Have executives simply marshaled power to such a degree as to claim they are beyond reproach? Is there any formal reasoning for contemporary executives to regard foreign policy as a presidential haven? And what role does the U.S. Supreme Court play in the transfer of power?

In principle, the Constitution establishes three distinct branches: the legislative, the executive, and the judicial. Each branch recognizes the metes and bounds of its powers and has the authority to check the actions of either of the other two. In practice, however, the limits of each branch's powers are vague or ambiguous, and the methods of exercising and checking authority have proven, at times, to be difficult to determine. This uncertainty is especially true in the management of foreign policy.

Pro-congressionalists argue that the Framers designed a Constitution that assigns to Congress the dominant role in the conduct of foreign policy. The Framers, pro-congressionalists assert, emphasized the long-term dangers to the Republic of concentrating foreign affairs in the hands of the executive, as doing so would leave the nation vulnerable to policy dictated by the impulses of one man. Instead, "to deter the abuse of power,"[7] they created a system that would foster discussions and debate to shape foreign policy and thus prevent exploitation. To support their position, pro-congressionalists cite the Supreme Court's early rulings favoring a strong legislative branch and regarding the president's involvement in the development of policy as secondary to Congress's.

In contrast, pro-presidentialists argue that the executive branch should be granted wide latitude in the management of foreign affairs and that in times of national crisis, the president should have the discretion to restrict individual rights. The executive branch is better suited, pro-presidentialists maintain, to meet the demands of a robust national agenda in international affairs. They also believe that the courts should be willing to endorse repressive governmental action that subordinates rights and liberties when the nation is threatened, arguing that such actions are within the president's "plenary and exclusive power."[8] In fact, pro-presidentialists maintain that the Supreme Court has enthusiastically sanctioned these claims. As Norman Dorsen maintains, "[N]ational security has been a graveyard for civil liberties for much of our recent history."[9]

Contemporary advocates[10] of unilateral executive power argue that presidential war making has occurred since the nation's founding.[11] John Yoo, for example, asserts that the bold decisions made by George Washington, Thomas Jefferson, Andrew Jackson, and Abraham Lincoln clearly demonstrate vigorous exercises of presidential power. These presidents, according to Yoo, acted broadly precisely because the Framers deliberately left the Constitution vague regarding the limits of executive power.[12] Presidents thus owe their "privileged position in foreign affairs . . . to the Constitution and to our first President[, Washington, for] establish[ing] . . . that the executive branch would assume the leading role in developing and carrying out foreign policy."[13]

But Yoo's observations are misplaced[14] and serve only to bolster the legal arguments put forth by contemporary executives who wish to support their positions of taking offensive measures during wartime, which they have also extended to national emergencies. The historical evidence demonstrates not only that the founding generation created a Constitution that gives Congress sole authority to initiate war but also that early presidents adhered to this principle.[15] Moreover, as pro-congressionalists note, early judicial decisions adhered to the original constitutional blueprint, and the path followed by the Supreme Court did not deviate from the established constitutional order.[16]

The assertions made by both of these schools of thought are valuable, but they overlook the Court's reach in redefining the scope of presidential powers vis-à-vis Congress. The Court's institutional position has expanded the legal capacity for presidents after Franklin D. Roosevelt (FDR) to claim unilateral prerogatives. In fact, the Supreme Court has provided a legal solution to a political problem. Prior to 1936, the Court decided foreign-affairs cases in favor of a strong legislature—a deliberative body that could collectively make a decision. This support in turn undermined presidents' claims to executive unilateralism. Yet the Supreme Court heard and decided a case in 1936 that would forever change the course of constitutional and political development in the conduct of foreign affairs generally and war making specifically. The Court's *Curtiss-Wright* decision reasoned that the executive has plenary powers and that this authority is not contingent on congressional delegation. In fact, Justice George Sutherland asserted that the president is the sole organ of foreign affairs. Absent *Curtiss-Wright*, the imperial president[17] would not have the same kind of leverage when claiming unilateral prerogatives to conduct our nation's foreign affairs. Over time, presidential ascendency is institutionally entrenched, normalized, and thus made routine,[18] and then it continues as the rule of law for future executives.[19] Ultimately, the Supreme Court transformed power, shaped politics, and redirected history.

FEAR OF UNBRIDLED EXECUTIVE POWER

It is well documented[20] that as orthodox republicans, the Framers inherited the well-established fear that the greatest danger to liberty lurked in the unchecked ambitions of the executive. Because of their deeply held fear of unilateral presidential power, the Framers embraced the principle of collective decision making,[21] the belief that the combined wisdom of legislators is superior to that of a single executive. Accordingly, the Framers designed a Constitution that assigns to Congress the dominant role in the conduct of foreign policy and the sole authority to initiate war. This distribution of power is evidenced by the "unambiguous textual language, almost undisputed arguments by Framers and ratifiers, and logical-structural inferences from the doctrine of separation of powers."[22] And the Court's early jurisprudence reasserted the dual nature of collective decision making between the president and Congress in a variety of cases, leaving the path dependency of the executive largely unchanged.

Among the Founders,[23] distrust of the executive was pervasive. A number of Federalist papers allay concerns about an overly robust executive branch, and in *Federalist* No. 75 Alexander Hamilton explains why the Framers rejected unilateral executive control of foreign affairs:

> The history of human conduct does not warrant the exalted opinion of human virtue which would make it wise in a nation to commit interests of so delicate and momentous a kind as those which concern its intercourse with the rest of the world to the sole disposal of a magistrate, created and circumstanced as would be a president of the United States.[24]

Steeped in English history, the Founders knew all too well, as James Madison stated, that "the management of foreign relations appears to be the most susceptible of abuse of all the trusts committed to a Government."[25] Seeking to attain the ideal of republican[26] government, the Framers[27] drafted a Constitution "that allow[s] only Congress to loose the military forces of the United States on the other nations."[28]

The delegates of the Constitutional Convention were committed to collective decision making, and their resolve to institute a system of shared powers in the area of foreign affairs would deliver, in James Wilson's words, "a security to the people."[29] Capturing the precise intent of the War Clause, Wilson stated that it "will not hurry us into war; it is calculated to guard against it. It will not be in the power of a single man, or a single body of men, to involve us in such distress, for the important power of declaring war is vested in the legislature at large."[30] This sentiment echoed the Framers' regard for collective decision making in the legislature, the republican principle that the "conjoined wisdom of many is superior to that of one."[31] This republican tenet had to come, then, at the expense of unilateral executive power.

The Framers' fear of unilateral authority led them to emphasize limitations on the executive rather than expansions. Thus, as Madison explained, they "defined and confined" the president's powers to ensure "that power not granted could not be assumed."[32] This decision was intended to "deter the abuse of power, misguided policies, irrational action, and unaccountable behavior"[33] of any one man. And the two branches, for constitutional as well as practical reasons, were expected to work in concert: once Congress declares or authorizes a war and provides troops, the president is then responsible for waging war and commanding the military.[34] The office, Hamilton asserts in *Federalist* No. 69, "would amount to nothing more than the supreme command and direction of the military and naval forces, as first General and admiral of the Confederacy."[35]

Article I of the Constitution consequently assigns "broad and exclusive powers" to Congress, including the power to regulate foreign commerce and to initiate all hostilities—skirmishes as well as full-blown, total acts of war, including letters of marque and reprisal. And the president, as commander-in-chief, may act in this capacity only "by and under the authority of Congress."[36] As Hamilton explains, the president's authority "would amount to nothing more than the supreme command and direction of the military and naval forces," but this power could be triggered only when war was "authorized or begun."[37] Essentially the title grants no war-making power to the executive.[38]

The Framers' preference for decision making with checks pervades the Constitution. In fact, there is no grant to the president of a unilateral policy-making power to conduct the nation's foreign affairs, nor is there any hint in the Constitutional Convention's records of an interest among the Framers to vest such authority in the executive branch. The Framers' fear of unbridled executive power ultimately led the convention, as Hamilton explains in *Federalist* No. 75, to withhold from the president the authority to conduct American foreign policy.[39]

THE COURT'S FIDELITY IN UNDERMINING PRESIDENTIAL UNILATERALISM

Early judicial decisions did not simply affirm the Framers' design for foreign affairs and war making; rather, they elaborated and explained the intricacies of war making between the two branches. In these early cases (*Bas v. Tingy*, *Talbot v. Seeman*, *Little v. Barreme*, *United States v. Smith*, and the *Prize Cases*),[40] the Court was constrained by the Framers' constitutional design and refrained from diverging from the established path.

Triggering several judicial decisions, the so-called Quasi-War[41] was one of the earliest sets of circumstances to clarify the prerogatives of Congress over war and the subsequent deployment of the nation's military force. The Supreme

Court determined in 1800 (*Bas*) and 1801 (*Talbot*) that Congress could authorize hostilities in two ways: by a formal declaration of war or by statutes that sanctioned an undeclared war. Military conflicts could therefore be "limited," "partial," or "imperfect,"[42] without requiring Congress to make a formal declaration. But, the Court asserted, Congress had the sole and exclusive power to declare either an "imperfect" war, understood as a limited war, or a "perfect" war, understood as a general war. The Court distinguished between the kinds of wars the nation could engage in but left it up to Congress to make the appropriate determinations, leaving the executive on the sidelines. And a year later, in the *Talbot* decision, the Court insisted that the Constitution vests war power in Congress.[43]

One must be cautious when reading either of these two cases, however. They do not suggest that "once Congress authorizes war, the President is at liberty to choose the time, location, and scope of military activities." Rather, "[i]n authorizing war, Congress may place limits on what Presidents may and may not do."[44] The Court took this opportunity to restate Congress's primary role in the authorization of war and to reaffirm the first constitutional order. The Court also addressed the role of the executive when called as commander-in-chief and determined that the president does not have the authority to govern the extent of military activities. These same points were reaffirmed three years later in *Little v. Barreme* (1804).

In *Barreme*, Chief Justice John Marshall concluded that President John Adams had acted illegally, because his orders to seize ships were inconsistent with an act of Congress. The plurality reasoned that when Congress announces policy "in a statute[,] it necessarily prevails over inconsistent presidential orders and military actions. Presidential orders, even those issued as Commander in Chief, are subject to restrictions imposed by Congress."[45] Essentially, the Court asserted that the president does not have "inherent authority" or "inherent powers" that allow him to ignore a law passed by Congress.[46] However, this constitutional foreign-affairs jurisprudence would not be sustained. Chapter 2 discusses how *Curtiss-Wright* repudiated Marshall's opinion by legally sanctioning an executive's claim to inherent powers and how Justice Robert H. Jackson's *Youngstown* concurrence did not exclude this kind of authority completely.

Just as the Supreme Court affirmed the constitutional blueprint outlined by the Framers, the lower courts were also establishing the first constitutional order through judicial decree. *Smith* (1806) was just one of many cases heard by the federal courts dealing with violations of the Neutrality Act of 1794. The courts defined congressional authority and restricted presidential action. Justice William Paterson—who wrote one of the serial opinions in *Bas*—held that the power to initiate hostilities was solely vested in Congress.[47] The Court stated resolutely that "the power of making war . . . is exclusively vested in [C]ongress."[48] Of course, if the United States were invaded, Paterson concluded, the president would have the constitutional authority and obligation to resist with force. There is, however, a "manifest distinction" between responding to a sudden invasion and going to war with a nation at peace. In the second instance, "it is the exclusive province of [C]ongress to change a state of peace into a state of war."[49] The president is not authorized to commence hostilities abroad on the basis of an executive assessment of the security of the nation, as the Court's *Smith* decision determined—this is a congressional prerogative. Moreover, the executive's power of self-defense does not extend to foreign territories.

Sixty years later, the Supreme Court once again addressed a president's exercise of military power "without first obtaining" congressional approval. In April 1861, with Congress in recess, President Lincoln was faced with an extraordinary situation, but his conscious frame was to favor preserving rather than observing the Constitution.[50] Addressing Congress in 1861, Lincoln asserted that the "war power" rested with the executive branch to suppress the rebellion. There was no other option, Lincoln claimed, "but to call out the war power of the Government and so to resist force employed for its destruction by force for its preservation." He did note that it was with the "deepest regret" that he was put in a position to draw on the "war power in defense of the Government forced upon him."[51] But when Lincoln asked for ad hoc legislation, he reminded Congress that the president "ha[d] . . . done what he had deemed his duty," adding, "You will now, according to your own judgment, perform yours."[52]

By invoking the "war power"—a union of executive and legislative powers—Lincoln effectively preserved the Union. Congress supported his resourcefulness, as did the Supreme Court in what are commonly known as the *Prize Cases*.[53] Yet even though the Court sanctioned Lincoln's initiative, Justice Robert C. Grier prudently limited this prerogative to internal defensive actions.[54] Even in these circumstances, the Court was unwilling to diverge from the established path.

Justice Grier's opinion, for a sharply divided Court, held that although the president "does not initiate the war," as that authority is reserved for Congress alone, he is compelled "to accept the challenge."[55] The Court thus justified the blockade imposed on southern ports by Lincoln. However, the president has no discretion, Grier cautioned. He must meet the crisis in the form in which it presents itself, "without waiting for Congress to baptize it with a name; and no name given to it by him or them could change the fact."[56] However, Grier cautiously constrained the executive's power to defensive actions only.[57] During oral arguments, the executive branch actually took this same position. Richard

Henry Dana Jr., who represented the president, acknowledged that Lincoln's actions had nothing to do with "the right *to initiate a war; as a voluntary act of sovereignty.* That is vested only in Congress."[58]

The *Prize Cases* Court legally sanctioned presidents' taking the initiative during emergency situations, against the law or in the absence of it, but with the requirement that they seek retroactive legislation from Congress at the earliest opportunity, as Lincoln had.[59] In this regard, the concrete effect of allowing ex post facto declarations is that executives in the future might feel liberated to act if they believe they can count on Congress to authorize their actions retroactively.

These early judicial decisions illustrate how the Court affirmed the Framers' principles of undermining presidential unilateralism and the constitutional design for the War Clause: Congress alone may "initiate hostilities, whether in the form of general or limited war, and the president, in his capacity as commander-in-chief, is granted only the power to repel sudden attacks against the United States."[60] As is evident, the Court left "little doubt about the limited scope of the President's war power."[61] These early decisions have never been overturned, but the *Curtiss-Wright* Court at a critical juncture significantly altered the trajectory of the executive's role vis-à-vis Congress in the management of foreign policy and war powers.

Without a formal declaration of war or statutory authority,[62] presidents have consistently used force against other nations to protect life and property. They have defended these decisions on the grounds that they have a duty to protect the nation that is inherent in the Constitution.[63] The constitutionality of this defense came before a circuit court in *Durand v. Hollins* (1860),[64] and it upheld the commander's actions, asserting that the duty of necessity "rests in the discretion of the president." When there is a threat of violence to the nation's citizenry or its property that cannot be anticipated, it might "require the most prompt and decided action" by the president to provide protection.[65]

When war has commenced, the reservoir of executive power fills up very quickly, as the legislature may delegate a variety of new responsibilities to the president, but the Supreme Court's fidelity remained with the constitutional order in these early judicial cases. The Court undermined presidential autonomy, favoring instead a strong legislative role. It took a formalistic or originalist approach and was thus not constrained by the political timing or external factors present in each case under review. These cases served two purposes: (1) the Court defined unambiguously Congress's role in war making and formally affirmed the first constitutional order, and (2) when the executive acted contrary to the first constitutional order, the Court served as a check.

Although the constitutional design is laid out in clear terms, the very fears held by the Framers have been realized. We have reached a time in our nation's history when the power of the presidency resembles the power of the British monarchy. This trend represents a sharp departure from early constitutional foreign-affairs jurisprudence and threatens the Republic.

CURRENT LITERATURE

Current studies generally focus on the legislative and executive branches or agencies to explain foreign-policy development.[66] Most credit FDR with ushering in the swift growth of presidential power and an ever-increasing presence in world affairs: the United States moved predominantly from a non-interventionist state[67] before World War I to a world power and global hegemon following it.[68] As the nation continued to become embroiled in armed conflict and to face national emergencies of varying kinds, the development of foreign policy took a more prominent place on the national agenda. While the political arena grappled with settling rising concerns (e.g., which branch is better equipped to effectively respond to emergency situations, war making, and foreign policy making more generally), the Supreme Court had a number of opportunities to address these uncertainties on constitutional grounds. These studies have therefore failed to include the instrumental role of the judiciary in reformulating the division of powers between the two branches in this area and how this allocation has influenced constitutional and political development over time.[69]

The first doctrinal shift acknowledged by legal scholars dates to either Justice Sutherland's decision in *Curtiss-Wright* (1936)[70] or President Harry Truman's assertion of unilateral authority to seize the steel mills in a time of war (1952).[71] The conventional view explaining this shift focuses primarily on either the internal or doctrinal world of the Court. Legal scholars simply note that a shift in power occurred and explicate how this change affected a president's authority to act unilaterally in foreign policy making. These studies generally focus on the role of the executive to claim broad inherent powers and largely regard the Court as passive and constrained.

Legal theorists model the *Curtiss-Wright* decision in the following ways. Attitudinalists[72] contend not only that the Court acts as a policy-making institution but also that each justice votes according to his or her policy preferences. But Justice Sutherland voted contrary to his typical behavior. In addition, without the Court's continued adherence to this new order in subsequent cases, *Curtiss-Wright* might be chalked up simply to one man's whims. Legal realists,[73] on the other hand, maintain that the Court is governed by legal rules and doctrines.[74] But in foreign affairs, the first constitutional order and the Court's fidelity (precedent) established in early judicial rulings did not hem in the Court.[75] Alternatively, the strategic model[76] asserts that when the

Court is trying to make good policy, it weighs the impact of its decisions against the interests of its audience, which was, in part, the case in 1936. The *Curtiss-Wright* Court weighed heavily in favor of the geopolitical impact of an encroaching and impending war over the defendant's claim that the embargo was an unlawful delegation of legislative power. Its evaluation of the geopolitical concerns (starting in 1936) raises questions on how precedent, polity, and individual rights inform judicial decision making.

Scholars bridging American political development (APD) and judicial decision making[77] show how these models and current studies do not accurately account for judicial decision making and how jurisprudence affects the world outside the Court. These approaches—attitudinal, legal, and strategic—overstate external influences over internal, and vice versa. Judicial decision making is not just about the attitudes or strategic behavior of the justices, the law, or political context; it is a more complex amalgamation of all these factors.[78] Simply put, we cannot treat "law as simply 'there' to be discovered by judges."[79] Utilizing the law and APD literature, I reexamine foreign-affairs cases to illustrate how the Supreme Court created a new constitutional order[80] in 1936 and redistributed the balance of power between Congress and the executive. As an agent of change, the Court successfully carved out and sustained a new path for the executive in this area, which better explains the developmental path of the imperial president.

A significant amount of work has been done to trace the Supreme Court's engagement with constitutional and political development,[81] yet the focus of much of this research has largely been on domestic issues,[82] with little discussion of foreign affairs.[83] Scholars evaluating foreign policy making[84] have limited their examination to Cold War civil liberties, which leaves the developmental narrative of foreign affairs only half told. While the political branches of government more overtly govern policy outcomes, the role of the Court is no less important. Countless foreign-policy questions concern constitutional interpretations, primarily regarding which branch is dominant in developing policy. Consequently, justices are presented with a constitutional moment;[85] the Court determines when the timing of a case necessitates or permits a possible redefinition of the existing constitutional order or whether fidelity to the current law should be maintained. As such, the Court constantly offers legal answers to political challenges.

Historical institutionalists assert that "legal doctrines had to be grasped as expressions of broader political ideologies, institutionalized in ways that constrained judges but also empowered them to give specific meaning to more general political outlooks,"[86] and this is true of judicial decision making in international affairs. Because legal doctrines are "expressions of broader political ideologies," when the conditions are ripe (balancing institutional needs while deciding whether to arbitrate politically controversial cases),[87] the Court can alter the developmental narrative of the executive branch.

By employing the theory of historical institutionalism, I show how significant "politics in time" is to understanding the trajectory of development; timing and sequence matter when examining the development of a particular policy area. Institutional politics "comprise multiple orders and patterns of intercurrence that often create unintended consequences, paradoxes[,] and disjunctures."[88] Before the Supreme Court renders a decision on the merits, there is a constitutional moment or space in which it has a number of power plays it can make. If the Court chooses to alter or overturn precedent,[89] it does so with the knowledge that the trajectory of the previously established course or path taken by the actors involved in the dispute might be forever changed; the political debate and actions taken may either have the legal backing to proceed or may progress without the Court's sanctioning.

The Court is institutionally advantaged to challenge the primary commitments of the governing elite, but not all judicial decisions are in direct conflict with the various institutions that constitute the dominant collective body.[90] And at times, collaboration with this ruling coalition can be quite difficult, especially if there is a divided national order. Essentially, the Supreme Court makes constitutional choices and selects between two alternatives. On the one hand, the Court can challenge the primary obligations of the majority coalition and the major political institution of the executive and vote against it in pursuit of its own political agenda;[91] see the Chapter 3 discussion of *Youngstown* for an example.

Alternately, the Court can choose a particular moment in which to partner with an institution—in this instance, the executive branch—and legalize the construction and stabilization of an asserted political order. Understanding when the Court chooses between these two options exposes the existence of a transforming relationship between law and politics. The Court is in a preferred institutional position to carve out its own path and ultimately become a self-governing lawmaker, at times aligning itself against the preferences of others.[92] When the Court hears foreign-affairs cases, certain conditions allow the justices more latitude to act. These conditions, which are not exhaustive, include exogenous factors—a compelling national interest in a perceived emergency, foreign policy making that does not encroach too severely on the domestic sphere (*Youngstown* [1952]), a direct challenge to judicial authority (detainee cases), and individual rights (Japanese internment). They also include endogenous factors, such as personal judicial bias and strategic positioning on the bench. Under these conditions, justices have the capacity[93] to institute a new constitutional order (*Curtiss-Wright*) as they balance claims to certain rights against their own policy preferences. Ultimately, the Supreme

Court, as a decision maker, does not operate independently from the political system.[94]

Examining development in the context of history and institutions assists in (re)conceptualizing the timing and options available to presidents who utilize the power and authority sanctioned by the judiciary and the impact that this newly defined role has on the formulation of foreign affairs. When action in the political arena is transformed into a constitutional issue, it is constrained by the norms and institutional boundaries of the judicial branch. However, a legally sanctioned assertion of unilateral executive power and authority facilitates the growth of presidential power and shapes future claims of presidential prerogatives.

This book demonstrates that although the timing and options available to the executive and the judiciary operate in two different spheres, they can influence, in profound ways, each other's developmental path; an interpretive turn or feedback mechanism exists between the branches. Feedback loops support the recurrence of a particular path, illustrating that the Court does not work in linear terms. Stephen Skowronek suggests that the executive branch experiences institutional thickening[95]—an institution having "shorter periods for successful innovation"—but this is not the case with the Supreme Court. In fact, successive benches have shaped—and at times broadened—presidential authority (see Chapter 5), which does not rest on party alignment or unified government. As such, presidents now have a "repertoire of powers . . . at their disposal"[96] that allow them to assert dominance in foreign policy, which rests on the legally justified reasoning of the Court in *Curtiss-Wright*.

THE COURT'S CONSTITUTIVE ROLE

The institutional prowess of the Supreme Court and how it embeds a new constitutional order that centers on unilateral executive prerogatives demonstrates that decisive moments can create conditions or constraints that generate or sustain a path or depart from a proceeding path of law. When we speak of moments, I refer to exogenous shocks[97] that can shift the debate from the political to the legal sphere when a constitutional question is raised. As such, the presidential narrative is reconfigured when we read the Court into the executive's development. As an agent of change, the Court challenges or collaborates with an institution in the construction and stabilization of a major political order.

Sutherland's opinion in *Curtiss-Wright* lays the foundation for executive ascendancy in the management of international affairs against the backdrop of the first constitutional order and the Court's original jurisprudence. There are several ways to evaluate why the Court would render such a decision. I posit two likely scenarios. First, it was simply a political choice on the part of the Court, to promote a united front between the legislative and executive branches to utilize an embargo. Second, it was the result of Justice Sutherland's advancement of his own political or attitudinal[98] agenda. Yet Chapter 2 demonstrates why neither of these scenarios accounts for the decision rendered. And if neither of these explanations is true, how do we construe change?

Path dependence is the development and permanency of institutions along a particular path that is either hard to break from or resilient to change. Individuals or groups generally design policies and institutions with the goal of permanence. To safeguard these policy goals, political actors set in place rules that make preexisting arrangements difficult for anticipated incoming rivals to reverse, because political uncertainty exists when regime change takes place.[99] Path dependence primarily employed in economics has been extended to political science to examine the process of increasing returns.[100] Paul Pierson notes that once a particular course of action is introduced, it may "be almost impossible to reverse."[101] Once policies are passed and implemented, they can be resilient,[102] and when the policy arrangements are wide-ranging, they can influence the motivations and resources of political actors.[103]

Four pathways that are essential to political environments typify the positive feedback or increasing returns of an entrenched path. In each of the pathways, any and all decisions over time can initiate a self-reinforcing response. In other words, longevity in a particular direction increases the costs of switching to some alternative path. Two barriers—the short terms of political actors and the status-quo bias[104]—inherent in the political sphere therefore "make path dependent effects particularly intense,"[105] which complicates increasing-returns processes in politics. These pathways therefore increase the complexity of trying to change the course down which political actors have already started. Moreover, Pierson's theory is conditioned by how institutions behave to safeguard increasing returns as the world outside the institution changes.[106] But Pierson provides no examination of how institutions might be influenced by external forces, such as judicial decision making. Instead, he offers only an assertion of anticipated and expected institutional reactions to the external world.

Although "entrenchments of certain institutional arrangements obstruct an easy reversal of the initial choice" of a path selected,[107] Margaret Levi suggests that there are moments during which a path may be changed. In an increasing-returns process, the likelihood of additional steps on the same path escalates with each and every move along that path. However, although the executive may experience a high cost in attempting to change the trajectory of this institution, the Supreme Court can facilitate a shift when it legally redefines the very path in question. Over time, this newly established path becomes."entrenched when successive Courts legitimate the switch in paths through judicial decree. In this respect, the process of increasing returns is therefore self-reinforcing: a positive feedback loop or interpretive turn reinforces a new path.

Another aspect of path dependence is Pierson's notion of "branching points." He suggests that particular factors bolster the "paths established at those points."[108] If we regard the Supreme Court as part of the broader political process and agree that its justices are not hemmed in like the president, then the Court has discretion and latitude when deciding cases. The Court, restructuring the political debate, closes off certain possibilities while opening up others. The path is essentially redefined and altered over time by successive benches (see *Dames*). Consequently, the theory of path dependence cannot satisfactorily account for the process and impact of judicial decision making in the management of foreign affairs and war making.

Karen Orren and Stephen Skowronek assert that if junctures are explained in terms of "exogenous shocks that disrupt established patterns," then path dependence is reduced to the unhelpful claim that "politics follows a particular course until something happens that changes the course."[109] Furthermore, path dependence works on the assumption that formerly viable options may be closed once a constant period of positive feedback has been established. And increasing commitments to an existing path change become problematic, as they "condition" the configuration in which any new divergence can emerge. But if path dependence is so difficult to reverse, how do we account for the Court's instituting change? Ronald Kahn suggests that a unique association exists between the "temporal sequencing" of judicial decisions and the course of a path.[110] Paths are thus far from clear, coherent, or even predictable, because the Court is in a favorable position to alter the direction of policies and actions taken.

The application of path dependence is therefore limited until the theory incorporates the interaction of the internal mechanisms (preexisting law and institutional norms) of the judicial decision-making process with external features—the "political process, institutional, cultural, intellectual, and social forces."[111] Evaluating how the Court weighs these internal and external forces reveals what constitutes transformation and how the Court plays a significant role in creating and sustaining change.[112]

The path dependency of the Supreme Court is very different from that of its political counterparts, so it is advantageously positioned to change the course of constitutional and political development for the political institutions and for subsequent courts. Why? Primarily because the Court does not experience the same costs associated with its political counterparts, it can act as an agent of change. One reason that the Court can behave in this dynamic way is that it does not have to make decisions on the basis of the perceived actions or reactions of others. While its role in foreign policy making has been largely regarded as inert and inhibited when certain conditions are met, the Court is in a preferred position to alter or amend a path through the development of time.[113] Alternatively, the Supreme Court can decide to disregard a path previously established when it strikes a balance between rights principles and the Court's position on a contested policy or action (see *Youngstown*, in Chapter 4, and detainee, in Chapter 6).

Scholars merging judicial decision making and American political development examine the conditions that preserve or trigger a departure from a preceding path in the law and the Court's role in these departures. These scholars demonstrate that the course of action taken by the Supreme Court is frequently governed by the placement of a case in a sequence of related cases over time. In addition, the meaning of a contested issue may change over time, which then fundamentally shapes American political development.[114]

For Kahn, precedent cannot necessarily be traced along one linear path,[115] and, perhaps more importantly, he reveals how divergences exist within paths. When conflicts arise, the constitutive decision-making process[116] might move out of alignment to such a degree with the external world of the Supreme Court that the likelihood of even a landmark case being overturned increases. The Court therefore chooses whether to overturn case precedent. Established paths are usually followed, yet at momentous points in time, the Court makes constitutional determinations that at times challenge rather than cooperate with the major commitments of the dominant political alliance.[117] And with the progression of time, Kahn argues, these patterns become more principled, because justices of the Court, with different political and legal attitudes, consent to the idea that social construction is a natural part of judicial decision making.[118] When the world outside the Court adjusts, justices can target previous cases to influence the present contestation where the Court can sustain the path or overturn prior holdings.[119] The social factors involved in a case are therefore relevant in evaluating judicial choice and the maintenance or alteration of a path.[120]

The multifaceted interaction between the internal and external[121] explored in this book suggests that paths are not necessarily predetermined by the institutional demands of the Supreme Court, because the Court is also concerned about the world outside its walls. These conditions, which include the geopolitical concerns of our nation's foreign policy and/or the perceived national emergency, yield the constitutional space or interpretive turn that allows the Court to act more freely. This ability does not mean that the Court always takes into account changes in the external world or that it always participates in Kahn's mutual construction process (discussed below). Rather, the justices are institutionally situated to govern more freely—having "fewer start-up costs"—than are political institutions when making constitutional choices and deciding whether to participate in the construction process[122] in international affairs. In this way, judicial decision making yields viable options for the broader political, economic, and social world.

Because the Supreme Court hears cases and controversies, it has a determinate set of "switching costs" for altering a path. As a case moves through the appeals process, those institutions and individuals outside the Court pose versions of what they believe the law says (detainee cases). But the Court can substitute its own interpretation of the law, thereby offering legal stability in its pronouncement. To draw this demarcation between the alternate readings of the law, the Court must participate in the construction and constitutive decision-making process.[123] In this sense, the Court does not hear cases unless there is the real possibility of a reversal of the present course or the necessity to reaffirm or broaden (*Dames*) earlier rulings.[124] Constructing and creating an avenue of legal alternatives is therefore part of the Court's regular business.

Paths are therefore "not preordained because of the complexity of Court decision making," and we cannot view change "as increasing returns because Court decision-making is neither simply a response to institutional needs from externalist factors, nor simply increasing returns for legalistic purity."[125] Instead, path dependency should be viewed as the outcome at a critical juncture that generates a feedback loop (a unique bidirectionality) supporting the repetition of a particular pattern in cases that are not contemporaneous.[126] This constitutive process can embed a divergent path, as the Court behaves in ways that are nonlinear.[127] This constitutive decision-making process was borne out in the resulting chasm in the early part of the twentieth century when the Court decided *Curtiss-Wright*.

Historical institutionalism regards public policy making and political change as a distinct process, typified by protracted or extended time periods of extensive stability, which is similar to path dependency. However, these time periods are interrupted by formative moments. Critical junctures[128] in the historical process expose many paths of development, and the Court may seize these junctures to define and redefine the executive's role in the conduct of foreign affairs. As Paul Pierson and Theda Skocpol demonstrate, feedback mechanisms are triggered by critical junctures, which in turn "reinforce the recurrence of a particular pattern into the future."[129] These feedback mechanisms sustain the Court's role as an agent of change.

Examining critical junctures—a feature of APD—exposes how and why the Supreme Court departed from the original constitutional order in the pivotal case of *Curtiss-Wright* and how the newly constituted order, and thus the subsequent path carved out by the Court, became entrenched. Further-more, it is during such formative epochs that public policy is ascribed a new purpose (see *Dames*, in Chapter 5, and detainee cases, in Chapter 6).[130]

Examining the Court in this way, we find that paths are malleable. The progression of negotiations between the Court and politics through develop-mental time leaves the direction of change itself open-ended.[131] The path is therefore penetrable by these negotiations. The temporal ordering of principles and law, combined with exogenous forces, significantly influences the trajec-tory of doctrine and the Court's position in the course of APD.[132] As Orren and Skowronek stress, development can occur when different institutions—in this case, the executive and the judicial branches—"come into conflict with each other or reinforce each other in new and transformative ways."[133] Al-though causality affects judicial decision making, I show that when political and legal time cross paths, change occurs.

The Court straddles the political world and a unique legal culture, and it must be sensitive to internal (legal norms) and external (political sphere) strategic concerns.[134] This intersection grants to the Court the constitutional space to insert its institutional prowess to reconstruct developmental time and, consequently, the path of another institution.

POLITICAL AND LEGAL TIME

The Supreme Court's legitimacy and actions (Constitution, precedent, and public opinion, for example) situate it in a distinct position institutionally com-pared to the immediately politically answerable branches of government. Rec-ognizing its institutional role, the Court shares space within the larger gov-ernmental sphere.[135] Consequently, it operates with "its own [set of] norms, dynamics, and institutional history"[136] and incorporates law (the Constitution and statutes) in the form of precedents, but external influences—politics in general, and political actors specifically[137]—also affect judicial decision mak-ing. This configuration of internal and external factors is unique to judicial de-cision making; the implications are such that when the Court decides questions of presidential authority to claim a unilateral role in foreign policy making, these decrees influence and change the trajectory of political and constitutional development.

Skowronek's theory of political time illustrates the institutional barri-ers (institutional thickening) that constrain the executive branch, but these constraints are not shown to bind the Court. Moreover, through the passage of time, there is "a waning of political time" that impedes a president's com-mitments, owed in part to the "thickening" of political institutions.[138] The result is intensified demands for and the anticipation of political change by the president. At the very heart of this idea is the notion of path development, which regards the status quo as a waning of political time.

Evaluating debates and rhetoric advanced by the executive branch and key political actors in response to a perceived emergency (political timing or the geopolitical concerns) in international affairs and war making demonstrates how policies evolve from political deliberations and action to the legal sphere in the form of a case or a controversy. Once the Supreme Court decides to hear a case, a "contested interpretive space"[139] is exposed. In this moment, the Court determines the shape and scope of the developmental path as it balances competing concerns (internal and external forces).

Keith Whittington asserts that Supreme Court justices have had power forced upon them, because politicians benefit from the Court's taking an active role in interpreting the Constitution and statutes.[140] Although the Court has no institutional authority to say what the Constitution means, and the politically accountable institutions of our government have no obligation to accept the "Court's reading of the Constitution as being the same as" their own meaning and understanding, "presidents and political leaders have generally preferred that the Court take the responsibility for securing constitutional fidelity."[141] Although presidents at times disagree with the Court and attempt to "alter the trajectory of constitutional law," rarely is there, Whittington argues, a "crisis of, or challenge to, judicial authority."[142] This is not the case in foreign policy making, however. Modern presidents, in this area, often challenge the judiciary's authority and reading of the Constitution and assert an alternative understanding—the unilateral authority to make foreign policy free of oversight and checks (see *Youngstown*, in Chapter 4, and detainee cases, in Chapter 6). When the Court does not adopt this alternative understanding, it asserts its own institutional authority to interpret the Constitution. In this way, the Court challenges the political regime in place.

The Supreme Court is acutely aware that it cannot make "compromises with social and political pressures," because it lacks "plausibility [precisely] because [it is] viewed as unprincipled, [which] place[s] the Court in the position of being viewed simply as a political body, and thus illegitimate."[143] As such, this process "must be transparent, well grounded in principle, and 'sufficiently plausible' to be accepted by the nation."[144] At first blush, this appears to be true of foreign-affairs cases. Sutherland's support of a strong executive is "sufficiently plausible," because it finds solace in Hamilton's support of an energetic executive. And by today's standards, the pro-presidentialists' position has certainly gained in strength, as executives purport to require more authority to handle increasing threats to our nation's security. But there is more to this story (see *Curtiss-Wright*, in Chapter 2, and Japanese internment cases, in Chapter 3).

Legal time, Pamela Brandwein asserts, is more open-ended than political time, because it brings the external world into the decision-making process, which means that law is not just internal.[145] So legal time is fluid and complex and is defined by how the Supreme Court interacts with the external world.[146] Essentially, as the Court considers external factors with internal norms, it may be constrained to find in favor of the executive (Japanese internment cases, in Chapter 3, but not detainee cases, in Chapter 6).

When presidents challenge judicial authority, the Court reaffirms its place institutionally[147] by asserting that it is "the primary and final authority to arbitrate, circumscribe, and legitimate" executive branch actions "through its power to establish 'legal[ly] binding rules.'"[148] The rule of law over government and constitutional law means that the Court is in a position to "limit the abuse of government power," which yields to it the "incentive[] to question the action[s] of political institutions" rather than to merely accept them.[149]

As such, the Court is in a politically insulated position vis-à-vis the executive, who is limited by the thickening of the political system. As Kenneth Kersch asserts, legal time is far less thick than political time.[150] Legal time is more transformative:[151] institutional norms that incorporate "a mutual construction process, an interpretive turn, and the social construction process" grant to the Court the discretion to act. This is particularly relevant when the Court assesses individual rights with polity principles while taking into account geopolitical concerns.

In times of crisis—wars, internal rebellions, or terrorist attacks—governments are inclined to suppress the rights and liberties of those living within their borders, a trend that has also been extended to enemy combatants (detainee cases), because national-security and military "necessity" necessarily dwarf liberty if governments are to be guarded and preserved. However, the discretionary power of the judiciary provides the Court with an opportunity to shape the political debate as it assesses rights claims, without being subject to the political costs of doing so.[152] When the Court engages in this way, it fundamentally reshapes constitutional and political development.[153]

Legal time is distinct from political time, yet in examining patterns of intercurrence between the Court and the president in foreign policy making, as this project does, I show that the transformative space produced when political time and legal time cross paths allows for change to be instituted by the Court. These disjunctures emphasize the Court's constitutive and less-constrained role, thereby giving the Court, or what some would call the counter-majoritarian Court,[154] legitimacy under our democratic values.[155] Just as James March and Johan Olsen contend, "[J]udges, like other institutional actors, actively g[i]ve 'meaning to the values they espouse' in politically consequential ways."[156]

Whittington's framework of regime theory[157] offers an alternate understanding of the fused process of legal and political time by uncovering which factors constrain judicial review and constitutional interpretation. Ultimately, reconstructive presidents, Whittington suggests, battle the Supreme Court over constitutional meaning. As drafters of "fundamental political change," Whittington claims, "reconstructive presidents appeal to the Constitution to help legitimate their enterprise."[158] This is not only a defining characteristic of reconstructive presidents (FDR and Ronald Reagan, for example) but also a commonly used tactic. These presidents "insist that theirs is an effort to save the Constitution from the mishandling of their immediate predecessors and the Court itself."[159] This argument suggests that as presidents define their own powers, they create an atmosphere of tension in which a challenge to the Court's authority is amplified. When reconstructive presidents—executives who put in place a new majority at a time when the regime is vulnerable to change[160]—are successful in their assertions, their interpretations of the Constitution prevail and ultimately legitimate present and future political practices. However, Whittington does not include a comprehensive analysis of foreign policy making, so this framework is not robust. For example, he maintains, affiliated presidents find allies on the Supreme Court.[161]

The Bush administration (2001–2009)—that of an affiliated president, or one who belongs to an existing regime—challenged the Supreme Court's authority by claiming to have the sole authority to determine the president's constitutional powers. Bush wanted to act unilaterally against the threat of terrorism and asserted that the Court had no power of review over the executive's actions (see the Conclusion). The Court, however, was not an ally of the Bush administration. In fact, it thwarted the executive's claims to unilateral foreign policy making, finding in favor of individual rights. Consequently, regime theory is complicated when we read the Court and its decisions in foreign-affairs cases into the narrative.

Skowronek asserts that regimes constrain executive decision making and that as each new regime is instituted (via critical elections), presidents have a tougher time effecting change (institutional thickening).[162] Fleshing out complicated periodizations shows how recurring patterns of behavior are "created by the past, alterable by the future and have a life of their own."[163] As fundamental shifts occur by way of critical elections, the political structure or party system determines whether the Court collaborates with the regime or is hostile to it. But this circumstance is not what we find with foreign affairs. Even though five (six, if you count the ideological realignment of President Reagan) critical elections—those that usher in new regimes—have occurred,[164] this study demonstrates that a stable period existed from 1800 to 1936 when the Supreme Court reaffirmed and defined the constitutional blueprint advocated by the Framers in a series of foreign-affairs cases. The Court then instituted a new constitutional order in 1936 and maintained it until it heard the detainee cases (Chapter 6).

The role of ideas is central to the selection of policies.[165] For ideas and belief systems to influence the trajectory of a policy, they must be communicated in such a way as to be included in the political debate. Understanding how ideas come to be and how they evolve helps explain institutional change. As such, this perspective exposes how ideas espoused by the Court have evolved not just across spatial time but also across political and legal time, and how judicial supremacy has reshaped the trajectory of the executive branch.

A path is ultimately shaped by the constant interplay between the different institutions or political forces that come into conflict with one another. These patterns of intercurrences, defined as "independent institutions shifting in and out of alignment with one another," then "form patterns of entrenched structural enduring and constant change."[166] A change in policy is likely when a political actor can subjugate a prevailing perception or frame and then offer an alternate interpretation that is viable. In the area of foreign affairs, the Court's constitutive role determines whether this new frame is practical and sustainable as it balances competing rights claims with geopolitical concerns. Ultimately, the Court acts as the catalyst of that change when a shift in the frame is observed, which is not based on regimes, the political timing of the president, or the internal norms of the Court.

LAYOUT OF THIS BOOK

Each chapter of this book covers a particular temporal period. The universe of cases includes decisions from the Supreme Court from 1800 to 2015 (and secondary cases[167] that further entrenched the constitutional orders). In each of the empirical chapters, it might first appear that as the definition of principles (polity and individual) develop, the Court merely changes its behavior accordingly. However, I show that the situation is more complex than a mere assertion that rights constrain the Court's jurisprudence. These chapters identify and explain the significance and consequences of the Court's efforts to settle uncertainties arising under exigent circumstances.

Chapter 2 begins the empirical narrative with a consideration of *Curtiss-Wright*. The *Curtiss-Wright* Court instituted a new constitutional order, for the first time establishing plenary powers that were not dependent on congressional delegation. Chapter 3 examines the issue of Japanese internment. This set of cases is usually framed as "race based," but I demonstrate the entrenchment of the new constitutional order and how presidential ascendency became institutionalized; executive power undermined individual rights and was given the widest of latitude to wage war successfully. The discussion of *Youngstown* in Chapter 4 illustrates that the Supreme Court was willing to check executive power and authority during a time of war. This case reaffirmed the Court's institutional prowess to draw a sharp distinction between foreign and domestic affairs as it assessed the role of the executive vis-à-vis Congress.

Dames and *Regan* are the next cases covered, in Chapter 5. In these instances, the Supreme Court insisted it was duty-bound to determine the extent to which the executive can make foreign policy despite various congressional attempts to rein in executive autonomy statutorily. Chapter 6 examines the detainee cases. Ultimately, the Court continued to operate within the newly established constitutional order as it handed down its initial rulings, but with political, public, and global backing, over time it rendered a more robust review of the Bush administration's detention policies as it weighed national-security concerns against the protection of individual liberty.

The Conclusion asserts that the Supreme Court is an unconstrained actor when it decides foreign-affairs cases. Through judicial decree, it can institute change—a move away from the established order. Over time, this ability has led to a comprehensive national acceptance "of the systematic legal entrenchment"[168] of an executive's acting autonomously in foreign policy making, which has come to include war making. The imperial president has been neither unchecked nor usurping power over developmental time. Rather, believing that the old constitutional order can no longer accommodate the practical necessities of our national foreign-affairs agenda, the Court has instituted and buttressed the recurrence of the sole-organ doctrine (executive autonomy) over developmental time. This chapter emphasizes the contemporary relevance of this study by speaking briefly to the Court's sanctioning of presidential unilateralism in *Zivotofsky* (2015).[169]

Courts are part of the broader political process.[170] Because the president is largely constrained by institutional thickening, the institutional costs of changing paths may be too high for the executive branch to attempt alone, but with the collaboration of the Supreme Court, these costs are minimized. Judges have interpretive leeway and actual power and authority to influence political questions, so not only are paths of development open to the Court; the judiciary can significantly change path trajectories and establish institutional change.

2

CURTISS-WRIGHT

The Court's Dynamic Role

Nineteenth-century deference to Congress in the area of foreign affairs gave way in the twentieth century to a distinct judicial conjecture favoring unilateral executive power in foreign relations. The *Curtiss-Wright* Court reasoned that although the Constitution does not explicitly vest in the president the authority to conduct foreign policy, it gives it implicitly through the commander-in-chief clause. Moreover, the Court stated, the president has "plenary" powers in the area of foreign affairs that is not contingent upon congressional delegation. This ringing endorsement transformed the developmental narrative of the executive and of future courts by redefining constitutional jurisprudence in the area of foreign affairs. By departing from the constitutional blueprint in the *Curtiss-Wright* decision, the Court demonstrated its lack of constraints, which in turn altered the path dependency of the presidency. In this respect, the Court was not passive; it did not merely sanction presidential assertions of unilateral powers. Inserting itself as an authoritative institution, the Court became an agent of change.

Curtiss-Wright was a catalyst for change. The Court held that the president's foreign-affairs powers are not only open-ended but also inherent in his position as the executive of a sovereign nation. Scholars have evaluated how transformative domestic politics was at this time, but the transformation of foreign policy making, although inherently different, is just as significant. While the Supreme Court served as a domestic check on Franklin D. Roosevelt's (FDR's) New Deal, it also played an instrumental role in (re)defining the allocation of powers of the executive branch in the conduct of international policy making. At every turn in national policy, where the cleavage between the old and new regime was distinct, FDR confronted a judiciary predominantly held over from the old order. These partisan differences have "been an estranging influence between the Court and the great Presidents"[1] with respect to domestic affairs, but that is not the case when international discourse is examined. The Court's constitutional foreign-affairs jurisprudence is not purely political or simply attitudinal.[2]

The Supreme Court is in a preferred position to institutionalize a new role for the executive as it balances rights claims in foreign policy making. In striving for a form of government stability, it recognizes the practical nature of presidents' wielding more authority to conduct our nation's foreign affairs. The Court's *Curtiss-Wright* decision therefore laid the foundation for unilateral executive powers to become entrenched constitutional law. Ultimately, the constitutional space in which the Court operates is predisposed as an avenue to create change and therefore has played a significant role in American political development (APD).[3]

REALIGNMENT USHERS IN NEW DEAL LIBERALISM

Walter Dean Burnham argues that when political actors and institutions are considered "maladjusted and politicized," critical realigning elections take place.[4] The party that wins one of these realignments ultimately sets the terms of the more-stable governing party voted into office.[5] The 1932 election ushered in the fifth realignment, known as New Deal liberalism. At this time, Congress and the executive branch were unified (Democratic), but the Supreme Court was a conservative carryover (1889–1937). Only after *Curtiss-Wright* did FDR appoint justices with left-wing leanings to the Supreme Court.

FDR was a pragmatist and an ideological liberal. As a pragmatist, he accepted a variety of subterfuges for restoring American economic health, and in his first term (1933–1937), there was scarcely time or occasion for anything else. He demanded "political independence from the existing state of affairs" and stressed "an expansive warrant for discarding received political formulas."[6] Pressing for change, FDR asserted that he could take control of the Democratic Party on his own terms, but he also wanted Democrats to move the party forward—but adhere to his agenda when doing so. FDR enjoyed a first term with steadfast party majorities and for more than two years experienced no well-formed opposition.[7]

However, this political reconstruction was not without institutional obstacles. In the summer of 1934, the first clear signs of dissatisfaction with the New Deal began to appear. By the fall, some of the privileged interests of the old regime, among them old-line Democrats, created the American Liberty

League as one of the first strategies of political resistance.[8] The New Deal faced sharp rebuke by the League, but the midterm election returns gave FDR a resounding popular endorsement. This public confirmation was short lived, however; soon, support for the old order intensified within the government. With the Supreme Court striking down the most important pieces of New Deal legislation, FDR found himself allied with popular support but facing a wall of opposing interests and institutions determined to defend the old ways.

By 1936, FDR was even more relentless in his resolve to oust the received political order and safeguard a broad-based substitute. His rhetoric of denouncing the old order and his overwhelming reelection victory essentially silenced the direct challenges to the legitimacy of the new order he was spearheading. The critical political shift in the construction of the New Deal regime, however, was the shift away from the National Recovery Administration (NRA) (and business) toward the National Labor Relations Act of 1935 (also known as the Wagner Act) (and labor), which became the cornerstone of the new ordering. But Congress ushered in the new state of affairs.[9] Moreover, in an interesting turn of events, the Supreme Court—working in the privacy of its own chambers—decided to reverse its opposition to the New Deal well before the president's Court-packing plan was disclosed.[10]

In FDR's second term, he chose a different track—reform was to be institutional, aimed specifically at the Supreme Court and the political-party system. The great holdover of conservatives on the Supreme Court struck down seven of the eighteen New Deal cases as unconstitutional. Presented with this institutional roadblock, the president challenged the Court's constitutional interpretation head-on. He asserted that the text of the Constitution should be given a "liberal interpretation" so that it could be used as an "instrument of progress."[11] The Court, FDR maintained, had been invited by the American people to play its "part in making democracy successful," and the people had an expectation that the Court would sanction the use of "legitimately implied" powers for the "common good."[12]

FDR's confrontation is not surprising. Reconstructive presidents,[13] such as he, establish a contested vision of the constitutional order, which is central to their political agenda.[14] Moreover, reconstructive presidents have "historically . . . asserted the authority to ignore the Court's constitutional reasoning and act upon their own independent constitutional judgments."[15] It is evident that FDR was displacing the old regime, yet by promoting the foundations of the New Deal, the Court was central in instituting the new regime.

From early 1935 to the spring of 1936, the Supreme Court handed out a string of adverse decisions that voided far more than the relatively unpopular NRA.[16] Justices George Sutherland and Owen Roberts both joined the 1935 "black Thursday" rulings against the National Industrial Recovery Act

(NIRA) and the Agricultural Adjustment Act and then in 1937 switched to favor such laws as those creating the Social Security Act of 1933.[17]

Liberal and conservative judges alike declared that the president's alternative to chaos had no lawful claims to order. So FDR was left with the choice of either abandoning his commitment of reconstruction or radicalizing it.[18] Despite this sharp rebuke from the Court, he bounced back and galvanized the ever-growing reform majorities that had united in Congress and even managed to solidify the basic commitments of what would ultimately become the new liberal regime. This renewed energy continued with his election campaign of 1936, where he once again won an overwhelming popular endorsement for the changes he advocated. By this point, political opposition to the New Deal was practically wiped out.

Given the magnitude of FDR's enterprise, domestically and internationally, success was wholly dependent on presidential supremacy, and that was a notion the original constitutional frame could not necessarily accommodate; the practical reality of the increasing geopolitical pressures and the required measure of deliberation between the executive and legislature were waning. With increasing pressures internationally, the nation was acutely aware of the prospect of the executive's seizing more power. As later presidents would do, FDR was implicitly rejecting the founding generation's view that dealing with foreign affairs is a shared power. The office Harry S. Truman inherited following Roosevelt's death in the spring of 1945 was immensely different from the one FDR acquired from Herbert Hoover in the spring of 1933.[19]

Not only was this a period of the modernization of the presidency; it was also a time that permanently ended what was considered a period of American isolation from European and world affairs. In the 1930s, Congress and the country were determined to remain an isolationist nation and stay out of the war raging in Europe. But FDR, acutely aware of the impact of Adolf Hitler's progression, attempted to ally with France and Great Britain against Hitler's regime. Fashioning a modern presidency during the New Deal bequeathed a critical zone of new power and independence to all future incumbents in the domestic arena.

Curtiss-Wright, which concerned the principles of governmental regulation of business and the hegemony of the executive in the management of international relations, was decided at a time when the cleavages between the old and new regimes were well defined. Acting with the authorization of a joint resolution,[20] Congress empowered FDR to place an embargo on shipments carrying arms to countries at war in the Chaco region of South America—specifically, Paraguay and Bolivia, because they were engaged in a cross-border conflict. Acting pursuant to the joint resolution, FDR issued Proclamation 2087 in May 1934,[21] which forbade the shipment of arms to the combatants in the Chaco region. The Curtiss-Wright Export Corporation was indicted for violating the embargo and charged with plotting to sell fifteen machine guns to Bolivia.

Because an adverse outcome against the Curtiss-Wright Export Corporation would ultimately result in substantial fines, lawyers arguing for the company asserted that the congressional resolution granting the president discretionary power was an unlawful delegation of legislative power. Therefore, both the embargo and the proclamation were invalid.

Consequently, the law under review was FDR's implementation of his discretionary power. This prerogative was a legislative determination, the Curtiss-Wright lawyers argued, and Congress was leaving this right to the executive's "unfettered discretion." This claim had judicial support. In *A.L.A. Schechter Brothers Poultry Corp. v. United States*[22] and in *Panama Refining Co. v. Ryan*,[23] decided one year prior to *Curtiss-Wright*, the Supreme Court struck down congressional acts on the grounds that they characterized unconstitutionally broad delegations of legislative power to the executive. However, congressional Democrats and the White House were relentlessly critical of the Court's decisions in both cases.

At first blush, the majority opinion of *Curtiss-Wright* is a crude story of the justices' willingness to tolerate the opinion's author, "Sutherland, to ride a favorite hobby-horse at the expense of doctrinal clarity."[24] On closer inspection, the story is complicated. Not only was the Court wrestling with which branch—legislative or executive—had supremacy over the conduct of the nation's foreign policy; it was also reevaluating its holdings in *Schechter Poultry* and *Panama Refining Co.* in the present case. Even though the Court had struck down legislative acts by reasoning that they were unconstitutionally broad delegations of legislative power, it now had to determine whether this characterization applied to *Curtiss-Wright*. Ultimately, the Court drew a sharp distinction between the precedent set in the two proceeding cases and *Curtiss-Wright* and reasoned that the executive branch was better equipped to conduct the nation's international affairs; the world outside the Court justified an assertion of executive discretionary authority when viewed in light of those rights claimed by the Curtiss-Wright Export Company.

POLITICAL UNDERPINNINGS OF THE CHACO WAR AND ROOSEVELT'S RESPONSE

The relatively low-level conflict in the Gran Chaco (now known as northern Argentina) turned into a bloody war when oil was discovered.[25] A Bolivian subsidiary of American petroleum giant Standard Oil organized in 1921 and 1928 discovered oil west of the Chaco, and many believed the Chaco would turn out to be rich in petroleum. Bolivia's interest in a port seemed to be a necessity when oil was found, but it feared that Argentine or Brazilian middlemen would absorb profits. As such, Bolivia responded with the placement of troops at newly built outposts. Paraguay believed these outposts were in its territory, so it responded militarily. Bolivia initially enjoyed a military advantage and access to an unlimited supply of oil. But incompetent generalship, a divide between the Bolivian elite, and a military coup at the end of 1934 undermined the legitimacy of the Bolivian political authority.[26]

A conflict in Latin America was significantly relevant to the political terrain and to the policy guiding the nation at the time. As the United States emerged as a world power, the Monroe Doctrine (1823) stated that any advances by European nations to colonize land or interfere with states in North or South America would be considered as acts of aggression necessitating American intervention. Following the Venezuela Crisis (1902–1903), President Theodore Roosevelt added a corollary to this doctrine in 1904, proclaiming American intervention in Latin America as a right in situations of "flagrant and chronic wrongdoing by a Latin American Nation."[27] This well-established doctrine and its corollary—a presidential initiative—had legislative support. The corollary was cited as granting the legal authority to intervene militarily to prevent the spread of European influence.

The Chaco War occurred at the height of FDR's New Deal reconstruction. Despite rising opposition, he reinvigorated the new order and succeeded in solidifying the basic tenets of the new liberal regime. His political career began with his commitment to a robust international role at the center of U.S. foreign policy. While FDR was influenced by Theodore Roosevelt's unabashed nationalism and Woodrow Wilson's idealism, by 1928, FDR had rejected the Roosevelt/Wilson view of inter-American relations because of "a newer and better standard in international relations" and stated, "Single-handed intervention by us in the affairs of other nations must end."[28]

In accordance with American ideals, FDR was committed to preventing war and settling international conflicts,[29] but he did not comment on how he would pursue these objectives. It should be noted, however, that he did not make policy as if he already had the constitutional power to engage the nation in war. Prior action did not promulgate legal precedents or an accepted historical practice of using the commander-in-chief clause to take the United States into war—unilateral presidential power to initiate war had not been the norm.[30]

In FDR's first term, his foreign policy was governed by two ideas: his Good Neighbor policy[31] and the deterrence of aggression. His position yielded policy requiring the United States to take an active role in seeking out international cooperation by compelling other nations to resolve international differences through peaceful multilateral action.[32] With the concerns of Hitler's increasing power, and the potential for conflict, FDR believed that he should have the authority to take peaceful steps to identify and punish aggression. Shortly after taking office, he submitted a piece of draft legislation that granted to the president discretionary power. The House passed the bill, but the Senate amended it, requiring the president to use embargos.[33]

Resolution of the 1933 legislative proposal set the stage for how the White House and Congress would interact when considering the issue of discretion. The Roosevelt administration regularly pursued discretionary power so that he could use arms embargos as a discerning tool of foreign policy, but a select group of senators and representatives continued to assert that any embargo should be even-handed and mandatory when war broke out.[34]

A proposal suggested by the Roosevelt administration in February 1934, requesting that discretionary arms embargo power pass the House, was once again amended in the Senate, denying any discretionary power to the president. Not content with this development, FDR intended to put the issue aside,[35] but the ongoing conflict in the Chaco War resulted in a truce between FDR and the powerful group of senators and representatives regarding the issue of presidential arms embargo authority.[36]

Concern over the sale of American arms and munitions[37] to Bolivia and Paraguay resulted in an investigation,[38] which also led to a bill being introduced on May 18, 1934. Six days later, it was pending FDR's signature.[39] He was keen to apply whatever restrictions Congress wanted to impose on both countries, La Paz, and the Asunción government, because he considered them both responsible for the war.[40] But long-standing treaties between the United States, Bolivia, and Paraguay did not permit an embargo on U.S. trade with either one of those countries. Therefore, legislation would need to be drafted carefully so that it did not violate any treaties or serve to damage precedent. The answer was a prohibition on the sale of arms and munitions in America to either Paraguay or Bolivia. This bill amounted to a domestic piece of criminal legislation and avoided an arms embargo; domestically, Roosevelt was in an optimal position. The result, albeit brief, was House Joint Resolution 347.[41]

Even though the Senate approved the Joint Resolution unanimously, ambiguity existed: did the president's authority depend on his determination of a fact, as the verb "finds" suggests in "if the President finds that the prohibition of the sale of arms and munitions of war," or did he have the authority to make discretionary judgment, as the optional phrase implies in "if . . . he makes proclamation to that effect"?[42] The legislative record does not speak to this ambiguity. Setting this opacity to one side, Congress did set the conditions under which the president could act. The lack of censure from the legislature implies collaboration between the executive branch and Congress. The bottom line is that the resolution assisted, in part, FDR's inclination toward discretionary control over the sale of American arms as a means to execute his foreign-policy objectives.

After signing the joint resolution into law, FDR also signed Proclamation 2047,[43] which suggested the narrower, fact-determination reading of the resolution. Regardless of whether the language was intentionally narrow, the impact of utilizing this authority to act, conferencing with the other governments, and granting statutory authorization gave the president the authority to act.[44]

IMPACT OF STATUTORY AUTHORIZATION

Clarence K. Webster, the president of the Curtiss-Wright Export Corporation, saw the Chaco War as a unique opportunity to capitalize on what the corporation could provide and supply to those fighting in it. By early 1933, Curtiss-Wright had a virtual monopoly on the sale of warplanes to Bolivia.[45]

Joint Resolution 347 and FDR's implementation of Proclamation 2087 threatened Curtiss-Wright's monopoly and its financial recovery following the stock-market crash. Five of its fighter planes and four bombers were seized in June 1934. Because the fighters were constructed before the proclamation had been issued, they could be sent to Bolivia, but the bombers could not be shipped, because they were finished after the proclamation and therefore fell within the president's scope of authority.

A scheme was devised to collect on the bombers; turning the aircrafts into commercial "air-liners" would allow them to be delivered to Bolivia under a fabricated corporation, and payment could thus be collected. The Department of State became aware of the arrangement and worked with the Peruvian government to prevent the completion of the bombers and their ultimate delivery to Bolivia.[46] The Justice Department and the U.S. attorney for the Eastern District of New York, Martin Conboy, saw the Curtiss-Wright scheme as warranting the application of Joint Resolution 347. As a result, Conboy indicted Webster, John Allard (Webster's successor), and the Curtiss-Wright Export Corporation on conspiracy to sell machine guns to Bolivia. The defendants asserted that there was no constitutional foundation for this indictment and claimed that it should be dismissed because the president did not engage in the required consultation with Congress.[47]

District Judge Mortimer Byers found in favor of the defendants.[48] His argument rested on the constitutional problem that judges had attributed to the Constitution since the time of John Marshall: Congress may not redelegate its authority to either of the other two branches of government, yet Resolution 347 did just that. The president had to act first and issue a proclamation;

in that event, the resolution would then be implemented, and the prohibition of arms sales would be imposed. The ambiguity inherent in the resolution rested in what steps the president would need to take to issue the proclamation. However, under the circumstances and the precedent already set, that question seemed to be of little value.[49] In fact, in a number of cases, the delegation principle had been utilized in an assortment of contexts, and the Supreme Court, up until 1934, had "never invalidated an act of Congress on that ground."[50]

In 1935, the Supreme Court addressed discretionary executive power when it decided *Panama Refining* and *Schechter Poultry*. It decided, virtually unanimously in both cases (Justice Benjamin Cardozo was the only justice to dissent in *Panama Refining*, but he wrote a concurrence in *Schechter Poultry*), that the statute under the NIRA had "violated the rule against delegation of governmental power."[51] Taken in unison, these two cases appeared to "substantially rewrite the constitutional law of delegation" and seriously questioned the validity of Joint Resolution 347. When Conboy reargued the *Curtiss-Wright* case, he stressed that if the law were invalidated, it would significantly impede "the successful conduct of the foreign relations of this government." Byers thought this to be a moot point, because he believed that the conduct of foreign affairs was not "necessarily involved"; therefore, this was a simple case of criminal prosecution of a situation that took place within the United States. Consequently, Byers found the joint resolution to be unconstitutional; as such, the president's invocation of the proclamation was null and void.[52]

The decision rendered by Judge Byers presented an apparent and direct threat not only to FDR's Chaco policy but, more importantly, to his long-term objective of acquiring the authority to implement embargos as a discretionary device in the conduct of U.S. foreign policy.

FDR's modified concept of neutrality[53] kept the nation out of war, but he also wanted the discretionary power to use as a weapon to deter or stop aggressors. He saw discretionary authority as a necessary component to deter aggression being waged around the globe. Discretionary power over trade was, for FDR, the most effective way to assert control and power, but he needed the authority to use this power at his discretion in whatever way and against whomever the national interest required at any given moment. Roosevelt and Congress contentiously quarreled over this matter for six years (April 1933 to November 1939), although in some pieces of legislation in the 1930s, Congress did grant FDR discretion. However, FDR most wanted the authority to exercise discretionary power over trade, especially over the traffic of arms. So, in 1935, when Congress ratified a compulsory arms embargo instead of granting discretionary power, requiring further that it be applied to aggressors and victims, FDR was quick to point out his frustrations, asserting that this measure might pull the nation into war instead of keeping it out.[54]

With mounting tensions worldwide, FDR was acutely aware that the nation at large and Congress were cautious about making bold moves abroad and that any attempt by the executive branch to push this point would jeopardize parts of his legislative program that he was attempting to guide through Congress in the summer of 1935. One way he wanted to counter Fascist advances was via discretionary control over neutrality. When the Anglo-French-Italian talks folded, Benito Mussolini initiated final arrangements for an attack, which put additional pressure on FDR and forced his hand—"believing that the time had come to 'make a vigorous effort' to enact the temporary arms embargo." While support for the bill was evident, the House Foreign Relations Committee had "unanimously opposed any grant of discretionary power to the President," deciding instead to back an impartial neutrality law by 11 to 3.[55] Two days later, an amended bill was presented to the Senate and approved without a vote of record. This bill gave the president the statutory discretion he was looking for.

Speaking more broadly, if Judge Byers's conclusion of *Schechter Poultry* was indeed correct, it would be extremely difficult for FDR to defend his vision of a government in general terms and of the executive branch more specifically by invoking broad concepts of "public interest" and "national purpose."[56] Consequently, the government appealed the case to the Supreme Court. In December 1936, the Court reversed Byers's ruling on the issue of delegation. Ultimately, the Court's pro-presidentialist decision institutionalized a change in the constitutional order by granting to the executive (and presidents to come) plenary powers in foreign affairs.

SUTHERLAND ESTABLISHES A NEW CONSTITUTIONAL ORDER

After issuing reproaches in the domestic arena (striking down significant pieces of the New Deal), the Supreme Court was now positioned to render another decision that might be in opposition to the commitments of the majority coalition. How would the Court read discretionary executive power? Would the Court be constrained by early judicial rulings? And did the external framing of the situation and the administration's asserted authority to act influence the Court?

The government's brief unintentionally affirmed its fear that if Judge Byers had read *Schechter Poultry* correctly, then Congress could not confer discretionary power on the executive. The administration was troubled not by the impact on the Chaco policy itself but rather by the applicability of *Schechter* in the case and, therefore, its subsequent impact on the dynamic role between congressional flexibility and executive discretion. It was this interest the administration asserted in its brief. The brief also noted that precedent, which now included *Schechter Poultry*, dictated "the proper test, and the only test, of the validity of authority vested by Congress in the executive [to be] the absence of free and arbitrary discretion."[57] While the Supreme Court used the invalidation of the NIRA, in *Schechter Poultry*, as a way to affirm constitutional limits on congressional power, the government reasoned that the precedent of *J. W. Hampton*, in which the Court discarded the argument that specific rules compartmentalized Congress's power to confer discretion, allowed Congress in the present case, within defined limits, to vest discretion in the executive. *Schechter Poultry* was therefore interchangeable with *J. W. Hampton* (1928), according to the government. It therefore came down to how limits were defined when delegating power.

The lawyers for Curtiss-Wright argued that in the area of foreign affairs, separation of powers between the legislature and executive could not be disregarded. But this claim was supported neither by principle nor by precedent.[58] The government maintained that Congress had the authority to grant to the president the ability to go to war if he believed that doing so would reestablish peace between nations that were at war. If this were the case, the executive and not the legislature would decide whether the nation went to war,[59] which is not in accordance with the first constitutional order. The joint resolution ultimately gave the president unfettered discretion. As such, if Congress could give the president discretionary authority on whether to bring legislation into effect, it would ultimately grant the executive what amounted to "a deferred veto—one that Congress could never vote or override and one not provided for in the Constitution." If lawful, the series of actions authorized by the joint resolution "would invest the [p]resident with a power far more effective than the constitutional veto."[60]

The most interesting facet of the substantive briefs filed is the subsidiary query of the role of the executive in exercising power in international affairs. Some of the lawyers in FDR's administration argued internally that the president should assert a stronger claim to executive independent authority in external affairs. For instance, Assistant Secretary of State R. Walton Moore argued that Congress should grant wide latitude for discretionary executive power, because "the [p]resident . . . is primarily responsible for our international affairs." Moreover, it was naïve to believe, Moore noted, that if the president used discretionary authority to impose an arms embargo, doing so would embroil the nation in a potential war without direct congressional approval, because the executive had unilateral constitutional authority by way of the commander-in-chief clause.[61]

Despite Moore's conviction, the lawyers' briefs made no such declaration. Rather, they asserted that the president's conduct of foreign relations was more limited and defined an area of legislation, whether due to settled principle, access to facts, or even the Court's own language, where the delegation principle was confined to the present situation.[62]

Nothing in any of the briefs suggested that *Curtiss-Wright* would become a foundation on which to show judicial support for the executive's control over foreign policy. The following discussion demonstrates how Sutherland's opinion fundamentally changed the political landscape of the executive branch by granting to the president broad unilateral authority in external affairs. With its *Curtiss-Wright* decision, the Supreme Court, at a critical juncture, permanently altered the path affirmed in early judicial opinions by evaluating competing interests.

The key to Justice Sutherland's expansive view of presidential authority to conduct foreign policy is found, in part, in his early and developing principles of the division between domestic and foreign-affairs powers granted to the government by the Constitution. Sutherland had long asserted that the United States should follow an active foreign policy at the hands of the president, which would isolate the position from the parochial trepidations that, according to Sutherland, governed congressional policy making. In Sutherland's view, politics should stop at the water's edge.[63]

Sutherland was a strict constructionist and tended to align with the conservatives on the Court.[64] In fact, Sutherland was part of the conservative "Four Horsemen," which included James McReynolds, Willis Van Devanter, and Pierce Butler, who were instrumental in striking down Roosevelt's New Deal legislation. (These four conservatives, holdovers from William Howard Taft's Court, often convinced Roberts to side with them, giving them the majority.) The Four Horsemen took a static view of the Constitution and ignored precedents that empowered government in favor of those that limited government. A sharp ideological division existed on the bench, and Roberts, the swing voter, switched positions and began upholding New Deal legislation, which gave the liberal justices the majority.

When Sutherland served in the Senate (1905–1917), he displayed a keen interest in and particularly fervent views on issues concerning constitutional power. He decried expansive interpretations of Congress's power to regulate interstate commerce, yet he supported Teddy Roosevelt's resilient approach to foreign policy, for example. In 1909 and 1910, Sutherland drew a distinction between foreign- and domestic-affairs powers granted to the government.[65] Examining "external powers—extent and limitations"[66]—Sutherland concluded that the United States was a "progressive nation in a progressive world," and although the Constitution does not change, the "things which fall within the scope of the Constitution constantly change." Sutherland was therefore suggesting that for those generations that came after the framing and adoption of the Constitution, the Constitution must have the "capacity for indefinite extension."[67]

Sutherland applied this reasoning on March 2, 1910, when he outlined his reasons for supporting a bill that would establish postal savings depositories. The subject of the bill itself is irrelevant, but Sutherland contended that the Constitution had not changed in meaning—only that its "application and scope ha[d] broadened." The Constitution could and should be applied to "new conditions, new things, [and] new activities" that had occurred since the Constitution was adopted. Furthermore, Sutherland insisted, a Constitution that was incapable of adapting "to the constant growth and constant change of a progressive and constantly changing people" would be useless, and an "impossible contrivance" would hinder and not encourage the development of the newly freed people of our nation.[68]

Sutherland's Blumenthal Lectures at Columbia (1918) further developed his theory of domestic and international powers as inherently different in source and scope. Through this development, we see how Sutherland would later elucidate a redefinition of powers granting to the executive sole plenary powers. As H. Jefferson Powell[69] notes, Sutherland essentially maintained that the Constitution enumerates and grants domestic power to the government, primarily to Congress.[70] But, Sutherland argued, the government's powers in the area of foreign affairs stemmed from the powers of international sovereignty, which originated from the Crown: "These powers passed directly to the Nation as the result of successful revolution." Sutherland added that although the Constitution does not grant those powers to the national government, it does regulate and distribute those powers among the branches of the newly formed government.[71]

There are several points of concern in this reasoning. First, at the time of the American Revolution, in practical terms, the British king was no longer sovereign; the English Civil Wars had led to parliamentary sovereignty. And while the Declaration of Independence addresses the Crown—the original thirteen colonies were each separately established by charters from the English Crown—the Articles of Confederation refer to the sovereignty of the states, which delegates authority over foreign affairs to the Continental Congress. Finally, Sutherland failed to explain how the power of foreign affairs then flows to the president. Simply stated, the president cannot be the "sole organ" of foreign affairs, because Congress is vested with numerous powers to regulate the nation's international relations.[72]

The Constitution is the supreme law of the land, so to claim that the president may derive power outside the Constitution distorts polity principles and the Framers' understanding of checks and balances and separation of powers. "Advocates of Executive power have long advanced notions of drawing power from outside of the Constitution, most notably Theodore Roosevelt—with his stewardship theory of the presidency—and Alexander Hamilton in Pacificus No. 1."[73] But this approach undermines the first principle of American constitutionalism, which asserts that the government has only that power granted to it by the Constitution.[74] It is not immediately obvious, then, why Sutherland redrafted his *Curtiss-Wright* opinion advocating "plenary and exclusive power," which would fall to the executive, unless he was influenced by his early writings and the geopolitical underpinnings of the case. The Supreme Court (7–1)[75] favored the theory opined by Sutherland; each justice, taking account of the geopolitical concerns and practical realities of the spread of fascism, believed that the president was in a better position to conduct the nation's foreign policy.[76]

According to Sutherland, sovereignty—containing foreign-affairs powers—passed automatically and without pause from the British monarchy to the union, to the government under the Articles of Confederation, and finally to the federal government under the Constitution.[77] And in the area of external affairs, Sutherland maintained, the federal government had the legitimate authority to do anything a sovereign could do legally under the confines of international law when there is no explicit constitutional prohibition.[78]

Sutherland thus rejected any assertion by the federal government that it could legitimately ignore a constitutional prohibition by appealing to its external powers. Simply stated, however, invoking extraconstitutional powers does not allow a direct violation of a constitutional limitation placed on the federal government. Sutherland's position that foreign-affairs powers were "extra-constitutional"[79] is fundamentally at odds with language found in some Court opinions but compatible with others.[80]

Despite these strong convictions on the distinction between domestic and foreign affairs, Sutherland said relatively little on the matter of presidential constitutional powers. What he did say, with only minor discussion, was that the president had the sole responsibility to negotiate with foreign powers. The Senate's role, Sutherland indirectly stated, when concerning the negotiation of treaties, lacked the means and the legitimate authority to directly participate,[81] so its role would be in an advisory capacity.

Sutherland had a distinct pro-congressional position when involving America in armed conflict.[82] Sutherland's assertions were far from advocating unilateral presidential authority in this area. Rather, he argued that the presidency "ha[d] grown in potency and influence to an extent never dreamed of by those who framed and adopted the Constitution" and that the executive's "domination . . . threaten[ed] the stability of the principle of departmental independence involved in the distribution of the several powers among the three branches of government."[83] With respect to war powers, Sutherland maintained, the sword and the purse were two essential requisites of war. When engaged in war, the government by any means necessary must strengthen the sword and the purse and use them in unison to protect the nation. With respect to the war power, it existed without restriction unless expressly prohibited by the Constitution. And if such a restriction existed, Sutherland argued, it should be applied at all times and under all conditions,[84] with the exception of times of international crisis. Sutherland pointed out that the American people were "coming to regard [the president] as the sole repository of their power, which, very decidedly, he is not."[85] The line between foreign affairs and war powers has unequivocally been distorted over developmental time. The norm had been that during armed conflict, the president had the leeway to act freely as commander-in-chief.[86] In fact, America's history is replete with presidential and congressional attempts, during times of urgency, to limit an individual's right to speak, publish, and even assemble; to regulate those rights given to the criminally accused; or to increase restraints on foreigners or those labeled as the enemy.[87] However, beginning with Sutherland's diminishing clarity in *Curtiss-Wright*, over time, the sole responsibility to negotiate with foreign powers, to make foreign policy unilaterally, and to restrict civil rights and liberties has been extended to the executive.

By the time Sutherland was appointed to the Supreme Court, his theory had matured, and the sharp distinction that had once existed between domestic and foreign affairs had far less clarity. In fact, Sutherland used *Curtiss-Wright* as an avenue to settle "the key problem facing conservatives who were also ardent nationalists and who somehow wanted strong national powers in foreign affairs but protection from certain states' rights in domestic affairs."[88] Sutherland valued the doctrine of stare decisis, but he argued that precedent was not a fixed pathway, because it was the opinion of only the person who came before who said where the pathway should be. Path dependency of precedent in constitutional law is therefore not a controlling factor, and constitutional decision making on the Court is based, in part, on a justice's personal policy preference or strategic objectives.[89]

Sutherland appeared to be the best prepared on the bench to handle the *Curtiss-Wright* case, given his theory on the distinction between domestic and foreign affairs. Chief Justice Charles Evans Hughes assigned to Sutherland the majority opinion, assuming that because of Sutherland's affirmation of a narrow-constructionist view of legislative[90] power in domestic affairs, he could avert other justices on the bench from dissenting, as they also supported Sutherland's general view. On the surface, Hughes was vindicated. The opinion was substantial and written quickly.

Yet upon reexamination, Sutherland's opinion offers an alternative interpretation to the old order; the constitutional blueprint is supplemented by a new order, one favoring the practical realities of a strong executive in international discourse. The Court seized this occasion by applying external factors to justify the plenary powers of the executive in this area. Over time, *Curtiss-Wright* has been institutionalized as courts and executive-branch lawyers have embedded the rhetoric in presidential claims of broad discretionary power.[91]

It is evident that FDR administration lawyers believed that the Court would not extend the 1935 delegation cases, which it had used for New Deal flexibility. On the other hand, the defendant's lawyers thought their best chance was to assert that the Court could use its discretion when applying the delegation doctrine that came from *Panama Refining* and *Schechter Poultry*. However, the only query the Court was prepared to answer[92] was based on which questions they certified: if—but not definitively deciding—the joint resolution, which was the challenged delegation, was restricted to internal affairs and determined to be invalid, could it still be found to be a necessary tool, because it was a remedy for a difficult situation within a foreign territory?[93]

With the question conveniently narrowed, Sutherland drew from his own theory and argued that the resolution, delegating power to the executive, might have been unlawful if it had only been applied to our nation's internal affairs. Foreign affairs were a different issue, Sutherland contended: different rules and standards applied. Essentially, "the powers granted to Congress could therefore be exercised or delegated to the [p]resident and were not limited to the express and implied powers constitutionally granted."[94] Any limitations were applicable only to internal affairs. Ultimately, the president exercised "plenary and exclusive power," which was independent of any legislative authority, because he was the sole organ of the federal government in the field of international relations.

Sutherland moved beyond the issue at hand and maintained, in what some have called "ill-considered dicta,"[95] that the role of foreign affairs rested exclusively in the hands of the executive. Sutherland relied on "Congressman John Marshall's reference to the president as the 'sole organ' of American foreign policy in a speech he delivered to the House of Representatives in 1800." Marshall had declared that the executive "was the 'sole organ' of communication."[96] But Sutherland's invocation suggested that the executive, as "sole organ of the nation in its external relations," could make foreign policy unilaterally.

Justice Sutherland also claimed that the executive had a broad prerogative, or extra-constitutional authority, ultimately derived from the English Crown. At the time of the American Revolution, Sutherland observed, the authority to conduct foreign affairs fell to the Continental Congress, which meant that states had no foreign-affairs powers. Sutherland asserted that with the construction of the Constitution, plenary authority over foreign-affairs powers naturally transferred to the president. This interpretation appears to be a reach, given the earlier discussion of Sutherland's theory of domestic and foreign affairs. However, as noted above, Sutherland argued that the president had the sole responsibility to bargain and negotiate with foreign powers, whereas the Senate lacked the means and legitimate authority to act. This assertion was in reference to treaty making, but the case could be made, Sutherland now reasoned in light of his reading of Marshall's "sole-organ" speech, that by implanting this theory with a general substantive policy-making role, the president was granted plenary authority in international affairs by way of the Constitution.

Sutherland's *Curtiss-Wright* argument demonstrates a change of heart from his 1919 defense of Congress's authority and role in foreign affairs vis-à-vis federalism and of the "narrow-construction attack to an assertion of the foreign-affairs authority of the president that stresses its independence of Congress."[97] This change of heart might be credited, as examined below, to the external factors—the government's argument and historical practice—that Sutherland's opinion embraced.

Upon initial reading of Sutherland's opinion, it is difficult to determine what his contentions have to do with the issue of delegation. However, relying on Powell's analysis of Sutherland's opinion and granting the justice some latitude, one can consider that if foreign-affairs powers do not originate from the Constitution, they cannot be defined by it and are therefore plenary except when they are limited by "applicable provisions of the Constitution." Continuing with this line of thought, Sutherland could then assert that the dissemination of these powers was not created; instead, the Constitution makes the president the "sole organ of the federal government in the field of international relations," putting few restrictions on the conduct of those affairs. The executive therefore has plenary powers when conducting foreign affairs that the legislative branch is not otherwise entitled to. Consequently, the president's power in this area is "delicate, plenary and exclusive."[98] If the executive is the primary decision maker in international affairs, responsible for formulating policy, then it naturally follows that a delegation rule constructed to protect Congress's role in defining policy is quite simply, and plausibly, according to Sutherland's assertion, inapplicable. Moreover, it is at this point that Sutherland incorporated components of the administration's claim; when Congress legislates in international relations, it undoubtedly takes into account the executive's power—both in principle and in practice—of intelligence, secrecy, and negotiation, which debatably are vital elements to the triumph of international policy making.[99]

Sutherland—relying fundamentally on a structural argument—pointed out the history of legislation that had been granted to the president, which gave the executive broad discretionary power over international trade and other interrelated issues. Even though Sutherland maintained that the Supreme Court was not bound by historical practice, he agreed with the government: if the Chaco Joint Resolution was determined to be unconstitutional, it would indirectly invalidate a "uniform, long-continued and undisputed legislative practice. . . . [E]ven if the practice found far less support in principle than we think it does, we should not feel at liberty at this late date to disturb" it.[100]

Ultimately, Congress could authorize the president to act in foreign affairs, on the basis of prediction and opinion, but the executive was given absolute discretion regarding whether to act at all. At the end of the day, the joint resolution was constitutional, because the action taken by Congress—declaring domestic-arms sales that aided Chaco fighters to be criminal offenses—was a modest congressional act that contributed, in a small way, to the overall power of the president to determine whether America should ban the sales as an effective function of U.S. foreign policy.

With the trajectory of Sutherland's theory and his preceding judicial opinions, his plurality opinion in *Curtiss-Wright* was plausibly an apparent evolution of his discernable schema, but it was not necessarily predetermined. Prior to *Curtiss-Wright*, the almost unanimous Supreme Court that decided delegation cases in 1935 suggested that the justices were fully prepared to stay the course. For example, the Court's *Panama Refining* decision revealed an unwillingness to depart from the Court's historical acquiescence in broad delegations of power in the realm of international trade.[101] And Sutherland's majority opinion in *Carter v. Carter Coal Co.* (1936) mentioned his theory but proclaimed that it was not an issue to be considered at that time.[102] Sutherland's majority opinion in *Carter Coal* limited the reach of Congress's power under the Bituminous Coal Conservation Act of 1935 under the commerce clause.[103] This decision initiated the slow entrenchment of executive dominance in this area. Six months later, *Curtiss-Wright* served as the jurisprudential vehicle by which to establish unfettered unilateral discretionary power.

IMPLICATIONS OF *CURTISS-WRIGHT*

In the immediate sense, *Curtiss-Wright* had no significant role to play in the tug-of-war between the executive and Congress over whether to grant to the president discretionary arms-embargo authority or to force a binding and impartial duty of neutrality in terminating American arms sales to warring states. Those opposing FDR had the upper hand; the Neutrality Acts denied the executive the kind of discretion advocated in *Curtiss-Wright*.

Youngstown (1952) is considered a bookend, but the ramifications of *Curtiss-Wright* have continued well into the twenty-first century. Executive-branch lawyers and the courts, to support claims of broad discretionary power—the authority to act without congressional authorization in foreign policy—regularly cite the sweeping language of *Curtiss-Wright*. Narrowly read, the data suggest that courts simply follow controlling precedent when the case involves a triggering event, such as the Cold War or the war on terror. However, this trend is better understood as demonstrating its evolution as precedent over time, which can be evaluated as a turning point only when development is examined after the fact.[104] When a case is decided, it merely deals with the specifics at hand. Its content is developed only later, as Courts wrestle with new cases (as shown in later chapters); the sole-organ doctrine, outlined by Sutherland, takes on prominence as time elapses and later Courts come to rely on Sutherland's position.[105] Judges therefore adhere to the new constitutional order established in *Curtiss-Wright*.[106] In fact, the courts have cited *Curtiss-Wright* 487 times (1936–2016), with the Supreme Court referencing the case 60 times (1936–2015). And the D.C. Circuit Court relied on the sole-organ dicta a total of five times when it decided *Zivotofsky* (2013).[107] Even in light of the Supreme Court's seeming denunciation of the sole-organ doctrine in *Zivotofsky* (2015)—it was supposedly jettisoned but was replaced by a near look-alike[108]—presidential ascendency is institutionally embedded and endures as the rule of law today.

The first time the Supreme Court cited *Curtiss-Wright*, in what was nominally a foreign-policy issue, was in *Ex parte Quirin* (1942). This case was heard during FDR's administration and addressed German spies' landing on American soil. During Truman's administration (1945–1953), the Court cited *Curtiss-Wright* thirteen times—the most of any administration. These cases all concerned foreign-affairs matters.[109] Perhaps not surprisingly, six of the sixty citations came during George W. Bush's administration and the Court's hearing of the detainee cases. And during Ronald Reagan's administration, the five citations recorded occurred during the Oliver North and Iran-Contra hearings.[110] North "relied heavily on explicit executive prerogative arguments to defend their actions during the crisis. In their view, the president had full constitutional power to authorize their actions whether or not those actions conflicted with statutory rules imposed by Congress."[111] *Curtiss-Wright* set the precedent for presidential prerogatives in international affairs and continues to be "used as ammunition in modern debates."[112]

Curtiss-Wright split from the established path by instituting a newly constructed constitutional order for executive supremacy in foreign affairs. Even though its significance was not immediate, *Curtiss-Wright* did set the stage for Sutherland to speak again to the role of the president in this area.

Unfettered discretionary power was reaffirmed in two contemporaneous cases (*United States v. Belmont*[113] and *United States v. Pink*[114]) and then utilized almost four decades later in *Dames and Moore v. Regan*[115] and *Regan v. Wald*.[116] This fidelity over developmental time established the new constitutional order. *Belmont*, decided only four months after *Curtiss-Wright*, concerned the legality of an executive agreement. Sutherland, writing for a six-justice majority, once again favored his modified version of the external and internal powers when he deduced that the national government had the power and authority to enter into such an agreement. Sutherland invoked the language of *Curtiss-Wright*, while not naming it specifically, when he wrote that "in respect of what was done here, the Executive had authority to speak as the sole organ of the [national] government."[117] (Sutherland retired from the Court in mid-January 1938, ending his personal role.) *Belmont* was contemporaneously aligned with *Curtiss-Wright*, but the Court's faithfulness to the newly constituted order was applied in *Pink* (1942), which influenced how the Court would strategically reengineer legislative history to find tacit consent to grant broad discretionary authority to the executive forty years later in *Dames and Moore*. *Dames* was a rights case (discussed at length in Chapter 5) that was resolved as a separation-of-powers foreign-policy issue. The principle in *Curtiss-Wright* limited legal advocacy until William Rehnquist's Supreme Court chose to take up the case. This strategic maneuvering illustrates that law and political power are intertwined. Law reconfigures and entrenches the scope and trajectory of political power. The Supreme Court's constitutional foreign-affairs jurisprudence determines the balance between polity and rights principles. Ultimately, the Court is an architect in providing the legal scaffolding for future foreign-affairs contestation.

The Supreme Court's *Pink* decision[118] reaffirmed *Belmont* by invoking the sole-organ doctrine and the executive's recognition power. *Pink*, relying on *Curtiss-Wright*, argued that the president had the power to make binding international agreements without Senate ratification. Yet again, *Belmont* and *Pink* (and *Eisentrager* [1950])[119] demonstrated the Court's continued adherence to Sutherland's disinclination to be "in haste"[120] to meddle with the executive's management of foreign affairs.

In the period following *Curtiss-Wright*, executive discretion and independent authority drastically increased in international affairs. *Curtiss-Wright's* rhetoric was beneficial to those claiming the executive to be the "sole organ" and that the "delicate, plenary and exclusive" power in the management of international affairs vested the president with the legitimacy of autonomous executive action. For example, Attorney General Robert H. Jackson quoted the whole of the "plenary and exclusive" paragraph from *Curtiss-Wright* when he wrote a defense for the president in the 1940 destroyers-for-bases agreement with Britain. Jackson did note that the executive's "plenary" power was not without limits, and he spent a considerable amount of time analyzing the discretion Congress had delegated to the president through germane statutes.[121]

Despite Jackson's later rebuff of *Curtiss-Wright* in *Youngstown* (discussed in Chapter 4) and the criticisms of today's scholars (pro-congressionalists), the impact of *Curtiss-Wright* and its rhetoric over time has well served those advocating the legitimacy of unilateral presidential action. Our contemporary understanding of presidential prerogatives is now quite discernable: the president single-handedly has the power and authority to manage our nation's foreign affairs, and when our national security is threatened (which is an assessment left to the Supreme Court),[122] the president is lawfully authorized to "override constitutional constraints to preserve and protect that security,"[123] but only at the discretion of the Court.

Justice Sutherland's opinion in *Curtiss-Wright* is often cited by the Supreme Court to support claims of "broad delegations of legislative power to the President" and also to claim "the existence of independent, implied and inherent powers for the President."[124] The first illustration of politicizing this enduring principle—the sole-organ doctrine—occurred during the Truman administration.[125] At *The President's News Conference* (1949), Truman was asked about his authority in relation to emergencies, in particular labor. He replied that he had "implied powers in emergencies that presidents before him ha[d] used." When pressed about whether "that [wa]s part of his power as President or Commander in Chief," Truman responded that it was "a combination of both."[126] These powers had long been claimed, but executives now had legal backing.[127] As Truman stated at the end of his presidency, the president has to make choices that affect the entire world, adding, as president, as commander-in-chief, he determines if the United States will have times of peace or war.[128] This assertion has been maintained over developmental time.[129] However, the Supreme Court is responsible for evaluating these claims in light of polity principles and individual rights claims in relation to national-security concerns.

This newly articulated prerogative has been discernable over time. President Bill Clinton, for example, aggressively used military force without obtaining congressional approval and asserted, when pressed, that he had unilateral prerogatives and constitutionalized politics.[130] Walter Dellinger (Office of Legal Counsel [OLC]), on behalf of the administration, articulated broad constructions of executive power in the area of war powers: the War Powers Resolution of 1973 "recognizes and presupposes the existence of a unilateral presidential authority to deploy armed forces into hostilities or into situations where imminent involvement in hostilities is clearly indicated by the circumstances."[131] Dellinger maintained that the War Powers Resolution acknowledges unfettered executive authority to use force on its own without the participation of Congress.[132] This continued trend has exalted presidential power far beyond the constitutional blueprint advocated by the Supreme Court prior to 1936 and placed the governance of foreign affairs into the realm of unilateral executive dominance.

In a number of key cases, the Supreme Court has expanded executive power and ruled in favor of "executive judgment" when taking into account the geopolitical concerns of war making. Decisions by the Court have not always invoked *Curtiss-Wright* directly, but the spirit of Sutherland's opinion has been embedded in law, which perpetuates the growth of presidential prerogatives and the claim that the executive is granted superior authority over foreign affairs.

For those committed to defending unilateral executive action in international affairs or to confronting legislative attempts to regulate presidential discretion in this area, Sutherland's profuse language is attractive:

> The President alone has the power to speak or listen. . . . Congress itself is powerless to invade . . . the very delicate, plenary and exclusive power of the President as the sole organ of the federal government in the field of international relations—a power which does not require as a basis for its exercise an act of Congress.[133]

Executive branch lawyers have therefore understandably not refrained. As Harold Hongju Koh observes, "Among government attorneys, Justice Sutherland's lavish description of the president's power . . . is so often cited that it has come to be known as the '*Curtiss-Wright*-so-I'm-right' cite—a statement of deference to the president so sweeping as to be worthy of frequent citation in any government foreign-affairs brief."[134] For example, in 1966, the State Department upheld "the legality of the Vietnam War in part" by maintaining that the executive "holds the prime responsibility for the conduct of United States foreign relations."[135] And thirty years later, a memo from the OLC would assert that the Whistleblower Bill for the Intelligence Community is unconstitutional,[136] partly because of the executive's position as "sole organ of the Nation in its external relations."[137] In 2001, *Curtiss-Wright* was further relied on to describe the executive's foreign-affairs power as "plenary and exclusive" when President Bush announced his authority to combat terrorists.[138] In 2006, the OLC sanctioned the power of the National Security Agency (NSA) to eavesdrop on all communications of alleged individuals linked to al-Qaeda or associated with terrorist organizations. The OLC, in its defense, called attention to "the President's well-recognized inherent constitutional authority as Commander in Chief and sole organ of the Nation in foreign affairs."[139]

And Barack Obama's administration laid claim to the sole-organ doctrine to defend its actions, in the face of congressional stalemate, to advance its policy toward the Islamic State in Iraq and the Levant (ISIL).[140]

Opponents of the sole-organ doctrine have fervently attempted to weaken Sutherland's plurality opinion, but they have ineffectively kept it out of administrative briefs and judicial opinions: "[F]or every scholar who hates *Curtiss-Wright*, there seems to exist a judge who loves it."[141] *Curtiss-Wright* instituted a discernible change in trajectory for the separation of powers in foreign policy making. The Supreme Court, at the juncture of legal time and its evaluation of the geopolitical construction of the case, asserted its authority to define presidential power. It is therefore in a preferred position to change not only the path trajectory of the presidency in the immediate sense but also administrations along the developmental path by providing the legal framework to claim broad prerogatives in war making and foreign policy making. Over time, the executive branch has come to rely on *Curtiss-Wright* to address (political-capital) foreign-affairs concerns more generally. And the judiciary has also utilized the broader principles of *Curtiss-Wright* (not simply the legal premises) to meet the demands of foreign-affairs problems. The geopolitical construction, then, is a two-way process: as executives lay claim to the authority to act, the Supreme Court evaluates these asserted prerogatives and determines whether they warrant judicial sanction. As the Court reevaluates the balance between rights and policy principles, the development of constitutional foreign-affairs jurisprudence is adjusted over time.

The Court's dynamic institutional role is profound, because the impact of *Curtiss-Wright* is what it reveals about, and what most would consider, the contestable issue of our day: what powers the executive vis-à-vis Congress has over foreign policy making generally, and war making specifically. Legal fidelity addressing the separation of powers and rights principles shapes the trajectory of politics and public policy even when they are not key to later cases on foreign-affairs matters. The Court's implicit rejection of the old constitutional order and the ever-more-pressing role of the executive have culminated in the imperial president in foreign affairs. In turn, the executive branch has the discretion to determine the trajectory of public policy and the political debate in relation to foreign affairs.

Curtiss-Wright set a baseline for future action: when executives make foreign policy, if they are not specifically prohibited by the legislative branch, those actions will be tacitly approved by the courts. The Supreme Court, acting as an agent of change, was not merely following the change that originated with the elites[142] populating Congress and the executive branch when it decided *Curtiss-Wright*. Nor was the Court falling in line with the newly instituted political regime. It is not beholden to any political regime—in fact, legal regimes do not map political regimes. Because *Curtiss-Wright* initiated the "switch in time that saved time," Sutherland's plurality opinion requires a reconceptualization of judges as legal actors who are institutionally bounded and historically contextualized.

Even with the dramatic shift in attention from domestic New Deal policy making to war preparation and conduct during FDR's sixth presidential year (1938), the same Court that declared New Deal policy unconstitutional under the commerce clause[143] and limited the president's power to remove members of independent regulatory commissions[144] produced a decision that granted broad affirmation of presidential foreign policy making.[145] Aided by the Court's broad reading of executive power, FDR carved out expansive presidential power in foreign intercourse that was every bit as sweeping as the domestic policy making he had advanced in the preceding six years.

Curtiss-Wright is a story of how the executive branch and the Courts utilized and reinvented the decision decades later, so that what the sole-organ doctrine stands for now has virtually nothing to do with the original case. As such, the Supreme Court wove itself into the very fabric of American foreign policy making, altering the course and political development of the executive branch. It did so by taking the lead in (re)defining the executive's scope and power in this area, with little institutional costs to either the executive or the judiciary. Unconstrained by path dependence, the Court successively closed off legal paths that were once entrenched and made available alternate paths, granting to future Courts the constitutional space to redefine presidential prerogatives.

Ultimately, the intersection of legal time and the geopolitical-construction process produces moments when the Supreme Court is constrained to act. However, the following chapters examine what happens when the Court is unconstrained. Regime theory, rights principles, and path dependency all suggest that the Court has no autonomy, but this analysis clearly illustrates how the Court acts contrary to these theories as it balances the geopolitical concerns of a case vis-à-vis polity principles and individual rights claims. Polity principles do not necessarily limit the depth of the geopolitical-construction process. In fact, as Chapter 6 illustrates, the Court's evaluation of right principles was insurmountable in light of the Bush administration's assertion of unreviewable unilateral decision making. The Court was unconstrained to find that the legislature and the executive acted unconstitutionally when denying detainees their fundamental rights. However, when addressing the key question of the constitutionality of the executive's war-making authority, the Court was constrained by the current constitutional jurisprudence.

In its discussion of Japanese internment, the following chapter shows how the Supreme Court, faced with public outcry, political demands for internment, and external social factors, allowed the national emergency to trump rights principles. The breadth of executive power thus depends on the Court's reading of exogenous factors. Furthermore, the Court's construction is not dependent on the congressional use of political pressures as a reason to support exclusion. Ultimately, when polity principles conflict with rights principles, the Court finds in favor of the president, but it also considers actions taken by Congress. While *Curtiss-Wright* did not involve race issues as Japanese internment did, these cases collectively contributed to the developmental path of the Court as it continued to recognize the realities of the executive's unilateral role in foreign policy making in times of emergency.

3

THE COURT DEFINES THE LEGAL NARRATIVE OF JAPANESE INTERNMENT AND EXCLUSION

A lthough it has a checkered past, the Supreme Court has found in favor of those seeking constitutional protection from laws infringing on their rights because of their race in a variety of areas. For example, the Court's *Strauder* decision (1880)[1] ruled that categorical exclusion of blacks from juries for no other reason than their race violates the Equal Protection Clause. The Court's *Smith* decision (1944)[2] held that primary elections must be open to voters of all races; it also declared that laws that enforce segregation on interstate busing are unconstitutional (*Morgan*).[3] The Court's landmark *Brown* ruling overturned *Plessy* (1896) by holding that segregated schools in states are unconstitutional, because they violate the Fourteenth Amendment.[4] But when the Court addresses race-based claims vis-à-vis foreign affairs, it is more likely to find in favor of the government if its appraisal of the geopolitical construction demonstrates a demonstrable leaning in favor of policy measures to safeguard the nation (e.g., Japanese internment). However, as the Court continues to grapple with questions of denying due process to those held solely on the basis of their race, we see the Court backpedaling (Chapter 6). The breadth of executive power, in the midst of a national emergency, depends solely on the Court's reading of the circumstances, and cases dealing with rights-based claims are no exception. It is the Court's province to determine constitutional foreign-affairs jurisprudence.

Despite scathing dissention from some justices, the incredible display of presidential power of Japanese internment and exclusion found favor with the

Supreme Court's majority. The constitutional space in which these internment cases were decided demonstrates that the Court's framing of the external weight of the war efforts and its evaluation of executive prerogatives to protect the nation from an attack undermined race-based claims. While raising significant constitutional questions (at the time and for future Courts) of the extent to which the government can intern and exclude on the basis of race, the Court transformed the political debate and legally justified executive actions as reasonably based, further institutionalizing presidential prerogatives.

Japanese internment occurred when many people in the United States, reeling from the attack on Pearl Harbor (December 7, 1941) believed that Imperial Japan was preparing to wage a full-scale attack on the West Coast. Given Japan's swift military defeat of a large portion of Asia and of Pacific nations between 1936 and 1942, some Americans believed not only that these military forces were unstoppable but also that the loyalty of ethnic Japanese living in America should be questioned. This doubt, fueled primarily by the racial prejudices of General John L. DeWitt, key White House administrative staff, the War Department, and the support of other prominent senior military officers and congressional members,[5] resulted in presidential proclamations designating Japanese, German, and Italian nationals as enemy aliens. Going one step further, Franklin D. Roosevelt (FDR) signed Executive Order 9066 on February 19, 1942,[6] authorizing military commanders to designate "military areas" at their discretion "from which any or all persons may be excluded." This authorization sent nearly 120,000 Japanese nationals and Japanese Americans to internment camps, resulting in four cases heard by the Supreme Court—*Yasui v. United States* (1943), *Hirayabashi v. United States* (1943), *Ex parte Mitsuye Endo* (1944), and *Korematsu v. United States* (1944)[7]—each addressing race-based claims and equal-protection concerns.

The totality of the external factors imposed an overwhelming set of constraints on the Court in balancing the president's unilateral claim of emergency powers out of military necessity during World War II with the suspension of Japanese Americans'[8] constitutional right to civil liberties. The Court, constrained by the geopolitical concerns, actively embedded the newly carved-out role of the unilateral executive established in *Curtiss-Wright*. Not only did the Court side with FDR, asserting that the president has statutory and constitutional authority to act during an emergency; the discourse between the justices also illustrates how the newly created role of the executive in warfare would be further extended in emergency situations when the Court heard the internment cases. These cases would demonstrate the dynamic nature of the Court as it advanced executive powers over the role of the legislature and, more importantly, over the civil-liberties claims of those bringing suit.

PRESIDENTIAL ACTION UNDER
EXIGENT CIRCUMSTANCES

A few weeks after FDR was elected to his first term, Secretary of State Henry L. Stimson visited him at Hyde Park to review the nation's foreign-affairs agenda. FDR agreed with Stimson that Japan had momentarily regressed "to the old position of a feudal, military aristocracy," which had now overextended itself in Manchuria.[9] As such, his policy toward Japan comprised a series of measures intended "to dissuade the Japanese from further militarization without provoking armed conflict." FDR's "strategy applied psychological and economic pressure, an intermittent and cautious forerunner of the "containment" policy."[10] He intentionally circumvented warlike conduct toward Japan,[11] while at the same time he prepared for conflict. Because FDR's attention needed to be fixed on the economic crisis in the United States, for a number of years, the Japanese American community resided on the periphery of the administration's agenda.[12]

Before the attack on Pearl Harbor, it was almost incongruous to most Americans that America would enter World War II. There were moments of public excitement after the gunboat incident in 1937 when the USS *Panay*, which was anchored in the Yangtze River outside Nanking, China, was attacked by a Japanese air strike. And Japan's coalition with the Axis alliance in 1940 was indicative that war might be just around the corner. However, Asian affairs went largely unnoticed.[13]

Following the attacks on Pearl Harbor on the morning of December 7, 1941, FDR delivered his war message.[14] He was not the first president to deliver a message of this kind, but he was confronted with a unique rhetorical[15] situation—his war message was the first to be broadcast via the radio. Not only was the president addressing Congress; he was speaking to an emotionally charged American public. FDR's audience was in a great state of shock, more so than previous presidential audiences. The war was unexpected, American territory had been attacked directly, and rumors[16] were escalating, so he had a lot to accomplish in a single speech. He had to not only console the nation but also speak to the engagement of the nation in a war, which required direct and immediate action on behalf of its citizens. Fueled by radio bulletins and special newspaper editions, the "sneak attack" outraged the country, and divisions between isolationists and interventionists that had existed became all but nonexistent. Americans now looked to the White House for unification and, more than anything else, direction and leadership.

FDR had to unite the nation, arouse optimism, and stimulate a war effort in which he now found himself. He was absolved from rationalizing a declaration of war with a long and aggressive discourse, but, given the growing level of hysteria of an impending attack on the coast of California and the nation's inevitable entry into the war, the president had to do more than simply arouse optimism and clarify the current situation.[17]

FDR's war address therefore utilized rhetoric that drove home the severity of the imminent danger surrounding the United States in the upcoming months—the "onslaught against us," a "premeditated invasion," "our people, our territory[,] and our interests are in grave danger." The unprovoked and deceitful attack from Japan ultimately gave him a mandate from Congress and the American people to do what was necessary to defend America and prevent this "form of treachery" from "endangering us again."[18] In addition, because of the implications of Japan's offense (i.e., threatening the nation's safety), FDR has the constitutional authority to attack: he stated that as "Commander in Chief of the army and navy I have directed that all measures be taken for our defense."[19] Note that FDR was speaking to his Article II authority to respond defensively to sudden attacks, which was a position advocated and upheld by the Supreme Court prior to 1936; early presidents understood defensive action, and the Court endorsed and legalized the commander-in-chief's role in repelling invasions. This speech set the stage for the American resolve of going to war and eventually helped sell the idea to the American public that a threat within U.S. borders required the internment of those that threatened Americans' safety.

Delivering a second message on December 9, 1941, FDR set the tone for how America should view the attack and the nation's response to Japanese nationals and Japanese Americans living in the United States—"[t]he sudden criminal attacks perpetrated by the Japanese in the Pacific provide the climax of a decade of international immorality." After cataloguing the events leading up to the Pearl Harbor attack, he stated that it was all one pattern,[20] which necessitated a unified front, because "we are now in this war."[21]

FDR warned the nation that the attack at Pearl Harbor might not be in isolation. Revealing that because the administration anticipated an attack somewhere along our coastlines, the nation's "industrial strength and our capacity to meet the demands of modern warfare" had been increased. FDR reminded the nation, "[W]e have learned a terrible lesson," which was that "[t]here is no such thing as security for any Nation." Powerful aggressors will attack without warning, and "we are not immune from severe attack."[22] FDR added that Japan was assured that if it joined the fight, it "would receive the complete and perpetual control of the whole of the Pacific area . . . and also a stranglehold on the western coast of North, Central, and South America." This logic would underpin the policy of internment. The American public, FDR concluded, must "realize that [the Axis powers] can be matched only with [a] similar grand strategy," because they were facing evil.[23] This sentiment resonated with Congress; the president secured a formal declaration of war, which passed both legislative houses with only one dissenting vote.[24]

In just a few short days following the attacks, anti-Japanese sentiment spread throughout the nation: on the streets, in the newspapers, and in government halls. Americans voiced their hatred and suspicion of the "treacherous Japs," and rumors spread of an impending invasion of the West Coast.[25] The first signs that FDR had any personal interest and involvement in controlling Japanese Americans by the military are found in a 1936 memo.[26] It highlights his willingness to "tolerate arbitrary action against Japanese Americans in the name of preserving security and his indifference to the constitutional rights of those citizens and aliens involved."[27] FDR's actions over time illustrate that he was ready to "assume that Japanese-Americans, whether alien or U.S.-born, were potentially disloyal" and that preventive measures were absolutely necessary.[28] Adding to his concerns was the War Department's conviction that the only threat to the nation's military bases came from the potential sabotage of local Japanese Americans.[29] As a result, the president signed a number of proclamations empowering the Federal Bureau of Investigation (FBI) with the authority to arrest aliens in the United States and to close land borders to all enemy aliens and all people of Japanese ancestry—whether alien or citizens of the United States. And in late November 1941, Roosevelt signed an executive order allowing the army to tighten surveillance and enforce restrictions on those individuals leaving and coming into the Los Angeles–Long Beach Harbor Naval Defensive Sea Area.[30]

While FDR's military advisers[31] recommended the exclusion of persons of foreign descent, including American citizens, from sensitive areas of the country as a safeguard against espionage and sabotage in late 1940,[32] the shock of the Pearl Harbor attack and the atrocities in the Philippines made apparent the immediate necessity of internment amid worsening race relations and concerns and fears on America's West Coast. Within three days of the Pearl Harbor attack, 1,200 arrests were made.[33] By late December 1941, former Attorney General Robert H. Jackson had authorized raids without search warrants on homes on the West Coast if at least one resident was a Japanese alien.[34]

Rumors and reports ran rampant from December 1941 onward regarding alleged sabotage by people of Japanese descent at Pearl Harbor and claims of Japanese submarine activity off the Pacific Coast. Embedding this claim even further, a government report prepared by then U.S. Supreme Court Justice Owen J. Roberts and released in late January 1942 alleged, without foundation, that espionage efforts helping the Japanese naval force attack Pearl Harbor had involved Japanese American citizens.[35] This report was taken as proof of Japanese American disloyalty and fueled harsh reactions among newspapers and politicians on the West Coast.

The developing situation on the West Coast took a turn for the worse at the end of 1941, when the U.S. military took an active role in pressing for the "coercive treatment of Japanese Americans, and popular pressure had grown for their removal from the coast."[36] General John L. DeWitt was one of the chief instigators of internment. While FDR was absorbed with the aftermath of Pearl Harbor and preparing the nation for war by developing a wartime strategy to conquer fascism, a coalition of alarmed groups "began to press for 'control' of the Japanese-Americans on the West Coast in the name of national defense."[37] The first appeal to emergency powers actually came from the West Coast Defense Command. As head of this command, DeWitt believed that Japan would invade the West Coast, and he told the War Department on more than one occasion that West Coast Japanese Americans were in communication with "the enemy and plotting sabotage."[38] He submitted a number of reports as proof; even though these reports were later discredited, they further fueled his concern and desire to take what he saw as necessary measures to safeguard the nation's security. As such, DeWitt discussed relocation options with his War Department superiors.[39]

As the Justice Department and military brass attempted to figure out how best to deal with the Japanese, interest groups, predominantly in Southern California, "organized a campaign to force all Japanese Americans away from the Pacific Coast."[40] It did not take too long before California's political officials began a campaign to have Japanese Americans evacuated, starting with congressional representative Leland Ford. In early January 1942, he sent a telegram to U.S. Secretary of State Cordell Hull asking for rigorous safeguards on the Japanese community: "I do not believe we could be too strict in our consideration of the Japanese in the face of the treacherous way in which they do things."[41] Ford also sent letters to U.S. Attorney General Francis Biddle, Secretary of War Frank Knox, and Stimson requesting the evacuation of Japanese Americans and stating that his constituents strongly favored this measure, given the number of letters he was receiving. Ford's correspondence effectively changed the debate from action to removal.[42] Biddle believed that while the Justice Department's Enemy Alien Control Program's officials were handling the situation, he did not see any legal way to relocate citizens short of suspending habeas corpus.[43] Late in January 1942, Stimson wrote to Ford that the relocation of Japanese Americans would be difficult and multifaceted, but the army was prepared to act, and facilities were available should they be needed.[44] Ford was soon joined by other "Pacific Coast congressmen in an ad hoc committee chaired by Clarence Lea, Dean of the California delegation and one of the chief instigators of the internment of Japanese-Americans." They met to determine "how to pressure the Justice Department into agreeing" to the internment of Japanese American citizens.[45] It should be noted, however, that FDR was insulated from these developments as he talked wartime strategy with Prime Minister Winston Churchill. By mid- to late January 1942, FDR once again returned to the issue of Japanese Americans, at which time, California political leaders and army officials were united in favoring the evacuation of Nisei, American-born and -educated children of immigrant Japanese (also categorized as Issei).[46]

FDR's State of the Union Address on January 6, 1942, spoke to the continued strength and spirit of the American people and the continuation of the present path to ensure security. He noted that the United States was a resolute nation, poised and ready to pursue a "total war effort."[47] To defend the sanctity of our basic freedoms, he argued, "we may have to pay a heavy price," because this is a war fought "for security, for progress, and for peace, not only for us, but for all men, not only for one generation but for all generations. We are fighting to cleanse the world of ancient evils, ancient ills." This was a fight, FDR admonished, that "our fathers have fought, to uphold the doctrine that all men are equal in the sight of God. Those on the other side are striving to destroy this deep belief and to create a world in their own image—a world of tyranny and cruelty and serfdom."[48]

He believed that the bipartisan appointment of Stimson to the position of secretary of war would help foster unified support for a war that FDR viewed as unavoidable yet needed to be won.[49] Stimson had mixed feelings over the constitutionality of removal,[50] but he advocated for the mass evacuation of people of Japanese descent from the Pacific Coast when he advised the president in early February.[51] FDR instructed Stimson to do whatever was necessary for the safety of the nation.[52] Within a couple of days of receiving Stimson's advice, the president had the full support of congressional representatives and citizens lining the West Coast.[53] Nationally syndicated columnist Walter Lippmann made a case for the upcoming administration's policy, which intensified the public's fear of sabotage by disloyal Japanese Americans.[54] And Department of Justice lawyers believed that the removal of people of Japanese descent from the Pacific Coast was a legal exercise of the executive's war powers.[55]

Claims of sabotage saturated the political sphere, propelling the need for immediate action. Within a few days of the U.S. Army's Western Defense Command's sending a memorandum to Stimson, advising him to evacuate "Japanese and other subversive persons" from the Pacific Coast area, FDR issued Executive Order (EO) 9066,[56] which granted discretionary power to the secretary of war, or any military commander, to designate military areas and exclude any and all persons from them.[57] FDR and his administration maintained that internment was a matter of military necessity and that the secretary of war would need the authority to implement the policy effectively. Moreover, the president seemed unconcerned about the possibility of any rebuke from the courts when he issued the order, because he believed that "the Constitution has not greatly bothered any wartime President."[58]

In mid-March, FDR issued EO 9102,[59] which established the War Relocation Authority (WRA). It authorized this agency "to provide for the removal from designated areas of persons whose removal [wa]s necessary [to] the interests of national security" by the military.[60] While the removal process was in full swing, local paranoia of potential sabotage was still clearly evident. For example, the governor of Wyoming went so far as to assert, "If you bring Japanese into my state, I promise you they will be hanging from every tree."[61] In an effort to tighten the current policy of internment and assist in curtailing rampant hysteria, the Western Defense Command issued several proclamations that severely restricted the movement of individuals of Japanese descent in military areas on the Pacific Coast, which also prevented them from moving out of those designated areas.[62]

A Progress of Relocation Report (1942) informed the president that "over 90,000 evacuees, or roughly 80% of the evacuated population, had been transferred to the 9 operating centers."[63] This report was evidence that the relocation program was successful and drove the rational and sustainability of the order. If those believed to be a threat to national security were confined to defined military areas, then Americans would be safe in the knowledge that the executive branch was doing all that it needed to ensure the safety of its land and its people. By August 1942, the Western Defense Command proclaimed the relocation of people of Japanese descent from the Pacific Coast military area to be complete.[64]

The totality of the exogenous factors (the political landscape and the geopolitical concerns) weighed heavy on the Supreme Court as it decided a set of cases that questioned the administration's internment policy.

Collectively, the internment cases confirmed Justice George Sutherland's assertion that the president can make foreign policy unilaterally (*Curtiss-Wright* [1936]). The Court not only sanctioned the new constitutional order established in 1936 but also, in the present cases, broadened the capacity of the executive to act in times of war; presidential prerogatives undercut individual rights. Moreover, in assessing the degree of legislative involvement, the Court determined that when the president and Congress sanctioned such action, military measures were "reasonably" based. This determination is not what we find when analyzing the detainee cases (Chapter 6).

AFFIRMATION OF THE NEW CONSTITUTIONAL ORDER— POLITY PRINCIPLES OUTWEIGH INDIVIDUAL RIGHTS

FDR's authorization to intern Japanese Americans via an executive order invoked a unilateral claim to emergency powers to safeguard national security. Because relocation had strong favorable political support and public deference, the policy agenda could be challenged only in the courts. The Supreme Court not only upheld the unilateral role of the executive to make foreign policy but also closed off alternative policy paths. It asserted that this ruling was a legal determination and not a political calculation, because the order was formulated out of necessity.[65]

The constitutionality of the curfews ordered by FDR, which applied equally to U.S. citizens, was legally challenged in *Yasui* (1943) and *Hirabayashi* (1943). *Yasui* involved Minoru "Min" Yasui's successful attempt to deliberately break the curfew law, issued on March 24, 1942, that required all "enemy aliens" and persons of Japanese ancestry to be indoors between 8:00 P.M. and 6:00 A.M.[66] It was the first case of its kind to directly challenge General DeWitt's orders—he had issued the proclamation—and it was also a chance for the WRA to defend its position on detaining Japanese Americans. If the WRA was successful, the *Yasui* case would be the scaffolding needed for the efficacious constitutionally determined defense of concentration camps, should the issue arise again.[67]

The argument that the government presented to the district court was grounded on race: the "racial characteristics" of Japanese Americans presented a real threat to national security. The government maintained that evidence showed organized work "of undisclosed and undetermined dimensions." Moreover, it claimed that the burden of providing proof came at a time when the nation was barely surviving. Government prosecutors advanced DeWitt's claim that it was "impossible during this period of emergency to make a particular investigation of the loyalty of each person in the Japanese community."[68]

Judge James A. Fee authored the opinion for the U.S. District Court for the District of Oregon, which agreed with Yasui's assertion that the curfew was illegally applied to American citizens. The curfew order was therefore deemed unconstitutional. However, Fee found that Yasui's employment at the Japanese consulate necessitated stripping Yasui of his American citizenship. This forfeiture of citizenship thus legally classified Yasui as an "enemy alien."[69] Consequently, Fee ruled, Yasui had violated the curfew.[70] Upon appeal, Yasui found himself grouped with fellow resistors Gordon Hirabayashi—the Supreme Court heard both cases in May 1943 and decided them simultaneously—and Fred Korematsu (decided in October 1944).

Hirabayashi directly challenged the curfew policy, and Korematsu directly confronted the internment and relocation policies. Solicitor General Charles Fahy defended the administration's policies in *Hirabayashi* and *Korematsu*,[71] asserting that the curfew and relocation orders were matters of "military necessity" and "military urgency."

Justice Department lawyers were confident that the judiciary would be sympathetic to the government's brief, yet they were concerned that if *Endo* (a case addressing the government's detention policy) was heard before *Yasui*, *Hirabayashi*, and *Korematsu*, it would derail a victory for the government in the present cases. To ensure that timing was not the key to unraveling the government's position, they asked the court of appeals for a "certification." This is a somewhat complicated and rarely used practice, but essentially if the appellate court raises a constitutional question, then the Supreme Court has to answer it. Here, the question raised concerned Yasui's citizenship status, which shunted this case to the head of the queue.[72]

Chief Justice Harlan Stone, author of the *Yasui* plurality opinion, reversed Judge Fee's decision. The Supreme Court determined that Fee had wrongly concluded that Yasui had forfeited his citizenship by working for the Japanese consulate, but it also stated that the curfew was valid and applied equally to U.S. citizens.[73] The application of the order was therefore constitutional. Stone's opinion was short, with no concurrences or dissents.

Behind the scenes, civil liberties lawyer Morris L. Ernst wrote to the president in mid-April 1943 to warn him that the Supreme Court was about to hear *Hirabayashi*.[74] Ernst had also written to Chief Justice Stone earlier in the year, asking him to join in the drafting of an "Anglo-American statement on the protection of civil liberties."[75] Stone responded that he was "uncertain how any document about the government's treatment of civil liberties could properly address 'the internment of our Japanese citizens.'"[76] Ernst took Stone's response as a direct sign of potential judicial opposition to the government's internment. As such, and without referencing this letter, Ernst warned FDR that he was confident the Supreme Court would find EO 9066 unconstitutional, at least with respect to the Nisei and Issei. The president, Ernst suggested, should prepare a new program. In agreement with Ernst, FDR quickly responded and began working on a new program that would readdress the internment of Japanese citizens. A pragmatic solution was martial law. He hated the very notion, but he also recognized its necessity: "[It] would solve the problem—a limited, local martial law could be made to stick anywhere we wanted."[77] FDR requested that Ernst "prepare a declaration of martial law in order to circumvent an adverse Court ruling." This request suggests that FDR, like DeWitt, continued to believe that all internees still posed a significant threat to national security. Even though the request was for limited local martial law, clearly envisioned as a practical answer to averting full-scale military rule, if implemented, it would have epitomized a dramatic assertion of arbitrary and blatant extraconstitutional power.[78] Despite Ernst's projection, the Supreme Court ruled in *Hirabayashi* that the curfew policy was constitutional, because it was a wartime emergency measure. The rather extreme alternative policy measure was therefore not necessary.

The Court's unanimous ruling in *Hirabayashi* affected more than one hundred thousand Japanese Americans—two-thirds of whom were natural-born U.S. citizens.[79] Again writing for the Supreme Court, Stone held that EO 9066 had been ratified and confirmed by Congress's Public Law 503.[80] The order was constitutional, Stone concluded, because Congress and the president jointly authorized DeWitt to protect the West Coast. Congressional and executive authority were "each an exercise of the power to wage war conferred on the Congress and on the President, as Commander in Chief of the armed forces, by Articles I and II of the Constitution."[81] Ultimately, the Court granted great deference to the fact that both institutions not only authorized the curfew (collaboration) measures but also acted within their own respective constitutionally conferred powers.

Furthermore, the Court found in *Yasui* and *Hirabayashi* that when the nation was at war, the application of curfews against members of a minority group were indeed constitutional. In the *Hirabayashi* decision, Stone added that the war power of the federal government was "the power to wage war successfully."[82] This war power, Stone reasoned, included "every matter and activity so related to war as substantially to affect its conduct and progress."[83] Faced with imminent or present dangers of war, Congress and the executive, Stone asserted, must be given the widest latitude of discretion and judgment. It was therefore "not for any court to sit in review of the wisdom of their action or substitute its judgment for theirs."[84] In addition, Stone's opinion made particular reference to the external factors that governed the necessity of the curfew order: the devastation at Pearl Harbor, Japanese advancement in the Pacific, and military "findings" that merited the need to meet threats of espionage and sabotage assumed of persons of Japanese ancestry, which would negate the nation's war effort and its safety.[85] These factors may have suggested mere judicial deference, but the Court's treatment of these contributory factors that led to the policies, an assessment of the actors involved, and the authority they drew on led the Court to determine the constitutional viability of the orders in question.

The Supreme Court's main concern was the scope of the federal government's war power, which it dealt with quickly by affirming the validity of the exercised war power rather than determining whether it was right or wrong, wise or unwise.[86] As such, the Court's lack of pronouncement left in place the assertion of presidential prerogatives under exigent circumstances. Stone noted that because of these findings, FDR, Congress, and the military had a solid foundation to provide support for their respective decisions and that each entity could "reasonably" determine that its actions were just and proper.[87] Ultimately, the curfew was within the limits of the war power at the time it was instituted. Moreover, DeWitt's curfew order was based on the constitutional delegation of legislative power and was a practical measure for securing national security.[88] The practical necessity of securing the nation outweighed the claim of any right's violation. With respect to Fifth Amendment rights, Stone argued that the amendment contains no equal-protection clause and therefore only restrains discriminatory legislation that denies due process of the laws.

Having quickly dispensed with a determination of the curfew's constitutionality,[89] the Court upheld the order, because it aided in contributing to the winning of the war, and the government "did not have ground[s] for believing" the curfew to be unnecessary.[90] In fact, at no point did the Court apply a close-scrutiny test to the actions and conclusions drawn by the president, Congress, or the military. Rather, constrained by the practical realities of war, the Court took two propositions as facts, which constituted a rational basis for the military's decision for the curfew order. In a time of war, the Court found, when residents have ethnic affiliations to the invading enemy, they may be a source of danger, and the perceived existential threat to the West Coast in 1942 did not grant the military the time to segregate and judge the American loyalty of people of Japanese descent on an individual basis. Similar claims would be made during the war on terror (Chapter 6), yet there, the Supreme Court would conclude that the George W. Bush administration overstepped its authority when it denied citizens their basic constitutional rights.

In short, the Supreme Court reviewed *Hirabayashi* with restraint.[91] Stone did not find any room to speak out against the decisions made by the administration, Congress, or the military, nor did the Court make any suggestions about whether limits should to be placed on war powers. In fact, Justice William Douglas's concurrence affirmed the Court's position, noting, "[W]e cannot sit in judgment on the military requirement of that hour."[92] Justice Frank Murphy's concurrence, on the other hand, was critical of the ruling. He rejected the idea that essential liberties could be put on hold by a state of war and believed that when an order singled out a group on the basis of color and ancestry, it went against the American tradition, its ideals, and its basic principles.[93]

The Supreme Court's opinion lent support to the government's evacuation policy, but the administration was well aware that the West Coast exclusion order and internment had not fully survived judicial scrutiny. For example, Murphy's concurrence, originally drafted as a dissent, asserted that the U.S. Army had moved "to the very brink of Constitutional power" when it instituted the curfews.[94] This contention suggested that the administration would have a difficult time if the internment policy were challenged head on. Moreover, it implied that the *Hirabayashi* decision could not be used to justify further expansions of unilateral power. However, this implication did not come to fruition; the Court determined that wartime measures must yield wide discretionary authority, which included the subversion of individual rights on the basis of race.

The Supreme Court under Justice Stone—not wanting to impede the prosecution of the war, but sensitive toward individual and minority rights—faced the dilemma of weighing the nation's security with the civil liberties of its citizens. The *Hirabayashi* decision was thus a calculated opinion toward "the formulation of a constitutional doctrine adequate to the needs of American society in its present state of siege."[95] The Court's geopolitical construction and a desire to unify the bench ultimately determined that the present state of war necessitated extreme measures, which could include the restriction of individual rights in favor of discretionary presidential prerogatives. Remaining sensitive to minority rights, the Court did not deal directly with the race-based claims present in the case due to a fear of imminent attack from those residing in the homeland. Generally, the justices agreed that the Court should focus on only Hirabayashi's violation of the order and leave the question of race-based orders, because the circumstances of the day (i.e., the war) made the order judicious.[96] But Stone also deemed it necessary to increase the government's power because of geopolitical concerns, and he had a majority.[97]

Justice Jackson aligned himself with the general theory of restraint, but he shared a similar conflict with Justice Felix Frankfurter in viewing the imposition of practical limits on power as the duty of the Court,[98] which is evident in his *Youngstown* (1952) concurring opinion. Essentially, Jackson maintained that judicial activism strips democratic government where "the attitude[s] of a society and its organized political forces, rather than its legal machinery, [are] the controlling force in the character of free institutions."[99] Given Stone's resolve to decide the case narrowly to unify a divided bench,[100] Jackson set aside this position and joined the *Hirabayashi* majority. It would not be until *Korematsu* that Jackson's concerns would come to the fore in his dissenting opinion.

Although he was a leading spokesman of judicial self-restraint,[101] Frankfurter maintained that the Court should not curb the effective exercise of the war power by sticking to the "due process of the law."[102] In *Blaisdell* (1934), he endorsed former colleague Chief Justice Charles Evans Hughes's position that "while emergency does not create power, emergency may furnish the occasion for the exercise of power."[103] As long as war-power measures were not unreasonable and military determinations were not unfounded, the use of war powers by the executive would be constitutional. Given the Court's deductions, Frankfurter joined the majority in upholding the current curfew order, finding sufficient grounds for believing that the war measures were necessary. Justice Hugo Black followed suit, noting, in line with Stone, "I want it done on the narrowest possible points."[104] However, Black expressed an alternative view when he wrote the majority opinion in *Korematsu*. The plurality evaluated Korematsu's claim broadly and, again, found in favor of the executive branch, reasoning that the welfare of a nation necessarily trumped the assertion of a right's violation.

The position of Justice Stanley Reed (a moderate and swing voter) in *Hirabayashi* and *Korematsu* also suggested deference to the war power. The only significant input made by Reed in *Hirabayashi* was his remark on Murphy's draft dissent: "Military protection only needs reasonable grounds, which this record has. You cannot wait for an invasion to see if [Japanese American] loyalty triumphs."[105] Reed's commentary illustrated how he was constrained (as the Court should have been) by the exogenous factors when balancing the internment policy with the race-based nature of the claims asserted in the case. Moreover, given the tenuous nature of the case, the Court needed only to employ a rational-basis test. Once the opinion was completed, Reed remarked to Stone, "You have stated a very difficult situation in a way that will preserve rights in different cases and at the same time enable the military forces to function."[106] Although the justices believed that individual rights should be protected, their consensus was that if the Court determined the viability of exigent circumstances, then the judiciary should provide the legal space for such measures to be carried out effectively.

The Court placed polity principles above individual rights violations when its *Hirabayashi* decision asserted that it did not need to address the question of whether the president had acted in accordance with the law to impose curfews, because Congress had given its support. Congress and the executive, the Court maintained, acted jointly to "impose restrictions as an emergency war measure."[107]

Even though Justice Douglas's concurrence highlighted unease with the case's implication of racial guilt—that is, that all Japanese Americans would be considered potential enemies—he restated that the narrow grounds upon which the case had been decided[108] could leave for the moment a decision on race claims. He concluded that the Court must grant the military good faith, because it was not the Court's duty to stand in judgment on the military's determination of the curfew order.[109] The "temporary treatment on a group basis was the only practical expedient" during national emergencies.[110]

The concurrence of Justice Frank Murphy (a crusader of minority rights)[111] initially appeared to go against the Court's findings; he all too readily noted that being in a state of war did not suspend "the broad guarantees of the Bill of Rights and other provisions of the Constitution in protecting essential liberties."[112] Murphy even censured "distinctions based on color or ancestry," which he noted were "inconsistent with our ideals."[113] However, although Murphy believed that the curfews were based on "a priori" assumptions of racial guilt, he was also willing to defer to military judgment.[114]

Murphy's concurrence began as a dissent, but the pressures of public opinion, Justice Frankfurter's letter, and the possible perception of a lone dissent in the middle of a war eventually swayed him into writing a concurrence.[115] Frankfurter's informal letter to Murphy stressed the importance of "closing the ranks." He reminded Murphy:

> [A dissent] has internal contradictions which you ought not to allow to stand. . . . [C]an't you write your views with such expressed tolerance that you won't make people think that when eight others disagree with you, you think their view means that they want to destroy the liberties of the United States, and lose the war at home?[116]

Appealing to the geopolitical construction, Frankfurter maintained that the Court must be constrained by the exogenous factors in political time when deciding the case in legal time. A real fear of attack and espionage loomed large, and the Court must be restrained to act by directly challenging the bounds of military discretion.[117] Murphy succumbed to Frankfurter's words and concurred on the narrow grounds purported by the Court: that a rational basis existed for discrimination at the time the order was applied.[118] When executive prerogatives would be called into question again in *Korematsu*, Murphy would have an opportunity to advance his concerns by writing a dissenting opinion.

Even though Justice Wiley Rutledge agreed with Stone's position that the judiciary should be restrained and should not scrutinize military discretion in military areas, he asserted that there were "bounds beyond which [De-Witt] cannot go and, if he oversteps them[,] . . . the courts . . . have power to protect the civilian."[119] Rutledge's claim highlighted the Court's capacity as an agent of change to circumvent the political process: while the Court maintained the narrative established in its *Curtiss-Wright* decision, that the executive has the authority to make foreign policy, it added that if the Court concludes that the policy "oversteps" its constitutional bounds, then the judiciary will intervene.

Hirabayashi set the groundwork for the inevitable majority and for the scornful dissenting opinions in *Korematsu*. As the justices jockeyed for position in *Hirabayashi*, the continued fear of immediate attack, presidential prerogatives, congressional maneuverings, and military action all served to constrain the Supreme Court to find in favor of broad prerogatives. Although the *Hirabayashi* decision established the rationale for the Court as it decided *Korematsu*, the dissenters reasoned that striking down racial prejudices should outweigh national-security concerns.

At the same time that the Court issued its opinions in *Yasui* and *Hirabayashi*—upholding the curfew—Tule Lake's relocation center was chosen as the place to house evacuees identified to be loyal to only Japan. Eventually, eighteen thousand people were housed at Tule Lake. In mid-February 1944, FDR issued EO 9423,[120] which transferred oversight of the WRA from the Office for Emergency Management to the Department of the Interior. FDR believed that the transfer to a cabinet would strengthen the position of the administration and the image of the WRA to Congress and the public. In turn, he thought, this position would yield continued support for the internment and relocation programs.[121]

Korematsu, an American citizen with Japanese ancestry (Nisei) who was born and raised in California, refused to report for relocation. He was arrested for violating DeWitt's exclusion order and prosecuted under Public Law 503 and EO 9066. The crux of Korematsu's argument was whether the exclusion order was a necessary war measure. And if it was, "was it a transgression of the Bill of Rights?"[122]

The Ninth Circuit Court of Appeals affirmed the lower court's ruling and upheld the conviction. Because the Supreme Court had upheld the notion of military emergency in its *Hirabayashi* ruling, Assistant Secretary of War John McCloy was convinced that the government had the advantage in arguing *Korematsu*. Consequently, he advised Justice Department lawyers not to do anything that could create any doubt between the two cases.[123] The Court granted certiorari and announced its *Korematsu* decision the same day as its *Ex parte Endo* decision. In *Endo*, the Court ruled that on statutory grounds, EO 9066 and EO 9102 could not be construed as giving the WRA "authority to subject citizens who are concededly loyal" to detention in a relocation center.[124] But Douglas's majority opinion also emphasized that the Japanese American program and the legal measures utilized would be in effect only during the time of the threat and that these individuals would regain their freedom after the threat subsided.[125] This argument is all too familiar; accommodation theory maintains that under exigent circumstances, the Constitution should be "relaxed or suspended."[126]

The *Korematsu* decision fractured the Supreme Court. In a sharply divided 6–3 ruling, the Court concluded that the government had acted constitutionally when it ordered the emergency exclusion of Japanese Americans. It thus rejected Korematsu's discrimination argument and upheld his conviction. Writing the majority opinion allowed Justice Black to expand upon the narrow findings of *Hirabayashi*. Siding with the government, Black determined that the U.S. Army had reason to trust that Japanese Americans presented a significant risk to the nation's national security.

Determining that EO 9066 was constitutional and that the government's policy to relocate citizens to protect against espionage was legally valid, the Court determined that the immediate threat of attack outweighed the rights violation asserted by Korematsu. The Court reasoned that the order and the actions it authorized were a constitutional exercise of the president's war powers: "[T]he curfew order [w]as an exercise of the power of the government to take steps necessary to prevent espionage and sabotage in an area threatened by Japanese attack."[127]

Solicitor General Fahy emphasized the constitutionality of the evacuation program and the value in averting sabotage and espionage.[128] He asserted that the evacuation was "reasonably related" to a victorious end to the war.[129] This reasoning resonated with the Court's holding when Black noted that the orders were reasonable to avert the genuine threat of danger.[130]

Black reasoned that Civilian Exclusion Order 34 was a necessary use of presidential power and that Korematsu was in violation of it. Considering Black's observations, with "the presence of an unascertained number of disloyal persons of Japanese ancestry[,] it was impossible to bring about an immediate segregation of the disloyal from the loyal . . . [so] temporary exclusion of the whole group was deemed a military necessity." Black concluded, "[I]n time of war[,] citizenship may carry with it heavier burdens and responsibilities than in time of peace; citizens must recognize the fact that the 'power to protect must be commensurate with the threatened danger.'"[131] Yet again, the majority holding favored the military necessity of safeguarding the homeland vis-à-vis rights principles.

In comparing the exclusion order in *Korematsu* to the curfew order in *Hirabayashi*, Black stated that both orders were reasonable ("not unfounded") and essential to prevent the dangers of espionage and sabotage. Black further asserted that because curfew was considered inadequate exclusion, it was therefore a logical and necessary measure.[132] Black also rejected Korematsu's argument that the exclusion order was invalid because it led to detention. Ad-

ditionally, he determined that *Korematsu* had nothing to do with racial prejudice, because "Korematsu was not excluded from the Military Area because
of hostility to him or his race." Rather, his exclusion was due to the fact that
"we are at war with the Japanese empire." Black concluded, "The power to exclude includes the power to do it by force if necessary. And any forcible measure must necessarily entail some degree of detention or restraint[,] whatever
method of detention is select[ed]."[133] Black found that the order was therefore
valid, even though evacuation and detention could not be separated.[134]

Even though Black was steadfast in preserving civil liberties, in times of
national emergency, he believed that "the welfare of the people is the supreme
law." During times of war, Black traditionally upheld governmental action, but
he tended not to do the same during "normal" times:[135] civil-liberties claims
often won out. But given the geopolitical construction, Black had faith that the
Supreme Court's determination was justified, considering the extraordinary
circumstances surrounding the case.[136] He therefore rejected the racial over-
tones of the exclusion order: "To cast this case into outlines of racial prejudice,
without reference to the real military dangers which were presented, merely
confuses the issue."[137] It was necessary, Black maintained, to trust the military.
He reiterated that during times of national emergencies, such as the one the
nation faced in the immediate sense, it was necessary to have such measures in
place to protect the nation's security.[138]

Even though strict scrutiny was applied for the first time in *Korematsu*,
the Court upheld the race-based exclusion order and internment, because it
found that strict scrutiny was limited to instances of de jure discrimination;
racial classifications must be written directly into the language of a statute.
One of the next times the Court would adhere to this doctrine would be in
Adarand Constructors (1995),[139] in which it would hold that race-based discrimination, including affirmative action, must pass the strict-scrutiny standard.

In an early draft, Black stated that "nothing short of apprehension of the
gravest imminent danger to the public safety can constitutionally justify either
curfew or detention at assembly centers." To which Stone retorted, "[I]t is
important for us to make it plain that we do not impose our judgment on the
military unless we can say they have no ground on which to go in formulating
their orders."[140] Ultimately, however, the Court determined that the national
emergency was sufficiently grave to warrant finding the orders constitutional.
This reasoning was again reiterated in Frankfurter's concurring opinion, in
which he maintained that the exclusion order was constitutional, because the
military deemed it necessary and found "some grounds" for anticipating the
danger of sabotage and espionage.[141] Exclusion was a suitable way to successfully conduct the war effort, according to the Court.[142]

Frankfurter's concurrence, which provided an expanded discussion of the metes and bounds in which the military might act constitutionally, lay between Black's majority opinion and the dissenting opinions of Roberts, Murphy, and Jackson. Adhering to judicial self-restraint, Frankfurter considered the *Korematsu* case within the context of war, arguing that military action

> is not to be stigmatized as lawless because like action in times of peace would be lawless. . . . [I]f a military order . . . does not transcend the means appropriate for conducting war, such action by the military is . . . constitutional.[143]

Essentially Frankfurter protected the strength of the war power.[144] In a late 1942 address, Frankfurter said that the main task of the United States was to facilitate the successful conclusion of a war and that, consequently, "any interest or issue that stood in its way should be put aside,"[145] including rights principles.

Despite the majority position of the Supreme Court, the three dissenting justices—Roberts, Murphy, and Jackson—found that issues of racial prejudice outweighed national-security interests. At the time when *Korematsu* was under review (late 1944), the geopolitical concerns appeared to be tipping in favor of Allied forces, and those dissenting believed that the Court's reliance on external pressures to find in favor of the government's actions should no longer be a constraining factor. Consequently, Roberts, Murphy, and Jackson were unwilling to uphold military decisions and actions without question as the other justices appeared to do. While the Court as a whole evaluated the external world, those in the majority and those in the minority weighed competing claims but drew two very different conclusions.

Roberts remained silent in the *Hirabayashi* case, but his dissent in *Korematsu* was influenced by his examination of the facts concerning the events leading up to Korematsu's detention. Roberts also used a factual analysis of the issues to draw his conclusions in *Endo*. He concluded that he did not trust the reasonableness on which the military based its actions. Moreover, he believed that the majority was willing to base its determination too broadly, which sanctioned the war power to infringe on civil liberties. Justice Roberts's dissent maintained that the Court's earlier defense of curfews could not be equated with placing citizens "in a concentration camp" exclusively on the basis of ancestry and without evidence of disloyalty.

The concerns Justice Murphy had with Stone's reasoning in *Hirabayashi* all but disappeared in light of Black's opinion in *Korematsu*. Murphy took a rather expansive view of individual liberties and believed in limitations on government action, which was evident in his *Korematsu* dissent. When Murphy learned of Black's decision to write his opinion using the principles advocated in *Hirabayashi* to uphold the exclusion order, Murphy's response was "[T]he Court has blown up on the Jap case—just as I expected it would."[146] Murphy was convinced that the concerns raised in *Korematsu* were significantly more serious than those raised in *Hirabayashi*. As a result, Murphy redrafted his original dissent in *Hirabayashi* when he wrote his dissent in *Korematsu*. He argued that the Court, in the present case, was sanctioning a "legalization of racism." Murphy believed that the Court failed to apply a necessary, tougher standard when it reviewed the military justification for the exclusion order: "This exclusion . . . on a plea of military necessity in absence of martial law ought not to be approved."[147]

While Murphy acknowledged the power of Congress and the president to grant wide discretion to the military in wartime, he believed that the exclusion order, whether "temporarily or permanently, [with respect to] all persons with Japanese blood . . . has no such reasonable relation" to sabotage and espionage and that the belief that "all persons of Japanese ancestry may have a dangerous tendency" was supported by "semi-military conclusions drawn from an unwarranted use of circumstantial evidence."[148] Murphy went one step further and cited expert independent studies that refuted the validity of a "good portion of the evidence and conclusions [that] DeWitt based his order on."[149]

Murphy further asserted that the exclusion order was based on unreasonable racial discrimination, which denied Japanese Americans the Fifth Amendment's equal-protection rights. Murphy reasoned that the segregation of Japanese Americans "goes over 'the brink of constitutional power' and falls into the ugly abyss of racism."[150] Moreover, he noted, the order resembled "the abhorrent and despicable treatment of minority groups by the dictatorial tyrannies which this nation is now pledged to destroy."[151] Ultimately, the exclusion order was about race and not an emergency:

I dissent . . . from this legalization of racism. Racial discrimination in any form and in any degree has no justifiable part whatever in our democratic way of life. It is unattractive in any setting, but it is utterly revolting among a free people who have embraced the principles set forth in the Constitution of the United States. All residents of this nation are kin in some way[,] by blood or culture[,] to a foreign land. They . . . [are] entitled to all the rights and freedoms guaranteed by the Constitution.[152]

Murphy's concurrence in *Endo* reiterated the "unconstitutional resort to racism inherent in the entire evacuation program," but he noted that Mitsuye

Endo's "unconditional" release gave her the freedom to move freely into California.[153]

Jackson's dissenting opinion in *Korematsu* aligned with Murphy's finding of inherent racism, but Jackson did not comment on whether he found DeWitt's orders reasonable.[154] He did conclude, in line with Roberts, that the two orders were contradictory, but he refrained from defining any kind of limits on the scope of the war power with regard to restricting civil liberties. So even in dissent, the metes and bounds of the power to conduct war were largely left intact.

The military action against Korematsu, Jackson reasoned, was unconstitutional, and he maintained that the Court mistakenly upheld as constitutionally valid a military order that he believed was extralegal and based solely on military necessity.[155] However, Jackson argued that courts "should [not] have attempted to interfere with the Army in carrying out its task."[156] Jackson's dissent ultimately rested on the assertion that the Supreme Court should not be used to police military action:

> [O]nce a judicial opinion rationalizes such an order to show that it conforms to the Constitution, or rather rationalizes the Constitution to show that the Constitution sanctions such an order, the Court for all times has validated the principle of racial discrimination.[157]

This reasoning is best explained by evaluating Jackson's unpublished opinion in *Ex parte Quirin* (1942),[158] a case contemporaneous with the internment cases (see Chapter 6). Jackson began the opinion "with the fixed presumption that the Court has no business reviewing military judgments in time of war."[159] He added:

> [W]e have no more important duty than to keep clear and separate the lines of responsibility and duty of the judicial and of the executive-military arms of government. Merger of the two is the end of liberty. . . . [W]e would do well to refuse to meddle with military measures dealing with captured unlawful enemy belligerents.[160]

Irrespective of how one views Jackson's analysis and his assumptions on the duties and responsibilities of the judiciary and the scope of executive power, this excerpt demonstrates Jackson's principle when thinking about judicial application. Even in dissent, Jackson refused to insist on judicial review of military matters, even when he believed the underlying executive actions were unlawful (*Korematsu*).

Although the Court applied the strict-scrutiny standard, which courts can employ to weigh an asserted government interest against a constitutional right or principle, it concluded that the government had met its burden. Some actions taken by decision makers may have seemed unjustified, but given the political climate surrounding the program of internment and exclusion, the Court reasoned that the nation was often faced with threats that called for extraordinary measures. Courts, at times, tacitly trust the good faith of executive officials to justify excusing civil-liberties concerns with the legal positions that government officials have devised.[161]

Even though *Korematsu*, in the immediate sense, did little to ease the situation of those interned, the Court unanimously determined in *Endo* that the government had no right to detain any loyal citizen without charge; due-process rights must be afforded to those detained. The end result was that "the government could no longer legally confine any loyal Nisei."[162]

World War II was fought to preserve freedom and democracy, yet it instigated one of the greatest suppressions of civil liberties in our history. America was fueled with hysteria, and FDR authorized the internment of tens of thousands of American citizens of Japanese ancestry and resident aliens from Japan, which resulted in the Supreme Court's finding in favor of the president and Congress when rights principles were violated. The management and direction of internment and evacuation were reconstituted to serve the administration's political agenda: securing the nation from imminent attack from within. The judicial branch's interpretation of the national emergency undermined rights principles in each of the internment cases. And the breadth of executive power ultimately depended on the justices' appraisal of the emergency and not on Congress's use of the political process (see Chapter 6).

CONCLUSION: AN UNCERTAIN PATH

When rights and polity principles collide, the Supreme Court asserts its autonomy to determine when military actions are "reasonably" based. To safeguard the nation, the Court determined that racial distinctions needed to be drawn to meet the exigencies of the time and that it was in the position to evaluate the politically charged decision making of the executive, Congress, and the military. The internment cases were chosen carefully by the Court, each one building on the other—*Yasui* and *Hirabayashi* evaluating the constitutionality of the curfew policy, *Korematsu* challenging the relocation policy, and finally *Endo* examining the extent to which citizens could be detained. Ultimately, the Supreme Court provided the legal justification necessary to ensure the continued safety of the nation during wartime. The presence of war was sufficient grounds for the Court to find in the government's favor: geopolitical factors outweighed the concerns of racism.

The suspension of Japanese Americans' constitutional right to civil liberties was, at best, deferred until the nation was no longer at war. A president's claim to unilateral powers and Congress's joint action during an emergency undermined the civil liberties of those individuals of Japanese descent. While the Court attempted to remain judicially restrained and say little, its silence on the practical limitations on the military's measure showed its deference toward the unlimited scope of the war power. FDR was given the latitude with which to act, and legally the Court backed him.

As legal time and geopolitical concerns cross paths, the Supreme Court evaluates the scope of executive powers in light of the exigent circumstances. Aware of the racial undertones of the policies under review in these cases, the Court offered a critical assessment of the president's use of executive power to assert unilateral authority to justify restrictive policies in the name of national security. Considering the practical realities of implementing particular measures that might otherwise be considered unconstitutional as a way to secure the nation's security, the Court allowed for the constitutional delegation of legislative power in the conduct of the war to the military.

The scope of executive power, according to the Court, needed to be determined on the basis of the reasonableness of the actions taken. During wartime, the Court asserted, the nation is faced with imminent dangers, and the executive's power must be given the widest of latitude to meet the challenges of the day.

As such, these cases collectively contributed to the developmental path of the Court as it recognized the practical realities of the executive's unilateral role in the management of foreign policy; the constitutional order established in *Curtiss-Wright* was further entrenched in the Court's treatment of Japanese internment. While the *Curtiss-Wright* decision established the executive as the sole organ of foreign affairs, this set of cases illustrates how the Court instituted the new constitutional order and established a set of parameters in which the executive could make decisions regarding foreign affairs.

Although World War II was a significant external constraint to warrant internment, when the Court would evaluate President Bush's war on terror, it ultimately would find the opposite to be true: the administration went beyond its capacity statutorily to establish military tribunals to deny enemy combatants of their basic constitutional rights. The judiciary's assessment of the geopolitical construction and internal legal norms leads to a determination of how foreign-policy measures proceed. President Donald Trump's executive order, which targets people from Muslim-majority countries who want to enter the United States, revives this political debate, as the U.S. Court of Appeals for the Fourth Circuit temporarily displaced the administration's current policy.[163] Attorney General Jeff Sessions appealed the decision to the Supreme Court (asking for a stay), asserting that the federal immigration law grants to the administration broad authority and that in national-security matters, the courts should defer to the executive. A decision is pending, as the Supreme Court granted certiorari for the end of its 2016–2017 term to review sections of the travel ban that remain temporarily blocked.

As the courts wrestle with developing individual and polity rights principles, judicial decision making restructures presidential authority and ultimately institutes a new model for executive decision making in the management of foreign affairs. FDR, a reconstructive president, appeared to find a responsive Supreme Court—a judiciary supporting the asserted claims of the administration that military measures were reasonable even if they targeted individuals on the basis of their race. However, although the Court aided the political regime in instituting the narrative that race-based claims during wartime necessitated courts' favoring the federal government, it tipped the balance in favor of Congress and the executive only after it evaluated the geopolitical construction. FDR made claims of broad authority to safeguard the nation, but the prowess of the Court provided the constitutional space for such military measures that undermined individual rights.

Justice Jackson's discussion of executive powers in his dissenting opinion in *Korematsu* is given further credence when we turn to his concurrence in *Youngstown*. Jackson's opinion was significant to the advancement of executive unilateral powers, but *Youngstown* illustrates a case when the Court determined that the Korean War, as defined by President Harry Truman, was not a sufficient justification for seizing private property. Drawing a sharp distinction between foreign and domestic affairs, and the extent to which an executive can claim authority to act to protect the nation's security, the Supreme Court, and not those political actors external to the bench, is ultimately responsible for making this assessment.

4

STEEL SEIZURE

A Practical Approach to Presidential Power

The *Youngstown Sheet and Tube Co. v. Sawyer* ruling (1952)[1] provided what some argue is the end point to the impact of *Curtiss-Wright*. This assertion is compelling, because those who contend this point highlight the fact that by 1952, the delegation issue[2] had retreated in significance, and the specific holding in *Curtiss* was no longer applicable. However, this is not an accurate account of the developmental history of the Supreme Court's institutionalization of the sole-organ doctrine[3] that ensconces presidential prerogatives. *Youngstown* is thus further illustration of the Court's domain to define the trajectory of constitutional foreign-affairs jurisprudence. The Court asserted its authority to interpret the Constitution upon finding that the case concerned polity principles. Ultimately, institutions define and redefine constitutional powers.

The steel-seizure case of 1952 marked an extraordinary moment when the Supreme Court, during a time of war, used judicial review to check executive power. On April 8, 1952, President Harry S. Truman announced that in the interests of the Korean War effort, the federal government was seizing the steel mills of all major companies involved in a labor dispute (and a possible strike with the United Steelworkers union). This announcement was met with uniform shock. Presidents of the past had seized plants, but never before had the government, during what was by all intents and purpose a time of peace, apprehended a major portion of an industry as central to the American economy as steel. Nor had a president laid claim to inherent executive powers under Article II of the Constitution to defend a seizure when a statute—in this instance, the Taft-Hartley Act[4]—provided an alternate and legal method for thwarting strikes.

Truman's seizure of the steel mills created a political and constitutional crisis that solicited fundamental questions about the role of the president and the nature of presidential power in a system governed by separation of powers and checks and balances. The crux of the case was the extent to which unilateral powers can be extended in the domestic sphere. In the end, the rights of the steel mills prevailed, and Truman's assertions were censured. The steel-seizure case afforded the country with a rare opportunity to reexamine the balance of authority among the branches. More importantly, it provided an occasion for the Court to reassess and potentially redefine the scope of presidential power in light of almost twenty years of unparalleled exploitation of executive authority. Truman's unprecedented action sparked a traditional, constitutional, and institutional debate—did the president act with legal authority? If he did not, what role, if any, did Congress play in passing judgment? And finally, did that judgment fall to the Supreme Court?

Although the Court drew a line in the sand between domestic and foreign affairs, Justice Robert H. Jackson's concurring opinion, over developmental time, provided an oversimplified set of rules for courts to determine the capacity in which the executive has the authority to act. The Court did not stand at the periphery and rubber-stamp Truman's actions; rather, the Court took an active role and provided a practical framework (Jackson's concurring opinion) by which to evaluate the executive's role vis-à-vis Congress. *Youngstown* was therefore another instance when the judiciary delineated the scope of executive power, outlining in what capacity the president had the authority to act, with or without congressional approval.

The developmental framework advocated by the Court's *Youngstown* decision—that the practical realities of foreign affairs often necessitated unilateral executive action—expanded on the new constitutional order. *Curtiss-Wright* legalized a transitional period of change (executives can legally justify unilateral decision making in the management of foreign policy), but *Youngstown* provided further insight into the feedback loop and mechanisms between legal and political time; as the Court defines and reconstitutes constitutional development, in this capacity the judiciary influences the political process over developmental time. *Youngstown* was thus a notable presidential-judicial interaction, illustrating how the Court takes opportunities to reaffirm its authority to interpret the Constitution[5] and to determine the scope of presidential prerogatives.

When separation of powers (or more broadly, polity principles) is legally challenged, the Court balances the need to usurp rights, as asserted by the administration, with the authority to act under exigent circumstances. The perceived emergency of the Korean War, which the Truman administration proclaimed was tantamount to unilaterally seizing the mills, did not serve to constrain the Court. It found that the president's military power did not extend to labor disputes; this distinction would prove to be clear for the Court when it balanced polity principles. In fact, the Supreme Court determined that Truman chose to seize the steel mills but did not invoke the national-emergency provisions outlined in any one of the three acts available to him, which may have provided him with the statutory authorization to seize and operate the mills.

Congress ultimately avoided making a decision, and the steel industry, wanting to retrieve its property, promptly brought suit. The resulting case of *Youngstown* invalidated President Truman's seizure of the steel mills. Even though *Curtiss-Wright* broadened the parameters of presidential prerogatives, *Youngstown* appeared to rein in the executive. However, an alternative reading of the steel-seizure case demonstrates not only the Court's resolve to use its geopolitical-construction process to determine when and to what degree the executive can act but also the fact that presidents and the Courts would use Jackson's concurrence to further advance broad claims of unilateral authority in foreign affairs.

The political, economic, and legal setting of the spring of 1952 shaped the Court's decision making in what some called an unexpected decision. The case came up against the backdrop of two decades when presidents had steadily expanded their power and the judiciary had all but sanctioned its continued growth.[6] This expansion of power provided what Truman thought was the legal foundation by which to assert that he had the authority to seize the mills. He believed this measure was necessary to safeguard the continued provision of supplies to American troops in Korea and would also support the nation's healthy economy. Truman appeared to be on solid legal ground, so why would the New Deal–Fair Deal Court, which had typically been so receptive to the exercise of presidential authority, restrain the use of inherent executive power in *Youngstown*? Contrary to Truman's assertion that the Korean War substantiated the seizing of private property in emergencies, it was the duty of the Court to determine whether the executive acted beyond his constitutional authority on the basis of its own examination of the exogenous factors surrounding the case.

Youngstown has generally been regarded as a sharp rebuke to President Truman's seizure and an attempt by the judicial branch to immobilize the accumulation of power by the executive. Upon reexamination, the Court's holding was not a simple case of rebuke and not as sweeping as its broad language may have initially suggested. Rather, the Court redefined presidential prerogatives on the basis of its evaluation of the exigent circumstances; the Korean War was not found to be a compelling interest that supported Truman's broad claims. This determination placed individual rights ahead of separation-of-powers principles. Furthermore, Jackson's concurrence provided the extent to which executives may assert their power to act by outlining their working relationship with the legislative branch.

POLITICAL UNDERPINNINGS OF TRUMAN'S COURSE OF ACTION

The key external factor of the spring of 1952 was the Cold War, and Korea quickly became a concern for the administration. In addition, the administration was also confronted with economic concerns, as reconversion faced severe opposition in the congressional midterm elections of 1946 and the mounting political imperatives of the 1948 presidential election. Truman also faced a postwar backlash against presidential power, which ultimately led to the Twenty-Second Amendment (establishing presidential term limits). The combination of these factors presented a volatile political climate in which the Truman administration had to act, and when some of these actions were legally challenged, the Court responded.

Truman, an affiliated[7] president, believed he had the unilateral authority to act. When affiliated presidents are challenged, they find allies on the Supreme Court and often look to the judicial branch for legal support. Truman did just that when he urged the Court to take on the long list of actions that his administration believed were necessary to combat Communism. Truman supposed that this appeal would find patronage on the Court.[8] Even though he made this judicial appeal, he did not believe he actually needed congressional approval to commit troops to Korea. In this particular instance, Truman attempted to reconstruct the powers of the executive by claiming the unilateral power to seize the private steel mills, which in his estimation were vital to the success of the war efforts.

In the area of foreign affairs, Truman was unconcerned with "continuing, extending, or more creatively reconceptualizing the fundamental commitments made by an earlier reconstructive leader."[9] Rather, he had to "call forth independent action, disruptive of previously established political and institutional arrangements," and he had to "establish legitimacy anew on his own terms."[10] In foreign policy making, Truman saw the Korean War—and more specifically, the impending steel strike—as an opportunity to assert unilateral executive powers, an occasion to confirm independent action and his authority to act unilaterally. But Truman's attempt to define his own constitutional authority was met by a Court unwilling to yield its judicial capacity to interpret the Constitution. Truman's authority thus hinged on the justifications of his actions drawn from the moment; the impending steel strike would cause a threat to the successful outcome of the Korean War and would deter securing the legitimacy that this particular action would give to presidential power—namely, a claim to unilateral power as an instrument of domestic policy making, which the Court would later claim as an inherently legislative role.

Even though the threat of Communist aggression had been talked about for years, the nation was surprised when North Korea invaded the Republic of Korea to the south in June 1950. The Truman administration believed that the Communists had to be repelled in Korea to dissuade them from using force elsewhere. To avert the outbreak of a third world war, Truman employed limited aggression[11] but decided not to confer with Congress.[12] Even without a formal declaration of war, a large number of American troops were committed.

Truman envisioned a quick end to the hostilities and thus downplayed the seriousness of the course of action taken. During a press conference, he definitively stated, "We are not at war."[13] Truman characterized the situation as a police action,[14] yet the Korean conflict soon became a war in every practical sense. As such, the term "police action" was an infelicitous description for the current situation. In fact, one congressman's reaction to the use of this phrase was emblematic. Harold Cooley (D-NC) noted, "Our countrymen are fighting and dying every hour of the day and the night. . . . Yet we sit here and seem to think that we are engaged in a kind of 'police action.' . . . Let us face up to the fact: This is no police action. It is nothing short of war."[15]

The gravity of the situation was evident, and several legislatures began to ask why the president had not sought congressional ratification of his actions.[16] Few, however, categorically stated that the war was illegal, as Senator Robert Taft did.[17] As the situation worsened, more congressional representatives joined Senator Taft,[18] which put Truman in a difficult situation. The administration did not have the cooperation of Congress, and many of its members were unwilling to act as though the nation were involved in an acute wartime emergency.[19] And the decision to proceed with measures commensurate with war without first acquiring formal approval from Congress in the steel-seizure case resulted in a sharp rebuke from the Supreme Court.

However, many members of Congress and the public agreed with Truman that the initial intervention and the decision to cross the 38th parallel were strategically the right moves. As intensity mounted thanks to the Chinese Communists' intervention to support the North Koreans in late 1950, Truman was forced to take retaliatory action. He realized that what had started as a police action would become a lengthier conflict requiring many more soldiers and more materials. This particular point turned out to be a decisive issue in the minds of a handful of justices when they deliberated over the president's decision in *Youngstown* (see Justice Fred Vinson's dissent, for example).

A month after the involvement of the Chinese Communists, Truman declared a "limited" national emergency.[20] This declaration, Truman knew, would trigger the employment of a variety of statutory provisions yielding to the president additional power to act in this ever-increasing crisis.[21]

Increasing defense expenditures meant the administration would need to reevaluate the economic policy promulgated after the United States entered the Korean War. From the beginning of the conflict, Truman did not pursue direct control from Congress over the economy. In fact, the administration believed the economy would not be seriously affected by the war and that inflation was best dealt with by indirect controls. This reservation to restrict economic controls, Truman decided, would minimize the fear that the nation was gearing up for another war.[22] Immediately after North Korea invaded South Korea, consumers and business owners alike stockpiled goods and materials they feared would be in short supply (a behavior known as "scare buying"). In response, speeches on the floors of both houses led to sponsoring standby authority for the president so that he could enforce wage and price controls as needed.[23]

The Defense Production Act of 1950 was passed with overwhelming majorities[24] and aligned with the general framework legitimized in *Curtiss-Wright*—that the legislature may grant to the executive discretionary powers. This act contained all the provisions Truman requested, including Titles IV and V, which dealt with price and wage stabilization and the ability to settle labor disputes. In conjunction with Title II (the power to requisition), these provisions granted him the authority to requisition property, or the use thereof, when he concluded "that the use of any equipment, supplies, or component parts thereof, or materials or facilities necessary for the manufacture, servicing, or operation of such equipment, supplies, or component parts, is needed for the national defense."[25] The legal action available to the administration in dealing with the steel dispute in 1951 and 1952 was therefore palpable. Congress set the parameters of the objectives to be achieved but left to the president's discretion the determination of appropriate means of achieving those goals.[26] Congress wanted an effective way to handle labor disputes that affected national defense[27]—Title V. Recognizing that price and wage stabilization would put an unfamiliar pressure on the collective bargaining process,[28] Congress thus authorized discretionary power to the president.[29]

Title V proved to be a weak source of authority for the president as he attempted to handle the labor disputes that arose during the Korean War. The steel strike of 1952 pitted the United Steelworkers against ten steelmakers, among which was U.S. Steel. Essentially, the unions held that during World War II, the National War Labor Board (NWLB) had unjustly held wages below the level of inflation, yet corporate profits had risen significantly. Several unions were determined not to feel the same kind of unfair treatment under the new Wage Stabilization Board (WSB); as such, representatives gathered to influence the WSB deliberative process. When deliberations did not go well, the unions went on strike.[30]

Executive Order (EO) 10161 (September 1950)[31] established the mechanism by which to implement the Defense Production Act of 1950.[32] However, in late September 1950, the military situation in Korea dramatically improved, and the scare buying subsided. The need for defense expenditures seemed redundant, but the Chinese Communists' intervention at the end of November quickly changed military and economic conditions. On a daily basis, the position of American troops grew worse, and at home, a second, concentrated bout of scare buying ensued. Truman thus had to amend his assessment on military spending, but he was faced with the ever-increasing pressure of economic inflation. Accordingly, he believed that vigorous measures would need to be taken to curtail this rising inflation.[33] Price controls were established because of the demand for critical defense production and the rising cost of living, affecting steel, copper, electric power, and food, for example. Because price controls were necessary in certain areas, wages would also need to be stabilized.[34]

Business owners and labor unions alike hurried to increase their prices and wages before the administration could impose what many believed were inevitable controls[35] that Truman warned were coming. On January 26, 1951, Truman implemented sweeping mandatory controls and further cautioned the nation of an impending general freeze.[36] In retaliation and as a way to demonstrate their dissatisfaction, labor members withdrew from the WSB in February 1951. A domino effect occurred, and labor representatives in all mobilization and stabilization agencies correspondingly resigned,[37] leaving Truman with a crisis.

To continue to successfully fight the Korean War, the Truman administration had to come up with a solution to the wage-stabilization crisis. It was widely contended throughout the executive branch that a halt in production in the steel industry could not be allowed to occur. Even though the administration maintained that the Korean situation was uncertain and that fighting was quite sporadic, it could not afford to discount the real possibility that military action would increase. Following a conference between Truman and his top advisers, he was even more determined to prevent the labor strike. With the increasing conflict in Korea, Truman was resolute in his efforts to preserve the integrity of his current economic policy, despite some of the concessions he believed that he had already made.[38]

When the Republican-led 80th Congress passed the Labor Management Relations Act (better known as the Taft-Hartley Act [1947])[39] and then overrode Truman's veto, union leaders who had wanted to see Truman defeated in 1948[40] quickly returned to the Democratic fold. The Taft-Hartley Act was passed to equalize the standing of labor and management vis-à-vis the government, but unions believed that it essentially tied their hands.[41] On the other hand, Congress—which had witnessed postwar union strikes—believed this act would curtail the perceived increased power of the unions. Even the Truman administration believed that some labor legislation was necessary,[42] but Truman, benevolent to the views of the unions, considered the Taft-Hartley Act to be too restricting and was keen to draw on the political capital of his veto.[43]

When labor withdrew from the stabilization boards, in 1951, the United Labor Policy Committee wanted to reconstitute the WSB, which would have the authority to settle labor disputes and oversee wage-stabilization regulations.[44] Organized labor was on board. Its representatives understood the administration's desire to have continuous production during the Korean conflict, but they also believed that the emergency did not warrant a "no-strike" assurance. And the Taft-Hartley Act did not include a provision by which to settle disputes. The business community opposed the creation of the board and proposed changes. Despite these objections, the WSB resumed operations.

In the meantime, President Truman commenced with military action in Korea and initially had the full support of the public and Congress. Senate Minority Leader Kenneth Wherry (R-NE), for example, applauded the president on his actions: "A sigh of relief has swept across the country. . . . [Truman] says to the Communist hordes, '[T]hus far and no further.'"[45] In July 1950, a public-opinion poll showed that 81 percent of those surveyed approved sending troops to Korea.[46] In addition, for the first time since Truman's second term began, his popularity increased, rising from 37 percent prior to the conflict in Korea to 46 percent after he sent troops.[47] But public opinion changed quickly. With Chinese Communists now occupying Korea, the public's faith in the president was weakened. Additionally, an increase in prices and continued military defeat undermined the Truman administration's policy and commitment to the Korean conflict.[48] Lacking the vision and charisma of the reconstructive president Franklin D. Roosevelt (FDR), Truman, now a war leader, could not inspire the public as FDR had. Truman's popularity faded fast when the Communists broke off truce talks in November 1951.[49]

At the time of the steel seizure, the Truman administration faced a low political standing thanks to the difficulties of the Korean War and the fervent concerns over economic controls. Moreover, 1952 was an election year, and Congress was deeply divided, ideologically and regionally. Senators and representatives faithful to the president could not withstand the coalitions of Republicans and Southern Democrats.[50] Acutely aware of his political standing, Truman announced on March 29, 1952, that he would not run for reelection. However, his status as a lame-duck president did not discourage him from using any means necessary to achieve the desired result in Korea. Truman ardently trusted in a robust executive branch. The president, he declared, was the guardian of American citizens as a whole and must therefore use all his powers, and powers not explicitly drawn from the Constitution, to safeguard their welfare:

> These powers, which are not explicitly written into the Constitution[,] are the powers which no President can pass on to his successor. They go only to him who can take and use them. . . . [I]t is through the use of these great powers that leadership arises, events are molded, and administrations take on their character. Their use can make a . . . Lincoln administration; their nonuse can make a . . . Grant Administration.[51]

The steel dispute occurred during the last year of Truman's presidency, and it gave him the opportunity to transform his theory of executive prerogatives into a practical approach. But the Supreme Court would be the ultimate test of this transformation.

Truman believed that the conflict between the steel companies and the steelworkers presented a threat to the supply of steel, which would severely jeopardize the Korean War effort. Truman definitively held that a strike in this industry could not be tolerated: "[I]t is of the utmost importance to prevent an interruption in the production of steel. Steel is a key material in our entire defense effort." So the "continuous production . . . is essential in order to meet urgent demands for steel—steel for weapons, for factories, for highways and hospitals and schools."[52] But the administration was faced with two powerful and hostile parties—the United Steelworkers and the steel industry. A reasonable agreement needed to be imposed, but a strike had to be avoided at all costs, because it could shut down most of the steel industry.

Steel companies were experiencing their most profitable period since World War I[53] and hoped to maintain this prosperity throughout the Korean conflict. The industry was agreeable to giving wage increases as long as it could raise the price of steel and sustain its current profits. However, the upshot of price controls going into effect was that profit margins would be vulnerable to the imposition of any additional costs. Consequently, new contracts would be negotiated with the United Steelworkers by the end of 1951. While the government was imploring the steel industry to increase its capacity to meet the current demands of the Korean conflict, it failed to take into account the investment per dollar of sales in the steel industry.[54] On the other hand, the United Steelworkers, fully aware of the profits being made by the companies, wanted to be rewarded for these profits. With each respective point of view having major stakes, the upcoming contract talks would culminate in the historic confrontation of 1952.

Current contracts were due to terminate at the end of 1951, and if new contracts were not reached by then, United Steelworkers, which had already given the required notice set by the Taft-Hartley Act, was legally permitted to strike. Benjamin Fairless, the president of U.S. Steel, signaled that no wage settlement would be reached until the government had indicated how much of a price increase it would allow the steel companies to impose.[55] But the government refused to give any assurance on a price increase in the initial negotiations. With the impending strike deadline, Truman decided it was best to refer the dispute to the WSB. Defending this action, Truman added, "The law and regulations assure that the steel companies will get price increases if they are entitled to them."[56] Appealing to patriotism, Truman urged that those parties involved would continue production and cooperate with the WSB, because "the national interest demands it."[57]

As negotiations unfolded between the steel industry and the unions, the president would not yield to the steel industry's demand for a price increase. As such, the negotiations became more intense, and the White House staff began to discuss other courses of action that could be taken to avert a strike. If the administration chose to seize the steel mills, the president had plenty of options: he could seek an injunction under the Taft-Hartley Act, seize the steel mills under Section 18 of the Selective Service Act of 1948, utilize the executive's inherent powers, or request seizure legislation from Congress. Moreover, because the process was lengthy and required meeting the needs of the steel crisis, the White House did not entertain the idea of sequestering the mills under Title II of the Defense Production Act.[58] In fact, Truman believed he had the unilateral authority to seize the steel mills (if necessary), so there was no reason to employ statutory authority. This rationale eventually led to the steel industry's challenging Truman's claim of discretionary power, which provided the constitutional space for the Supreme Court to evaluate Truman's assertion of power.

The Taft-Hartley Act, the administration held, did not receive any serious consideration, because Truman implied its use was unwarranted in the present situation.[59] Under the advice of Milton Kayle, a member of the White House staff, and his legal advisers, Truman believed a strike would have an adverse effect on the Korean War. He advocated using the executive's inherent powers to unilaterally achieve his ultimate goal of a successful outcome in stopping the spread of Communism.[60] Kayle and Justice Department lawyers seriously considered, as a legal defense, relying on the inherent powers of the executive, under Article II of the Constitution. This tactic had obvious advantages, for no statutory restraints would exist governing the manner and timing of seizing the mills. Once an executive order was issued, according to Kayle and the lawyers, the government could take over the steel mills. Furthermore, any compensation—required per the Selective Service Act of 1948—would not be relevant. The tactic's major drawback was the uncertain legal basis for such a claim.[61]

After much discussion of the options available to the president, Justice Department attorneys concluded that if seizing the mills was indeed necessary, then Section 18 of the Selective Service Act was the authority on which to base the president's actions.[62] However, Defense Department representatives were steadfast in their opposition to utilizing this provision. Employing the executive's inherent powers, they asserted, would be less vulnerable to attack in court.[63] Moreover, this option would take less time to implement and would be less complicated for the administration. If the case went to court, the Defense Department claimed, the action could be defended on the grounds that neither Section 18 nor the Taft-Hartley Act was practical or reasonable in the situation of the steel conflict.[64]

In April 1952, Truman addressed the nation and noted that he was instructing Secretary of Commerce Charles Sawyer to take control of the steel mills on behalf of the government.[65] The country faced a national emergency, Truman stressed, and its security depended upon its capacity to maintain its defense production, with steel as the major component. Truman went one step further and laid blame with the steel companies for the dispute that had ensued, claiming they were uncompromising.[66]

The White House was attempting to play a strategic game. Threatening to increase steelworkers' wages while the government had control of the mills would apply the necessary pressure on the steel companies to settle with the unions at no cost to the administration's stabilization policy. Because the production of steel was a necessity, and the only way to secure that production was by seizing the mills, the steel companies would be left with no leverage to receive the price adjustments it was holding out for during negotiations.[67] This move would turn out to be a big gamble for the administration, because the steel companies actually had the upper hand. With the support of Congress and aided by the press, the steel companies helped change the focus of the seizure, which the Supreme Court took due notice of.

Instead of focusing on the issue of collective bargaining, the seizure became the source of a great constitutional debate. The steel companies would not back down, even though Truman continued to assert that their demands for price increases were unreasonable and that seizure was undoubtedly necessary. Due to the legal maneuvering by the steel companies, discussed below, the administration had to defend itself against the accusation of dictatorship. Ultimately, the labor dispute was sidelined, with the focus of the debate resting on the extent of executive power.

The steel industry was, unsurprisingly, stunned and upset by the impending seizure, but the reaction by the national press was unparalleled. Newspapers were visibly brutal in their attacks of the president's actions; even those that had been previously supportive of Truman reprimanded him for abusing the powers of the office. The *Nation*, for example, reported that the president had "exaggerated the crisis and exaggerated even more the 'inherent powers' with which the Constitution has invested him. . . . [W]e don't like the arbitrary exercise of executive authority."[68]

To take control of the situation and garner support,[69] Truman sent a special message to Congress to find legislative backing. He reasoned that the only other option available was a complete shutdown of the steel industry. Alternately, he maintained, Congress could write a bill outlining the "specific terms and conditions" for government operation of the steel mills. But in the absence of such a bill, Truman noted, he would continue to take responsibility for ensuring that steel mills remained open and functioning as he attempted to settle the dispute.[70] The response from Congress, for the most part, was to support Truman's plan to seize the mills. However, a group of congressional representatives began introducing legislation related to the takeover of the mills. Before these bills[71] gained any traction, the judicial branch heard a direct legal challenge to the executive's claim of inherent power when it ruled on *Youngstown*.

POSITION TAKING

Within minutes of Truman's seizure speech,[72] lawyers for the Republic Steel Corporation and the Youngstown Sheet and Tube Company submitted a motion for a temporary restraining order (TRO) and a permanent injunction.

As the administration defended its actions against the criticisms mounted by Congress and the press, the Justice Department championed Truman's actions in the courts. Truman believed that this judicial course was auspicious. Given the Supreme Court's generous construction of presidential power during wartime (see Chapter 3), Truman and his administration were convinced the courts would uphold his authority to seize the mills.[73]

Arguing on Sawyer's behalf, Assistant Attorney General Holmes Baldridge's argument rested on two key issues. First, he emphasized the limited nature of the seizure. While the United States had temporary and nominal ownership of the companies, the actual operations of each plant remained in the hands of the previous owners, and business was to go on as it always had. Second, the plaintiffs' request for a TRO was "untimely," because the steel companies had an "adequate remedy at law."[74] The government maintained that the seizure was a "legal taking under the inherent executive powers of the President" and that if the steel companies could prove they had suffered any damages as a consequence of the seizure, they were entitled to just compensation under the Fifth Amendment of the Constitution.[75]

Baldridge maintained that the provisions of Article II of the Constitution ultimately granted the president all executive power that was not specifically assigned to others elsewhere in the Constitution. When pressed by District Court Judge Alexander Holtzoff to explain what he meant by "executive powers," Baldridge answered, "[A]mong other things[,] it is the power to protect the country in times of national emergency by whatever means seem appropriate to achieve the end."[76] Baldridge, on behalf of the government, was asserting broad authority under exigent circumstances, a claim drawn from *Curtiss-Wright*.

While technically the TRO applied only to the secretary of Commerce, the effect would be to proscribe the performance of Truman's executive order. Consequently, Judge Holtzoff reasoned, "the court should not do by indirection what it could not do directly." If there was no "vital" reason, the court should not restrict the president's attempt to prevent a national emergency, Holtzoff concluded.[77]

Dissatisfied with the decision, four companies—Youngstown Sheet and Tube, Republic, Bethlehem, and Jones and Laughlin—appealed to have a hearing on the merits. Federal District Court Judge David A. Pine presided over the hearing. Appearing before Pine, Baldridge stated, "[O]ur position is that there is no power in the Courts to restrain the President and . . . Secretary Sawyer is the alter ego of the President and not subject to injunctive order of the Court."[78] Following Baldridge's bold assertion, senators who had supported Truman turned on their heels and formally denounced the view that the president's power was unlimited.

Without convening the court, Pine filed his judgment.[79] He ruled that the government's position was devoid of legal justification and thus rejected the doctrine of inherent powers. Pine maintained that the seizure would result in irreparable damages for the steel companies, and because the seizure had no authority in law, the companies could not recover any damages in the Court of Claims, as suggested by Baldridge.[80]

Pine allowed preliminary injunctions enjoining the seizure to all the petitioners except for U.S. Steel. U.S. Steel had verbally amended its original motion, requesting an injunction preventing the administration only "from changing the terms and conditions of employment while it was in possession of the mills." Due to this modification, Pine declined to issue such an injunction. He reasoned that if he granted U.S. Steel's motion for a limited injunction,[81] it would be tantamount to implicitly saying there was a valid basis for the seizure.

Pine's opinion created a pressing crisis for the administration. Before the injunction could be signed, the United Steelworkers launched a strike. The administration was not prepared for this development and had to act fast to avert a prolonged interruption in the production of steel. The White House decided that the only course of action was to seek a stay of Pine's decision and go straight to the Supreme Court. The Justice Department requested that the Court grant writ and hear the case immediately, because Judge Pine's decision presented a rather uncertain situation; the fact that the case dealt with national security necessitated a swift resolution of the issues presented in the petition.[82]

As the court of appeals reached a decision on the request to alter the stay order, the government's petition for certiorari was taken to the Supreme Court on May 2, 1952. With a vote of 7–2, the Court granted cert[83] and scheduled the steel case to be argued. It also stayed the initial injunction order of the district court.[84]

There was ample reason to dismiss the immediate crisis, the necessity of the continued production of steel, as not being as severe as the Truman administration claimed. In fact, some members of the White House staff were aware even before the Court's decision that steel supplies were more than sufficient. White House staff noted that the Supreme Court knew it too: "The proposed message stresses once again the need for uninterrupted steel production. Yet the fact is that the public has never believed this contention, and in the face of recent releases of steel for race tracks and bowling alleys, they are even less likely to believe this now."[85] In this context, the Court's majority could not find any reason to uphold an exercise of inherent power. However, this opinion was couched in sweeping terms.

The positive reaction to Judge Pine's decision left the Court in a difficult position: it could not rule on any grounds less broad or less easily understood than a lack of power granted to the executive to seize the mills. If the Court had tried to cut back Pine's absolutes, it might have been construed as attempting to soften the blow for Truman and signaling a lack of independence on the part of the Court—the final arbiter. Moreover, the 1936 *Curtiss-Wright* ruling had depicted presidential power in broad and sweeping terms. In short, absent the presence of a genuine emergency, the Court was averse to shroud an exercise of inherent power with the authority of law. While the Court outlined the parameters of what constituted a genuine emergency, it closed off the possibility that claiming an emergency as an instrument of domestic policy would be constitutionally upheld.

The Court's stay relieved the pressure to resolve the dispute, but an agreement could not be reached until it made a decision on the basic issue—the legitimacy of the seizure. Before we turn to a full evaluation of the Supreme Court's decision, we should briefly discuss the brief filed by the government, because it aids in understanding the administration's effort to frame the crisis and the legal questions at the center of the assertions made by the president regarding inherent power to act in such circumstances.

The government's brief narrowly defined the issue on the merits, describing the issue as "whether seizure [was] a method available to the President, in the exercise of his constitutional powers, to avert a crisis of this type."[86] The brief proclaimed it was redundant to identify an explicit clause of the Constitution as the one from which to derive the president's power to seize the steel mills. Instead, the brief concluded, the historical record demonstrated the president's authority to act in any situation, which stemmed from several of the grants itemized and taken simultaneously in Article II. Congress could have authorized the seizure, but the question was whether the president's order of the seizure was an appropriate executive reaction to an exigent situation. The brief noted numerous examples of executives' seizing private property in times of war or during national emergencies, and the legislature and the courts had accepted these actions as legitimate ways to meet the crises of the day.[87]

While parties to the suit were waiting on the Supreme Court's decision, Truman held a press conference and made clear that his authority was unreviewable: "The President *has* the power [to seize], and they can't take it away from him."[88] When pressed as to whom "they" referred to, Truman responded without any hesitation that he spoke of Congress and the courts: "Nobody can take it away from the President, because he is the Chief Executive of the Nation, and he has to be in a position to see that the welfare of the people is met."[89]

Immediately following the press conference, Joseph Short, the White House press secretary, released a statement clarifying Truman's comments: "[N]either the Congress nor the courts could deny the inherent powers of the presidency without tearing up the Constitution." While the Court "might properly decide that the conditions existing did not justify the use by the President of his inherent powers," a decision of this kind "would not deny the existence of the inherent powers." It was clear the administration believed not only that the president had the authority but also that, irrespective of the Court's decision, the executive would define its own constitutional powers. This assertion directly challenged judicial supremacy—the Court's asserted authority to determine the scope and parameters of constitutional authority—and in these moments, we find the Supreme Court more willing to address the issue in question.[90]

Even though the political climate did not appear to support Truman's broad claims of unilateral authority, the president believed that his actions had legal grounds; thus, he did not expect that "the Court would decide otherwise than that he [had] acted properly."[91] Despite his unfavorable public and political support, few expected Truman's actions to be invalidated, so the country was startled when the Supreme Court reached its decision.[92]

Recent decisions by the Court (*Curtiss-Wright*, *Belmont* and *Pink*, and the internment cases) had suggested that the judiciary would not curb unilateral executive authority. But Truman went beyond the assertions of the presidents evaluated thus far by claiming inherent powers to intervene in a domestic strike and framing the act as a necessary measure for the war efforts. Given the Court's jurisprudence, few (including Truman) believed[93] that the bench of 1952, composed of five justices appointed by FDR and four by Truman,[94] would be the mechanism by which to bring the accretion of power by the executive branch to a possible standstill. Moreover, although many believe that justices' views on presidential power match those of the presidents under whom they are appointed,[95] the Court's decision would belie that opinion.

Individual backgrounds and justices' records are often indicative of how they might vote.[96] FDR and Truman had appointed these men, each of whom (except for Felix Frankfurter) had experience in government—in either the legislative or the executive branch—during the New and Fair Deals. It was therefore not a stretch to assume that these justices held views of presidential power akin to those of the presidents in whose administrations they had worked. This study, however, challenges these assumptions. Justices balance geopolitical concerns and through their own analyses determine the reach of presidential prerogatives when individual rights are transgressed.

Justice Hugo Black, an ardent FDR supporter and his first nominee to the Supreme Court,[97] interpreted the words of the Bill of Rights literally to thwart government intrusion with personal liberties, but during wartime, civil-liberty claims had to give way to the needs of the government. This had been the case when Black authored the 1944 *Korematsu* opinion: when the war powers of the government conflict with individual rights, the safety of the nation necessitates the sacrifice of the latter. *Korematsu* thus upheld the appropriate exercise of the war powers. Given his standing, it was not unthinkable to expect Black to sustain Truman's seizure of the steel mills, considering the administration's framing of the hostilities in Korea, the international concerns, and the necessity of steel to the successful outcome of the war, the nation, and its allies. However, as illustrated below, it is not the framing advocated by the administration that influences judicial decision making but rather the Supreme Court's determination of the geopolitical construction and the assertion of executive power.

Stanley Reed, an FDR appointee, was also expected to vote in Truman's favor. For most of his career, he been deferential to the legislative and executive branches, believing they were the best judges of their own power and the policies they would enact.[98] This theory of departmentalism would be heavily asserted by the George W. Bush administration when his policies on detention were challenged in Court (see Chapter 6). And just as the Bush administration would be statutorily denounced by the Court, so too was Truman when he claimed presidential prerogatives.

Frankfurter was a little more unpredictable, but he was still perceived as likely to uphold Truman's assertion of power.[99] During World War II, Frankfurter had consistently championed the government's war powers. His concurrence in *Korematsu* underscored his jurisprudence that the Constitution provides Congress and the president adequate powers to carry out a war: "Therefore, the validity of action under the war power must be judged wholly in the context of war."[100] However, Frankfurter, in the present case, avoided ruling on the general powers of the executive, concluding only that Truman's seizure violated the express will of Congress.

In contrast, William O. Douglas, FDR's fourth appointee, infrequently allowed uncertainties concerning the exercise of judicial power to affect his need to meet the issues head on.[101] By the time the steel-seizure case reached the Court, few believed that Douglas would be sympathetic to their claims, but other aspects of his jurisprudence would influence his judgment.

Douglas might have deemed Truman's seizure of the steel mills to be an unconstitutional usurpation of the steel companies' rights. However, his notion of war powers was unrestrained. In fact, during World War II, he regularly voted with the majority to support the government in cases that infringed on personal freedoms.[102] Douglas was seen as likely, then, to frame the power to seize the mills in the context of the Korean War. However, he ruled against the administration.

Justice Jackson's earlier record on executive power suggested that he was a sure vote for Truman.[103] But once on the Supreme Court, he became more conservative.[104] His position on war powers was thus inconsistent. As illustrated in Chapter 3, Jackson joined a unanimous bench in the *Hirabayashi* ruling, which determined that military necessity superseded individual rights infringements. However, as noted, Jackson's concerns over the practical limits of power led to his *Korematsu* dissent. In this instance, he was reluctant to legally sanction a military action that was undoubtedly unconstitutional during peacetime, because approving such action would create a mischievous precedent. Given this position—balancing the government's expansive view of executive power alongside Jackson's more incredulous attitude—it was difficult to predict how he would decide the emergency averred by the government in the present case. As noted below, Jackson's three-tier schema did not overtly reflect inherent powers, but the zone of twilight and subsequent use by the executive branch suggested that this framework had been utilized to advance this theory.

Many expected that the four Truman appointees would unwaveringly support the president. Each appointee had a record of generally upholding government action irrespective of the issue, and they often voted the same way. Chief Justice Vinson, for example, resolutely believed that the popularly elected branches of the government should be allowed to rule and that the Court should be restrained in judging their actions.[105]

Truman's appointment of the Republican Harold Burton had been a tactical move intended to foster good relations with the opposition party. Burton was a promising nominee, because he was not highly partisan in his conduct and had an amenable approach when reviewing significant issues.[106] And Tom C. Clark firmly and consistently believed in the inherent powers of the president to act during emergencies, so Clark was another justice perceived as likely to vote for Truman in the steel-seizure case.[107]

The record of Sherman Minton,[108] Truman's last appointee, as both a judge and as a senator led many to think that he would become part of the Black bloc when he joined the Court. Yet this alliance did not materialize; Minton became a practitioner of judicial restraint. Few believed that Minton would question Truman's power to seize, given his construction of the liberal powers of the elected branches with his restraint of the role of the judiciary.[109] These few were vindicated when Minton joined Justice Vinson's dissent in *Youngstown*. Ultimately, Vinson determined that there was validity to Truman's framing of a steel strike as harmful to national security. As such, Vinson's dissent clearly endorsed presidential action. Of the four Truman appointees, only Reed and Minton found in favor of the executive; FDR appointees Douglas, Black, and Jackson ruled against the president.

The steel-seizure case could have been disposed of in a number of ways that would have avoided the Court's striking down Truman's seizure order. First, as Frankfurter and Burton advised, the Court could have voted to deny cert, which would have sent the case to the court of appeals to be reheard. This action may have allowed enough time for the companies and the union to then reach an amicable settlement, thus revoking the seizure.[110] Even after granting cert, the justices had a number of options. At the top of the list, the Court could have decided that the issues in the case presented a political question. Cases regarding the scope of presidential action in the conduct of foreign affairs have been dismissed as involving political questions, because, by the Court's own admission, it lacks the necessary information required for a reasoned decision (for example, *Goldwater v. Carter* [1979]),[111] or because judicial decree might embarrass the nation in the international sphere.[112]

Black wrote the majority opinion, but every justice in the majority also wrote separate concurring opinions, yielding seven opinions in total. Jackson's concurrence, a schema outlining executive power vis-à-vis Congress, has gained in prominence over developmental time, but this broad framework has been significantly misconstrued, particularly with respect to the zone of twilight.

Justice Black's opinion rejected each and every point raised by the administration and invalidated the seizure of the steel mills.[113] Ultimately, the political climate and the political process utilized by Congress, the executive's relationship with the legislature, and the scope of authority was what mattered to the majority, not the textual approach advanced by Black.

ADVANCING A PRACTICAL FRAMEWORK

Court decisions are reached after justices apply the geopolitical-construction process. In recalling his days as a law clerk for Jackson during the steel-seizure case, Chief Justice William Rehnquist noted that the Truman administration was on solid ground with respect to legal precedent.[114] So why did Truman lose by a 6–3 vote? Ultimately, his delineation of executive power was too sweeping; in light of unfavorable public opinion as well, the Court deduced that the power to seize was beyond Truman's constitutional authority.[115] Rehnquist pointed out, "[T]his is one of those celebrated constitutional cases where what might be called the tide of public opinion suddenly began to run against the government[,] . . . [which] had a considerable influence on the Court."[116] Presidential power is therefore contingent on the Court's evaluation of the geopolitical construction, which includes the general approval of the public. This prerequisite places a heavy burden on individual citizens, however: it requires them to be cognizant of the use of executive power, to express their trepidations, and to demand that the legislative and/or the judicial branch hold presidents accountable by reining in broad assertions of power.

Not long after the Supreme Court's judgment was announced, the president responded. Truman sent a letter to Secretary Sawyer instructing that the steel plants be returned to their owners. Sawyer quickly informed the companies that possession had been relinquished, which resulted in the United Steelworkers' striking.[117]

The Court sided with Congress against the president's assertion of unilateral power, because the case concerned action taken by the executive against private property. Moreover, the very act of seizing the mills was the overt exercise of legislative power, and the Korean War, the Court determined, did not provide for the grant of inherent executive power. It reasoned that the president's military power did not extend to labor disputes. Black noted, "[T]he President's power, if any, to issue the order must stem either from an act of Congress or from the Constitution itself."[118] This assertion essentially excluded inherent power as a separate category of authority.

Black's opinion personified the Court's holding, but the justices did not agree on the course of action to resolve the legitimacy of President Truman's order. There are two diverging opinions on how to understand the way the Constitution structures federal power. Black's opinion embodied the formalist approach, whereas the concurring opinions of Justices Jackson and Frankfurter denoted a functional approach.[119] Despite these diverging methods, both agreed that Truman's claim of inherent authority was too sweeping and that presidential power must rest on either a statute or the Constitution. Simply stated, the political climate did not warrant broad presidential authority, according to the Court.

Black's formalist position was modest. The order seizing the steel mills to keep them operating was an exercise of legislative power. In response to a national emergency, however, Congress could have delegated power to the president, thus allowing him to seize the steel mills. As Justice Antonin Scalia would later explain in *Loving v. United States* (1996),[120] *Youngstown* did not exhibit a delegation of constitutional legislative power, because the core power of Congress is constitutional legislative power that may not be delegated. The first constitutional order adhered to this notion (*Schechter* [1935] and *Panama Refining* [1935]).

Truman's order was therefore invalid, because Congress did not statutorily delegate such authority, nor was it authorized by a constitutional grant of power. In fact, according to the Supreme Court, Congress had explicitly rejected the idea that seizure could be used as a method of solving a labor dispute when it voted down a seizure amendment during its debate on the Taft-Hartley Act.[121] Consequently, if EO 10340 was going to be upheld, the Court would have to find a clause in the Constitution authorizing the president's power.

The government admitted, Black pointed out, that no specific language in the Constitution authorized the seizure. However, the government insisted that the power could be implied from the sum total of powers granted to the president by three key sections of Article II. Despite the government's insistence, Black rejected this claim. Truman's seizure of the steel mills could not be upheld, Justice Black argued, as a function of the president's military power as commander-in-chief. The government's analogy of the seizure's being equivalent to taking possession of private property by military officials engaged in combat, which had been upheld by the Court on numerous occasions, was unconvincing, Black argued. Expanding on this unsuccessful comparison, Black asserted, "A 'theater of war' [can] be an expanding concept."[122] But the Court did not find the Korean War sufficiently constraining to grant this broad authority to seize.

The formalist approach thus rejects the presence of inherent power. If, for example, the president had inherent powers as well as statutory and constitutionally stated or implied powers, then showing that Truman lacked the statutory and constitutional power to issue the order would be a necessity; however, doing so would not demonstrate that the president lacked power, because the executive might still be able to confirm the order because of inherent power. Therefore, because Black regarded the lack of a favorable grant of power as adequate to provide Truman's order as being beyond the president's legal capacity, Black's formalist reasoning excluded the claim that Truman therefore held inherent power.

The constitutional provisions that granted executive power to the president, Black asserted, could not support EO 10340. Presidential powers differ inherently from the authority to make laws; the lawmaking function assigned by the Constitution is granted solely to Congress, and the president is limited to recommending, vetoing, and executing laws. The order to seize the mills was, for all intents and purposes, a piece of legislation. The order read like a statute in every way, promulgating policies and sanctioning a government official to execute them. Black reasoned that only Congress had the lawful power to prescribe such a policy. In short, Black concluded, "[T]his seizure order cannot stand."[123]

Justice Black drew a line in the sand between executive and legislative powers and asserted that they were rigid and precise. For Black, even grave emergencies, such as the Korean War, could not grant to any branch of government the authority to exercise the powers granted to the other—in this instance, to create and execute a legislative statute. It was clear the Court struck a balance in determining constitutional power when such assertions of authority encroached upon domestic policy.

Of the justices in the majority, only Douglas shared Black's opinion that the doctrine of separation of powers was unequivocal and unyielding. For Douglas, the Court needed to determine whether a crisis existed to then determine whether Truman's seizure of the steel mills was legal. The Court also needed to evaluate, more generally, the distribution of constitutional powers between the legislative and executive branches.[124]

The Constitution, Douglas asserted, gives all legislative power to Congress. Consequently, the legislature was the only branch of government that could permit a seizure or sanction one that the president ordered. For Douglas, seizure or sanction in the domestic arena needed to yield a stringent standard of separation of powers. But this standard had some flexibility if the Court were to conclude that the president's claims of authority lay squarely in the interest of national security.

The remaining four justices definitively rejected the absolute position that Black and Douglas advocated, viewing the separation-of-powers doctrine as too simplistic. The functions of the three branches of government did not fit so neatly into the compartments that Black and Douglas outlined, according to Frankfurter, Jackson, Clark, and Burton.

Justice Frankfurter was particularly inclined to address this problem. He reasoned, "The Constitution is a framework for government[,]" but it was "an inadmissibly narrow conception of American constitutional law to confine it to the words of the Constitution . . . disregard[ing] the gloss which life has written upon them."[125] To prevent a dictatorship, Frankfurter concluded, it was absolutely necessary to check unauthorized, although well-intentioned, assertions of power. However, it is the Court's responsibility to check this power, which is facilitated by its evaluation of the geopolitical construction.

Although Frankfurter believed that it was the Court's duty to steer clear of making decisions on the basis of broad constitutional interpretations,[126] he also believed that it was imperative to determine the relationship between the powers of Congress and those of the executive. Reluctant to make any sweeping statements on presidential power, he would consider only the issue at hand—Truman's assertion of having the power to seize in the specific circumstance—and not the general powers the president would have if Congress were to ratify statutes affecting labor disputes and seizures.

For Frankfurter, the most important issue surrounding the case was the congressional legislation concerning the topic, which included the Taft-Hartley Act and the path to its ratification. Frankfurter drew two conclusions. First, Congress had sufficiently dealt with the issue of national-emergency strikes and concluded that if such a situation should arise and the act did not adequately bring about a resolution, then Congress would decide what, if any, action was necessary by the government. Second, during the Taft-Hartley Act debate, Congress had considered giving the executive the authority to seize but had intentionally decided not to include this power. Making a conscious choice, Congress wanted to provide the authority on an ad hoc basis if a seizure were necessary.[127] Essentially relying on legislative intent, Frankfurter concluded that the seizure was in complete violation of Congress's will and displaced the constitutional balance of power between the legislative and executive branches. Even though he determined that Truman's decision was for the good of the nation, he could not dismiss the significance of legislative intent and thus had to find against the president's assertion of power.

These opinions demonstrate that the Court was unconvinced by Truman's framing of the situation: the Korean War necessitated seizing the steel mills to avoid a national emergency, and a steel strike would have a direct effect on the successful outcome of the war. The Court instead saw the act as legislative in nature and Truman's seizure as the taking of private property. This interpretation squarely placed Truman's actions in the domestic arena, an area in which the Court believed the president could not claim inherent authority. And the justices agreed that it was their role, and not the president's, to make this determination.

Jackson split from the purely textual approach advocated by Justice Black, deducing that the "actual act of governing under our Constitution does not and cannot conform to judicial definitions of the power of any of its branches based on isolated clauses or even single Articles torn from context." Executive powers, Jackson added, "are not fixed but fluctuate, depending upon their disjunction or conjunction with those of Congress."[128] Jackson's reasoning turned on the separation-of-powers doctrine, except his opinion focused more on the practical realities of governing under the Constitution rather than on the theoretical considerations of actions themselves.

However, Jackson's concurrence did not dismiss entirely the practical use of inherent powers; in fact, his opinion has shaped contemporary constitutional analysis. This concurrence demonstrates how Courts carve out the constitutional space to provide a practical framework for future executives in the management of foreign affairs. This schema, institutionalized by subsequent courts, also illustrates that the judiciary, when needed, will create branching points to the initial path established by *Curtiss-Wright* to Jackson's oversimplified concurrence and Rehnquist's finding of tacit authority (Chapter 5) to expand further the scope of the unilateral executive.

By Jackson's own admission, this framework was "somewhat over-simplified,"[129] yet it has been relied on by the courts and by administrations in a number of instances. For example, when it was discovered that the Bush administration had been conducting warrantless domestic surveillance,[130] his actions were initially placed in the lowest ebb (tier three) and then recategorized by the Justice Department to fall within the highest type (tier one); in other words, statutory legislation was determined to provide the necessary authority to act.[131] As the war on terror developed and as challenges were brought against the Bush administration, the district court in *Rumsfeld v. Padilla* (2004) moved away from the constitutional questions to issues of statutory interpretation, which the Second Circuit later confirmed (see Chapter 6).[132]

While Jackson's concurrence criticized and rejected George Sutherland's *Curtiss-Wright* opinion, noting that the language used by Sutherland merely insinuated that "the President might act in external affairs without congressional authority, but not that he might act contrary to an Act of Congress,"[133] it was merely a prescription for the sole-organ doctrine. This schema has been utilized to claim the same broad assertions that Jackson denounced: extraconstitutional powers for the president.[134] This was an interesting claim, given Jackson's endorsement of the "plenary and exclusive" paragraph in his defense in support of the president in 1940.[135]

The Supreme Court's *Youngstown* decision attempted to emphatically reject the subsistence of inherent power when it considered Truman's actions, but despite Jackson's rejection of Sutherland's opinion, his concurrence has taken on prominence. Future Courts would address the inadequacies of the new constitutional order (*Curtiss-Wright*) with the practical realities (*Youngstown*) of having a strong executive presence in the management of foreign affairs. This three-tier analysis encourages Courts to conduct their own examination of the relationship between the two branches in light of the geopolitical concerns. Through this process, justices control the evolution of constitutional jurisprudence and thus determine institutional and political development.

Jackson divided the president's authority into three distinct categories. Tier one asserts that presidential power is at its zenith when the "president acts pursuant to an express or implied authorization of Congress," because "it includes all that he possesses in his own right plus all that Congress can delegate."[136] In such a situation, the executive is dependent on presidential powers as well as those delegated by the legislative branch. Tier three provides that presidential power is at its lowest ebb when it is "incompatible with the expressed or implied will of Congress," as the executive may rely on only his own constitutional authority.[137] Under this circumstance, the president depends on the office's constitutional powers, excluding whatever constitutional authority Congress might have over an issue. In this case, the Court can uphold the executive's action only by finding that Congress could not act in the situation. However, tier two, known as the "Twilight Zone," maintains:

[W]hen the President acts in absence of either a congressional grant or denial of authority, he can only rely upon his own independent power, but there is a zone of twilight in which he and Congress may have concurrent authority, or in which its distribution is uncertain. Therefore, congressional inertia, indifference or quiescence may sometimes, [as] a practical matter, enable, if not invite, measures on independent presidential responsibility.[138]

In this instance, if the president's power is in doubt, the legality of executive action is "likely to depend on the imperatives of events and contemporary imponderables rather than on abstract theories of law."[139] But it is the Court's duty to make this determination.

It was evident, Jackson stated, that Truman's taking of the steel mills fell into tier three. Jackson could not place the seizure in the first tier, because, by the government's own admission, Congress had not authorized it. Nor did the seizure fit into the second tier, because Congress was not silent on the issue; the legislature purposely denied giving the executive the authority to intervene (via the Taft-Hartley Act and the Selective Service Act). Because Truman chose not to utilize either act, Jackson concluded, his actions fell into the third tier and could be upheld only by finding "that seizure of such strike-bound industries is within his domain and beyond control by Congress."[140]

Of the claims made by the government, the reliance on the commander-in-chief clause was of particular concern for Jackson. The solicitor general insisted that the president had sent troops to Korea by an exercise of his constitutional power and that from that undertaking, Truman derived the power to then seize the mills to guarantee an uninterrupted supply of steel for the troops. This, Jackson believed, was a destructive doctrine. By designating the president as commander-in-chief of the army and the navy, Jackson argued, the Constitution does not suggest that the executive is commander-in-chief "of the country, its industries and its inhabitants."[141] Moreover, and most significant for the Court, Jackson noted, the president could not control the use of the war power "as an instrument of domestic policy,"[142] as this was within the purview of the legislative branch.

Jackson denied any intent to delineate or shrink the constitutional role of the executive. In fact, he believed the control function of the chief executive should be furnished with the greatest latitude, which fell in line with the reasoning of *Curtiss-Wright* regarding when military power has to be instigated against other nations for the security of the nation. But, Jackson noted, "when it is turned inward, not because of rebellion but because of a lawful economic struggle between industry and labor, it should have no such indulgence."[143] On the basis of this reasoning, the Supreme Court could not uphold the executive's assertion of seizure power grounded in the commander-in-chief clause, because this action attempted to control unilaterally a domestic interest that naturally fell within the domain of the legislature.

With respect to the issue of inherent powers, the government claimed the same rhetoric and practice of previous administrations to demonstrate a trend that powers not explicitly granted to the president in the Constitution had become an accepted norm and also a necessary and proper function of the office. One of these powers was the authority to act in perilous situations. However, as convincing as the inherent-powers theory might appear, it would be imprudent, Jackson noted, for the Court to legally sanction its employment and substantiate presidential action during an emergency situation. Rather, Jackson argued that Congress had at its disposal a set of mechanisms to meet the current demands of the emergency. Similarly, Burton's concurrence asserted that Congress set aside for itself the prerogative of authorizing a seizure if the need should arise.[144] Congress could grant to the executive additional powers to deal with the immediate crisis. The current situation was no worse than any of the other situations that previous executives had faced, during which Congress had willingly granted the necessary power to manage the crises they confronted. Consequently, Jackson could not support Truman's utilization of such a power without the obligatory statute from Congress.[145]

Jackson counseled, "'Inherent' powers, 'implied' powers, 'incidental' powers, 'plenary' powers, 'war' powers[,] and 'emergency' powers are used, often interchangeably and without fixed or ascertainable meanings,"[146] thus significantly distorting presidential powers. But courts are culpable, as they have led the way in redefining and institutionalizing alternative interpretations of presidential prerogatives. In fact, advocates of immense presidential power now claim implied constitutional powers, which exposes how Jackson's observations were realized. This interchangeability of asserted powers is further explored in subsequent chapters.

Jackson's opinion suggested a fluid relationship between Congress and the executive: "While the Constitution diffuses power to secure liberty, it also contemplates that practice will integrate the dispersed powers into a workable government. It enjoins upon its branches separateness but interdependence, autonomy but reciprocity."[147] It is a relationship confined by the parameters of politics, but only the Court's determination and redefinition of that partnership redirect the balance of polity principles over developmental time.

On the issue of inherent powers, Burton was cautious. He believed that the current situation offered no occasion to exercise inherent powers, yet he did not completely renounce the doctrine. He merely maintained that the Court was not considering the issue of what the executive's powers might be in "catastrophic situations."[148]

Moreover, Justice Clark, disagreeing with Black, maintained that the majority opinion appeared to invalidate the presence of any kind of inherent power for the executive to act in emergencies. Clark stated, "The Constitution does grant to the President extensive authority in times of grave and imperative national emergency. In fact . . . such a grant may well be necessary to the very existence of the Constitution itself." Clark added, "I care not whether one calls it 'residual,' 'inherent,' 'moral,' 'implied,' 'aggregate,' 'emergency,' or otherwise."[149] Clark could not sanction the seizure under the theory of inherent power of the executive, because, he concluded, Congress had supplied several alternative methods that the president could have utilized in the current crisis.[150] Clark rejected the absolutist approach of Black and Douglas, asserting that the president did have some inherent power to act and that those circumstances would include grave and imperative national emergencies, but he fell short of defining these boundaries.

Clark was troubled over his reading of the majority opinion as closing off the presence of inherent powers for future executives to act in emergencies, although this was not the case. This concern, however, speaks to the notion that the Court can close certain paths and thus viable legal narratives to future Courts. This fear also underscores the Court's role in changing paths because of its capacity to redefine and renegotiate constitutional politics.[151] If the Court's *Youngstown* decision had definitively closed the path of inherent power, a different developmental narrative would exist. Even though Jackson's concurring opinion acknowledged that the executive should have the widest latitude when commencing military forces for the safety of the nation, in the present case, he found that Truman could not use this kind of power as an instrument of domestic policy.

The dissenters had been persuaded by Truman's argument that this emergency was real: "[T]he vital disagreement was over premises" between "the two divisions of the Court."[152] Ultimately, the division on the Court came down to how individual justices perceived the emergency. Justice Vinson, joined by Justices Reed and Minton, delivered a ringing endorsement of inherent power: Truman acted in accordance with his constitutional responsibilities. Vinson, Reed, and Minton adhered to the new constitutional order established in *Curtiss-Wright* and, in fact, reasserted the current trend. Considering the crisis in Korea, the dissenters found that Truman's seizure of the steel mills avoided risk to national security and also sustained the status quo, thereby allowing the legislative branch time to review the crisis of a strike.[153] For Vinson, national-security concerns outweighed Truman's intrusions into the domestic sphere when claiming the unilateral authority to act.

Taking into account the geopolitical concerns of the Korean War, Congress's reaction to the war efforts, and the executive branch's attempt to carry out the congressional defense program, Vinson concluded that a steel strike of any kind doubtless would be disastrous to national security. For the chief justice, the seriousness of the crisis facing the president—and, indeed, the nation—was a factor the justices in the majority should not have disregarded. The plain facts of the case suggested no foundation for charges of "arbitrary action, unlimited powers[,] or dictatorial usurpation of congressional power."[154] For Vinson, Truman acted in harmony with his responsibilities under the Constitution.

The *Youngstown* ruling appeared to place some serious limits on the president's claim to emergency powers and cast doubt on the constitutionality of seizing property under a presidential order during previous wars. It also seemed to argue that Congress, not the president, had the power to act in emergencies and that the executive had authority to act only when an act of Congress or the Constitution expressly or implicitly granted that authority. But given Jackson's practical concurrence and Clark's and Vinson's endorsement of inherent powers, *Youngstown* ultimately stayed the course of presidential prerogatives.

The *Youngstown* decision pleased many.[155] Truman's seizure of the steel mills seemed to be the move of an imperial president. The press, Congress, and steel-industry executives praised the Supreme Court for protecting the nation from executive dictatorship. In fact, the press characterized the majority opinion as "a redefinition of the powers of the President. Under this opinion the trend toward an indefinite expansion of the Chief Executive's authority is deliberately checked."[156] Even the *Chicago Sun-Times*, generally regarded as liberal, pointed out that the holding was a "stinging rebuke to President Truman" and suggested that government by executive fiat was a far greater danger than the steel strike.[157] Only the *New York Post* examined the detrimental effects of the strike and indicated that the Court's decision amounted to resolving nothing with respect to the steel dispute itself.[158]

Only the White House appeared concerned about the practical costs of the decision. Truman had clearly expected an auspicious ruling. Events over the prior twenty years had suggested that the Court would not restrain presidential power. He therefore took the decision as a personal censure,[159] and his opinion never changed; the decision, he believed, was simply wrong.[160] The *Youngstown* ruling was regarded as a huge loss not only for Truman but also for future claims of inherent powers.

In terms of importance, Black's majority opinion has been eclipsed by Jackson's concurrence. Jackson's three-tier analysis has become the standard by which to evaluate presidential actions, as it offers the practical realities of foreign policy making and not the theoretical realities advanced by the plurality opinion, and it is not a yardstick for limiting presidential prerogatives.[161]

IMPACT OF *YOUNGSTOWN*

Contemporary executive-use and foreign-affairs cases illustrate how Jackson's framework has advanced inherent powers. Courts have utilized the schema to further entrench the new constitutional order articulated in the *Curtiss-Wright* decision. Administrations intent on championing inherent power have relied on Jackson's assertions that the scope of presidential power depends on where it falls among three possible tiers.[162] If the administration in question can successfully demonstrate to the Court that the twilight zone is where the president draws his authority, then the Court upholds broad claims of executive unilateral power.

Presidents since Truman have successfully relied on the zone of twilight. A case in point is *Goldwater* (1979). When President Jimmy Carter declared his intention to unilaterally terminate a defense treaty with Taiwan, his legal authority to terminate a treaty without the advice and consent of the Senate was called into question. Justice Lewis Powell, echoing Jackson's concurring opinion, stated that if Congress "chooses not to confront the President, it is not our task to do so."[163] Carter's actions against Iran, which included freezing assets and suspending claims pending in America's judicial system, were affirmed by the Supreme Court in part because Congress acquiesced: presidents have wider latitude in foreign affairs "where there is no contrary indication of legislative intent and when, as here, there is a history of congressional acquiescence in conduct of the sort engaged in by the President."[164] A similar decision was reached in cases involving the Ronald Reagan administration. Members of Congress repeatedly went to the courts to challenge his administration over its use of the war power in El Salvador, Nicaragua, Grenada, and the Persian Gulf.[165]

In *Sanchez-Espinoza v. Reagan* (1985), Judge Ruth Bader Ginsburg (for the D.C. Circuit Court) noted that Congress "has formidable weapons at its disposal—the power of the purse and investigative resources far beyond those available in the Third Branch, but no gauntlet has been thrown down here by a majority of the Members of Congress." Rather, "Congress expressly allowed the President to spend federal funds to support paramilitary operations in Nicaragua."[166] Ginsburg concluded that Jackson's practical concurrence influenced the decision-making process; courts must evaluate presidential actions in light of congressional delegations. Ginsburg's assessment relied on whether the legislature acted to grant to the executive the authority to act, which she determined it did. The actions thus fell squarely into Jackson's first tier. Assessing polity principles in this way and factoring in the world outside the court, Ginsburg ultimately found that executive decision making must be afforded wider court deference.

The third situation outlined by Jackson—presidential actions incompatible with the expressed or implied will of Congress—was exemplified by Reagan's role in the Iran-Contra affair. To justify its actions, the Reagan administration relied on extraconstitutional powers. At the time, aides to the president utilized the teachings of *Curtiss-Wright* and extended the notion of executive power beyond what Justice Sutherland had counseled. During the Iran-Contra hearings, Oliver North argued that the president had the power to authorize and conduct covert actions with nonappropriated funds—funds acquired from private parties from foreign governments.[167] North justified his own actions by invoking *Curtiss-Wright*, stating that "it was within the purview of the President of the United States to conduct secret activities and to conduct secret negotiations to further the foreign policy goals of the United States."[168]

It should be noted that the *Curtiss-Wright* decision did not deal with the issues addressed in the Iran-Contra affair, and the reasoning to support the necessity of secrecy and confidentiality in foreign affairs did not apply to the assertions made by North. Sutherland's *Curtiss-Wright* opinion did speak to secrecy, for he remarked that "information gathered by [presidential personnel] may be highly necessary, and the premature disclosure of it productive of harmful results."[169] With respect to the Iran-Contra affair, the accusation against the Reagan administration was that the gathering of information and safeguarding the disclosure of said information did not justify the actions taken: providing weapons to Iran and offering help to the Contras in Nicaragua. The administration was found to be in violation of the Boland Amendment, but North had referenced the *Curtiss-Wright* decision as authorizing the president to "do what he wants with his own staff," including the National Security Council (NSC). This assertion meant that the Boland Amendment could not restrict the activities of the NSC.[170] However, nothing in Sutherland's opinion authorized the president to use personal staff to defy statutory proscriptions.[171] In fact, FDR was acting pursuant to statutory authorization, and the issue at hand in *Curtiss-Wright* was whether Congress had delegated its authority too broadly. *Curtiss-Wright* and Jackson's framework had been used to advance the scope of executive unilateral prerogatives to include staff and administrative agencies under the president's directive.

It is worth noting that Jackson's concurrence said nothing about war or foreign relations as a special category of controversies. Nevertheless, Jackson's concurrence has been used to justify presidential decision making in international foreign affairs, because it divided the commander-in-chief's power along an outward-inward axis: "the widest latitude of interpretation to sustain his exclusive function to command the instruments of national force, at least when turned against the outside world for the security of our society." But when power is "turned inward" on the domestic sphere "not because of rebellion[,] . . . it should have no such indulgence."[172]

Works by Harold Koh and Michael J. Glennon[173] illustrate a continued effort to compare the broad sweeping theoretical model presented in *Curtiss-Wright* to the practical model in *Youngstown*. Koh notes the appearance in *Curtiss-Wright* of "*unchecked executive discretion* [that] has claimed virtually the entire field of foreign affairs as falling under the President's inherent authority."[174]

In contrast, the Supreme Court's *Youngstown* decision, handed down in the midst of the Korean War, overtly rejected the Truman administration's assertion that it was necessary to seize the steel mills for the successful prosecution of the war. Foreign affairs, the Court noted, were not an executive prerogative. Rather, in exercising its own powers, the Court reined in presidential action and observed Congress's power to authorize or proscribe presidential action. The Court reasoned that the power to seize private property was largely considered a legislative act to be retained by the legislature, a power that was intentionally withheld from the executive. Black saw a clear distinction between the situations in *Curtiss-Wright* and *Youngstown* and thus could not apply the *Curtiss-Wright* precedent. Consequently, Koh argues, *Youngstown* ultimately "rejected the *Curtiss-Wright* vision of unrestrained executive discretion in favor of a normative vision of the policymaking process in which the three branches of government all play integral roles."[175] However, the exigencies of the world outside the Court would inform later decisions, as presidential war and foreign-affairs powers continued to be asserted and, at times, challenged in the courts. Jackson's opinion identified the practical realities of executive decision making in international affairs, but *Curtiss-Wright* led the way for administrations to lay claim to the sole-organ doctrine, which was settled legal doctrine until *Zivotofsky* (2015).

Curtiss-Wright and *Youngstown* can coexist as equal precedent. *Curtiss-Wright* was the institutional forerunner to Jackson's tripartite system that attempted to outline a fluid, albeit complex, partnership. Political context and the Court's role in ascertaining the distinctions between foreign-affairs policy making and continued presidential claims of war powers have led the Court to utilize *Curtiss-Wright* and *Youngstown* as it evaluates polity principles.

The circumstance surrounding Truman's seizure of the steel mills was exceptional.[176] The Court was unconvinced by the president's assertion that the crisis confronting the nation was grave enough to justify his claim to inherent power to seize private property. The steel mills asserted a rights claim, but the case was decided on the basis of an evaluation of polity principles, which outweighed the perceived national emergency as advanced by the Truman administration.

The Court did not discount the impact of the crisis—it just did not believe one existed in this instance and believed that it had the authority to disagree with Truman on this particular point.[177] It concluded that the problems facing the nation because of the Korean conflict and the Cold War could not yet be analogous to those faced by the nation during the Civil War and the two world wars. In addition to analyzing the perceived crisis, the Court also took note of public opinion. As Arthur Schlesinger Jr., points out, the Court "registered the sense of Congress and the nation, volubly expressed in the two months since the seizure, that Truman and Vinson had it wrong and that this was simply not an emergency calling for drastic recourse to inherent presidential power."[178]

The Court applied sufficient rigor as it evaluated the president's actions and determined that the constitutional structure constrained such actions, rendering them subject to judicial and congressional restraints. The decision appeared to emphatically reject Truman's claim to inherent powers, but Justice Clark granted that the president could act in moments of exigent circumstances, pursuant to inherent powers, and Jackson's discussion of inherent powers was under the guise of the zone of twilight. Vinson's dissenting opinion (joined by Reed and Minton) endorsed Truman's actions, because the external security concerns of the Korean War necessitated the broad claim of power. And Burton and Frankfurter stated they would not pass judgment on the issue of inherent powers, because the steel-seizure case did not require them to do so.

Pro-presidentialists advocate that we operate under a one-branch model of foreign affairs, in large part because of the Court's instrumental role in facilitating this split in the original constitutional jurisprudence. The Court has defined and carved out the scope of executive authority in this area. *Youngstown* has been employed to provide a workable framework in which to understand the dual nature of shared powers. This schema has also created constitutional ambiguity (zone of twilight) when evaluating separation of powers, which gives advocates the legal positioning by which to expand presidential authority.

Justice Jackson's overall position, aside from the framework, was ambiguous. He appeared to outright reject the theory of inherent powers and underscored that only the legislature should make laws, yet his zone of twilight—where power is not clearly apportioned and where "the imperatives of events" determine the criteria in which to judge the legality of any action—allowed room for the executive to utilize inherent powers.

The outcome of the Court's ruling was that while the opinion declared illegal any and all unauthorized "legislative" acts of the president, seven justices supposed that future acts of the executive in emergency situations should be adjudicated on an ad hoc basis and the Court's duty would be to serve as the final arbiter of those asserted powers.[179]

The Frankfurter-Jackson approach was harmonious with the realities of the day—the three coordinate branches share a variety of powers, a practical framework in which to rationalize the reach of executive power. While the nation was faced with the pressures of international affairs and diplomacy, the Supreme Court was charged with evaluating Truman's claim to inherent power. As Justice Clark stated, "Where Congress has laid down specific procedures to deal with the type of crisis confronting the President, he must follow those procedures in meeting the crisis,"[180] but it was the Court's responsibility to stand in judgment of whether and in what capacity Congress had acted and whether the president had complied. Truman could have decided to use any of the three methods prescribed by Congress to avert a steel strike, but he could not go beyond those provisions outlined by the legislative branch, according to Clark. As Corwin notes, "Clark[,] . . . guided by Marshall's opinion in . . . *Barreme*, [concluded] that with Congress having entered the field, its ascertainable intention supplied the law of the case."[181]

In the years following the *Youngstown* decision, the tripartite schema was analytically helpful to lower courts' decision making in the late 1970s and early 1980s.[182] Lower courts acknowledged that the president has access to inherent and extraconstitutional powers in a zone of twilight. *Youngstown* therefore did not impede the possibility of courts' holding that inherent executive power exists, which rests on the established sole-organ doctrine of 1936—*Curtiss-Wright.*[183]

As an equal branch of government, the Supreme Court welcomed the opportunity to make a decision on the merits.[184] As a political institution,[185] it took the occasion to assert itself and proclaim that "presidential action is not immune to judicial review."[186] The nation, embroiled in the Korean conflict largely due to the fact that Truman had committed troops without a declaration of war by Congress, now faced a steel strike.

This pattern of orchestrated events unquestionably stirred the justices, as Truman declared he had the authority to seize private property to avoid a strike whose effect might detrimentally affect military forces in Korea. As Jackson stated, "No doctrine that the Court could promulgate would seem to me more sinister and alarming than that of a President whose conduct of foreign affairs is so largely uncontrolled, and often even is unknown, can vastly enlarge his mastery over the internal affairs of the country by his own commitment of the Nation's armed forces to some foreign venture."[187]

As an affiliated president, Truman's assertion of independent authority yielded to the Court an opportunity to insist upon "their own interpretive authority." He launched a vigorous rhetorical and unilateral administrative tenor when he advanced his foreign-affairs campaign. But the Court's decision in *Youngstown* "[re]articulat[ed] the constitutional commitments of the dominant coalition" and "enforce[d] and extend[ed] those commitments, perhaps in ways that are not readily available to legislative leaders who must cope with fractious coalitions and crowded agendas."[188] Because the regime at this time was resilient (Truman inherited the reconstruction regime of the New Deal), the Court's interpretative authority was regarded as a source of strength,[189] which was further buttressed by Truman's outrage over the ruling. Yet in foreign affairs, irrespective of whether a regime is collapsing or resilient, when the Court's authority is directly challenged, the Court lays "claim to a larger space of operations," which is usually, according to Whittington, available to Courts operating within the framework of the regime. And Jackson's innovative schema has allowed constitutional politics to be "creative"[190] over developmental time, because the Court has had substantial autonomy to elaborate or even rein in constitutional meaning as it has balanced polity and rights principles in light of perceived exigent circumstances.

Judicial authority is not in any danger of losing political support, because the Court utilizes a broad practical framework when it evaluates the sole-organ doctrine. As such, constitutional authority and constitutional settlements are developed over time; the Court's reframing is institutionalized as accepted paths of beliefs and ideologies transform power, politics, and history into law.

The *Youngstown* decision illustrated, quite clearly, the prowess of the Court in defining the parameters in which a president may act. It also showed that the Court could initiate and embed a branching point, if and when necessary, to the constitutional foreign-affairs jurisprudence. The Court moved from the new constitutional order instituted in *Curtiss-Wright*, which outlined the executive's broad plenary power in foreign affairs, to signaling that executives should be cautious when exercising authority in the domestic realm. The Court used its institutional positioning to determine whether the executive met the judicial bar of demonstrating a significant international threat. Irrespective of where a president was in political time, according to Skowronek's cyclical theory, the Court was predisposed to scrutinize executive claims, evaluate the political mechanisms utilized by Congress, and examine rights claims before reaching a decision.

Reframing presidential prerogatives as the *Youngstown* Court did provided for the operational space of the executive branch to broaden its capacity and role in making foreign policy over political time. But an executive's framing of a crisis must meet the threshold of judicial scrutiny, withstand the pressures of public opinion, and ensure that if Congress acts to block the executive, then the administration must be able to demonstrate why it has worked around or despite such action. Executive authority thus hinges on the justification of the president's actions drawn from the moment, which influences the ability to secure the legitimacy that a particular action would have on presidential power. The Court's decision making in legal time has profoundly guided American political development as it has shaped and controlled the relationship between the coordinate branches of government and subsequent constitutional claims by the executive.

The judicial branch's autonomy and subsequent authority to shape the political space in which the executive and legislature share power would be examined further in *Dames*, a case discussed at length in Chapter 5. *Dames* would be the next time the Court would hear a case questioning the broad authority of the executive and adopt Jackson's schema as controlling. Reevaluating an executive agreement that froze Iranian assets after the president asserted a national emergency, the Court would engineer a shift in authority as it relied on two cases decided shortly after *Curtiss-Wright*—*Belmont* (1937) and *Pink* (1942).

5

DAMES AND REGAN

Engineering a Shift in Authority from Congress
to the President

The first time the Supreme Court relied on *Youngstown* was in the *Dames* decision (1981). The *Dames* Court institutionalized Robert Jackson's broad schema, and the prominence of his concurring opinion would take on developmental significance. James Earl (Jimmy) Carter—a disjunctive president[1]—declared a national emergency and froze Iranian assets by way of an executive agreement in 1980, and the Court ruled that the president's authority to issue such an executive agreement was statutorily grounded. Relying explicitly on Jackson's *Youngstown* concurrence, the Court held that the absence of congressional disapproval of the president's actions could be construed as approval. Moreover, the Court rested its opinion on *Belmont* (1937) and *Pink* (1942), two cases that reaffirmed George Sutherland's sole-organ doctrine. *Dames* thus entrenched presidential control over the nation's foreign affairs.

Three years later, the Court heard *Regan v. Wald* (1984), which involved reconstructive President Ronald Reagan's restricting travel to Cuba, despite Congress's enacting provisions to fence in the far-reaching scope of presidential authority. The *Regan* Court concluded that the president had the unilateral authority to restrict travel, favoring national-security concerns over individual rights.

Taken in unison, these two cases show the extent to which the Court's interpretation legitimized a president's claim of broad unilateral authority in foreign policy making. The Court deliberately shifted authority from Congress to the president by finding exceptions to justify and sanction the executive's broad discretionary authority. These exceptions not only broadened the scope of presidential powers but also continued the slow entrenchment of the pro-presidentialist framework. For example, President Dwight D. Eisenhower "laid the statutory foundation for the executive prerogative interpretation, going to Congress for open-ended delegations of foreign policy power."[2] And President Richard Nixon's use of prerogative power raised the bar— "prerogative interpretation rose to new heights, both in its articulation and its execution." Having fewer constitutional limitations, Nixon maintained, enabled the executive branch to better safeguard the nation as it responded to exigent circumstances.[3]

Moreover, a revisionist reading of the Pentagon Papers illustrates the Court's acceptance of congressional delegations of power to the president in international affairs. The Court sanctioned the president when it concluded that the legislature unequivocally repudiated the executive's prerogative claim, but some justices overtly noted that without a clear denial by Congress, the judiciary would be disposed to find in favor of the prerogative privileges asserted by Nixon.[4] Nixon's employment "of the prerogative interpretation demonstrated . . . that one could not isolate foreign policy (and foreign policy powers) from domestic affairs." Effectively, the necessity "to act freely abroad was said to justify similar prerogative powers at home." The trend was clear: "[I]n foreign affairs[,] the president alone had final authority, and when the national security was imperiled (a judgment left to the executive)[,] the president was legitimately entitled to override constitutional constraints to preserve and protect that security."[5] However, although the Court's ingenuity fortified this trend, it was also disposed to harness the extent to which presidential autonomy in foreign affairs could extend to the domestic arena.

Dames and *Regan* were decided when the United States was involved in the Cold War, in which the United States (with the North Atlantic Treaty Organization [NATO] among its allies) and the Western Bloc never met in direct military combat, but both were assured of destruction because both possessed nuclear weapons. The political pressures placed on the administration of this war necessitated a number of wide-ranging policies. Under these circumstances, the Court contended that the executive had a significant role in the conduct of the nation's foreign policy as the president attempted to contain the spread of Communism. The Court, reengineering authority, clearly asserted its prowess in settling which branch and by what measure foreign policy was conducted. However, Justice William Rehnquist asserted that when it came to international affairs, the vast majority of executive action was "not neatly in one of three pigeonholes, but rather at some point along a spectrum running from explicit congressional authorization to explicit congressional prohibition."[6]

The *Dames* Court's reasoning in legal time and its finding in favor of the executive complicated Stephen Skowronek's theory of political time and his assertion of Carter's ineffectiveness. Carter, Skowronek argues, "was a nominal affiliate of a vulnerable regime projecting a place in history in which liberalism would prove its vitality through hard-nosed readjustments of its operating assumptions."[7] At the end of the day, he was considered as a political incompetent and was politically frustrated for four years; the Iran hostage crisis was his last chance to vindicate his leadership role as president. His response was strategic, and as a disjunctive president, Carter had a lot to prove. Initially, he had great latitude with the Iran hostage situation,[8] but in political time, Carter could not successfully get the hostages released. However, in legal time, Carter was vindicated; he had the legal authority to institutionalize policy measures as a bargaining chip. Skowronek's cyclical theory thus does not account for the constitutive role of the Court. By broadening the decision-making capacity of a disjunctive president, the Court was an agent of change that reconfigured Carter's leadership.

On July 2, 1981, the *Dames* Court judicially ended the fourteen-month Iran hostage crisis of 1979 to 1981. Sixty-six American nationals had been taken hostage on November 4, 1979, by Iranian militants at an American embassy in Tehran in response to the former shah's entering the United States for medical treatment. Reacting to the seizure of the U.S. embassy and American nationals, President Carter had declared a national emergency and froze Iranian assets[9] by invoking the International Emergency Economic Powers Act of 1977 (IEEPA).

Iran had then entered into continued negotiations with the United States that led to the signing in Algeria of two executive agreements[10] on January 19, 1981, by Deputy Secretary of State Warren M. Christopher, which resulted in the release of fifty-two American hostages. These agreements stipulated that approximately $3 to $4 billion of Iranian assets frozen in the United States would be returned to Iran. Upon the release of the hostages in 1981, the United States and Iran had entered into another agreement that required the termination of all legal proceedings in U.S. courts involving claims of U.S. nationals against Iran.[11]

The *Dames* Court's determination "gave legal effect" to the Algerian Accords, as it sanctioned the transfer of Iranian assets from the United States by July 19, 1981.[12] The majority—Justice Rehnquist was joined by Justices Warren Burger, William Brennan, Potter Stewart, Byron White, Thurgood Marshall, and Harry Blackmun—unequivocally held that the IEEPA[13] yielded to the president the express power to invalidate attachments on foreign assets in declared national emergencies and gave the executive the authority to transfer them out of the country.[14] Moreover, the Court reasoned, Congress had tacitly consented to the presidential use of international executive agreements to resolve the claims of American nationals against foreign governments and agencies.[15] The plurality ultimately saw its responsibility as ascertaining the degree and type of congressional approval of executive action (this same determination would be seen again in *Hamdi* [Chapter 6]).

The *Dames* Court exalted presidential control over Congress to conduct the nation's foreign affairs. Justice Rehnquist held that the president's claim to an executive agreement was grounded in statutory authorization, because Congress had "tacitly" endorsed the president's agreement—the "general tenor" of two statutes allocated broad discretionary authority to the executive. Rehnquist asserted that "past practice does not, by itself, create power, but 'long-continued' practice, known to and acquiesced by Congress, would raise a presumption that the [action] had been [taken] in pursuance of its consent."[16]

Dames walked a fine line between *Curtiss-Wright* and *Youngstown*. The *Dames* Court's grant of wide latitude further entrenched the constitutional order established in *Curtiss-Wright*, and its employment of Jackson's practical categorization of presidential power acknowledged that the executive branch has at its disposal unilateral policy-making tools—executive agreements and treaties—with which to conduct foreign policy.

By sanctioning the transfer of American claims, the Court grounded its decision on exceedingly scarce power.[17] The IEEPA, the Court maintained, granted to the president the unilateral power to control foreign assets to end a national emergency, which the Court asserted that the president alone had the sole discretion to declare.[18] While the IEEPA granted explicit authority to the president, no express constitutional clause permits the president to make use of international executive agreements to achieve these ends. *Dames* sanctioned broad authority in foreign affairs (echoing *Curtiss-Wright*) and, through its evaluation of congressional-presidential relations, determined that the president had statutory authority to act (utilizing the *Youngstown* framework). The *Dames* decision thus demonstrated an engineered judicial recognition of authority. Rehnquist's opinion rested on statutes that did not directly talk to the issue at hand, so the holding also illustrated the Court's continued entrenchment of broad presidential power in foreign relations.

CARTER'S STRATEGIC RESPONSE TO THE IRAN HOSTAGE CRISIS

Carter took office in 1977 and served one term. While he was in office, his administration was faced with, among other events, international stagflation (1977–1981),[19] an energy crisis (1979), the Three Mile Island nuclear accident

(1979), the Soviet invasion of Afghanistan (late 1979), and the Iran hostage crisis (1979–1981). By 1980, Carter's popularity had significantly declined, but he survived a primary challenge against Senator Ted Kennedy (D-MA) for the Democratic Party's nomination in the 1980 presidential election. However, he lost the election to Republican candidate Ronald Reagan. Mere minutes after Carter's term ended on Inauguration Day, the remaining fifty-two U.S. hostages held in Iran were released, thus ending the 444-day Iran hostage crisis.

When Carter entered the Democratic Party presidential primaries in 1976, the centerpiece of his campaign platform was his insistence on government reorganization. This platform was further enhanced by the fact that he was thought to have "little chance against those nationally better-known politicians," because he had a name-recognition factor of only 2 percent. However, he had the distinct advantage of being an outsider; given the recent Watergate scandal, voters were looking for a candidate with some distance from Washington, D.C. Carter's two-prong strategy helped him become an early front-runner by winning the Iowa caucuses and the New Hampshire primary. In the South, he ran as a moderate. In the North, he appealed largely to conservative Christian and rural voters, although he did not have the numbers to win a majority in most of these states. Ultimately, Carter proved to be the only Democrat with a truly national strategy, which, in the end, sealed the nomination.[20] Carter won the popular vote by 50.1 percent to 48.0 percent for Gerald Ford,[21] who was in a weak position in the wake of Watergate.

Domestically, Carter had the challenge of inflation and recession as well as an energy crisis. Internationally, Carter was instrumental in signing the Camp David Accords, returning the Panama Canal to the Panamanians, and creating the SALT II nuclear-arms-reduction treaty with Soviet leader Leonid Brezhnev. However, the final year of his first term was marred by the Iran hostage crisis, which ultimately contributed to his losing his bid for reelection in 1980. The Iran hostage crisis was, by all accounts, an occasion for Carter's "third rebirth."[22] As a voice for the American people and their frustrations,[23] he instructed his administration to focus all of its energy on freeing the captive Americans.[24]

Carter wasted no time in making this situation a true test of his leadership.[25] He wanted to show the kidnappers that he would remain firm but patient in his resolve to gain the successful release of the hostages.[26] As the election year drew near, Carter believed that the only other issue that should be on his agenda and the nation's was the Soviet invasion of Afghanistan, calling it "one of the most serious threats to World Peace since the Second World War."[27] As such, Carter's responsiveness to the Cold War rapidly increased.

With the public's view that Carter had an issue that he could define and fully command, "the political effect was immediate."[28] They widely believed that the job of the White House was to resolve the hostage crisis, which gave Carter the impregnable political clout necessary to get the job done.[29] Democrats who had favored Senator Kennedy in the summer of 1979 now favored Carter; by early March 1980, the tables had turned,[30] and Carter held a lead of 2 to 1.[31]

Yet over the course of the hostage crisis, the political landscape began to look quite different. Carter set strong standards for how he would handle the crisis, but as time went on, pressures to act intensified. The White House became inundated with charges that it was manipulating the crisis for political advantage. So the administration decided to employ the military, but attempt to rescue the hostages failed.

Instead of this crisis's being Carter's "rebirth," this "late-regime affiliate" became the most frustrating situation of his presidency.[32] Ten days after the capture of sixty-six American hostages in Tehran on November 14, 1979, Carter, under the authority granted to him by IEEPA sections 1701–1706,[33] issued Executive Order (EO) 12170,[34] which stopped the withdrawal of all Iranian property and interests from the United States.[35] In accordance with this order, the administration decreed Treasury regulations on November 15, 1979, that obliged attachments on Iranian assets to be licensed by the Treasury Department,[36] adding that these licenses could be rescinded at any time.[37]

A CHALLENGE TO EXECUTIVE STATUTORY AND CONSTITUTIONAL AUTHORITY

The corporation Dames and Moore filed suit in the Federal District Court for the Central District of California against the Atomic Energy Organization of Iran on December 19, 1979, alleging that it was owed money per their current contract.[38] In an attempt to secure judgment, the Federal District Court directed an attachment on certain Iranian property, pursuant to the Treasury clarification of December 19.[39] On January 19, 1981, the Algerian Accords were signed, which provided for the transfer of Iranian assets out of the United States and terminated all litigation against Iran.[40] On the same day the accords were signed, President Carter issued EO 12276 and EO 12285, which implemented the terms and conditions of the accords.[41] Barely a month after President Reagan took office in 1981, he supported the accords by requiring the suspension of all American claims against Iran, except for those already appearing before the International Arbitral Tribunal, which had been established by the second Algerian Accord.[42]

Dames and Moore had been awarded summary judgment against Iran, but enforcement of the judgment was halted pending an appeal. Furthermore, prejudgment attachments were lifted because of the accords and the executive orders.[43] As such, Dames and Moore filed suit against Treasury Secretary Donald T. Regan in an attempt to prevent enforcement of the accords. The company charged that the president had exceeded the bounds of his statutory and constitutional authority, which adversely affected the corporation's claims against Iran.[44] The District Court denied the petitioner's motion and prohibited the transfer of Iranian property.[45] Because the Iranian crisis was an exigent matter, the appeal was taken directly to the Supreme Court, which granted certiorari.[46]

Arguing on behalf of the federal respondent (Treasury Secretary Regan), Rex E. Lee outlined the position and arguments invoked by the administration. In open court, Lee and C. Stephen Howard (arguing for the petitioner) discussed at length the congressional authorization of the IEEPA that granted to the president the statutory authority to take the necessary steps to meet an emergency by freezing assets. Acting pursuant to statutory authorization, Howard conceded, the president acted constitutionally.

Addressing the president's power to act alone, the government presented the Court with a long line of historical references demonstrating the executive's authority to act as in the present case. The government also asserted that the president had the authority to act by way of the IEEPA; specifically, the president had the authority to move it "out of the judicial track and put it in the diplomatic" by stopping the "lawsuit and [lifting] your attachments."[47] In response, Howard argued that for the executive to assert that he had the authority to stop a lawsuit, it would have to be dragged out of the statute.[48] But Lee maintained that this was not necessarily the case; context mattered. He asked the Court to consider the circumstances leading up to the freezing of assets: the government had reacted to the likely threat of the "Government of Iran withdrawing its funds" with an order issued by President Carter in January and Reagan's reaffirming order a month later. This request reminded the Court that exigent circumstances and the president's framing of the situation—volatile and requiring a definitive response—were necessary components of judicial decision making. The Court contemplated these two factors when reaching a verdict.

To lend further credence to Carter's actions and ground his assertions, Lee drew on Court precedent and the leadership of the executive. Lee reminded the current justices of the Court's earlier decision in *United States v. Pink* (1942), which determined that "this kind of authority in the President has a much broader use than just the assurance of the rights of American claimants."[49] He added, "[T]his is one of the bargaining chips, if you will[;] this is part of a leverage that the President can and should use in achieving the normalization of relations with foreign countries." When Justice Stewart pushed

Lee to reveal why this kind of action was a useful policy tool for the executive, Lee noted, "[T]he proposition that this was used solely as a bargaining chip for the release of the hostages does not tell the entire story." He maintained that the legal issue undercutting both causes for concern in the suit (the power to nullify attachments and transfer assets and the power to settle claims) was the power "to act in an international crisis whose nature and magnitude are such that if it [is] to be resolved[,] it has to be resolved by one person and one person alone, and under our system of argument[,] that person is the President."[50] Drawing on *Curtiss-Wright*, Lee added that the executive could act with sole authority in the area of foreign affairs when responding to a crisis.

In defense of the president's transfer of the assets and nullification of the attachments, Lee not only stated that the authority was covered under the statutory authorization of IEEPA but also invoked Jackson's tripartite schema, suggesting that the president's actions and congressional sanction had placed the executive in tier one.[51] Lee contended that although Howard asserted that the category was broad, this category spoke to the president's taking question and did "not pertain to the President's power." Moreover, Lee noted, the precedent of *Pink* and *Curtiss-Wright* showed the Court's "deference in these matters of delegations of broad authority to the President." And the IEEPA granted to the president this power with the understanding that it "will be exercised only with respect to an unusual and extraordinary threat which amounts to a national emergency," which the government asserted that the present situation amounted to.

Furthermore, Lee argued, Jackson's framework "indicate[d] that you get the additional force of Article I power added to Article II power when you have the implied approval of Congress." Adding implied power was not "characterized by contention and by inter-branch struggle." Instead, this was an "area in which there has been a continuing recognition by Congress of the existence of claims settlement authority and periodic enactments to support it." And with respect to *Pink*, Lee pointed out that the Court "characterized it as a modest implied power of the President as to which effectiveness in handling the delicate problems of foreign relations requires no less." He added, "[I]t is a practice that is well recognized, well established, recognized not only by the decisions of this Court in Pink."[52] The *Dames* Court relied on this point when it asserted that the president acted within his authority.

To distinguish between those powers that resided with the president and those that were acquired, Justice Rehnquist asked Lee, "[D]o you disagree, then, with Justice Frankfurter's statement in the Steel Seizure case that just because the power does not reside in the President doesn't mean that the Government as a whole doesn't have it, and just because the Government as a whole has it doesn't mean that the President by himself can exercise it?" Lee responded,

"I do agree with that statement." His reliance on Jackson's framework demonstrated the strength of the government's assertion that the president's power was at its zenith. This position was compelling, as Rehnquist referred to this point in his majority opinion.

Regarding the steel-seizure decision, Rehnquist argued that "President Truman's order was posited on the emergency that he felt existed and he shut down the steel mills in the Korean conflict. Yet this Court decided against him." As Chapter 4 points out, although the majority appeared to render a decision that was in sharp rebuke to Truman's decision to seize the steel mills, Jackson's opinion became the cornerstone to determining executive power vis-à-vis Congress and how succeeding presidents would defend unilateral authority. In fact, as Lee argued, this case "is either a category two or category one," because Carter had acted with more than just his own Article II power, although that alone "would have been sufficient." The bottom line, Lee noted, was that the executive had acted with the authority of Congress as well as with his own authority, because he had been responding to a rare occasion of crisis.[53]

The *Dames* majority emphasized two central issues. First, did the president have the power to invalidate the attachment of assets? And second, could the president use executive agreements to compel the transfer of American claims from domestic courts to an international tribunal? Rehnquist relied heavily on Jackson's *Youngstown* analysis when discussing the first issue, because this circumstance, according to the three tiers, was when the president's power was at its zenith. However, when Rehnquist discussed the implied congressional delegation of power to settle claims by an executive agreement, a power that could be categorized in the "zone of twilight" or even in the "lowest ebb" tier, he virtually disregarded *Youngstown*.[54]

The *Dames* Court originally framed the second matter as whether the president could suspend claims pending in American courts, as Reagan had claimed in EO 12294.[55] But the Court broadened its discussion and asserted that "international agreements settling claims by nationals of one state against the government of another 'are established international practice reflecting traditional international theory.'"[56] The Court observed, "Though these settlements have sometimes been made by treaty, there has also been a longstanding practice of settling such claims by executive agreement without the advice and consent of the Senate."[57] It further contended, "Congress has implicitly approved the practice of claim settlement by executive agreement."[58] It is evident that the Court took judicial notice of historical practice as it evaluated the claims of the administration and the circumstances of the crisis when it determined that individual rights claims were undermined by the executive's employment of bargaining chips to resolve said crisis. It determined that the executive must be able to act freely abroad when national security was in such peril.

The majority held that the IEEPA not only conferred to the president the express authority to invalidate attachments but also did not limit his power to act in national emergencies.[59] Resting on Jackson's *Youngstown* concurrence, the majority concluded that the president had acted pursuant to specific, express congressional authorization. And from a public-policy standpoint, the Court argued that the president needed the freedom to act—in this case, to use frozen assets as "bargaining chips" in delicate negotiations.[60] The Court declared that if such a power were not granted to the executive, "the Federal Government as a whole [would] lack . . . the power exercised by the President."[61]

On the issue of the constitutionality of executive agreements, the Court asserted that neither the IEEPA nor the Hostage Act of 1868[62] specifically authorized the suspension of American claims against foreign entities.[63] The Court stated that the reality was that because Congress had never formulated a clear system for claims settlement, it implied legislative approval of unilateral executive action.[64]

The Court relied on a case decided three days prior to *Dames*. Its holding in *Haig v. Agee*[65] was instrumental in how the Court dispensed with *Dames*. In *Haig*, it reasoned that the State Department had appropriately revoked Philip Agee's passport, even though Congress had not given the executive branch express authorization to take such action. Drawing on *Haig*, the *Dames* Court decided that the "failure of Congress specifically to delegate authority does not, 'especially . . . in the areas of foreign policy and national security,' imply 'congressional disapproval' of action taken by the Executive."[66] Moreover, the *Dames* Court concluded that Congress's adoption of the International Claims Settlement Act of 1949 gave tacit legislative approval.[67]

Reinforcing the Court's prior decision, Rehnquist stated that "prior cases of this Court have also recognized that the President does have some measure of power to enter into executive agreements without obtaining the advice and consent of the Senate."[68] Interestingly, the "prior cases" Rehnquist referred to consisted of only one case—*Pink*, a case raised by Lee during oral argument. It reasoned that Congress's failure to oppose explicitly the use of executive agreements could be understood to establish a rule of customary constitutional law validating unilateral presidential agreements. Quoting *Youngstown* directly, the opinion concluded that there was "'a systematic, unbroken executive practice [of using executive agreements], long pursued to the knowledge of Congress and never before questioned.'"[69] So if Congress had a problem, it could have intervened. In not taking any steps, Congress had tacitly consented to the continued practice. And if Congress had sanctioned such practice, albeit implicitly, the inclination might be to suggest that the Court must go along. But the rationale and impact of the Court's decision were more complicated.

The *Dames* Court sustained the broad reach of executive power but also shaped the scope and parameters of the president's utilization of powers in the area of foreign affairs. To understand how it did so, whether at the behest of the executive branch or per its own initiative, the following discussion shows that the Court's reliance on the IEEPA grounded the president's authority to "attach and nullify attachments of foreign assets." Second, the Court's determination of the executive's framing of the situation resulted in claiming the president had broad authority. And finally, even though the Court granted broad prerogatives, this determination shaped how far-reaching these powers were; the Court sanctioned the use of international unilateral executive agreements to settle claims of American nationals against foreign governments and their entities. In these ways, the Court marshaled evidence and reconstructed history to ground its decision and reach its conclusions, all the while entrenching the sole-organ doctrine by employing the complex and unclear tripartite system.

MARSHALING EVIDENCE AND RECONSTRUCTING HISTORY

After pointing out that Section 1702 (a)(1)(B) of the IEEPA[70] included, verbatim, Section 5(b) of the Trading with the Enemy Act of 1917 (TWEA),[71] the *Dames* majority concluded that the legislative record of both acts and relevant case law supported the continuation of presidential nullification of attachments on foreign assets.[72] The case law referenced by the Court resulted in only one citation, *Orvis v. Brownell* (1953),[73] to explain historical support for this kind of executive power. The majority made no reference to either statements or committee reports in the *Congressional Record*, which would have informed the Court of the legislative purpose in passing the IEEPA. It did, however, concede that "Congress intended to limit the President's emergency power in peace time."[74]

The Court's dependence on the IEEPA's legislative history was, perhaps, unnecessary, but it did give the Court cause to illustrate that the statute did little in the way of placing sufficient limits on the president's power to conduct foreign affairs. The statute clearly granted the president the power to "compel, nullify[,] . . . prevent[,] or prohibit, any acquisition, holding, . . . [or] transfer . . . of . . . any property in which any foreign country or a national thereof has any interest."[75] An expansive definition of the word "holding" could realistically include "attachments"; because the *Dames* majority concluded that the president had worked under a specific congressional grant of authority,[76] the "widest latitude of judicial interpretation"[77] conceded a broad definition.

It should be noted that the legislative history of the IEEPA did exhibit that Congress was troubled with the reach of presidential power in foreign affairs. In fact, the statute was envisioned to give the executive "narrow . . . powers subject to congressional review in times of 'national emergency' short of war,"[78] because the executive, prior to the act, had enjoyed unilateral power to declare such emergencies without conferring with Congress.[79] The act was not meant to "t[ie] the President's hands in times of crises,"[80] because Congress's adoption of the IEEPA conceded the necessity of presidential flexibility to respond to real emergencies, a classification that could include the Iranian crisis. Despite this rather paradoxical legislative record, the IEEPA was enacted in 1977, and its implementation over time influenced the president's utilization of power and legislative development, subsequently influencing the Court's determination as it balanced presidential prerogatives against the rights of the claimants.

At issue was Section 5(b)(1) of the TWEA, which postulated in part, "[A]ny property or interest of any foreign country or national thereof shall vest . . . in such agency or person as may be designated . . . by the President, and upon such terms and conditions as the President may prescribe."[81] This particular provision, however, was excluded from the IEEPA, which stated, "[T]his grant of authority does not include . . . the power to vest . . . foreign property."[82]

The *Dames* Court could simply have noted that the IEEPA did very little to limit the president's power in the area of foreign affairs, because Section 1702 (a)(1)(B) relied upon by Carter when he issued EO 12170 was taken word for word from the TWEA.[83] And this particular section was not aimed to alter the scope of the president's authority. In fact, as Felix Frankfurter wrote in his *Youngstown* concurrence, "It would be not merely infelicitous draftsmanship but almost offensive gaucherie to write . . . a restriction upon the President's power in terms into a statute"[84] that clearly confers that power upon him. But the *Dames* Court seemed disinclined to consider a major substantive difference between the language of the pertinent TWEA provision and the germane passage in the IEEPA. Conceivably, if the Court had admitted to the clash, it would have significantly undermined the Court's reliance on *Orvis* as the authority for the executive's actions under consideration in *Dames*. Stare decisis, then, is applicable only when the Court decides how it will frame the issues and questions in the present case, and then it will decide whether and when case precedent is employed and to what degree.

Orvis was the only precedent used by the *Dames* Court to uphold the president's powers under the TWEA. In *Orvis*, the property of Japanese nationals was vested in an "Alien Property Custodian" after an executive order stopped all transfers of Japanese property in the United States.[85] During the time between the executive order's issuance and its implementation, the petitioners in the case got an unlicensed attachment and judgment. The question before the Court was whether the attachment created a property interest sufficient to deny title in the custodian and grant it in the petitioners.[86] Interestingly, the *Orvis* Court's opinion acknowledged that although the attachment of assets was not sufficient to deny the "guardian" of the property,[87] "the executive freezing order did not prevent such an attachment from creating rights between the judgment creditor and the enemy debtor whom the Custodian had elected to succeed."[88] Because the vesting power was explicitly nullified by the IEEPA, the portion of the *Orvis* opinion that upheld the superior right in the custodian, an executive official, was decisively challenged. Consequently, the opinion in *Orvis* suggested that a creditor who attained an attachment lien had the ultimate right to the attached property after recovering judgment.[89]

But the *Dames* Court's interpretation opposed the *Orvis* reasoning. *Orvis* did not suggest "that an American claimant may not use an attachment that is subject to a revocable license that has been obtained after the entry of a freeze order to limit . . . the actions the President may take under § 1702 respecting the frozen assets."[90] The *Dames* opinion noted, however, "Although it is true the IEEPA does not give the President the power to 'vest' . . . the assets, it does not follow that the President is not authorized . . . to otherwise permanently dispose of the assets."[91] Congress unmistakably indicated that presidential action was appropriate when a "national emergency [is] declared and emergency authorities [are] employed only with respect to a specific set of circumstances which constitute a real emergency."[92] In political time, the events in Iran were not questioned as to whether they constituted a real emergency. The IEEPA was therefore adopted in recognition of the executive's necessity for "standby emergency authority to deal with unusual and extraordinary economic crisis."[93]

So what does this all mean? Generally speaking, the language of the IEEPA allowed the president the definitive authority to attach and dispose of foreign assets. In a national emergency, the executive, pursuant to express statutory authorization, could freeze foreign assets as a bargaining chip in negotiations and revoke licenses, at any time, to attach these assets. Aware of the implications of upholding the president's ability to use such a power, the Court was constrained by the accelerated briefing schedule. It consequently noted that there was a "necessity to rest [the] decision on the narrowest possible ground capable of deciding the case."[94] It legally upheld the politically motivated policy tool—freezing foreign assets as a bargaining chip—so the executive could successfully respond to a national emergency.

Although the Court upheld the power of the executive to resolve claims through the process of international executive agreements, its opinion never discussed the basis of the power from which to draw its conclusion. Rather, the majority cited four Court cases: *Curtiss-Wright* (1936), *Pink* (1942), *Youngstown* (1952), and *Haig* (1981). The Court inferred implied congressional acquiescence in the presidential use of executive agreements:[95] "'a systematic, unbroken executive practice, long pursued to the knowledge of Congress and never before questioned . . . may be treated as a gloss on 'Executive power' vested in the President.'"[96] Because the Constitution does not yield an express grant of power to authorize the utilization of international agreements other than by the treaty process, the Court considered the executive's power to carry out an executive agreement to be inherent, implied, or delegated.[97]

The Court could use an array of sources to justify these springs of power, such as the intent of the Founders, congressional power, and the recognition power. A brief overview demonstrated there was no such evidence. Consequently, the Court reconstructed history and rationalized evidence to ground its *Dames* holding.

The very text and history of the Constitution are instructive on the nature and possibly the source of power exercised by the president in the Algerian Accords. Even though the express words "executive agreement" are not found anywhere in the Constitution,[98] the president is not necessarily limited to purely enumerated powers.[99] For example, as Raoul Berger noted, "Madison stated in the Federal Convention that it was essential 'to fix the extent of the Executive authority' and to give 'certain powers' to the executive, and that the executive power should be 'confined and defined.'"[100] So although executive agreements are not expressly discussed in the Constitution, the Court could have asserted that the enumerated-powers doctrine did not apply to the field of foreign affairs.[101] If the Founders had intended to vest the national government with plenary authority in international affairs—this kind of authority would be implied unless it were specifically limited by the Constitution[102]—constitutional silence on executive agreements might reveal the intent of the Founders, which, as the *Dames* Court suggested, was to give the executive the capacity to act. This point is particularly debatable, because the scope and nature of implied powers continue to be contentious.

Another source of power allocated in the Constitution is congressional. The *Gibbons* Court (1824)[103] recognized the exclusive powers of Congress, but in the international arena, a modern Court might recognize concurrent instead of exclusive power in either of the branches designated with the authority to conduct foreign relations. So when the *Dames* Court held that the legislative branch had acted through the adoption of the IEEPA and the International Claims Settlement Act (ICSA), the executive had then simply acted pursuant to a congressional delegation of power. The president had not seized Congress's commerce-clause power when he issued the executive agreement.

Another possible source of constitutional power is the president's power of recognition. The *Pink* Court (1942) directly addressed this issue and was the primary source of authority for the conclusions drawn in *Dames*. The Constitution vests in the president the authority to "appoint Ambassadors, other public Ministers[,] and Consuls"[104] and to "receive Ambassadors and other public Ministers."[105] Even though Alexander Hamilton thought this power was "more a matter of dignity than of authority,"[106] it has, over time, come to serve as a source "for the authority of the President to recognize foreign governments and to enter into recognition agreements."[107] A case in point is *Zivotofsky* (2015), which is discussed in Chapter 6. The recognition power, judicially inferred (*Belmont*) from the power to receive ambassadors, has broadened the metes and bounds of executive authority and thrust the president far beyond the first constitutional order.

The Court first upheld the validity of executive agreements in *Belmont*. Not only did the *Belmont* Court take judicial notice of the sequence of events; more importantly, it relied on *Curtiss-Wright*: the Litvinov Agreement was implemented in accordance with the 1933 recognition of the Soviet government, so executive agreements derive their legitimacy from the president's role as sole organ of foreign affairs, and the executive has the authority to recognize foreign governments. At the time, Sutherland's *Curtiss-Wright* opinion added that Senate consultation was not required, as the president had sole authority to conduct the nation's international discourse. *Belmont* reaffirmed this position, so the *Dames* Court had the precedent it needed to render its decision.

Belmont was decided in 1937, but evidence of its doctrinal effect would not be realized until forty years later. The current Republican *Dames* Court reaffirmed Sutherland's opinion (a decision rendered at the heart of the New Deal era) by utilizing the *Belmont* precedent. This evolutionary narrative illustrates the Court's prerogative in adopting prior, not contemporaneous, decisions to substantively influence the trajectory of executive authority. The Court rereads and reapplies cases, even ignoring others (e.g., Jackson's rejection of *Curtiss-Wright* that is the bedrock of *Belmont* and subsequently *Pink*), when determining the scope of presidential prerogatives in the conduct of international affairs.

In 1942, the *Pink* Court reaffirmed *Belmont*. *Pink* involved New York state courts' rejecting to give effect, under state law, to the Litvinov Agreement.[108] The question before the Supreme Court was whether, under the supremacy clause,[109] a state law could constitutionally supersede an executive agreement that disposed of claims in return for recognizing a foreign government. The *Pink* Court upheld the Litvinov Agreement by invoking the sole-organ doctrine (*Curtiss-Wright*) and the recognition power (*Belmont*). However, the opinion writer Justice William O. Douglas went one judicial step further by holding that Congress had "tacitly" approved of the executive agreement. *Pink* was therefore interpreted to mean that the executive had the authority to implement executive agreements without first obtaining the advice and consent of the Senate.[110] The *Dames* Court relied on this legal reasoning.[111] The *Dames* majority employed *Pink* as precedent, but the holding of the Court suggested that *Pink* could be employed to uphold *any* executive agreement.[112]

Narrowly interpreted, *Pink* suggested that "complete power over international affairs is in the national government and is not and cannot be subject to any curtailment or interference on the part of the several states."[113] However, the *Dames* Court interpreted *Pink* broadly by unequivocally distinguishing the president, and not Congress, as the primary authority in foreign relations.[114] Consequently, the *Dames* Court found that "[p]ower to remove such obstacles to full recognition as settlement of claims of our nationals . . . certainly is a modest implied power of the President[,] who is the 'sole organ of the federal government in the field of international relations.'"[115]

For foreign policy to be expeditious, the Court combed through legislative history, looking for any attempts that directly or indirectly settled on policy initiatives that provided the president the unilateral authority to act in international emergency situations. But the Court argued that the legislative branch "cannot anticipate and [respond by] legislat[ing] with regard to every possible action the President may find it necessary to take."[116] This claim clearly demonstrated a preference for accommodating rather than creating friction between the political branches by demarcating a set of parameters in which the two branches could utilize their reserved authority to act in foreign affairs.

The *Dames* Court maintained that the executive did not intrude on congressional prerogatives in deciding the Algerian Accords, because Congress not only expressly[117] but also incidentally[118] had consented to the action procured by the executive to acquire the release of the American hostages. The Court, unwilling to check the president in resolving "a major foreign policy dispute between our country and another,"[119] readily seized on a version of congressional support to ground its decision.

The *Dames* majority, seemingly at ease with the prospect of plenary executive power in foreign affairs, endorsed the president's attachment of Iranian assets by proclaiming that it found congressional cooperation. Even though the IEEPA furnished the executive with *express* authority to attach assets, the

Court concluded that the ICSA[120] yielded *implied* power for the president to use executive agreements to dispose of them.[121]

The Court accepted that the ICSA was meant to establish a commission in the State Department to distribute to American claimants funds obtained through executive agreements with foreign countries.[122] This seemingly limited purpose, the Court asserted, suggested congressional resolve to approve the employment of executive agreements.[123] As such, the Court concluded, "Congress did not question the fact of the settlement [of claims by executive agreement] or the power of the President to have concluded it."[124]

Legislative history, however, is silent on the executive's power to employ executive agreements. Rather, Congress appeared to be more concerned with how to distribute funds acquired through settlements instead of the process by which the funds were obtained. So even though the ICSA offered some context, it[125] should not be interpreted as implied authorization for the president to resort to executive agreements, because the circumstances were dissimilar to those prescribed by the act, which distinguished the remedy available for the situation. However, the Court's determination of the crisis and its reading of legislative history granted broad authority to the president. Interestingly, references in the congressional record demonstrated Congress's acknowledgment of the presence of executive prerogatives in the area of claims settlement.[126] Members of Congress not only acknowledged these powers but also recognized that the Court had the authority to make this demarcation. Broad executive prerogatives were thus legislated by Congress, legalized by the Court, and institutionalized over developmental time.

The Court's inference of authority for unilateral executive agreements from the ICSA and legislative history was reminiscent of Justice Jackson's "zone of twilight." Recall that Lee referenced *Youngstown* and placed the president's actions squarely in tier one. To apply Jackson's categorization, the *Dames* Court had to establish whether presidential power was contingent on the exigencies of a specific emergency or on the requirements of an express provision to endorse the use of unilateral executive agreements.[127] It determined that "congressional inertia, indifference[,] or quiescence may sometimes . . . enable, if not invite, measures on independent presidential responsibility."[128] On the basis of this rationale, the Court was equipped to turn its attention to the seemingly ambiguous issue of delegated powers, an issue buttressed by the only case of unparalleled validation of executive authority, *Curtiss-Wright*.

The *Dames* majority maintained that "'long continued practice, known to and acquiesced in by Congress, would raise a presumption that the [action] has been [taken] in pursuance of its consent.'"[129] The Court effectively created a new standard that allowed Congress to delegate to the executive, over the course of time, the power to settle claims of American citizens by issuing an executive agreement. This delegation, however, did not need to be overt, because the legislative branch could, as the Court surmised, "implicitly [sanction] the practice of claim settlement by executive agreement."[130] This reading of legislative history effectively broadened the Court's holding in *Curtiss-Wright* (that the ruling against delegation by one branch to another does not apply to foreign affairs)[131] as it sanctioned the delegation of power from one branch of government to another through implication alone. In effect, the Court created legislative space where the executive might act through an implicit understanding of the practical necessities and power required to respond to situations that were international in scope, such as a crisis.

This determination disregarded the executive branch's theory that the lack of express power in Congress to unilaterally employ international agreements necessarily prevented the legislative branch from delegating that kind of power to the president.[132] The Court reasoned that Congress had, in fact, delegated this power by implication alone. It maintained that foreign-affairs powers were concurrent,[133] yet it fell short of assigning this power between the two political branches and from restricting the executive from acting on personal initiative.[134] Consequently, the Court also fashioned political space, allowing the two branches to continue to negotiate the terms of their concurrent powers. At the same time, the Court did not close off the possibility of the executive's personal choice to act while managing foreign affairs.

Relying on *Curtiss-Wright*, the *Dames* Court asserted that the executive possessed the power of the "sole-organ" doctrine to legitimate unilateral presidential action in foreign affairs, but it also accepted the hesitancy of the *Youngstown* Court to broaden such considerable power of the executive in the domestic arena.[135]

The *Dames* Court solidified the trajectory of *Youngstown*; after *Dames*, Jackson's concurrence was the law and no longer considered just dicta.[136] The *Youngstown* Court explained at length the separation of powers between the legislature and the executive.[137] To recap: Justice Black rejected the inherent-powers theory asserted by the government and held that Congress had clearly dismissed the notion that the president could seize domestic property in emergency situations.[138] Black argued that neither the executive's authority as commander-in-chief nor his authority to execute the laws provided the president "the ultimate power . . . to take possession of private property in order to keep labor disputes from stopping production."[139] However, Justice Rehnquist's majority opinion in *Dames* misconstrued Black's holding. Citing Black, Rehnquist noted that the validity of Truman's seizure of the mills during a nationwide strike illustrated that "the President's power, if any, to issue the order must stem either from an act of Congress or from the Constitution itself."[140] This reference steered the majority into finding the necessary statutory authorization to sanction Carter's actions. Rehnquist added that Jackson's framing, in a general way, asserted "the consequences of different types of interaction between the two democratic branches in assessing Presidential authority to act in any given case."[141] Even though Rehnquist reaffirmed the utility of Jackson's schema, he maintained that the Constitution has not neatly divided the powers between the two branches of government.[142] Presumably, neither could the *Dames* Court.

Rehnquist also drew from Frankfurter's *Youngstown* concurrence. He did not go into detail, but it is evident, given his own conclusions, that Frankfurter's assertions guided Rehnquist's line of argument. For example, Frankfurter argued that simple recognition power was national in nature and not automatically allocated to Congress or the president.[143] He added that inferences could be made from congressional silence: "[A] systematic, unbroken, executive practice, long pursued to the knowledge of the Congress and never before questioned, engaged in by Presidents . . . may be treated as a gloss on 'executive Power' vested in the President."[144] And Jackson's concurrence noted further that the executive branch controlled only those powers delegated to the president, with one caveat: these powers should be broadly construed.[145] Jackson recognized Congress's power to delegate extraordinary emergency power in times of crisis,[146] but he cautioned that "emergency powers are consistent with free government only when their control is lodged elsewhere than in the Executive who exercises them."[147]

Rehnquist gave judicial weight to Frankfurter's, Black's, and Jackson's pronouncements. The *Dames* Court underscored two points raised in *Youngstown* that were essential to its analysis and the majority ruling in the present case. First and foremost, Jackson's *Youngstown* opinion asserted that "in the framework of our Constitution, the President's power to see that the laws are faithfully executed refutes the idea that he is to be a lawmaker";[148] this legislative function was Congress's alone. Second, Jackson added, even if presidents had seized private property in the past without congressional consent, Congress remained the exclusive lawmaker.[149]

The *Dames* majority expanded on Jackson's view so that it could give "the strongest of presumptions and the widest latitude of judicial interpretation"[150] to the president's actions. The Court concluded that the executive had acted with the concurrence of specific legislative authorization.[151] This resolve held weight and could be legitimately applied to the IEEPA, but the fact remained that Congress did not expressly approve executive agreements. Additionally, because Congress was the sole lawmaker and international agreements had been recognized as having the same legal status as treaties,[152] an executive agreement was, in all actuality, an act of legislation and would therefore necessitate congressional involvement. Moreover, the Court had never concluded that the president's foreign-affairs power granted the authority to issue orders that had the force of law in which they could directly regulate property within the United States.[153]

Moreover, the plurality added, "usage has long been regarded as an inadequate source of constitutional authority."[154] The track record of presidential action regardless of constitutional disinterest was insufficient authority for the formation of a "customary constitutional rule of law." The legislative branch's failure to implement its acknowledged powers did not permit another branch not granted those powers to act in its place.[155] Simply stated, Congress's failure to employ its concurrent foreign-affairs power did not automatically authorize unilateral presidential decisions.[156] Although Congress had not voiced any specific concern over the Algerian Accords,[157] it had repeatedly expressed objections to executive agreements in general.[158] Consequently, the *Dames* Court provided the executive with a legislative function (in the form of an international agreement) at worst or a shared power at best (with the advice and consent).

The *Dames* majority also confronted the difficulty of depending on *Youngstown* as the standard by which to determine whether Congress's knowing acquiescence to past presidential actions necessarily implied its approval.[159] However, the Court asserted that legislative inertia in foreign affairs enabled the president to act unilaterally. Because *Dames* did not encompass express congressional approval of executive agreements, the *Dames* majority rejected Jackson's three-tier analysis with respect to their constitutionality. The *Dames* Court concluded that the legislative branch's failure to pass a statute articulating disapproval was tantamount to an invitation to the executive to act with autonomy.[160] For the *Dames* Court, congressional silence was equivalent to the sanctioning of presidential initiatives. The *Youngstown* Court, however, refused to imply approval from Congress's failure to yield to Truman the authority he had requested.

By asserting that the ICSA exhibited implied congressional approval of claims settlements by executive agreement,[161] when neither express language nor legislative history authorized such agreements, the *Dames* Court effectively relied on Frankfurter's *Youngstown* opinion: "[S]ecreted in the interstices of legislation [is] the very grant of power which Congress consciously withheld."[162] *Youngstown* advised that a lack of an express grant of authority to the president might not be manipulated to create that kind of power implicitly. Accordingly, the ICSA's silence on executive agreements did not create the approval of such agreements. But if Jackson's categorization of power were employed and granted to the president the use of executive agreements regardless of congressional objection, this power would be "at its zenith," because it would be read as an Article II power.[163]

On no occasion did the *Youngstown* Court question the executive's ability to depend on his own independent constitutional powers.[164] And the *Dames* Court maintained that the executive had the necessary power, whether implied or express, to take action in response to the Iranian crisis, because the emergency involved foreign affairs. The disparity in *Youngstown* stemmed from the mere fact that Truman had taken action in a domestic issue that fell outside the scope of the executive's independent authority. But the powers challenged in *Dames* were concurrent, and when power was considered concurrent, the executive's power to act, while disagreeable to some, would be unchallenged by the Courts.[165]

The *Youngstown* Court limited the president's authority to act with regard to domestic circumstances, but the holding's effectiveness as a limit on executive power in foreign affairs was infinitesimal, because the majority did not speak directly to the question of whether the president retained inherent powers in the international arena. *Youngstown* did not speak explicitly to the issue of inherent powers, but the *Dames* Court adopted Jackson's concurring opinion when it determined that the president may possess inherent powers when responding to international emergencies.

Curtiss-Wright recognized that in the area of foreign affairs, the president enjoyed far broader powers than in the domestic arena because of the "important, complicated, delicate and manifold problems"[166] inherently related with foreign relations. Similarly, the *Pink* Court maintained that the executive must be granted the implied power to settle claims to successfully "handle the delicate problems of foreign relations."[167] And even though Jackson warned against the "ready pretext for usurpation"[168] of power by the president, which emergencies allow, the Court retained the clout to appraise the assertion of these broad prerogatives as it evaluated the political timing of a case rather than the constitutional considerations of the executive's actions under exigent circumstances.

The *Dames* Court was no exception. It recognized that the claims settlement agreement under consideration was essential to the resolution of a major foreign-policy dispute[169] and admitted that its decision was "one more episode in the never-ending tension between the President exercising the executive authority in a world that presents each day some new challenge."[170] The Court also acknowledged that *Dames* concerned an international crisis, "the nature of which Congress can hardly have been expected to anticipate in any detail."[171] This framing fit squarely into Jackson's tripartite framework. The Court embraced a public-policy justification that invalidated the efforts by individual claimants that would complicate delicate negotiations and therefore impede the safety of American citizens. The Court was consequently unwilling to allow any kind of weakening of the value of the president's ability to deal with the unstable Iranian situation.[172] Accordingly, the Court came to a decision over the tension between the executive and the Constitution in favor of the president.

The Court gave these political considerations more weight in this case than in previous cases (except for the Japanese internment cases). In this instance, the relationship between the United States and its negotiating counterpart[173] underwent close scrutiny—the discussions with Iran were precarious and extended over a period of fourteen months. This period witnessed several oscillating advances and setbacks by the executive and legislative branches in the United States and with Iran. Consequently, the Court was sensitive to the exigencies of international politics. Furthermore, the volatility of the Iranian situation further accentuated the necessity of relying on the secrecy of the executive branch instead of having such sensitive discussions over intense hostilities playing out in the public arena. The realities of the day (overseeing the crisis) demanded a determination by the *Dames* Court to find in favor of the president; the safety of U.S. citizens superseded the claimants' rights to retrieve their invested assets. Consequently, the executive needed to be given wider plenary power to manage a successful outcome, as provided by *Curtiss-Wright* or *Youngstown*.

There is no direct evidence that the Court considered the national will, but it is evident that the *Dames* Court was fully aware of the precariousness of the Iranian crisis. It was of "imperative public importance"[174] that the president acted to ensure the "resolution of a major foreign policy dispute."[175] As such, the Court was sensitive to the fact that President Carter had enjoyed[176] general widespread support for the actions taken to resolve the Iran hostage crisis, despite the occasional criticism. It would have been ill-advised for the Court to disregard the national will and attempt to restrict Carter's actions in this particular situation.

What was quite unique to the situation in *Dames* was the need to conclude an agreement before the end of the Carter administration. This necessity resulted from the uncertainty of whether the succeeding Republican administration would implement an agreement with which it was ideologically at odds. However, Carter's order was reaffirmed by Reagan,[177] which by all accounts politically sanctioned the outgoing regime with the incoming change of establishment.

Dames demonstrated that the Supreme Court, not Congress or the executive branch, draws the lines when determining the extent to which the president might act in times of emergency. *Curtiss-Wright* illustrated a shift from demanding congressional collaboration, but the *Dames* Court embedded this shift by asserting that Carter, and Carter alone, could act due to the sensitivity of the matter. The *Regan* Court would entrench the trend of relying on congressional silence, thus facilitating the developmental narrative of broad executive prerogatives.

EXECUTIVE POWERS ARE FLUID

Regan sanctioned President Reagan's unilateral restriction on travel due to national-security concerns. The Court argued that the president had statutory authorization to act, because congressional silence and practice implicitly delegated to the president the emergency authority to restrict travel unilaterally. While this ruling seemed contradictory—how can statutory authorization exist in the face of congressional silence?—the following discussion illustrates how the Court played fast and loose with its reading of the TWEA.

Restrictions on travel to Cuba had been a key and often-controversial factor in U.S. efforts to isolate the Communist government of Fidel Castro for much of the past fifty-plus years. Throughout that time, several changes were made to the restrictions, but only for five years (1977–1982) were restrictions lifted on travel to Cuba.[178]

The United States first imposed an all-inclusive trade embargo against Cuba in the early 1960s; since then, policy changes on restrictions to Cuba have been extensive. The embargos did not ban travel specifically; rather, they placed restrictions on any financial transactions related to travel to Cuba, which in actuality resulted in a travel ban. In response to Castro's alignment with the Soviet Union during the Cold War, President John F. Kennedy imposed a trade embargo against Cuba by Proclamation 3447.[179] Following the Cuban Missile Crisis, Kennedy quickly imposed travel restrictions on Cuba under the TWEA with the Cuban Assets Control Regulations (CACR) on July 8, 1963,[180] in reaction to the Cubans' housing Soviet nuclear weapons. Under these restraints, Cuban assets in the United States were subsequently frozen. The Organization of American States (OAS) later imposed multilateral sanctions in July 1964, which were not annulled until July 1975.

From 1963 to 1977, travel to Cuba was essentially banned under the CACR issued by the Treasury Department's Office of Foreign Assets Control (OFAC).[181] Then in 1977, the Carter administration made some modifications to the regulations that effectively lifted the travel ban. In 1982, the Reagan administration again modified the CACR; it allowed travel-related transactions for certain categories of travelers:[182] U.S. government officials, employees of news or filmmaking organizations, persons engaging in professional research, or persons visiting their close relatives were allowed to travel to Cuba. The restrictions did not allow for travel by ordinary tourists or businesses that had been previously allowed by the Carter administration in 1977. Others looking to travel to Cuba for "humanitarian reasons" or "for the purpose of public performance, exhibitions[,] or similar activities" had to ask the Treasury Department for a specific license. Travel for any other reason was, therefore, barred.[183]

Since 1978, President Carter and President Reagan had determined that it was in the best interest of the nation to continue to exercise the TWEA authorities with respect to Cuba, North Korea, Vietnam, and Cambodia.[184] However, Carter let the restrictions against Cuba lapse in 1977, but in May 1982, the Reagan administration declared that because Cuba had continued to engage in activities hostile to the interests of the nation, Regulation 560 within the CACR would be amended, and the general issue in 1977 would be revoked.[185]

The Reagan administration stated that since 1960, a major objective of U.S. policy with Cuba had been to deny the Cuban government the financial means for conducting a program of violence against third-world countries that was, and still is, adverse to the security interests of the United States.[186] The amendment of Regulation 560, the administration argued, was specifically intended to thwart Cuba's plan to increase its hard-currency circulation by attracting tourists from the United States.[187] The administration reasoned that Cuba had rapidly expanded its tourist industry during 1981 and early 1982 and planned to continue to increase this important source of revenue.

The TWEA, passed in 1917, was a response to the U.S. entry into World War I.[188] Initially, Section 5(b) of the TWEA gave the president the authority to regulate economic transactions with foreign nations only during times of war.[189] In 1933, the TWEA was amended to permit the use of Section 5(b), economic powers, during peacetime national emergencies.[190] Since the passage of the TWEA in 1917, Section 5(b) has been described as a "catch-all" authority invoked by presidents when they lack the necessary authority to justify their conduct in the foreign-affairs arena.[191] From 1933 to 1977, powers granted under Section 5(b) were accessible to the executive during times of war or any other periods of national emergencies declared by the president. This broad grant of power gave the executive virtually unchecked despotic powers without any statutory provision for legislative review.[192]

Apprehension about the enduring state of national emergencies when they were initiated and the affiliated power granted to the president pressed Congress to enact the National Emergencies Act of 1976 (NEA).[193] The NEA's function was to ensure that executive power applied under existing declarations of national emergency would conclude two years from September 14, 1976.[194] The act also stipulated new procedures for the declaration, management, and conclusion of future national emergencies.[195]

A grandfather clause, protecting the authorities under Section 5(b) of the TWEA that were being exercised on July 1, 1977, provided that the executive could prolong those existing emergency powers for successive one-year periods beyond September 14, 1978, the date stipulated by the NEA for ending all existing emergency authorities.[196] If the president determined that an extension was necessary because of national interest, the grandfather clause, Section 5(b), could be invoked as granting this authority. Consequently, the government exercised its TWEA authority with respect to Cuba in enforcing the CACR.[197] With such restrictions on travel, a lawsuit was inevitable. However, the Supreme Court's pronouncement came as a surprise.

Two months after the Reagan administration reinstated restrictions on travel to Cuba in June 1982, the Center for Constitutional Rights (CCR), the National Emergency Civil Liberties Committee (NECLC), the American Civil Liberties Union (ACLU), and the National Lawyers Guild (NLG) contested the restrictions on behalf of a number of individuals, including the Cuba Resource Group and the Center for Cuban Studies. The petitioners argued that the restrictions deprived persons of their constitutional right to travel guaranteed by the due-process clause of the Fifth Amendment and that the embargo was at odds with a 1978 amendment to the Passport Act. Moreover, the president did not have the authority to impose the 1982 restrictions on travel-related economic transactions contained in Regulation 560. In addition, the TWEA's grandfather clause did not exempt Regulation 560 from IEEPA procedures, because the 1982 prohibition went beyond the power applied on July 1, 1977. Therefore, the restrictions breached the requirements outlined in the IEEPA and were without statutory authority. Furthermore, the plaintiffs asserted that the prohibition had been ratified without conforming to IEEPA review procedures.[198] The defendants contended that the executive did not have statutory authorization to restrict travel, but the administration asserted that national-security concerns and indirect assistance to countries being bullied by Cuba granted Reagan the unilateral authority to act. Specifically, the administration believed that tourism between the United States and Cuba was generating revenue for Cuba to continue its mission of violence against third-world countries. And addressing this issue, the administration concluded, was within the purview of the executive branch: directing foreign policy to curb behavior through sanctions.

The trial court denied a preliminary injunction,[199] and the U.S. District Court for the District of Massachusetts referred the case to a magistrate, who found in favor of the president and said the grandfather clause furnished the executive with the power to amend Regulation 560.[200] The magistrate concluded that although there were few restrictions on travel-related transactions with Cuba following the amended Regulation 560 by President Carter in 1977, some power was still being employed under a general licensing scheme. Consequently, the executive could amend the general license to levy tighter controls on economic transactions without being restricted by IEEPA's procedural requirements.[201] This ruling was affirmed by the District Court, which consequently denied the request by the petitioners for a preliminary injunction.[202]

The U.S. First Circuit Court of Appeals reversed the ruling, concluding that the restrictions were invalid and issuing a preliminary injunction.[203] A three-judge panel unanimously concurred that there was no statutory authority for Regulation 560, because the grandfather clause of the IEEPA had not maintained the authority to declare new restrictions on travel-related economic transactions with Cuba.[204] The court had two lines of thought. First, it concluded that travel-related restrictions were not being exercised on July 1, 1977, within "the meaning, intent, and purpose of the grandfather clause."[205] Second, the court reasoned that even if the statutory language and history of the grandfather clause were vague, constitutional deliberation and the objective of other related existing statutes reinforced interpreting the grandfather clause in favor of the plaintiffs.[206]

The court of appeals judged that an "exercise" of power to limit travel was qualitatively different from the power to restrict the influx of Cuban commodities; it concluded that the authority to restrict travel-related dealings was not, therefore, grandfathered in.[207] Furthermore, the clear intent of the grandfather clause was to be narrowly construed, as legislative history indicated. The clause permitted the president only to continue those prohibitions actually in effect on July 1, 1977,[208] an assertion supported by key legislative spokespeople for the IEEPA who had rejected draft language that would have maintained the idle authority of the president under Section 5(b) of the TWEA.[209]

Moreover, because the Supreme Court had explicitly instructed lower-level courts to "'construe narrowly all delegated powers that curtail or dilute' the right to travel," the court of appeals was constrained in its interpretation,[210] but it maintained that it would not render the executive powerless to act in response to Cuba.[211]

The government's response to the First Circuit's opinion was to petition the Supreme Court for a writ of certiorari. Upon issuing the writ, the Supreme Court, in a closely divided 5–4 decision, determined that the 1982 regulation was consistent with federal law and the Constitution and was therefore "justified by the weighty concerns of foreign policy."[212]

WEIGHTY CONCERNS OF FOREIGN POLICY
NECESSITATE A BROAD READING

Justice White and Justice John Paul Stevens, the former a moderate and the latter a liberal, joined the three conservatives on the Court—Rehnquist (who wrote the majority opinion), Sandra Day O'Connor, and Chief Justice Burger—and reversed the First Circuit's decision. The majority asserted that a "constricted reading of the grandfather clause does violence to the words chosen by Congress,"[213] which ran contrary to the directive the Supreme Court had issued to the lower courts.

The Court grounded its argument on a number of cases as it determined whether the president had the authority to restrict U.S. citizens from traveling abroad. And a brief discussion of case precedent (*Kent v. Dulles* [1958], *Zemel v. Rusk* [1965],[214] and *Haig v. Agee* [1981]) not only illustrates the doctrinal development but also offers a richer construction of how far-reaching the decision was with respect to executive authority. Two cases (*Kent* and *Zemel*), settled in roughly the same period as *Youngstown*, significantly influenced the Court's decision in *Regan*.

The *Kent* Court held 5–4 that the right to travel was essentially an inherent element of "liberty" that could not be denied to American citizens. Even though the Court held that the executive could regulate travel practices, the president could not impose any restrictions that denied American citizens basic constitutional notions of liberty, assembly, association, and personal autonomy. Furthermore, the Court decided that Congress had not envisioned that the secretary of state would be granted the discretion that officeholder John Foster Dulles claimed to have: the authority to deny passports to individuals with alleged Communist beliefs and associations. Even though the Cold War has been dated to 1945, when it was asserted that Morris Kent was affiliated with the Communist Party, the *Kent* Court did not find this association to be a constraining factor to deny American citizens the right to travel. This outcome seemed likely, because the defendant was traveling to England.

Even though *Kent* involved foreign policy, by finding in favor of the plaintiff and not the executive, the Court showed its determination that basic constitutional rights could weaken executive authority to restrict travel (a conclusion seen in the detainee cases).

The significance of *Kent* was that the Court held that any restriction to the passage of travel must be pursuant either to specific delegation or by way of administrative practice that was clearly embraced by Congress, which would imply delegation of its lawmaking function. In either case, delegation would be narrowly interpreted. However, the *Regan* Court departed from this position. Utilizing *Haig*, the Court held that the president needed only to assert, rather than demonstrate, established practice (*Kent*), which was the creation of its own directive to show that the executive was, in fact, conforming to the condition of congressional awareness.

A few years after *Kent*, the Supreme Court heard *Zemel* and denied an individual the right to travel. In 1962, Louis Zemel, an American citizen holding what had been believed to be a valid passport, applied to the State Department for a passport to travel to Cuba as a tourist. His application had been denied, because he had not met the travel standards prescribed. One year prior to Zemel's passport request, the United States had broken diplomatic and consular relations with Cuba. Consequently, the Department of State had excluded Cuba as an area not requiring a passport and declared all passports to be invalid unless travelers were already in Cuba. Therefore, travel to Cuba necessitated requesting a passport, which would be granted only if the secretary of state endorsed such travel.

The Supreme Court under Chief Justice Earl Warren heard the case and this time held 6–3 that the secretary of state had the statutory authority to refuse to validate passports of any U.S. citizen to travel to Cuba. Furthermore, the exercise of that authority was constitutionally permissible. In this instance, the Court distinguished between these findings and those of *Kent*, concluding that administrative practice was sufficiently substantial and consistent to warrant the deduction that Congress had implicitly approved it. With respect to Zemel's Fifth Amendment due-process right to travel and his First Amendment right to freedom of expression and association, the Court asserted that although the right of due process should be considered, because the government was imposing a constraint on the defendant's constitutional right to travel, it also had to consider that the restriction was necessary due to geopolitical concerns—Cuba's ties to the Soviet Union and the consequences of such association.[215]

In considering the exigent circumstances, the Court maintained that this case was supported by the weightier considerations of national security. In the spirit of *Curtiss-Wright*, Chief Justice Warren maintained that national-security needs permitted restrictions on travel, but they did not infringe upon due process of the rights of the individual.[216] The Court reasoned that Zemel's claim that the secretary of state's refusal to validate his passport for travel to Cuba deprived him of the rights guaranteed by the First Amendment was quite different from the issues raised in *Kent*.[217] Simply stated, the refusal to validate Zemel's passport did not result from any expression or association on his part, so he was not being forced to choose between membership in an organization and the freedom to travel.

The standards established in *Kent* and *Zemel* were, by all accounts, overruled in *Haig v. Agee*, but enforcement was recognized by the *Regan* Court as one means of ascertaining congressional awareness and approval of regulation. The *Regan* Court likewise claimed, in the spirit of *Dames*, that courts could also find support from congressional silence about long-standing executive practice. Thus, a new standard was fashioned in *Regan*. The Court's observations in *Haig* that the executive branch needed only to assert a creation of its own regulation to demonstrate compliance with the requirement of congressional awareness was a departure from the Court's rejection in *Kent*; the *Kent* decision held that only an established departmental practice could persuade the Court that Congress was satisfactorily aware of the asserted authority. *Regan* was a calculated and engineered shift by the Court to expand executive power.

Using a sleight of hand, the *Regan* Court modified a standard of congressional approval from one established practice to an assertion of authority to sanction executive action. Under Rehnquist, the Court continued down the established path of legally authorizing executive autonomy but moved beyond congressional collaboration in restricting travel aboard, justified by the perils of national-security concerns (*Zemel*).

The *Regan* Court asserted that the regulation presented no constitutional difficulty. It argued that time-honored deference to executive authority in foreign affairs since *Curtiss-Wright* provided the necessary justification under the due-process clause for limiting travel. In this case, because there was no claim that travel was being limited on the basis of affiliation or political belief, the Court reasoned that the restriction was applied fairly. Moreover, the president's decision (and framing in political time) to limit the flow of hard currency to Cuba to impede that country's backing of armed violence in the Western Hemisphere[218]—a position that the administration believed warranted the restriction—further justified the regulation. The claim, the Court concluded, justified reading Congress's silence broadly.[219] In fact, the Court held that through congressional silence and administrative practice, Congress had implicitly delegated emergency authority to the president.

Reinforcing its conclusion, the *Regan* Court asserted that travel-related limits were a function of the overall power granted to the executive to regulate property transactions.[220] Consequently, the president was simply implementing his broad authority under Section 5(b) of the TWEA to control property transactions through Section 201(b) of the CACR, which had been in effect since July 1, 1977.[221]

Evaluating the express language of the grandfather clause, the *Regan* Court concluded that if Congress had wanted to freeze existing restrictions, it could have quite easily inserted that phrase instead of the term *authorities*.[222] Although the Court recognized the clear support for a narrow interpretation of the clause,[223] it nonetheless concluded that even if this were the only sign of legislative intent, it would not be adequate evidence to affect the "clear, generic meaning of the word authorities."[224] Ultimately, given the Court's full consideration of the legislative history, the judiciary backed a broad reading of the grandfather clause.[225]

Examining the purpose of the grandfather clause, the Court subsequently rejected the notion that it was penned exclusively to preserve "bargaining chips" with affected countries.[226] It asserted instead that the clause was designed to keep the IEEPA from becoming too contentious, because disagreement would have delayed the passage of the act. Therefore, the majority argued, the legislative branch had chosen to focus on refining procedures for future uses of emergency powers instead of revising current uses.[227] The key issue for the Court was that limiting executive power to only revision of an existing license, in response to increased tensions with Cuba, would have produced the kind of controversy the grandfather clause was intended to avoid.[228]

Presidential powers are not fixed. They ebb and flow, depending on the executive's disjunction or conjunction with legislative powers,[229] as the Court evaluates this relationship when determining executive authority in international affairs. To establish whether the president had exceeded the bounds of his authority,[230] the *Regan* Court evaluated which tier the president's actions fell under. To make this determination, it examined the legislative grant of executive authority and the *Dames* precedent.

Alarmed by the ambiguous scope of presidential authority, and yet acutely aware of the possible ramifications of impulsively terminating long-standing presidential powers, the legislature had passed the 1977 amendments to the TWEA and the IEEPA. The Emergency Controls Hearings of 1977 had demonstrated Congress's concern over unchecked executive emergency authority.[231] This suggests that Congress's intention, when it amended the TWEA and enacted the IEEPA, was to restrain what had been considered as the president's ample and unrestrained authority to exercise broad powers that could affect future domestic and foreign economic affairs.[232] Justice Blackmun's account—discussed below—of the legislative history also suggested that Congress had attempted to place limitations on executive power.[233] The *Dames* Court asserted that although the IEEPA afforded Congress procedural control over the president's use of peacetime international emergency economic power, the IEEPA did not restrain the executive's substantive exercises of that kind of power.[234]

The *Dames* Court agreed that the legislative history and subsequent cases interpreting the TWEA showed that when the executive was acting under a statutory grant of authority, the breadth of his power was to be read broadly.[235] The Court asserted that the president had acted strategically: using Iranian assets, which were at his disposal, as a "bargaining chip" had facilitated a successful negotiation to end the declared national emergency.[236] The Court affirmed that the IEEPA explicitly authorized the president's actions and granted the widest judicial latitude, which aligned with *Curtiss-Wright*'s endorsement of the "delicate, plenary and exclusive power" of the executive as the sole organ of foreign affairs.[237] The necessity to negotiate successfully as well as the executive's exclusive access to sources of confidential information demanded "a degree of discretion and freedom from statutory restriction which would not be admissible were domestic affairs alone involved."[238]

The *Regan* Court concluded that the president was employing his authority under Section 5(b) of the TWEA by regulating travel-related economic transactions with Cuba through the 1977 general license. The Court therefore maintained that the grandfather clause presented an acceptable statutory basis for the 1982 amendment.[239] Congressional silence therefore had statutorily sanctioned the executive's position to act.[240]

Blackmun's dissenting opinion pointed out the discrepancies in the majority opinion. He[241] offered a completely different reading of the history and purpose of the grandfather clause, finding that it did not grant statutory authority for the 1982 amendment of Regulation 560.[242] His analysis of the general purpose of Public Law 95-223[243] led him to conclude that Congress had meant for the statute to restrain an unjustified expansion of presidential power that had been unintentionally authorized by the TWEA.[244]

Blackmun discarded the idea that use of the term *authorities* signaled intent for a broad interpretation of the grandfather clause. He asserted that the legislative record discredited that kind of a position,[245] adding that the word *authorities* was used instead of the term *prohibitions*[246] because Section 5(b) gave the executive the authority to conduct investigations as well as to freeze assets, neither of which could have been understood if the term *prohibition* had been used. As such, Blackmun noted, "the very pieces of legislative history that the Court cites to justify" congressional silence "clearly support the contrary view."[247] In fact, Blackmun noted, expert witnesses testified before the House subcommittee and expressed "a general consensus" that there were "no practical constraints" that restricted presidential action and that the authority granted to the president was ultimately "used as a flexible instrument of foreign policy in nonemergency situations."[248] Subcommittee hearings thus demonstrated, for Blackmun, that the "combination of legislative permissiveness and executive assertiveness" had fashioned "a significant shift in the functional allocations of constitutional power to regulate foreign commerce," and, therefore, that "checks and limitations on executive powers" were necessary.[249]

While Blackmun concurred with the majority that the grandfather clause was penned to avoid controversy, he maintained that the majority had misinterpreted which parts of the IEEPA were possibly contentious.[250] For example, he insisted that the grandfather clause was designed to prevent an "examination of current controls," the necessity "to declare new emergencies when none actually existed," and "ending restrictions without receiving something in return from the affected countries."[251] These assertions, Blackmun concluded, illustrated that the restriction of travel-related transactions did not fall into any of the aforementioned preclusions addressed by the grandfather clause.[252] As such, Blackmun found it remarkable that the majority had determined that Congress had chosen to give the executive greater flexibility in light of the mounting tensions with Cuba, when, in fact, Congress had expressed unequivocally that the situation with Cuba did not represent an emergency situation.[253]

Despite Blackmun's dissent, *Regan* illustrated not only the exceptions found by the Court to justify presidential autonomy to restrict travel abroad but also the Court's duty to ascertain whether the invocation of national-security concerns advocated by the executive necessitated broad leeway. Despite a clear separation-of-powers assertion by Congress (asserting a dominant role by enacting provisions to "tie the hands" of the president), the Court concluded that the executive had the authority to act in this instance. In granting more authority to the executive, the Court stripped power from the legislature. Its demarcation of power and authority clearly showed that even though Congress had attempted to rein in the president, the judiciary retained the authority to define and redistribute powers.

IMPLICATIONS: COURT REENGINEERS UNILATERAL AUTHORITY

The Supreme Court faced Reagan, a reconstructive president who was instituting change to the political order, and *Regan* aided in entrenching the new regime. Even though "reconstructive presidents tend to be departmentalists," their strength is reduced when they assert their own authority and attempt to ignore the Court's constitutional reasoning. However, in the area of foreign affairs, presidents, irrespective of their place in the cyclical pattern of presidential leadership, have found favor with the Court's general tenets of advancing executive authority. Certainly as the national-security state has become more prominent, executives have made stronger assertions to claims of power and even challenged the Court's authority to define presidential prerogatives (since *Curtiss-Wright*). But the Court has remained steadfast in deciding the scope of executive authority as it evaluates separation-of-powers principles and rights claims (for example, Truman and George W. Bush).

Finding that congressional silence was sufficient to grant the president unilateral power, the Court engineered a new standard, and its advancement of a newly created shift in power complicated Jackson's tripartite schema. Since the *Dames* decision, the Court and the executive branch have manipulated the framework to advance executive power by placing presidential prerogatives in any one of the three broad categories.

The deference afforded the executive by the Court since *Curtiss-Wright* in the area of foreign affairs was a lucid progression toward validating the Court's finding in *Regan*. This deference, however, was not static. As the *Dames* Court determined, reading statutory language in a narrow way would deprive the president of the necessary flexibility in international affairs, which Congress had intended to preserve. The Court asserted that when there was uncertainty in the legislative record of a statute relating to the president's authority in foreign affairs, it must be interpreted to support a grant of authority—uncertainty by Congress induced an expansive interpretation.[254] Consequently, if a conclusion were to be drawn that the legislature meant a different result when enacting a provision to maintain executive authority, it would necessitate clear undeniable proof—not proof of ambiguity. As a result, the Court determined that because the president's authority to regulate travel-related economic transactions with Cuba was grandfathered,[255] his power was at its zenith; the president had acted pursuant to the express authorization of Congress.[256] As Jackson's framework has been reinterpreted, successive Courts and presidents have legally manipulated the schema to suit their needs, which the Justice Department attempted when it relied on Jackson's model to find a statutory basis for the Bush administration's use of warrantless domestic surveillance. Consequently, *Curtiss-Wright*, *Youngstown*, and its progeny have provided feedback loops to expand presidential power, which were extended with the *Dames* and *Regan* decisions.

Although there is no constitutional grounding for executive agreements, the *Dames* Court provided the political and legal space for presidents to use them at their disposal. When the executive acts pursuant to the express or implied will of Congress, as occurred in *Dames* and *Regan*, the president's power is at its fullest.[257] These case decisions were not straightforward applications of the *Youngstown* framework, but they did reinterpret it. As Rehnquist noted, the real purpose and range of Jackson's schema followed a fluid "spectrum" of presidential action—moving from unambiguous "congressional authorization" to explicit "congressional prohibition"—that was unequivocally necessary when dispensing with cases involving international emergencies that Congress could not have foreseen.[258]

It appeared that the *Regan* Court deferred to Reagan's judgment and the petitioner's assertions fell short of meeting the burden of overcoming the autonomy granted to presidential authority in foreign affairs, but the Court drew the line on just how far discretionary executive power could extend. Despite the fact that Congress had enacted provisions to fence in the far-reaching scope of presidential authority, the Court's evaluation of national-security needs led it to conclude that through congressional silence and administrative practice, Congress had implicitly delegated emergency authority to the president. Ultimately, the Court determines when polity principles undermine rights principles and which branch is better equipped to deal with the case or controversy at hand.

The political exigency of the Iran hostage crisis suggested that the *Dames* decision was at least correct politically, if not constitutionally. Congress was kept abreast by the outgoing Carter administration and the incoming Reagan administration during all stages of the final negotiations of the Iran hostage situation. As a result, if Congress had desired to intervene, it could have done so; its resounding silence, the *Dames* Court concluded, illustrated that in the hostage crisis, Congress had deliberately refrained from recording its characteristic objections to the president's use of executive agreements.[259] This absence could thus be construed as approval.

Similarly, the *Haig* Court held that a failure of Congress to give the president authority for executive actions, "especially in the areas of foreign policy and national security," did not imply congressional disapproval of these actions. This rationale was utilized again in *Crockett v. Reagan* (1983),[260] when several members of the legislative branch claimed that the president had violated the War Powers Resolution (WPR)[261] by providing military assistance to El Salvador. The Court of Appeals for the District of Columbia Circuit found that before a court could intervene, Congress needed to take explicit action to apply the WPR to the matter at hand.[262] And then in *Regan*, the Court extended that power to also include restricting travel abroad. In fact, Rehnquist concluded that the president had a broad mandate to impose comprehensive embargoes on foreign countries as one means of dealing with peacetime emergencies and times of war—a claim that Rehnquist defended by asserting that "travel-related transactions" as determined in *Dames* "were specifically made subordinate to further actions which the President might take."[263] Presidents since the *Regan* decision have certainly adhered to this declaration. In fact, in June 2017, the Donald Trump administration rolled back the Barack Obama administration's relaxed Cuba policy, stating that tourism funds the Castro regime, which will not be supported by the current administration. Then, in November 2017, the Trump administration tightened restrictions by setting new regulations on businesses and travel by individual Americans meant to steer economic activity away from Cuba.

In *Dames* and *Regan*, the Court found in favor of a disjunctive president and a reconstructive president. It looked beyond the officeholder[264] and considered the developmental narrative of the institution and the sole-organ doctrine when it assessed the division of powers between the legislative and executive branches. The Court cannot overlook the enduring and comprehensive implications of its decisions in the conduct of foreign affairs, which necessarily affect the occupant of the office.

As such, the Court is institutionally advantaged to create a hospitable environment for oppositional executives who face a divided, hostile, or failing regime when it resolves constitutional claims rather than allow a president to face the possibility of a legislative injunction. The warrants of authority asserted by a reconstructive leader similarly find a friendly Court. While reconstructive leaders speak "on behalf of a relatively united and dominant political coalition against a collapsing political order," historically they challenge or even ignore the Court's constitutional interpretation, favoring their own independent constitutional judgments. In the management of foreign affairs, however, these departmentalists[265] face an institution intent on securing judicial supremacy and, at the same time, preserving its interpretation of the sole-organ doctrine.

The Court's duty resides in reconciling its interpretation of the Constitution inside and outside the Court. Constitutional interpretation is therefore dependent on the Court's analysis of the political framing of the circumstances. As Keith Whittington notes, "Judicial authority to interpret constitutional meaning must be related to the ongoing practice of constitutional politics."[266] If the Court concludes that an emergency exists that necessitates the unilateral role of the executive, the institutional capacity of the Court allows judges to redefine the scope of presidential prerogatives and ease any institutional costs of a branching point. It does so because it alone determines the severity of the emergency faced by each respective president; in these two cases, it concluded that Carter and Reagan had acted appropriately.

Carter's leadership role in the hostage crisis was the one challenge that would be a testament to his "competence as a political leader." The hostage crisis was largely unrelated to the issues frustrating the administration for the three years prior. If Carter had accomplished his goal of freeing the hostages before the election, he might have vindicated his leadership: "[T]he modern presidency harbored this change for Jimmy Carter, the chance to manipulate fate and escape political time."[267] While Carter has been cast as a disjunctive president in political time, in legal time, he found success when the Court ruled in *Dames*. In determining a national emergency, the Court found tacit congressional consent and upheld Carter's executive agreement. The Court, relying on *Belmont* and *Pink* to ground its decision, asserted that the president was the sole organ of foreign affairs. Given Carter's unsuccessful assertion of leadership in political time,[268] the *Dames* Court looked beyond the officeholder and focused on the institutional capacity of the president in foreign policy making.

Maintaining the constitutional order established in *Curtiss-Wright* and reaffirmed in *Belmont* and *Pink*, the Court was friendly toward Carter and thus provided a favorable platform for establishing leadership support. He ultimately "push[ed] against the limits of affiliated leadership,"[269] and the Court, in this instance, was an asset to the dominant coalition. Even though Carter was unsuccessful in freeing the hostages, the *Dames* decision "enforce[d] and extend[ed] those commitments" of the regime. Moreover, the affiliated Court, amid fractious coalitions, maintained the constitutional order established in 1936 by engineering a shift in the doctrinal development of the executive's role in foreign affairs to incorporate and legally justify the use of executive agreements. On the heels of Carter's failure in the political arena, Reagan faced a receptive Court, at least in issues of foreign affairs. The judicial decisions are institutionally intuitive, as the Supreme Court does not map political regimes. In the management of international relations, it helps facilitate the collapse of a regime and/or aids in entrenching a new one.

Constitutional politics is more creative when the Court is faced with a reconstructive challenge[270] (e.g., *Dames* and, more specifically, *Regan*). Reagan ushered in a new regime when he replaced Carter,[271] and the Court marshaled evidence to support an engineered shift in defining the scope and direction of executive autonomy in exigent circumstances. This positioning provided the Court with an opportunity to create the practical and constitutional space for presidents to employ bargaining chips (*Dames*) to rescue hostages and to restrict travel to a country allegedly using tourism revenue to fund a campaign of violence (*Regan*).

When considering weighty concerns of external emergencies, the Court continues to favor the executive. Its constitutive role reshapes constitutional jurisprudence as it grants more authority to the executive branch through judicial legitimization. Furthermore, political development is reconstituted; presidents can rely on a claim of tacit statutory authority to act and need only assert that power rather than demonstrate historical practice.

As we turn to the next chapter, we find the Court faced with one of the more pressing sets of questions of our time: how far-reaching are presidential prerogatives during a time of war? Is institutional deference necessary for a successful war campaign? And can enemy combatants' basic constitutional rights be suppressed during a war? Ultimately, with the failure of traditional assumptions, the Bush administration's actions launched concerns over the nation's foreign and domestic security that have continued to this day.

6

DETAINEE CASES

*A Definitive Statement of the President's Monopoly
in War Making*

The terrorist attacks of September 11, 2001, and the subsequent response by the U.S. federal government raised a new and rich conversation for understanding the politics and constitutionality of America at war. Initially, it appeared that the George W. Bush administration would show deference to the courts. As White House counsel Alberto Gonzales said of the administration's policies, "While being 'respectful' of constitutional rights, the administration's job 'at the end of the day' is 'to protect the country.'" "Ultimately," he added, "it is the job of the courts to tell us whether or not we've drawn the lines in the right places."[1] However, Bush quickly moved outside the customary constitutional authority in the management of the war on terror, and the legislature "stepped back, yielding to the prevailing winds of wartime discretion."[2] This grab for unprecedented executive autonomy resulted in a set of cases challenging presidential prerogatives vis-à-vis individual rights during a national emergency. "The existential tension at the heart" of the resulting detainee cases involved the essential "constitutional guarantee that no person (including non-citizens) shall be deprived of liberty without due process of law."[3] As a result, the courts shouldered a crucial role in defining the boundaries between the government and the rights of those detained.

The Bush administration mounted an offensive war against what it defined as a nontraditional enemy and thus framed it as a new kind of war: "Today we face a dynamic threat. . . . [O]ur tools to deter them must also be dynamic and flexible enough to meet the challenges they pose." As a result of these pleas, Americans "accepted [for the time being] the pendulum swing that war can bring, tolerating the wartime Constitution, secure in the knowledge that the peacetime Constitution will be waiting . . . ready to be retrieved and revived."[4] In a similar vein to other conflicts, the war on terror "encouraged and permitted the executive to demand deference from the other branches."[5] And in the name of national security, Bush claimed the authority to make decisions without conferring with or even informing either the courts or Congress, which suspended customary restraints on executive power. Bush distorted "the relationship not only between the branches but also between the government and the public." As the executive "navigated treacherous political waters," the "nation struggled to find a shared language and[,] beyond that[,] a shared vision of how to proceed in bringing the war on terror to a resolution that provides both a sense of security and a trust in the inviolability of the law."[6] With secrecy at every level, "national security concerns, and the administration's publicly announced willingness to use law enforcement in [total] disregard of an American tradition of civil liberty," frightened the American public into "political paralysis."[7]

Just as Bush predicted, the war on terror promised to be "a long campaign";[8] as such, "the pendulum-swing back to constitutional normality" hung in defiance of returning to the status quo, "waiting for a sign that such a return is viable."[9] Initially, the courts shared the administration's position:[10] the judiciary does not possess oversight, and only the president can exercise any discretion in deciding who to capture and detain and what legal processes to use. But just how far that deference extends "beyond that which peacetime principles find tolerable and results in postwar retrenchment"[11] would be the Supreme Court's sole determination. And as time went on, the Court would render a robust review of the administration's detention policies as it balanced the national-security framing advanced by the administration with the rights and procedures of those detained.

Rasul v. Bush (2004),[12] *Hamdi v. Rumsfeld* (2004),[13] *Rumsfeld v. Padilla* (2004),[14] *Hamdan v. Rumsfeld* (2006),[15] and *Boumediene v. Bush* (2008)[16] demonstrated the mechanisms—internal (the Supreme Court) and external (changing political climate and exigency)—examined by the Court as it found in favor of rights principles. As we have seen, individual rights were marginalized in previous cases (except for *Youngstown*), but in these instances, the Court concluded that rights principles were too important to relegate to the sidelines. Moreover, these decisions yielded the most definitive statements yet on the administration's claims—and, more generally, executive action—of unreviewable action, which is a clear demarcation of the separation-of-powers model; the Court would not be backed into a corner. Despite Congress's statutorily authorizing military commissions, the *Boumediene* Court did not consider congressional authority to be "the be all and end all" in the emergency context. While the Court constrained the Bush administration statutorily, it did not categorically challenge his constitutional authority.

This chapter examines the Court's continued role in determining the developmental narrative of the executive's formulation of foreign policy. As Bush's momentum of asserting extraordinary amounts of power became marginalized, with a turn in public opinion in the United States and globally,[17] and as criticisms mounted, the Court maintained the institutional position to redefine the statutory parameters of the executive in the conduct of the war as it assessed basic constitutional rights. The Court rejected by the slimmest of "margins some of the more extreme positions of the Administration,"[18] while maintaining respect for civil liberties.[19]

AN UNPRECEDENTED WAR AND UNPARALLELED CLAIMS TO EXECUTIVE AUTHORITY

In 2001, al-Qaeda terrorists destroyed the World Trade Center in New York and damaged the Pentagon, placing the United States in a state of emergency[20] and on the brink of an inevitable war. The Bush administration began filtering its discourse through a continued appeal for national unity and the possibility of an impending war. Bush was resolute in fighting and winning an unprecedented war, but he reminded the nation that doing so would require nothing short of a blank check. This appeal empowered the administration as it built a legal defense to justify executive actions. Establishing a frame of emergency and calling for unity in unprecedented times created for the administration an atmosphere suggesting that Bush had a mandate to act without limits to combat terrorism. Given the political climate, the administration's appeals found favor as he asserted unparalleled authority; Congress overwhelmingly supported the president's use of force (98–0 in the Senate and 420–1 in the House).

Bush followed up with several executive orders that discharged the U.S. military force against the Taliban regime in Afghanistan, established military tribunals for the prosecution of suspected terrorists, froze millions of dollars in foreign assets in the United States belonging to individuals believed to be assisting terrorists, and greatly expanded the authority of the Central Intelligence Agency (CIA) and other intelligence organizations. With the full support of his legal advisers, Bush claimed he was legally unrestricted in protecting the nation, so there was limited consultation between the administration and the legislature.[21]

On September 20, 2001, Bush addressed a joint session of Congress. He asserted a discourse of determination because the United States had been unexpectedly struck by an enemy that compelled the defense of freedom. Bush added that while Americans' grief was profound and had metamorphosed to anger, that anger had transformed into resolution. He was committed to bring justice upon those who had brought tragedy to American soil: "[W]hether we bring our enemies to justice, or bring justice to our enemies, justice will be done."[22] These words resonated with Congress and the American people. A resounding call for justice stemmed from the terrorist attacks, ironically uniting a nation and supporting a president who had been struggling in the polls.[23] Bush was now riding the coattails of a crisis to high approval ratings.

Given the severity of this new kind of war, the administration pushed for a new way of thinking; the nation must be resolved to do whatever it took to continue to be a free nation and safe from attacks for generations to come. The administration's rhetorical crusade, which portrayed these individuals not as people with a cause but as evildoers, murderers, and extremely dangerous persons, enabled Bush to pledge that they "must be found[,] . . . stopped[,] and . . . punished: terrorists . . . operate in the shadows. . . . But we're going to shine the light of justice on them."[24] While a frame of evil appealed to the sensibilities of religious fundamentalists, it was the framing of a unique war that grounded the legal argument adopted by the administration and justified unilateral decision making: a nontraditional war thus demanded actions contrary to traditional standards. This rhetoric of repudiation established a framework that aligned American citizens with the administration's policies—those who resisted this restructuring were guilty of having a deplorable "pre-9/11 mind-set."[25]

On the one hand, Bush was the quintessential stay-the-course president (as were Truman and George H. W. Bush),[26] as he governed over a conservative majority fashioned by Ronald Reagan. Generally, when it concerned domestic issues, Bush's conduct with the judicial branch squared with Keith Whittington's analysis of an executive who is tied to an assertive majority party. In line with an affiliated leader in political time, Bush indicated no interest in confronting the courts. On the other hand, Bush asserted executive power that invoked a departmentalism stance as he challenged, at every turn, the courts' review over his management of the war on terror. Bush thus acted as an affiliated and as a reconstructive president.

This unique display of deferential and transformative actions ran contrary to Stephen Skowronek's cyclical theory and further complicated Whittington's account of how presidents view their relationship with the courts. Affiliated leaders generally regard the Court as an ally to the political regime and thus tend to support the power of judicial review.[27] Reconstructive leaders, who come to power "when party loyalties are breaking down," and their transformational leadership challenge the outdated dogma and fashion a new constitutional baseline,[28] yet they are more likely to confront judicial suprema-cy and make departmentalist claims. Reconstructive presidents do this, Whit-tington contends, because they view the Court's justices as obstructionists to the formation of a new political regime.[29] Bush's presidency and the Court's reproaches illustrated the duality of his approach. Bush not only attempted to maintain his conservative legacy but also sought to implement destabilizing policies aimed to combat a war on terror.[30]

During wartime, Congress has commonly deferred to the president, and the war on terror was no exception. In fact, the Authorization for Use of Mili-tary Force against Iraq Resolution (AUMF) of 2002[31] was little more than a blank check. The resolution, which invoked the War Powers Resolution (WPR) of 1973,[32] authorized Bush to use the armed forces "as he determine[d] to be necessary and appropriate" in an effort to "defend the national security" of the nation "against the continuing threat posed by Iraq; and enforce all relevant United Nations Security Council Resolutions regarding Iraq."[33] In effect, Bush was granted the sole discretion, sanctioned statutorily, to conduct the war.

Since 1936, as evidenced by some notable cases, the Supreme Court has legally determined that the executive has unilateral authority to conduct the nation's foreign affairs, which invariably trumps individual rights (*Curtiss-Wright*, the internment cases, *Youngstown*, *Dames*, *Regan*, and *Goldwater*). The Court has even broadened the scope and breadth of presidential prerogatives in international discourse. With this legal grounding, Bush's legal advisers advanced his claim. Deputy Assistant U.S. Attorney General John Yoo, from the Office of Legal Counsel (OLC) was instrumental in defining the ad-ministration's legal justifications to claim unilateral prerogatives. In January 2002, Yoo advised Bush that al-Qaeda and the Taliban were "non-state ac-tors," so national security could not be used as a "one-size fits all rationale for expansive presidential powers."[34] But Yoo ignored the rejection by the Court in *Youngstown*, favoring instead precedents that directly supported the poli-cies of the Bush administration. Yoo reasoned that Congress had deliberately crafted a joint resolution (the AUMF) to explicitly authorize the executive to deploy the military.[35]

Pursuant to the AUMF, the president could arbitrarily, without limita-tions or consequence, use all necessary force against those whom *he* identified as having attacked the United States in the September 11 attacks. Conse-quently, "the resolution . . . tilts the balance of power between Congress and the president and grants the president more power than he can derive from the Constitution,"[36] but the administration embraced and dismissed parts of it. The administration embraced the AUMF's authorization "to detain any sus-pected al Qaeda members or associates wherever they might be, to hold them indefinitely and without counsel wherever it chose, and . . . to interrogate them using methods and techniques that would otherwise have been prohibited by U.S. and international law." And as dismissive as the administration was, even without this resolution, Bush would have had all the same powers: as "the sole holder of executive power and as commander-in-chief, the president had the inherent constitutional right to do what was necessary to defend a nation under attack—a power that Congress might confirm or even enhance but lacked the power to restrict."[37] Together, the AUMF and the USA PATRIOT Act[38] yielded to the president a wealth of power by which to act without the metes and bounds of the rule of law when combating terrorism.

The administration declared, "America will act deliberately and decisively,"[39] and securing justice would necessitate unconventional action. As such, the Bush administration and his legal team "embraced the shattering of established rules and norms" by departing "from previously settled law to defend coercive interrogation techniques, to redefine torture so narrowly as to allow for techniques accepted from medieval times[, and] . . . to denounce proper judicial processes, both in the military and the civilian context, as posing unaffordable risks to national security."[40] Facing a constitutional void, Bush responded by asserting his authority to elucidate first principles on security issues. Relying on inherent power and the commander-in-chief clause, the Bush administration made audacious interpretive claims[41] against Congress and the courts.

Reneging on basic rights and liberties that are traditionally guaranteed to Americans posed a significant threat to preserving the due process of law, partially repudiated, Gonzales maintained, by the fact that in a time of terror, concerns over constitutional guarantees are "quaint" and "obsolete."[42] For the administration, determinations regarding rights were at the executive's discretion in a time of war, but the defense representing those detained insisted that "creat[ing] unheard-of categories of prisoners and . . . constantly chang[ing] the rules for their treatment threatens overarching principles of legality, both domestic and international."[43]

In addition to utilizing structural checks to combat terrorism, the administration firmly advocated a constitutional grant of power to act unilaterally. The executive branch "was using the tools of law without abiding by the laws of war; Bush placed himself above the law by claiming power immune to check from Congress or the Court."[44] This "penchant for evading legal limits played" right into the hands of the defense. In fact, the executive branch resisted any oversight or constraint. By denying judicial review, the administration "held suspects incommunicado in secret prisons, rounded up thousands of Arabs and Muslims in the U.S., held hundreds of immigration proceedings behind closed doors, and authorized secret and warrantless wiretapping."[45] As the Court justices were writing their opinions for *Rasul*, *Hamdi*, and *Padilla* in June 2004, the most sensational document came to light—the "torture memo."[46] In the summer of 2002, White House counsel Gonzales requested that the Justice Department query whether U.S. personnel involved in the war on terror were restricted by federal law, which bans "cruel, inhuman, or degrading treatment" of detainees on or off American soil. In August, senior officials Jay Bybee and Yoo offered Gonzales a distorted and narrow definition of torture, which they defined as "severe physical or mental pain or suffering." Bybee and Yoo asserted that the president had inherent authority to bypass the statute and order any interrogation technique he believed was necessary to extract information from hostiles. The disclosure of the torture memo while the three cases were pending before the Court further called into question the administration's credibility. As Joseph Margulies (Shafiq Rasul's lawyer) recalled, after the story broke, "[t]hese photos proved to be the most powerful amicus brief of all."[47]

To provide further support for these measures, the administration insisted that the Geneva Conventions and the Constitution did not apply to foreign detainees in the war on terror and added that as commander-in-chief, the executive could ignore any legislation that did not advance a favorable resolution. As the administration reasoned, every action taken since the attacks had been "not only justified by national security concerns in an age of terrorism, but consistent with the president's historically expanded powers during wartime."[48] Many of these counterterrorism policies were largely regarded as lawless, so the courts were called upon to step in and assess the balance between the rule of law and "law-free zones."

Bush's comprehensive military order issued on November 13, 2001, governed the treatment, detention, and trial of specified noncitizens in the war on terror.[49] In January 2002, the military began transferring prisoners from Afghanistan to Guantanamo Bay. Secretary of Defense Donald Rumsfeld labeled these prisoners as "unlawful combatants."[50] At the center of the Bush administration's policies was the creation of a new category of person, which was applicable to U.S. citizens as well as to noncitizens. *Unlawful combatant* was a designation that "mixes confusingly several legal and military concepts."[51] The term referred to prisoners in the war on terror who could not be labeled as conventional prisoners of war, but it ultimately "conflate[d] previously well-defined categories" (especially "enemy prisoner of war," "combatant," and "civilian combatant").[52]

In "creating this nebulous class," the executive manipulated the ambiguity in international law. Although this class was "not part of any written international law or code, the idea has long been recognized in practice." Furthermore, "legal interpretation, military protocol, and case law have all led to the widely shared acceptance of the distinction between" lawful and unlawful, a "distinction that has specific implications for the legal treatment of prisoners in either group."[53] From the onset and throughout Bush's two terms, the OLC drafted a number of memos asserting that not only the "Geneva Conventions on the categorization and treatment of prisoners" but the conventional guarantees of due process were "quaint" and "obsolete." The administration did note that although no law obliged the government to provide detainees with the protections guaranteed by the Geneva Conventions, the detainees were being afforded many of them.[54]

While government lawyers were making these claims, they attracted little notice and even less controversy, at first, from the American people. Bush was delivering on his promises; suspected terrorists were being captured, transferred, and held at Guantanamo Bay. Issuing Military Order 1 in November 2001,[55] Bush established military tribunals to try alleged war criminals. Not only would the "Executive branch be judge, jury, and executioner"; the courts would have no power of review.[56] By January 2002, more than seven hundred prisoners were held at Guantanamo, accused of being al-Qaeda or Taliban members. Bush's crusade was quickly chalked up as a win. But continued internment without the rights of due process can "only take place if the culture, the press, and the political climate" allow it.[57]

The first criticisms started to emerge in January 2002, when the Guantanamo facility was opened. Disapproval at home and international outcry led to a lack of confidence in the administration's counterterrorism policies by the spring of 2003. Most Americans were insulated from the war's actual effects, leaving them more vulnerable to presidential persuasion.[58] As such, Bush responded to his critics by launching a public-relations offensive from 2005 to 2006.[59] The administration's poll data suggested that if eventual victory could be achieved, Americans would support a continued military offensive in the Middle East. The president's speeches thus emphasized this idea, and support for his policies increased.[60] The White House achieved a public-relations success when opposition to Bush's Iraq policy was temporarily muted despite the casualties, uncertain war objectives, and substantial evidence of mismanagement and duplicity on the administration's part.

The administration's fashioning of an unusual legal category for those suspected of terrorist activity rendered them neither criminal defendants protected by the U.S. Constitution nor prisoners of war protected by the Geneva Conventions, which require humane treatment of all wartime detainees. Rather, their treatment and detention fell under military-commission procedures, because they had been classified as "enemy combatants." In fact, the Bush administration maintained that detainees were not American citizens, and because they were held in Cuba, which had ultimate sovereignty over the U.S. Navy base, the lawsuits were comparable to a lawsuit filed by a foreigner from a battlefield overseas, which would not be condoned in an American court. As the first detainee case marched through the federal courts, public hysteria following the attacks faded, and sentiment over the conduct of the war made the claims by Guantanamo detainees seeking habeas appear more plausible.

Since *Curtiss-Wright*, the clear trend in case law has been to approve of presidential assertions of emergency and war powers.[61] During exigent times, the courts—and Congress—have nearly always favored the executive over rights claims. Those wanting to protect civil liberties and human rights following the September attacks faced a considerable hurdle, because neither history nor the law was on their side. The challenge faced by detainees was perhaps more daunting than previous challenges: civil-liberties and human-rights violations during the war on terror included "preventive detention, unfair trials, torture, and other cruel interrogation techniques, illegal abductions or 'renditions,' excessive secrecy, dragnet surveillance, ethnic and religious profiling, and the punishment of speech and association."[62] As the administration set the agenda of the direction of the war with its various initiatives, those defending rights violations had to show that national security did not supersede due process. This appeared to be an uphill battle, because national security is predominantly "a federal prerogative, and federal security programs cannot be challenged for transgressing state laws."[63]

The discretionary latitude afforded the president has been particularly evident, given the response of the federal courts. The Court, however, reined in presidential power—if not constitutionally, then statutorily—when it heard *Rasul, Hamdi, Hamdan*, and *Boumediene*. But given the path of constitutional jurisprudence in foreign policy making, why did it do so? Why did the Court break from the new constitutional order and rule against the executive? Constitutional jurisprudence dictated the results of the four cases before the Court: *Eisentrager* offered strong support for the administration in *Rasul* and later in *Boumediene*, and *Quirin* supported the administration's position in *Hamdan*.[64]

These Supreme Court cases all drew upon the rhetorical superstructure advanced by the Bush administration. The administration's legal standing rested on an "alternative constitutional understanding" of the president's power and authority to act. And "as their memoirs underscore, Bush and Cheney are entirely unapologetic about the tactics" they employed to counter terrorism.[65]

In June 2004, in three related cases—*Rasul, Hamdi*, and *Padilla*—the Court addressed the president's anti-terror initiatives and executive claims of unilateral power. In two of the three cases, the Court placed some statutory limits on executive authority.[66] To accept the administration's assertion that Bush had unfettered authority to detain without judicial oversight "would have looked dangerously like the excessive deference employed in *Koremat-*

su."[67] And by the time *Rasul* and *Hamdi* reached the Court, the issue was no longer about the terrorists versus the administration. Instead, "it was the mainstream American, British, and international legal communities against the U.S. government,"[68] which was unprecedented; in prior wartime cases, "there was no similar marshaling of professional opinion."[69]

In *Rasul*, *Hamdi*, and *Padilla*, all nine justices agreed that the nation was at war and that the executive's powers needed to be measured from that vantage point. In fact, not one justice was concerned that Congress had never declared war. And none of the justices in any of the three detainee cases embraced the argument that the "power to wage war successfully"[70] was a power that "stems from a declaration of war."[71] Moreover, the justices were not concerned that the government had not charged any of the detainees for crimes. The Court accepted the administration's position of detention until the conflict was over, because it had statutory merit: Congress's authorization to use "necessary and appropriate force" included "the authority to detain *for the duration of the relevant conflict*, and [the Court's] understanding is based on longstanding law-of-war principles."[72] However, the Court delineated important distinctions between the types of prisoners and the rights afforded to each of these types when it decided the three cases.

Weighing competing claims evidence suggested that some justices were influenced by revelations of U.S. troops' abusing prisoners in Iraq. Consequently, the Court ruled against a definitive declaration of absolute denial, by the executive, of procedural rights to individuals when held by the American military. External factors were found to be constraining, but the Court found against the president on statutory grounds, although these same factors did not compel the Court to redefine unilateral executive powers in formal constitutional terms. However, this was one of the first times the Court posed a distinct challenge to unreviewable presidential authority, which provided the first fissure in the developmental path of discretionary executive powers.

Interestingly, once cert was granted in *Rasul*, *Hamdi*, and *Padilla*, the Bush administration implemented some changes. After detaining Yaser Hamdi and Jose Padilla for two years with no access to legal counsel, the administration conceded and allowed them to meet with their lawyers. In addition, Secretary Rumsfeld revealed that the military would form "administrative review boards" to assess the status of each detainee at Guantanamo. Despite this concession, the administration maintained that the prisoners had no right to this procedural safeguard; instead, it was afforded "solely as a matter of discretion and does not confer any right or obligation enforceable by law."[73] The administration's position remained steadfast: the war on terror afforded the prisoners no rights, and a day in an American court was indefensible.

RASUL

Rasul was the first habeas corpus case. It involved four British and twelve Australian citizens captured by the American military and transferred to Guantanamo Bay. They were denied access to an attorney and held indefinitely without a court hearing. Their families filed suit in the federal district court, seeking a writ of habeas corpus to declare their detentions unconstitutional, as they violated their Fifth Amendment due-process rights.

The administration asserted extralegal authority—the authority to set aside the laws the nation is governed by to deal with the present crisis—adding that federal courts did not have the jurisdiction to hear the case, because the detainees were not American citizens. Moreover, the administration argued, because these detainees were being held in Cuba, the United States did not have sovereignty and thus had no jurisdiction.

Agreeing with the government, the district court dismissed the case. And the Circuit Court of Appeals for the District of Columbia,[74] relying on *Eisentrager*, deferred to the administration's reading of the status of enemy combatants held at Guantanamo Bay (as outlined in Bush's military order, which formalized the administration's reason to specifically detain alleged members and supporters of al-Qaeda or the Taliban). The circuit court thus rejected the plaintiffs' motions of habeas. As David Cole notes, "Politically, the detainees' case was no stronger. Memories of the collapsing World Trade Center towers and of the many people who had leapt to their deaths in desperation were still raw, and there was little sympathy for anyone said to be associated with the perpetrators of that heinous act. Moreover, the only people the government imprisoned at Guantanamo were foreign nationals, so the rights of U.S. citizens were not implicated."[75]

Case law appeared to support the administration. The *Eisentrager* Court had ruled after World War II that enemy prisoners of war could not seek habeas corpus review in U.S. courts.[76] Robert Jackson had asserted, "Nothing in the text of the Constitution extends such a right, nor does anything in our statutes." According to Jackson, this allowance would divert a field commander's "efforts and attention from the military offensive abroad to the legal defensive at home."[77] Given this jurisprudence, the Bush administration felt confident about how these habeas petitions would fare, but the Supreme Court, to everyone's surprise, reviewed the case and determined that the individuals had a claim. Even though the plurality, analogous to Anthony Kennedy's concurrence, factually differentiated *Eisentrager*, it did not depend on this factual examination; rather, it turned to a statutory analysis.

The John Paul Stevens[78] plurality (6–3) asserted that the degree of control exerted by the United States over the naval base in Guantanamo was significant to trigger the application of habeas corpus rights.[79] The Court embraced and adopted the position advanced by the *Rasul* petitioners: "They are not enemy aliens, but citizens of our closest allies who allege they have committed no wrong against the United States, and whose allegations at this stage must be accepted as tr[u]e."[80] While the Court concluded that the federal habeas corpus granted jurisdiction in federal district courts to hear challenges of aliens held at Guantanamo, it did not decide what those proceedings might include,[81] nor did it decide what the litigants would win—it only stated that the lower courts had jurisdiction.[82]

In referencing case law, Stevens distinguished *Eisentrager* by relying on *Braden*,[83] which essentially altered the interpretation of the habeas statute's rules with respect to who could be sued. However, nothing in *Rasul* required "any habeas protection for Iraqis captured in Iraq or Afghans captured in Afghanistan, as these are by definition nationals of countries at war" with America.[84] The administration was therefore legally obligated to provide detainees with hearings in an attempt to refute the evidence brought against them. But the Court did not indicate what procedures were due these noncitizens during their hearings.[85]

Even though the Court appeared to censure the administration's assertion of unreviewable actions, it was not clear how the Court's decision would ultimately affect the thousands of foreigners detained in such places as Iraq and Afghanistan. What was clear was that when presidents chose to reject the Court's power (e.g., *United States v. Nixon* [1974]),[86] the judiciary would reaffirm its institutional capacity to legally sanction and stop a path in its track—in this case, unreviewable authority.

Antonin Scalia clearly supported the administration and presidential prerogatives in general and not the Court's determination. He scolded the majority for its interpretation of the habeas statute: "Congress is in session. If it wished to change federal judges' habeas jurisdiction from what this Court had previously held that to be, it could have done so."[87] For Scalia, the Court did not go far enough to utilize the institutional process that was, according to him, a viable option.

In addition, Scalia vehemently rejected the idea that habeas could be extended around the world. In fact, he pointed out, the habeas statute for the first time had been extended beyond the sovereignty of the United States and beyond the "territorial jurisdiction" of its courts. As such, "today's clumsy, countertextual reinterpretation . . . confers upon wartime prisoners greater habeas rights than domestic detainees."[88]

Scalia charged that the Court had no jurisdiction[89] over the conduct of war and its detainees. Essentially, he accused the Court of attempting to "trap" the executive. With more than six hundred detainees, he stated, each one would have complaints about the circumstances surrounding their capture and detention, and if federal courts were to review these kinds of petitions, they would not only challenge events and actions from abroad but also force the courts to examine the conduct of war by an executive.[90] For Scalia, when individual rights claims challenged the executive's authority, the Court needed to be restrained, because "departure has a potentially harmful effect upon" the war efforts.[91]

In fairly quick succession, the Court decided three more equally noteworthy enemy combatant cases, which proved to be "a wholly unprecedented run of losses for a President during wartime."[92] On the same day that *Rasul* was decided, the Court's *Hamdi* decision rejected the administration's argument that it could hold a U.S. citizen in military detention as an "enemy combatant" without a hearing. Given the Court's finding, the administration released Hamdi on the condition that "he return to Saudi Arabia and remain there."[93]

HAMDI

The *Hamdi* Court ruled, in part—partially on procedural grounds, as it articulated the procedures required for U.S. citizens—that these procedures should be extended to aliens, as they are in no better position than American citizens would be, to give the alleged combatants a "meaningful opportunity to contest the factual basis for [their] decision."[94] Despite the plurality opinion, Bush continued to present a position of unchecked executive authority that was not subject to oversight. The dissenters were split, to some extent; some advocated for the rights of U.S. citizens, and others pushed for the extralegal authority of the executive.

Hamdi, captured by American forces in Afghanistan and brought to the United States, was incarcerated at the Norfolk Naval Station and classified by the administration as an illegal enemy combatant. Yet he was a U.S. citizen who was being held indefinitely and denied his civil rights, including the right to counsel.

Appealing to statutory and constitutional powers, the Bush administration maintained that it had the authority during wartime to declare people who fought against America to be "enemy combatants," making them ineligible for ordinary legal protection by way of the AUMF, which granted considerable latitude to the president. Furthermore, Bush advanced the constitutional claim that as the sole organ of foreign affairs, he possessed inherent power as commander-in-chief to protect the nation's security interests by conducting a successful military campaign. As such, it was necessary to deny detainees civil liberties to effectively wage a war on terror. And a denial of basic constitutional rights, the administration maintained, ensured that these individuals would no longer pose a threat to the nation.

The federal district court scheduled a hearing on Hamdi's habeas petition and ordered that he have access to unmonitored counsel through a federal public defender. The Fourth Circuit Court of Appeals reversed this ruling,[95] holding that the district court had failed to give proper deference to the government's intelligence and security concerns and should therefore have proceeded with a deferential examination.[96] Relying on *Curtiss-Wright*, the Fourth Circuit asserted that when assessing "foreign relations and national security" concerns, the president wielded "plenary and exclusive power."[97] In addition, the court asserted deference, because the Supreme Court's precedents necessitated that in "sensitive matters of foreign policy, national security[,] or military affairs," the judiciary must find in favor of the executive.[98]

Relying on Jackson's *Youngstown* concurrence, the district court found that the plenary and exclusive power of the president was superior when the executive acted with statutory authority. The court did not indicate which of these statutes might authorize the president's actions, but it affirmed Bush's constitutional power (as determined by the *Prize Cases*, *Quirin*, and *Dames*) to conduct military operations, classify enemy combatants, and determine the rules governing the treatment of such individuals. The president had virtually unfettered discretion to deal with emergencies, the court concluded, and it was inappropriate for the judiciary to saddle presidential decisions with what the court called the "panoply of encumbrances associated with civil litigation."[99] Clearly, the principle of separation of powers, the district court held, prohibited courts from becoming involved in cases that pertained to national security.[100] The lower court was clearly following the constitutional order established and reaffirmed by the Supreme Court in cases up to and including *Dames*. This time, however, the Supreme Court followed a different track.

The Court "reversed both the trial court and the Fourth Circuit, finding that the former required too many procedural safeguards[,] while the latter required too few."[101] Unlike *Rasul*, *Hamdi* produced no majority opinion, but Sandra Day O'Connor's opinion on the narrow question did (William Rehnquist, Kennedy, and Stephen Breyer joined O'Connor's plurality). The Court was in a precarious situation, as its membership was set to change in 2005 (John Roberts would replace Chief Justice Rehnquist [2005], and Samuel Alito would replace O'Connor [2006]). Therefore, securing at least five votes was essential. David Souter filed a separate opinion (joined by Ruth Bader Ginsburg) but joined the plurality with respect to the procedures to "give practical effect" to the Court's judgment and to "remand on terms closest to those

[they] would impose."[102] And Clarence Thomas's dissent would have allowed the administration to detain Hamdi without any further procedures; Bush, acting "with explicit congressional approval," had classified Hamdi as an enemy combatant, which allowed the military to detain him, and the Court should not "second-guess that decision."[103]

O'Connor's plurality acknowledged the administration's characterization: an enemy combatant was "an individual who, allege[dly], was 'part of or supporting forces hostile to the United States or coalition partners' in Afghanistan and who 'engaged in an armed conflict against the United States' there."[104] As such, the plurality answered only the narrow question of "whether the detention of citizens falling within that definition is authorized."[105] In short, the Court responded in the affirmative.[106]

The plurality rejected the assertion that a federal statute (Section 4001(a) of Title 17) banned Hamdi's detention,[107] because Congress had authorized it:[108] the AUMF empowered the president to "use all necessary and appropriate force against . . . nations, organizations, or persons that he determines planned, authorized, committed, or aided" in the September 11 attacks.[109] However, the Court maintained that Hamdi had a right to a hearing. While the Court read the AUMF broadly, Souter disagreed with this interpretation. He maintained that simply as a matter of statutory interpretation, the AUMF did not authorize Hamdi's detention.[110]

The *Hamdi* decision generated important implications for the Bush administration. O'Connor's plurality opinion was scathing and highlighted her growing estrangement from the administration. She reminded the administration and the nation that "[i]t is during our most challenging and uncertain moments that our Nation's commitment to due process is most severely tested; and it is in those times that we must preserve our commitment at home to the principles from which we fight abroad."[111] Consequently, O'Connor determined that executive power could not be "a blank check" in "a state of war." As such, enemy combatants had at least some rights; "due process demands that a citizen held in the United States as an enemy combatant be given a meaningful opportunity to contest the factual basis for that detention before a neutral decision maker."[112] This conclusion is important, because it theoretically denied Bush the authority to hold detainees with no formal review. Interestingly, Scalia, the archconservative, and Stevens, the ultraliberal justice, believed that when a U.S. citizen was on U.S. soil and the courts were open, that individual had to be tried as a criminal in a regular trial and not be held as an enemy combatant. This position did not, however, carry the day.

Conceding to the claim of a civil-liberties violation, O'Connor noted that although Congress had expressly authorized detention in "narrow circumstances," if the nation did not have checks on a system of detention, there was the real potential of "oppression and abuse of others." In fact, even the dissenting Scalia conceded that indefinite imprisonment by the administration cut at "the very core of liberty."[113] Drawing on the first constitutional order, O'Connor declared "that unlimited power, wherever lodged at such a time, was especially hazardous to freemen." With the administration's continued assertion of unreviewable discretionary authorization, O'Connor reminded Bush that the judiciary was not a rubber stamp for a president attempting to "*condense* power into a single branch of government"[114] to such egregious standards. Finding for the weightier concerns of individual rights, the plurality directly challenged Bush's wartime measures.

The Court argued that the necessary procedures were not particularly burdensome: a searching inquiry was not needed, but there must be *some* inquiry, and it must take place before a neutral decision maker, who could be a member of the military court;[115] and evidence presented could include hearsay and even "a presumption in favor of the Government's evidence," but the petitioner needed to have a fair opportunity to rebut.[116] These "core elements"[117] were not devised to punish or determine war crimes or to determine whether these combatants presented some future danger, the Court contended. Rather, these rules were simply to prevent falsely incarcerating individuals who were not, in fact, combatants.[118] The one caveat was that the process did not apply to initial captures on the battlefield; the parties agreed that the "process is due only when the determination is made to *continue* to hold those who have been seized,"[119] and then the truncated procedure must be employed for U.S. citizens held on American soil.

The Court found the least intrusive way as it created a procedure to balance individual rights with separation of powers during wartime: this process "meddles little, if at all, in the strategy or conduct of war, inquiring only into the appropriateness of continuing to detain an individual claimed to have taken up arms against the United States."[120] In summarizing *Quirin*, the O'Connor plurality held that the military could detain American citizens during wartime (even if undeclared) if the legislature authorized the detention (which, the majority determined was the case) and if the administration provided combatants "a meaningful opportunity" to refute their detention before a neutral decision maker.[121]

This was a distinct shift by the Court to check an executive's claim to unilateral authority to conduct a war, but the plurality's conclusions illustrated the Court's capacity to weigh competing rights claims and make its own determination on whether the executive had exceeded presidential authority. The Court concluded procedurally that the claimants had rights, but it did not formally check the president constitutionally.

The dissenters, on the other hand, adhered to the practical framework advocated by Jackson's *Youngstown* concurrence, which invoked the implied authority advanced in *Curtiss-Wright*. Thomas was the only justice who did not oppose the detention policy as applied to U.S. citizens: "[T]his detention falls squarely within the Federal Government's war powers."[122] In accepting the administration's position, Thomas reasoned that the president's action was grounded not only in his constitutional powers but also in "explicit congressional approval," which legitimized the detention of Hamdi. The combination of these powers, Thomas argued, precluded any second-guessing on the part of the Court due to its lack of expertise.[123] Judicial interference would, in effect, "defeat the unity, secrecy, and dispatch that the Founders believed to be so important to the warmaking function."[124]

Consequently, Thomas contended, the plurality failed to effectively take into account the "basic principles of the constitutional structure as it relates to national security and foreign affairs." The "federal Government's war powers can't be balanced away," as O'Connor attempted to do in her evaluation of the competing claims of national security and civil liberties, Thomas concluded. National-security concerns must outweigh civil-liberties considerations, because, "[o]f all the cares or concerns of government, the direction of war most peculiarly demands those qualities which distinguish the exercise of power by a single hand."[125] This had certainly been the constitutional foreign-affairs jurisprudence of the Court following *Curtiss-Wright* right up until it heard the detainee cases.

Thomas agreed with the Court that the AUMF provided the executive with statutory authority, but he invoked Jackson's concurrence to advance a second, and affirming, legal claim of authority—that of inherent power.[126] Inherent power, in Thomas's view, demanded that "executive action 'would be supported by the strongest of presumptions and the widest latitude of judicial interpretation, and the burden of persuasion would rest heavily upon any who might attack it.'"[127] Consequently, Thomas concluded, the Court failed to assess "the Government's compelling interests . . . [in securing] the Nation."[128] Thomas's determination meant that the president's war powers were beyond judicial reproach, which necessarily challenged judicial supremacy.

Due process, the *Hamdi* plurality determined, applied to the detained enemy combatant, but in a subdued way—a suspected terrorist could be detained, but he or she was entitled to some form of muted habeas hearing in which the administration must demonstrate that the detainee was a combatant.[129] In making this determination, the administration would provide the jurisdictional tie to remove said individual from the federal courts. O'Connor made it clear that the administration could establish military tribunals to serve this purpose,[130] but in the event that it did not do so, federal habeas proceedings would be utilized. However, muted procedural guidelines must still be applied. Alternatively, the administration could choose to prosecute the individual in federal court only if it chose to pursue criminal law charges.

While *Hamdi* spoke to whether detainees were entitled to due-process rights, the Court did not speak to the kind of tribunal these individuals would be entitled to, only that a tribunal could be established. This issue would wait until the Court heard *Hamdan*, because *Padilla* would never reach the merits of the case, as it would be dismissed on jurisdictional grounds.

PADILLA

Padilla was suspected by the government of conspiring with Islamic terrorists to explode a radiological "dirty bomb" in the United States. Under a presidential directive, Rumsfeld was ordered to detain Padilla as an enemy combatant after his arrest at O'Hare Airport. The Justice Department determined that even though Padilla was an American citizen held on American soil, because he had been declared an enemy combatant, he was therefore subject to indefinite detention with no legal rights. And the District Court for the Southern District of New York reasoned, in line with the administration, that the president, acting as commander-in-chief, had the authority to detain citizens and classify them as enemy combatants when they were captured on American soil during wartime. Similarly, the U.S. Court of Appeals for the Fourth Circuit concluded that Bush possessed the necessary authority to detain Padilla as an enemy combatant.[131]

On appeal, the Supreme Court asserted that presidential actions were, indeed, subject to judicial scrutiny, which placed some constraints on the president's unfettered power. At the same time, however, it affirmed that the president's single-most-important prerogative was the unilateral authority to categorize individuals, including U.S. citizens, as "enemy combatants" who could be detained by federal authorities under adverse legal circumstances. But the Court declined on procedural grounds to rule on the *Padilla* case.

Chief Justice Rehnquist delivered an attenuated opinion maintaining that the Court was confronted with only two questions. First, had Padilla properly filed his habeas petition in the Southern District of New York? Second, did the president possess the authority to detain Padilla?

Pursuant to settled habeas law,[132] Rehnquist asserted that the case represented "a simple challenge to physical custody."[133] Because Padilla had not properly filed his petition, the Court lacked jurisdiction to hear the case and therefore did not reach its merits. Accordingly, the Court refused to order

Padilla's release and dismissed his habeas petition without prejudice to his filing a new petition elsewhere.[134]

The Court did not decide whether the president had the authority to detain Padilla militarily,[135] but the O'Connor plurality in *Hamdi* spoke to that issue. First, the AUMF authorized such detention,[136] and second, the Court confirmed *Quirin*. Consequently, the *Hamdi* plurality confirmed that the administration could continue to detain Padilla, as long as the government used the same truncated procedural protections afforded Hamdi. This determination was based largely on O'Connor's endorsement of the *Quirin* precedent to authorize the military detention of U.S. citizens who were determined to be enemy combatants.[137]

IMPACT OF *RASUL, HAMDI,* AND *PADILLA*

The amalgamation of *Rasul, Hamdi,* and *Padilla* provided the most definitive statement yet of what powers are afforded the president during wartime. Rather than mere security and liberty interests, the political process and institutional collaboration between the president and Congress were crucial to the Court's decision making, whereas judicially settled constitutional rights were less of a concern. For example, the *Hamdi* Court was predominantly concerned with the extent of legislative authorization of the detention of enemy combatants, discarding a comprehensive reading of presidential autonomy. And in *Padilla* and *Rasul,* the Court utilized process-orientated justifications to the harm of "substantive determinations of first-order constitutional rights."[138]

These three detention cases thus articulated significant differences between the classifications of prisoners and their rights. First, not one justice asserted that those detained had any rights to habeas in American courts just because the United States was holding them. Second, the Court carefully split combatants into two types: a plurality maintained that those detainees held outside the United States could not access federal courts, and those held at Guantanamo who were not citizens of countries the United States was fighting may have a right to some kind of hearing, but if they were held on U.S. soil, then they were entitled to a hearing to contest their detention. Finally, American citizens captured and detained on American soil (*Hamdi*) were entitled to a pseudo-habeas hearing and, in a show of good faith, the administration needed to keep each individual remanded to one and only one jurisdiction.[139]

The Court upheld presidential authority in one significant area. The *Hamdi* plurality conceded that Congress, by way of the AUMF, had authorized the executive as commander-in-chief to detain U.S. citizens as "enemy combatants," and this authority had judicial grounding.[140] But the plurality maintained that the administration did not have the authority to prevent U.S. citizens from challenging their detentions.

For the administration to show that it could hold individuals incommunicado without any time limit, it labeled them illegal enemy combatants, which stuck: the "term makes them more than ordinary criminals and less than soldiers in any enemy army."[141] The AUMF, the Court concluded, authorized Bush to "detain such combatants until the end of hostilities—which could be indefinitely."[142]

The Court's composition had not changed in just over ten years, not since Breyer had replaced Blackmun in 1994. Rehnquist's passing and O'Connor's retirement—a crucial swing seat on the Court—gave Bush two seats at a very crucial time. Replacing Rehnquist alone would have been noteworthy, but a Bush appointee in that seat would not have changed the balance of power on the Court in any dramatic way. Filling O'Connor's seat would; a swing-voter replacement on the Court would give Bush an opportunity to change the dynamics of the bench. The conservative counterrevolution frustrated for years, and often at the hand of O'Connor[143] herself, might finally have a chance to succeed.

In filling Rehnquist's seat, Bush wanted a transformative appointee, a justice who would move the Court sharply and instantaneously to the right.[144] Bush was reeling from O'Connor's 2004 scathing rebuke to the administration's detention policy (*Hamdi*), which mandated some kind of due process for the detainees. Roberts was not necessarily the obvious choice, even if it seemed he was genetically engineered to be a Supreme Court justice.[145] Before taking a seat on the bench, John Roberts had joined a three-judge panel for the U.S. Court of Appeals for the District of Columbia Circuit (2005)[146] that approved Bush's plan, which had been developed in response to O'Connor's censure. Roberts and his colleagues had asserted that the executive did not have to comply with the Geneva Conventions, because they were not judicially enforceable. And on July 15, 2005, the day Roberts was to interview with Bush, the D.C. Circuit upheld the administration's plans for the use of military tribunals for the prisoners held at Guantanamo.[147]

For Vice President Dick Cheney and President Bush, no issue was more important than the preservation of presidential unilateral power, particularly in light of the current war on terror. With the D.C. Circuit Court's holding, Roberts had proven himself worthy of a nomination by the administration, and he was overwhelming confirmed by the full Senate (78–22). Evidently, the administration was hoping that a structural change to the Court would yield favorable decisions in the continued judicial evaluations of the ongoing war efforts. However, this would not be the case. Even when the bench changes, it is ultimately the Court as an institution that decides whether the executive has the power and authority to act. For example, a conservative New Deal Court sanctioned Franklin Roosevelt's actions in *Curtiss-Wright* and in the internment cases.

During Roberts's confirmation process, the political climate was changing; Iraqis held their first free elections since the start of the war, and the voters became symbols of a hopeful emerging democracy.[148] But in a few short months, chaos ensued, and American troops continued to lose their lives daily.[149] Domestically, the nation faced the devastation of Hurricane Katrina, and the federal response was widely viewed as indifferent at best and incompetent at worst. Bush's approval ratings plummeted from around 60 percent favorable at the time of his reelection to around the same percentage unfavorable within a year.[150] In this political atmosphere, the president made his second nomination to the bench.[151]

Everyone agreed that Judge Samuel A. Alito Jr. represented a guaranteed conservative voice.[152] As soon as Alito was nominated, it was evident that he would survive the most important test of any Bush nominee to the Court, or what might be called the Republican primary—that is, the approval of the conservative base. The full Senate posed no real problems for Alito, but the only way Democrats could stop the confirmation was to filibuster.[153]

Alito's confirmation hearing followed the *New York Times* story that revealed the administration had engaged in warrantless wiretapping of phone calls to and from outside the United States. The secret was out and was the lead in all news media across the country. Bush held a news conference on December 19 to justify his actions: he had the "constitutional responsibility and authority to protect our country . . . to effectively detect enemies hiding in our midst and prevent them from striking again."[154]

Following Alito's successful confirmation, it appeared that he would be an ally to the Bush administration when the Court decided *Hamdan*. When questioned on the subject, he declined to say much during the hearings, but he did note, "I don't think that we should look to foreign law to interpret our own Constitution." This remark fell in line with the administration, as it maintained that the Geneva Conventions did not govern how detainees should be treated. And the newly appointed Justice Roberts had expressed a similar sentiment during his own hearings.

The new Court bench would now be left to answer the important questions that had remained unanswered by the Rehnquist Court regarding the kind of legal process that enemy combatants should be afforded. The Roberts Court was now poised to determine the legality of the military commissions in *Hamdan* and *Boumediene*. The questions included the following: Could a military commission strip federal courts of jurisdiction over habeas? Was the Military Commissions Act of 2006 (MCA) a violation of the Suspension Clause (*Boumediene*)? Were detainee rights, as protected by the Geneva Conventions, enforceable in federal courts through habeas corpus (*Hamdan*)? And were detainees entitled to Fifth Amendment rights (*Boumediene*)? The *Hamdan* and *Boumediene* Courts ultimately concluded that individual rights (i.e., some form of due process) and the role of judicial monitoring of legal and criminal justice were more pressing than the polity principles raised by the administration, whereas in prior cases, polity principles carried greater weight than individual rights.

The holdings in *Hamdan* and *Boumediene* were quite profound. The *Hamdi* Court determined that the military did not have to charge a detainee with a crime,[155] but the *Hamdan* Court found that if the military wanted to punish an individual, it must utilize properly constituted military tribunals to do so.[156] In effect, the *Hamdan* Court determined that the government could not hold individuals in a place where no law would protect them; the president responded by establishing tribunals in Guantanamo.

The Supreme Court had effectively shut down the legal system and access to federal courts for claimants in *Dames*. Yet in *Hamdan*, the Court argued that the courts must be accessible to individuals. These two decisions were reconciled by the Court's assessment of individual and policy principles. In *Dames*, the key to denying access to the courts was to ensure the executive's ability to use bargaining chips to provide the safe return of hostages. And in *Hamdan* and *Boumediene*, the key to providing access to the courts was the judiciary's check on polity principles. Those detained were entitled to first-order principles (the right to counsel and the right to be heard, for example), but the Court's definition of what tribunals were constitutional was for it alone to make. Even though the Court was somewhat restrained by the war, it was more than prepared to place limits on the president.

These military commissions, the Bush administration admonished, could potentially constitute a "breach of the constitutional right to equal protection of law[,] because military commissions are not part of the judicial power laid out in the" Constitution. Rather, "they are constitutionally grounded in the war powers allocated to the political branches of government."[157] As such, "commissions are not subject to judicial oversight," the administration asserted, as they "do not adhere to the same standards of proof that apply in the civilian court system."[158] In effect, "commissions [are] simply an instrumentality for the more efficient executive of the war powers vested in Congress and the power vested" in the executive in the president's capacity as commander-in-chief in war.[159]

Assessing these claims, the *Boumediene* Court once again found against the administration—this time on procedural grounds. The Court returned to finding in favor of the weightier concerns of individual rights. Essentially, these decisions weakened "the authority of Congress and jeopardize[d] the constitutional separation of powers,"[160] as the Court maintained judicial oversight. In the end, the *Boumediene* plurality did "not consider congressional authorization the be-all and end-all in the emergency context." Moreover, Kennedy "found that restricting the reach of habeas review to places within the U.S. borders would undermine the constitutional separation of powers by allowing the Executive to turn constitutional limitations on and off at will."[161]

HAMDAN—COURT AS MEDIATOR

The *Hamdan* plurality (2006) outlawed military commissions, at least temporarily. The Court concluded that these commissions lacked the power to move forward, because their structure and procedures violated the Uniform Code of Military Justice (UCMJ) and the Geneva Conventions. In fact, the UCMJ, the AUMF, and even the Detainee Treatment Act (DTA) of 2005[162] prohibited them, according to the Court.[163]

Even though the military commissions were ultimately challenged and subsequently found to be an unconstitutional suspension of a prisoner's right to Habeas (*Boumediene* [2008]), *Hamdan* exemplified the Court's acting as a mediator between the two branches. Moreover, the Court offered a course of action that the executive should take to not only accomplish his agenda but do so with express authorization from Congress.

Taking into account external constraints, the Court used structural checks to compel the president to obtain authorization from Congress. Judicial intervention therefore had a decisive impact on the relationship between the executive and the legislature, as it forced them to work together. The Court's ruling thus established its institutional authority to determine the scope and direction of the executive in war making. In addition, these decisions reaffirmed the Court's jurisdiction to weigh separation-of-powers principles in light of individual rights under exigent circumstances. While finding in favor of individual rights, the Court did recognize the role of the executive during wartime, but it presented the administration with a corrective measure—securing a more direct legislative role. Insisting that Congress play a more prominent role illustrated the Court's ability to force another institution to act for it to sanction, statutorily, the actions taken by the administration. Consequently, because the president had sought and Congress had approved statutory authorization, the *Hamdan* decision did not pose a demonstrable challenge to presidential power.

When the *Hamdi* Court rejected the administration's claim that detainees were outside the American legal system's jurisdiction and did not have the legal right to bring such a case, Bush responded by unilaterally setting up secret military review panels (Combatant Status Review Tribunals [CSRTs]),[164] to determine whether detainees were really enemy combatants. The Republican-controlled Congress then passed the MCA in 2006,[165] which barred federal district courts from hearing any detainee challenges, including those already filed.[166] Detainees were given "limited rights to limited tribunals, in which secret evidence may be used and the verdict [is] rendered by . . . the same military that brings the charges."[167] *Hamdan* opposed this system of abbreviated trials.

The district court granted Salim Ahmed Hamdan's habeas petition and ruled that before a military tribunal could try the petitioner, he must be granted a hearing to determine whether he was, in fact, a prisoner of war under the Geneva Conventions. The Circuit Court of Appeals for the District of Columbia, however, determined that the Geneva Conventions could not be enforced in federal courts, consequently reversing the district court's decision. The circuit court also concluded that because Congress had authorized military tribunals, they were constitutional.[168]

At the heart of the administration's argument was whether the Geneva Conventions applied equally to the prisoners held at Guantanamo. With O'Connor no longer on the bench, Justice Kennedy's vote would be the one to observe. Scalia, Thomas, and the newly confirmed Alito were likely to align themselves with the administration, leaving Justices Souter, Breyer, Stevens, and Ginsburg to side with the plaintiff—Roberts recused himself, because he had already sided with the executive when he heard the case on the D.C. Circuit.[169] At conference, Kennedy joined the four liberals, voting to strike down the administration's policy.

The Court (5–3) rejected the government's use of military tribunals, finding that the tribunals were not authorized by the AUMF in their current form. However, the majority's split on various points created a complicated line of reasoning—Stevens spoke for the majority on most issues and the plurality on other issues.

Stevens held that special military tribunals either must be established by statute or, if created by presidential order, must follow rules and procedures consistent with the UCMJ and the Geneva Conventions. The mere assertion of inherent powers did not grant the president the authority to establish these commissions, Stevens maintained. Consequently, because tribunals were not authorized through statute, the procedures did not provide the detainees with the rights and safeguards they were entitled to. Hamdan had been excluded from certain parts of his trial, because the military tribunal had classified him as an enemy combatant; this exclusion was illegal, Stevens concluded, as it violated the ordinary laws of war.[170] Stevens theorized that even if Hamdan were the most dangerous individual and had the potential to commit "great harm or death to innocent civilians," the executive was still required to "comply with the prevailing rule of law" when trying him.[171] The Court added that the military could prosecute under the UCMJ on one of two conditions: if steps were taken similar to those in a court-martial or if Congress permitted the administration to use entirely different procedures. *Hamdan* was thus a statutory interpretation and not a constitutional decision.[172]

The Court rejected the executive's appeal for being restrained on prudential grounds. It assumed that the AUMF provided the statutory authority for the president's war powers[173] and that "those powers include[d] the authority to convene military commissions in appropriate circumstances,"[174] but "nothing in the text or legislative history of the AUMF even hint[ed] that Congress intended to expand or alter the authorization set forth in Article 21 of the UCMJ."[175] Consequently, no act of Congress could be found to authorize the creation of military commissions; by relying on the Geneva Conventions (Common Article 3), the Court concluded that military commissions were not a "regularly constituted court" but that a court-martial would be.[176]

Stevens stated that the same procedures used to try American soldiers under court-martial were to be used in military commissions unless the administration could show that these procedures were not "practicable." If the administration could demonstrate the impracticability of court-martial, it would "strike a careful balance between uniform procedure and the need to accommodate exigencies that may sometimes arise in *the theatre of war*."[177] The justices concluded that the administration's claim of military necessity was therefore inconclusive.

Stevens maintained that the use of military commissions was premised on the fact that they were needed to "dispense swift justice, often in the form of executive, to illegal belligerents captured on the battlefield." However, the executive had failed "to satisfy the most basic precondition" for its establishment—"military necessity."[178] Kennedy reiterated this point: no exigency, practical need, or military necessity mandated the divergence from normal procedures of providing due process. "Practicable" did not permit nonconformity based on convenience or expediency. Moreover, the structure and procedures of the military commissions violated the UCMJ and the Geneva Conventions,[179] and the rules to protect classified information[180] (exclusion of the accused and the lawyers from proceedings) infringed on one of the "most fundamental protections," the "right to be present," which, the Court concluded, was judicially enforceable.[181]

Stevens's opinion was a more systematic reproach of the administration than the Court had issued two years earlier. *Hamdan* illustrated that it was the sole authority of the Court to set the parameters and define or redefine the path of the president. Essentially, procedures could not be written for the military commissions unilaterally—Congress had to approve them. Nor could the procedures ignore the Geneva Conventions—they had to be in compliance. On this point, however, Stevens did not have a majority for all parts of the Geneva analysis: Stevens and Kennedy differed on the proper role of the Geneva Conventions, which may have left available a potential branching point if future Courts grapple with this question again.

Kennedy's concurrence (joined by Souter, Ginsburg, and Breyer) also raised concerns over separation-of-powers principles (part I): the risks of one branch controlling all elements of a case and how that affects avenues of redress (appeals and review). The Court agreed, and Kennedy concurred, that "regularly constituted courts" could include military commissions, but the executive would need to show "some practical need" to depart from courts-martial.[182] However, "no such need has been demonstrated here."[183]

The Court set aside the so-called jurisdictional limitations of the DTA:[184] "no court, justice, or judge" had the jurisdiction to hear habeas claims from Guantanamo detainees.[185] Congress had enacted the DTA that afforded a set of procedures for reviewing the status of detainees, but the Court found them to be an inadequate and ineffective substitute for habeas. Consequently, Section 7 of the MCA[186] operated as an unconstitutional suspension of the writ. While the commissions were not necessarily categorically prohibited, Breyer reasoned, because the president could return to Congress and ask for the necessary authority,[187] Kennedy maintained that the Court would not address whether the president had the authority to detain these petitioners nor hold that the writ must be issued.

For the dissenters (Scalia, Thomas, and Alito), the Court had no jurisdiction to review or decide whether the executive's power to take appropriate military measures was permissible. The executive was, after all, acting pursuant to congressional authorization. The Court, the dissenters asserted, "has appointed itself the ultimate arbiter of what is quintessentially a policy and military judgment."[188] Siding with the president, the dissenters maintained that Bush had the power to establish military commissions in "exigent and nonexigent circumstances" and that it was not the Court's duty to determine the necessity of those actions. The dissenters reasoned that the Court had a "well-established duty to respect the Executive's judgment in matters of military operations and foreign affairs."[189]

The conflict facing the nation, Thomas pointed out, had been determined by the executive to date to Osama bin Laden's August 1996 "Declaration of Jihad against the Americans,"[190] if not earlier. Thomas's adoption of the executive's description of the conflict, which alleged overt acts in "Afghanistan, Pakistan, Yemen[,] and other countries" taking place from 1996 to 2001, satisfied the temporal and geographic prerequisites for the exercise of law-of-war military-commission jurisdiction.[191] Thomas clearly invoked the spirit of the sole-organ doctrine when he argued that these judgments, which pertained "to the scope of the theater and duration of the present conflict[,] [we]re committed solely to the President in the exercise of his commander-in-chief authority."[192]

Using a departmentalist position, Thomas urged the Court to be governed by the political branch's determination of its own authority when confronted by a particular conflict—a position the Bush administration had long asserted. The Court's decision, Thomas maintained, would impede the president's ability to effectively confront and defeat the enemy and, more importantly, undermine the nation's ability to thwart future attacks. In Thomas's view, exigent circumstances were and should be controlling factors. If the Court had been restrained and found in the president's favor statutorily, it would have reaffirmed the post-1936 doctrinal thread.

The dissenters and those in the majority recognized *Hamdan* as a crucial case, not just because the detainees in Guantanamo were facing the real possibility of execution but because the ruling by a changing Court could redefine the meaning of the Constitution in an age of terror. Recognizing the magnitude of this case, Breyer wrote, "Where, as here, no emergency prevents consultation with Congress, judicial insistence upon that consultation does not weaken our Nation's ability to deal with danger"; instead, "that insistence strengthens the Nation's ability to determine—through democratic means—how best to do so. The Constitution places its faith in those democratic means. Our Court today simply does the same."[193] Here Breyer reminded the administration of the Court's prowess in determining when it would and would not grant broad authority. For the Court, the truncated DTA process was not an adequate substitute for habeas and was therefore an oversight of the surfeit of due-process violations occurring as a result of the CSRTs conducted at Guantanamo. And in recognizing the dangers facing the nation, the Court decides, through democratic means, which measures implemented by the president and/or Congress best served individual and polity principles when combatting exigent circumstances.

Hamdan was not an obvious challenge to presidential power during wartime; rather, *Hamdan* illustrated a branching point from the path established in *Youngstown*. Because the Court, acting as a mediator, required Bush to obtain statutory authorization before taking further action, it altered the constitutional boundaries of presidential authority in terms of Jackson's three-tier schema. Essentially, the Court said that the president did not have the authority to act unless Congress legislated. This determination may have appeared to be at odds with Rehnquist's determination in *Dames* and *Regan*, as the

Court concluded that the president could find tacit authority in congressional silence. However, while *Hamdan* and *Boumediene* found the substitute statutory authority of military commissions to be an unconstitutional suspension of a prisoner's right to habeas corpus, the Court relied on Jackson's counsel.

The Court was compelled to find in favor of individual rights, because the combined wisdom of the executive and the legislature resulted in an unconstitutional act (not much was changed in the rules between *Hamdan* and the procedures requested by Bush): presidential prerogatives were consequently trumped by individual rights, as the Court was unwilling to embrace the administration's assertion of setting aside the law to deal "effectively" with a national crisis. It was imperative that a system of checks and balances be in place to secure effective governance during emergencies, which the Court concluded would not jeopardize the stability of government or the conduct of the war. The Court rejected the view of judicial deference when the president and Congress worked together. If that joint action was unconstitutional, the Court would make that determination.

Fallout from *Hamdan* demonstrated the raw politics of executive power in Congress. In fact, by Bush's second term, his legal team had "systematically locked down a series of advisory opinions and policies that expanded presidential power, freeing the presidency from the burden of obeying statutes and treaties." Appealing to a reservoir of inherent powers, the administration "declared and demonstrated the power to bypass a warrant law, unilaterally create military commission trials, [and] pull out of treaties without consulting Congress."[194] And acting pursuant to the Court's counsel, the president asked Congress for the authorization to create special tribunals, but these commissions would operate under basically the same rules (adding "aggressive interrogation methods") and procedures as those declared unconstitutional in *Hamdan*. Congress acceded to Bush's request by passing the MCA. This request was also a hasty plea for national-security legislation just before a scheduled recess, a recognizable political tactic. The administration had used this strategy to win quick authorization to go to war in Iraq, and Bush used it again in August 2007 when the administration's "preferred version of the Protect America Act" passed both chambers of Congress.[195]

The culmination of these the DTA and the MCA amended the federal statute eradicating habeas jurisdiction for any enemy combatant held by the United States. The Bush administration pressed forward with protecting and expanding presidential power as it attempted to once again change the fundamental institutional balance between the branches. Despite their lame-duck status in late 2007 and the challenges of dealing with Congress when the opposition party held majorities in both chambers, Bush and Cheney were resolved to move forward with their agenda and pressed even harder with their assertion that a reservoir of powers belonged to every president, including Bush.[196]

In 2008, in a pair of consolidated cases, the *Boumediene* Court reaffirmed the rights of Guantanamo detainees to judicial review but added to *Rasul*'s statutory-rights finding that they also had a constitutional right that not even Congress could deny unless habeas corpus was formally suspended. In this way, the *Boumediene* Court formally checked the executive and Congress during wartime.

BOUMEDIENE—A ROBUST REVIEW

In 2002, Bosnian police captured six Algerian natives, including Lakhdar Boumediene. U.S. intelligence officers suspected them of being involved in a plot to attack the U.S. embassy in Bosnia; they were subsequently classified as enemy combatants and moved to Guantanamo. Boumediene's petition for a writ alleged that his constitutional due-process rights had been violated and that his detention violated statutes, treaties, and international law.

The district court, siding with the government, dismissed all claims, arguing that Boumediene had no right to a habeas petition, because he was an alien detained at an overseas military base. The U.S. Court of Appeals for the D.C. Circuit affirmed the ruling, even though the Supreme Court had previously reversed this reasoning in *Rasul*. Boumediene appealed.

Kennedy's majority opinion (5–4) aligned with Boumediene's claim, recognizing this as an exceptional case, given the plaintiff's lengthy imprisonment without a trial. The Court held that the habeas statute extended to noncitizens at Guantanamo, as guaranteed under the Constitution. Furthermore, the MCA represented an unconstitutional suspension of the federal courts' jurisdiction[197] to hear habeas applications from detainees who had been labeled as "enemy combatants" by the administration.[198] For Kennedy, "the laws and Constitution are designed to survive, and remain in force, in extraordinary times. Liberty and security can be reconciled; and in our system they are reconciled within the framework of the law."[199] However, it was the Court's duty to balance liberty and security.

While accepting the unique practice of imprisoning noncitizens at Guantanamo without trial, the Court concluded that no precedent or historical case existed that clearly fit the present situation. As such, the Court turned to what it considered to be the fundamental principle at the heart of a habeas lawsuit: whether the courts should act as a check on the perceived abuse of executive power. The Court noted that even from "an early date, it was understood [that] the King, too, was subject to the law."[200]

In short, Kennedy rejected the government's argument comparing the habeas restriction under the MCA to those affected by the Antiterrorism and Effective Death Penalty Act (AEDPA) of 1996,[201] which was ruled constitutional after the Constitution's Suspension Clause (Article I, Section 9, Clause 2) was challenged. The Court explained that the AEDPA's restrictions on habeas review were not a complete suspension of the writ but simply procedural limitations—for example, limiting the number of successive habeas petitions a prisoner can file or mandating a one-year time limit for the filing of federal habeas review that begins when the prisoner's judgment and sentence become final. The main distinction between the MCA and AEDPA, the Court went on to explain, was that the AEDPA applied in practice to those prisoners serving sentences after having been tried in open court and whose sentences had been upheld on direct appeal, whereas the MCA suspended the application of the writ to those detainees whose guilt had not yet been legally determined.[202]

From the outset, Kennedy emphasized, the Suspension Clause was designed by the Founders to "protect against the cyclical abuses of the writ" by either the executive and/or Congress. "Freedom from unlawful restraint," the Court emphasized, was a "fundamental precept of liberty." Central to this protection, then, was the Court's duty and indeed authority to question and hold accountable either branch that attempted to violate this constitutional safeguard. And when its institutional integrity was challenged, the Court carefully determined whose rights to favor: the executive's extralegal rights or an individual's fundamental guarantees. Adopting a practical approach, the Court examined the extraterritorial application of the Constitution to those detained at Guantanamo. It was highly critical of Congress and the president for their attempt to proclaim that because Guantanamo Bay was outside the sovereign territory, the Constitution did not apply to those being detained, which in turn disavowed judicial oversight—a point to which the Court was unwilling to adhere.

Criticizing the establishment of the CSRTs, Kennedy argued that they were "inadequate."[203] The plurality reasoned that these tribunals gave the political branches the power to "switch the [C]onstitution on or off" and would therefore "lead to a regime in which they, not this court," would "say what the law is."[204] This was a sharp reproach to the administration's assertion that it alone could offer an alternative constitutional understanding of executive powers. Clearly the Court would not allow its institutional integrity to be challenged, for it had an obligation to define constitutional jurisprudence.

Several factors merited the application of the Suspension Clause, the plurality concluded. First and foremost, the petitioners, who were noncitizens, disputed their status as "enemy combatants," as determined by CSRTs in a prejudicial proceeding. Second, the United States had exclusive jurisdiction and control over Guantanamo Bay. And last, there were no credible arguments that indicated habeas proceedings would obstruct any military mission as a result. So, effectively, governance during wartime would not be impeded. The Court thus determined that individuals held at Guantanamo had the right under the Suspension Clause to challenge their detention. The Court's reasoning provided the constitutional space for those individuals in a similar position to challenge their detentions in the future. As such, the Court not only sided with the rights of the accused but also refused to have its institutional authority challenged by either of the other two branches.

Procedurally, the majority concluded that DTA review was not an adequate substitute for a habeas petition. The Court reasoned that any habeas proceeding and therefore any substitute, such as the DTA, must provide the petitioner an effective way in which to correct his or her detention. In this instance, the petitioner needed to be able to challenge the government's evidence, detention, and label of enemy combatant.

Kennedy suggested that for habeas or even its substitute to work effectively, a proper remedy must be in place, and the executive (and for that matter, Congress) could not remove the federal courts from that process: the judiciary must be allowed to review executive decision making. The Court again counseled the political branches of their possible remedies; the Court used to conduct "habeas proceedings must have the means to correct errors that occurred during the CSRT proceedings," which would include "some authority to assess the sufficiency of the Government's evidence against the detainee." In addition, this Court must also have the "authority to admit and consider relevant exculpatory evidence that was not introduced during the earlier proceeding." Finally, Kennedy asserted, "when the judicial power to issue habeas corpus is properly invoked[,] the judicial officer" must have the authority with respect to relevant law and the facts to develop and issue the necessary orders for relief, which would include the release of a prisoner.[205]

Kennedy's pragmatism was evident. He took a practical approach to the case and firmly depoliticized the legal questions raised. The majority opinion illustrated the Court's unwavering resolve that it, and not the political branches, defined constitutional jurisprudence, which redefined the metes and bounds of the executive. The Court does not merely follow politics, as so many critics of law and courts have asserted. What is more, it is the Court's duty to redefine Congress's role, if the justices agree there has been a constitutional violation. In these ways, it is evident that the Court continues to act as an agent of change.

The dissenters, on the other hand, defended the administration's position, asserting that the prisoners were not entitled to the writ and that the rights they were entitled to were fulfilled by the very mechanism that Congress had authorized in the DTA. In fact, Roberts's[206] dissent emphasized that Congress had devised a system that protected the rights of detainees, and the Court therefore had no authority to review this case.

The focal point for Roberts was whether the DTA afforded the petitioners an adequate substitution for habeas protections, and in his view, it did. In fact, he maintained that the government had devised a deliberate and careful system of procedures for those detained in the ongoing military conflict.[207] Consequently, he argued, the Court was "strik[ing] down as inadequate the most generous set of procedural protections ever afforded aliens detained by this country as enemy combatants."[208] So detainees' right to the Suspension Clause, Roberts concluded, was moot. Even if the detainees had that entitlement, Roberts asserted, their rights were not being violated.[209]

For Roberts, the Court not only rejected the procedures; more importantly, it failed to "say what due process rights the detainees possess" and how "the statute fails to vindicate those rights."[210] Roberts accused the Court of assuming responsibility for "sensitive foreign policy and national security decisions from the elected branches to the Federal Judiciary," an exercise that the administration, on several occasions, had asserted *was* the responsibility of only the elected branches.[211] A case in point was designating detainees as enemy combatants, which came only after "multiple levels of review by military officers and officials of the Department of Defense."[212] As such, drawing on Jackson's *Youngstown* concurrence, Roberts determined that because the president and Congress had worked together, the executive's power was at its zenith, and the government's provision of a system of procedures should have allowed the Court to find in favor of the weightier concerns of national security.

Hamdi held that detainees were constitutionally guaranteed only *basic* procedural rights, and securing those rights could not come, Roberts reminded the Court, at the expense of burdening the executive during ongoing military conflict.[213] In other words, the *Hamdi* precedent was "consistent with the Government's interest in avoiding 'a futile search for evidence' that might burden warmaking responsibilities."[214] Consistent with Bush's counterterrorism measures, Roberts echoed the administration's framing that this war must be left in the hands of the executive, because he alone could balance the security of the American people with a war waged under unique circumstances against an enemy without boundaries.

Evaluating external constraints, Scalia's dissent used "rather apocalyptic terms"[215] to recall how "the enemy brought the battle" to the United States, "killing 2,749 at the twin towers," and now the military was fighting "against the enemy in Afghanistan and Iraq. Last week, 13 of our countrymen in arms were killed."[216] Scalia added that the "disastrous consequences" of the Court's opinion would no doubt lead to "more Americans [being] killed. . . . [T]he

Nation will live to regret what the Court has done today."[217] Scalia was obviously concerned about the ramifications of placing individual rights above national security, but the plurality believed that extending rights to the individuals detained would not derail military measures; national security would not be threatened.

The detainee cases could not be ascribed to judicial hostility to the administration. *Rasul*, *Hamdi*, and *Padilla* were all cases decided by the Rehnquist Court, which was the same Court that put Bush in office (*Bush v. Gore* [2000]).[218] And then the Roberts Court, which included two Bush appointees (Roberts and Alito), decided *Hamdan* and *Boumediene*. Both Courts were conservative, and conservatives generally endorse presidential prerogatives—but neither Court blindly followed this path. Rather, they found, on procedural grounds, in favor of civil liberties. These rulings were not, however, a blanket rejection of inherent executive power. Given the lack of deference, something other than collaboration with the political regime in place, the policy preferences of the justices, or even the necessity of an "energetic" president[219] during wartime caused the Court to rule as it did. It balanced the legal norms with the external political and social factors and ultimately censured the president and Congress quite severely on statutory terms that left intact the executive's constitutional power and authority (by not ruling against inherent powers); however, this was the first time the Court had seriously questioned the actions of the executive as the president implemented policies to safeguard the nation. The Court carefully negotiated this path as it strategically[220] decided each case by carefully choosing the questions it wanted to resolve.[221]

THE COURT CHALLENGES PRESIDENTIAL ASCENDENCY

On the one hand, military exigencies have afforded executives great latitude, demanding and even compelling Congress to grant extra powers or requests to set aside laws to effectively deal with the emergencies. On the other hand, war has brought with it political mobilization that has given groups in Congress the opportunity to forge political alliances that have empowered them to challenge the administration and attempt to recover some of their powers.[222] The significance of this political recourse—an important mechanism—has not always been to keep presidents in check, however. The modern president has built institutions and set in place procedures that insulate presidential decision making in wartime, which does not depend on popular mobilization.

At the onset of military exigencies, Congress and the public at large have thus given presidents enormous freedom to conduct foreign affairs and implement security measures. In fact, scholars have condemned Congress for rescinding its constitutional responsibility to serve as a check on the executive branch during national emergencies and wartime.[223] But how courts define the appropriate balance between security and liberty has the potential effect of constraining the executive. Adjudicating competing concerns over the security of the nation and the liberty of the individual presents a more significant challenge for the courts than simply resolving domestic-policy disputes. Many times, courts examine executive decision making while legislative involvement remains at the sidelines—acquiescing its constitutional responsibility—so the president acts alone when implementing measures to secure the nation from future attacks. Bush's war on terror, however, presented a different set of challenges for the Supreme Court, and the judiciary utilized a mutual construction process as it evaluated the intersection of legal and political time.

The war on terror led to national-security powers that unavoidably encroached on domestic issues with the USA PATRIOT Act and the newly formed, multifaceted Department of Homeland Security. This war has been a long, drawn-out effort that has become a seemingly permanent part of Americans' political reality, just as the Cold War did. As the president's ever-expanding powers take on greater domestic prominence, the line between foreign and domestic policy becomes blurred, which leads to direct confrontations of a president's monopoly over foreign policy making—as we saw with the steel-seizure case.

The Supreme Court is supposed to be impervious to public opinion and popular mobilization and be politically isolated from the executive, allowing it to defend its prerogatives from presidential incursion. However, the Court's judicial tilt toward the executive suggests that the judiciary often defers to the president, because presidential exercises of power frequently generate change in the world that the federal judiciary feels powerless to invalidate.[224] When it comes to decision making by the executive under exigent circumstances, the federal courts are tolerant, but they have not granted unfettered discretion. And when President Bush claimed that the Court lacked the power of review, an institutional power play between the judiciary and the executive was borne out, which was felt by the administration. As Yoo maintains, *Hamdi* and *Rasul* were "an unprecedented formal and functional intrusion by the federal courts into the executive's traditional powers" that will take the courts "far beyond their normal areas of expertise."[225] The Court took umbrage to the claim that it lacked the competence to evaluate the legality of military tribunals.

When the Court is challenged on the supremacy over constitutional interpretation, it confronts the primary commitments of the majority coalition and (re)establishes its institutional legitimacy. The detainee cases therefore demonstrated that the Court was not an institution willing to back down in the face of a president attempting to commandeer the executive role in defining constitutional jurisprudence. While typical stay-the-course presidents champion the declarations of judicial supremacy, because their long-term political interests are aligned, the transformational leadership of the Bush presidency actually faced an uncooperative affiliated Court.

Whittington's examination of judicial supremacy demonstrates that the interests of an affiliated president find favor in the Court, but Bush attempted to exploit the judiciary in a way that redefined a faithful supporter of an inherited regime. It quickly became clear that the Bush administration made a robust challenge to judicial supremacy as he proclaimed the sole responsibility to manage the nation's foreign affairs following the September 11 attacks. By accepting the Court's constitutional judgments, Bush, an affiliated president, undermined his presidential authority in this area. Bush therefore went beyond Skowronek's definition—a second-order interpreter pursues incremental change to the established principles he inherits—and Whittington's theory of the presidential-court relationship as he moved from using the courts to manage his coalition by blurring the lines of accountability[226] to completely rejecting judicial supremacy. In each of the detainee cases, Bush advanced an all-encompassing stance of his interpretive authority as he attempted to undermine the Court's authority to interpret the Constitution. This stance was in harmony with Skowronek's reconstructive president in political time, but this classification would be incomplete without a discussion of international affairs. Party politics is not a closed system. As the lines between domestic and foreign affairs are muddied, particularly in light of the domestic-security state, our conception of political time must necessarily include a wholesale discussion of foreign affairs and a realization of the proper role of the Court. The events of September 11 have influenced U.S. law and institutions,[227] and the Court has been an integral player in that evolution.

The detainee cases reflected the jurisprudential effect of a more combative judicial review process. The Court scrutinized presidential and congressional actions during a time when national security was heightened,[228] which resulted in severely limiting or depriving rights principles altogether. In response, the Court upheld the rights of those detained over the executive's claim to inherent, extralegal powers. The Court provided a real critique of the policy measures implemented by the executive and Congress. It outwardly rejected the view that judicial deference to presidential action was to be provided when the president and Congress united. In terms of Jackson's schema, when both institutions (executive and legislature) violate constitutional guarantees, the Court will not approve of such action. Practicalities alone do not govern the Court's actions on issues of presidential war making.

Even though it rebuked presidential prerogatives statutorily, these decisions did not adequately address the core war-making powers of the president.[229]

Traditionally the balance of power returns to the status quo at the conclusion of a war, thus revering the Bill of Rights and respecting the basic constitutional principles. But *Rasul, Hamdi*, in part *Padilla, Hamdan*, and *Boumediene* presented us with a new understanding of the politics and constitutional jurisprudence of America at war.

The detainee cases reflected the Court's balancing the suspension of individual rights with the president's authority to effectively conduct the war. The constitutional space within which the Court operates afforded the judiciary with the institutional capacity to define the province of the executive when implementing its foreign-policy measures. As the Court evaluated each case in light of the external factors and within the confines of internal legal norms, it determined to what degree the executive could usurp authority, deny individual rights, and assert departmentalism.

The Supreme Court posed the greatest challenge yet to the executive's constitutional position when claiming the unilateral authority to act in wartime as it decided the detainee cases. It came to a critical juncture and provided a branching point to the constitutional order established in *Curtiss-Wright*. Essentially, when the executive reaches too far, the judiciary will rein in presidential prerogatives. The Court is therefore instrumental in the constitutional and political development of the executive and provides the most telling statement of how far the president's reach might extend when individual rights have been violated.

Despite these pronouncements by the Supreme Court, headway appeared sluggish "to the point of being imperceptible." In fact, "the D.C. Circuit Court threatened to bring [the process] entirely to a standstill."[230] The circuit court "had not proved a friendly venue for Guantanamo prisoners, commonly rejecting habeas appeals." But by 2012, the circuit court had thrown out Hamdan's conviction, and by mid-2015, "four of the eight convictions had been overturned" as well.[231] Even with these executive setbacks, the Court remained in a prominent institutional position. In fact, the Court's *Zivotofsky* decision (2015)—see the Conclusion—would illustrate its capacity to once again redefine presidential prerogatives as it returned to the constitutional order established in 1936.

CONCLUSION

*Constitutional Change Instigated
outside the Legalized Constitution*

Presidents argue that the Constitution vests in them the exclusive plenary authority to conduct the nation's international affairs. However, these claims draw from the revisionist constitutional jurisprudence of 1936 (*Curtiss-Wright*). The executive is a key actor but not the only participant. The Supreme Court itself is a crucial player in contending and instituting its own interpretive authority, and the legislature aids in generating the strategic milieu in which the executive and the judiciary contend their own assertions for authority. In foreign affairs, the Court's constitutional choices not only legalize the construction and stabilization of the asserted political order[1] but also can shape the political development of the two corresponding branches.

The Court's interpretative review forever alters the jurisprudential framework in which constitutional decisions by its justices take place, which provides for the malleability of laws and development over time. The Court is not simply a reactionary adversary of enlarging national powers; rather, it is an architect of expanding and contracting such authority. As the Court responds to changing circumstances that produce innovative legal questions, it does so without altering the essential context of its own governing principles or the formal process of judicial review. Judicial independence means that the "Court doesn't exist outside of political time, but rather both helps determine political time and occupies a position within it."[2] In foreign affairs, the Court establishes important precedents for future legal cases as well as constrains policy options and shapes future executive legal disputes. Its role in this developmental narrative is consistent and coherent. This constitutional transformation does not have to mean that democracy, generally speaking, is slipping. The Court does not discount the long-term and wide-ranging implications of its decisions. While the Founders' vision of checks and balances to prevent a concentration of power is being transformed, even with the expanding concept of presidential conduct in international discourse and war making, the Court checks the commander-in-chief's assertion of ultimate power. The extent of executive authority is therefore subject to judicial action.

A significant and fluid institutional relationship exists between the executive and the Supreme Court. Prior to 1936, the Court favored American foreign policy established by democratic debate over the interests and the responsibilities of the Republic. When balancing competing claims, the Court advanced a strong legislature and limited the scope and parameters of the dual partnership between Congress and the executive, which undermined presidential unilateralism. Over time, a collective disaffinity with republican ideals of shared powers triggered the Court into changing the legalized Constitution.

After 1936, the pragmatic realities and the relative authority of the executive vis-à-vis Congress to conduct international discourse fundamentally shifted. The Court's legal reformulation of early judicial decision making instituted a new constitutional order when it decided *Curtiss-Wright*. It was neither unintentional nor insignificant that the *Curtiss-Wright* Court and its progeny reinterpreted the Constitution as it evaluated which branch should bear ultimate responsibility for the nation's foreign policy. Over developmental time, the Court delineated the constitutional and political space that allowed presidents to have the authority and the legislature to have the power to cooperate in a way that met the practical necessity of handling the ever-intensifying realm of international relations. The Court's independence and authority to interpret the Constitution ultimately transformed power and authority, politics and history as it continued to balance rights and national security in high-stakes cases that were directly related to foreign affairs and war making.

Many claim that exceptional times demand exceptional measures and that giving a defendant standard constitutional rights during a national threat puts the nation at unacceptable risk. This argument has enjoyed widespread support at times, but it is the Court's responsibility to determine when heightened national security demands the restriction of rights. Because "rights-oriented and process-oriented dimensions seem to operate in different domains and at different times, and often suggest different outcomes,"[3] the Court strikes this balance by evaluating external factors in line with internal norms. At times, it places institutional checks on the democratic branches, which can narrow or broaden individual rights vis-à-vis polity principles. The judiciary thus redirects the sphere of politics when it decides that national-security goals violate claims of power and authority *and* basic constitutional rights. The executive's reading of the office's own constitutional powers and authority are ultimately bounded by the Court's determination of those powers. Democratic politics is malleable in the conduct of foreign affairs as it embraces the Court as an agent of change. As such, the Court alters the constitutional text and structure over developmental time by instituting a reservoir of inherent presidential powers that it checks.

Judicial decision making that utilizes cases that are nonlinear but contextually relevant produces patterns of regime building, feedback loops, and a long-term effect on presidential politics and constitutional jurisprudence. Contrary to Stephen Skowronek's cyclical theory, presidents are not bound by their positions in the regime, whether it is the reconstructive leadership of Franklin D. Roosevelt (FDR; who faced a hold-over Supreme Court and extreme external forces) or Ronald Reagan (who confronted the collapse of a regime and precarious foreign relations), the disjunctive leadership style of Jimmy Carter (who commandeered a strategic response to a delicate hostage crisis), the affiliated (although questionably reconstructive at times) leadership of George W. Bush (who led an unprecedented global war on terror), or the preemptive governance of Harry Truman (an affiliated leader who faced a distinct divisive Congress). Foreign-affairs policy making disrupts the flow of political time when the Court decides these cases in legal time. As a result of the Court's supplying the legal foundation for the ensuing political debate, presidents are not constrained by the institutional context of their leadership efforts based on their predecessors.

The developmental narrative, as pronounced by the Court, dictates the executive's capacity to command a unilateral position in formulating international affairs. Consequently, there is no waning of political time, as Skowronek suggests, because the Court has ushered in an expanded role for the president. This interpretative turn provides a new notion of constitutional dexterity, which has had considerable practical ramifications on the nation's foreign policy. As justices respond to changing external factors, the Constitution changes, too. The Constitution is thus an adaptive document; judges substantively change its meaning to reflect the context and values of the times.

Even though the executive has been a strong opponent to the interpretive authority of the judiciary, in international affairs, it is important to recognize that the institutional positioning of the executive within the American constitutional system requires recontextualizing constitutional politics. During times of reconstructive politics, the Court resolves significant questions. And in times of normal politics, the Court remains steadfast in clarifying and extending those values and obligations, "independently but often in dialogue with other government officials."[4] Consequently, the Court aids in enunciating the "tenets of the dominant regime."[5] But it forges its own path in international discourse that can thwart and exasperate political leaders as it carefully balances the dominant regime's obligations with regard to individual rights against the backdrop of national-security concerns. When the Court aids the executive in accomplishing presidential leadership tasks, the judiciary in effect shares in the president's agenda while at the same time decreasing the pressures on the administration's alliances. Keith Whittington attributes this help to affiliated presidents, but in making foreign policy, the Court can be "an alternative policymaking resource" for any kind of president in political time to "secure [the president's] constitutional commitments."[6]

American national security and foreign affairs have profound legal and policy implications. For example, Democrats generally and the Barack Obama administration specifically depicted the Republican "[George W. Bush] lawyers as having illegitimately signed off on extreme and implausible legal pronouncements in order to facilitate unwise and illegal actions," such as torturing and wiretapping without warrants.[7] The Bush administration was unconcerned with what the legislature said the rules should be, because the executive could devise his own.[8] This kind of blanket rejection of congressional power sharing begs the fundamental question of what it means to obey the rule of law.

As new legal questions arise, the executive branch vies for the privilege of directing American foreign policy. As Charlie Savage contends, "[T]he laws of war were designed for traditional contests between well-organized nation-state armies clashing on literal battlefields, or for civil wars within a single country." Today, these same laws "are being applied to an armed conflict against a transnational, loose-knit network of zealots who move from country to country, and which lacks a leader who can sign a peace treaty."[9] As such, "interpreting and applying national security law to such turbulent and rapidly changing conditions has created an unending series of novel dilemmas."[10] For Edward Corwin, the Constitution sets up a "struggle for power in this field" that is inevitable[11] in more contemporary times.[12] "Conflicts over authority," Corwin maintains, "are seldom resolvable by resort to constitutional law. . . . Nor do the applicable principles of constitutional law help much in resolving such a quarrel."[13] However, the Supreme Court's response to this tension between the branches and the "unending series of novel dilemmas" provides workable solutions for resolving future contestations. Presidents must persuade the voters that their interpretations of the Constitution are better than the divergent positions of the Court, and they must also discard judicial supremacy. The Court need only defend its prerogatives against presidential intrusion, while at the same time being unyielding on its substantive precedents. Although precedents are complicated, sometimes the Court breaks from the established path, as it did in 1936. Precedent is not fixed and therefore not a controlling factor.

The theory of path dependence is thus challenged when the Court is not read into the discussion. When the Court asserts judicial supremacy in foreign-affairs cases, beginning with the establishment of the sole-organ doctrine (*Curtiss-Wright*), it transforms future cases in which federalism, separation-of-powers issues, and individual rights are complicated. Switching costs are minimized, because the Court has the institutional latitude to extract meaning from broad and indeterminate constitutional principles through glosses, which lead to equivalent legal principles. The court system has therefore reduced decisional transaction expenditures more than legislatures or executives, which can shield an executive and Congress by removing volatile disputes from the political realm completely.[14] Consequently, change is possible, despite Paul Pierson's contentions that positive feedback occurs along a path (path dependence). As institutions and political forces come into conflict (intercurrence),[15] the Court's determinations of the extent of executive hegemony when legal and political time intersect provide branching points or a complete change in the path. This juncture creates the constitutional space for the Court to assess and decide whether it will secure the benefits of executive energy and unity of purpose, while at the same time evaluate legislative action (e.g., passage of legislation) with the competing claims of individual rights in light of effectively dealing with exigent circumstances.

In deciding constitutional questions, judges act in a similar way to political actors who attempt to resolve questions of public policy. Just like those actors, "judges have ideological agendas and are mindful of their constituents, and like those actors, their ideological inclinations and their awareness of constituent pressures affect their decision-making."[16] These "political inclinations and goals of judges have a decisive effect on constitutional law" and American political development, because the collective Court "rejects[] as antiquated or misguided" (as the *Curtiss-Wright* Court did) any path that no longer meets the current demands of exigent circumstances. As such, judges, as constitutional interpreters and agents of change, must be considered simultaneously with the authority of the Constitution's text and "the authority of those [individuals] given the power to interpret it."[17] And changing external factors necessitate judicial monitoring.

Judges do not simply recite and follow the imperatives of the Constitution's text. Rather, judges wield political power as they modify and change developmental paths. In evaluating individual rights alongside polity principles, the Court takes judicial notice of endogenous and exogenous factors when reaching decisions, which naturally changes constitutional foreign-affairs jurisprudence. The meaning of the Constitution is therefore "synonymous with the current interpretations of its provisions by judges, and those interpretations are affected by political events and political pressures."[18]

In short, justices utilize their institutional position to carefully mold their writings to serve their contemporaneous legal purposes of ruling in a current situation, while at the same time serve their political purposes of redefining and, at times, enlarging the scope and direction of presidential powers. And because the line that separates policy and politics from law has grown indistinct, the Court is at the forefront of determining the province of the executive in international discourse and war making over developmental time.

National-security legal policy occupies a rather precarious place between what *should* be done and what *can* be done. Interagency legal debates provide policy makers with a set of parameters to aid in their decision making, but in practice if lawyers offer the legal space to take some other contested action that might reduce the risk of an attack, policy makers will find it difficult not to heed their counsel. As a result, the legal debate can be a locum for the policy debate. The Court is inherently intertwined with the political system,[19] so it is not a simple case of merely interpreting the Constitution by discerning existing constitutional principles and applying them to new cases. Rather, the Court revises and reconstitutes constitutional jurisprudence.

The Court's reading of the Constitution thus requires judges to evaluate policy controversies as political disputes (by examining what is prudent for the nation) and at the same time address how those decisions have legal resolutions. A case in point: The Obama administration inherited from the Bush presidency "a system that used the law to hunt for two types of messages: those linked to terrorists and those linked to foreign governments." Consequently, the Obama administration sought to circumvent "judges in the regular judicial system from scrutinizing the [Foreign Intelligence Surveillance] Act [FISA]," while simultaneously taking measures to drastically increase "warrantless surveillance under that law."[20] In gaining the FISA Court's approval, the Justice Department under Obama began "tracking people suspected of trafficking in biological, chemical, or nuclear weapons."[21] The floodgates were opened as other expansions followed.[22] In October 2009, the Obama administration again succeeded in winning the "FISA Court's approval for the FBI to keep and use its own copy of certain raw messages collected under the FISA Amendments Act." Two years later, the administration again "won a further loosening of the rules: NSA [National Security Agency] and CIA [Central Intelligence Agency] analysts [could] search for Americans' incidentally collected messages." And while "those analysts had to have a 'foreign intelligence' purpose when conducting that search," it was essentially considered a backdoor search.[23]

Even though presidents appear to win substantial ground in the courts, the Supreme Court does not merely sanction claims of unilateral executive decision making. Rather, it determines on pragmatic grounds if and when national-security legal policy and war making supersede individual rights and polity principles. Sensitivity to the president's authority to use executive power effectively does not mean granting unconstrained executive power in every case.

Over developmental time, the Court has strategically adopted the vague language of executive power established in *Curtiss-Wright*. This adoption has altered the Court's doctrinal posture by replacing realism with formalism. The *Curtiss-Wright* Court provided a well-defined doctrinal thread that provided institutional and moral support for the national executive in ominous and deeply troubled times. On its face, *Curtiss-Wright* was read as a separation-of-powers case, but over time, it has been read for the proposition that in the formulation of foreign affairs, executive power is not just plenary but also exclusive. The Court has therefore played a significant role in apportioning war powers under the constitutional separation of powers instead of merely acceding to the government in general and to the executive specifically.

Relying on *Curtiss-Wright*, subsequent courts have established plenary executive control of foreign relations. *Belmont* (1937), in the midst of a constitutional revolution, illustrated Justice George Sutherland's "determination to deconstitutionalize foreign affairs jurisprudence"[24] as it reaffirmed the new constitutional order. The impact of this decision brought to light the first signs of concern for the breadth of Sutherland's revisionist position.[25] Justice Harlan Stone, for example, wrote a separate concurring opinion in which he distanced himself from Sutherland's conclusion, believing that the majority was wrong in drawing the conclusion that in "all international negotiations and compacts . . . the state of New York does not exist."[26] But by the time *Pink* (1942) was decided, Sutherland's reformed notion of executive discretion had become conventional wisdom, and the Court's orthodox constitutional foreign-affairs jurisprudence has evolved ever since.

When we read the Court into foreign-affairs policy making, our current understanding of the developmental narratives of the executive and judicial branches are complicated: legal and political regimes do not map quite as crudely as studies have suggested.[27] While previous studies assert that the Court is marginalized and remains largely passive, in foreign-affairs jurisprudence, the Court is institutionally unconstrained to alter the developmental paths of the executive and Congress. Judicial supremacy in this area provides a continuous and constitutive dynamic relationship between the judiciary and the political branches of government, which yields to successive presidents the legal positioning to advance broad claims.

CHALLENGES TO THE CONSTRAINED
COURT THEORY

Traces of inherent power have emerged over time.[28] Constitutionally endorsed executive agreements with foreign states along with the suggestion of "'inherent' national foreign affairs powers in the Chinese Exclusion Case (1889) and the Insular Cases (1901) resulted in a growing perception" of inherent power. However, constitutional foreign-affairs jurisprudence was twofold. On the one hand, "it was constitutional, governed by the same boundaries, categories, and judicial" deciphering "of enumerated and reserved powers that existed in the domestic arena." And "on the other hand, it was 'international,' [as it] concerned . . . the growing role of the U.S. as a sovereign nation, participating in world affairs and operating within a body of international law."[29]

Discrete authority was not ushered in until the Court's 1936 broad pronouncements of inherent power and its continued support for plenary and exclusive power. But even with these broad pronouncements, presidential prerogatives have remained subject to judicial limitations. In fact, the Court does not employ an exclusionary rule whereby it reads the Constitution in light of foreign affairs to exclude Congress entirely. Congress may enact legislation that backs or empowers the executive to carry out the president's foreign-affairs agenda more effectively. This so-called fast-track legislation makes it easier for the administration to implement the executive's power to protect the nation. Moreover, when the Court balances policy principles with individual rights as it weighs foreign-affairs concerns, it may favor presidential decision making, which might then undermine constitutionally protected individual rights. Alternatively, the Court might conclude that the executive has no independent authority to make law. In the domestic sense, the Court has decided that governmental policies that regulate, prohibit, or punish private behavior must originate from legislation or treaty (*Youngstown*). And in the war on terror, the Bush administration could not suspend basic constitutional rights.

Scholars asserting that presidents usurp power and that the Court merely grants superior authority in foreign affairs are fundamentally challenged here. Despite Justice William Douglas's (1952) avowal that the Court could not "expand Article II of the Constitution" by "rewriting it to suit the political conveniences of the present emergency,"[30] *Curtiss-Wright* marked the first step toward the methodical legal entrenchment of the executive's acting unilaterally in formulating foreign policy. This decision exhibited the Court's creativity in its interpretation of the Constitution.

In many ways, *Curtiss-Wright* "marked the end of an era." Sutherland's theory was a radically more liberal approach[31] to his interpretation of federal foreign-affairs powers from his Columbia lectures. Gaining significant momentum with successive judicial decisions, the Court ushered in an expanded role for the executive. This claim of authority has had a distinct judicial conjecture in foreign-relations jurisprudence, which is the most visible example of a constitutional revolution. As a number of elements were coalescing, *Curtiss-Wright* set a new precedent for how the Court (re)defined presidential authority and how it regarded the legislature as a secondary institution to that of the executive.

Extraconstitutional arguments offered by those supporting a powerful executive have a sturdy legal foundation stemming from *Curtiss-Wright* to support such claims. The extraordinary powers of the president have been consolidated to the point where limits are perceived as evaporating. This trend has exalted presidential power far beyond the constitutional blueprint advocated by the Court prior to 1936 to enter into the realm of unilateral executive dominance with the new constitutional order instituted by the Court. Judicial decisions have not always invoked *Curtiss-Wright*, but the spirit of Sutherland's sole-organ doctrine has been infused with the techniques invoked by the Court.[32] Even with the 2015 *Zivotofsky* ruling, the spirit of *Curtiss-Wright* remained in place because of its malleability to current situations.

It was not until *Hamdan* (2006) that the Court admonished (but not in formal legal terms) the legislative branch to be a more active participant in the formulation of national-security policy making. Even though the theater of war can be an expanding notion, it was clear that the Court would not allow the commander-in-chief to have unfettered and unreviewable power.[33] Consequently, the Court has become the definitive overseer of executive foreign-policy decisions and the extent of legislative involvement, which is a revisionist undertaking.

Obama's utilization of unbridled unilateral powers claimed by so many presidents[34] before him faced the Court head on. In contrast to its response to Bush, the *Zivotofsky* Court was hospitable to Obama's[35] unilateral claim to the power of recognition. It determined that executive authority trumped an individual's claim to his or her birthplace. The Court appeared to have abandoned the sole-organ doctrine, but it actually fashioned a new standard that will allow future Courts to exalt executive power above Congress in this area.

Even though Justice Anthony Kennedy's majority opinion noted that the Court "declines to acknowledge the unbounded power" that the *Curtiss-Wright* case asserted, he left "the sole power to negotiate treaties"[36] in the hands of the executive. This assertion drew on *Curtiss-Wright*'s holding that "the Senate cannot intrude; and Congress is powerless to invade." The *Zivotofsky* Court added that "the Executive had authority to speak as the sole organ of this government,"[37] which was a direct quote from the *Curtiss-Wright* ruling that the current Court was purportedly denouncing. Consequently, *Zivotofsky* left the path open to future claims of unilateral executive powers. At the hands of the judiciary, presidential ascendancy has thus remained intact.[38]

The relevance of *Curtiss-Wright* has been seen in its evolution as precedent over developmental time. *Curtiss-Wright* has been a lynchpin or cornerstone to many of the executive branch's subsequent claims of the power[39] to act without congressional authorization in the conduct of international affairs. And as this revisionist constitutional jurisprudence becomes embedded in future presidential claims of broad discretionary power,[40] judges will wield political power as they remain steadfast in adapting the Constitution to changing times; it is a reinterpretation that belongs squarely within their domain.

BALANCING INDIVIDUAL RIGHTS CLAIMS WITH NATIONAL SECURITY CONCERNS

The employment of judicial review is said to pose fundamental concerns in a representative democracy, as countermajoritarianism is said to thwart the will of the people as active courts articulate innovative and often contentious constitutional interpretations. Judicial supremacy does solicit normative concerns, but the Court's articulation of constitutional jurisprudence is in response to the "broader political and constitutional regime, the broader outlines of which have been established by political actors."[41] In foreign policy making, the executive is at the forefront of constitutional leadership as the president attempts to pronounce a constitutional vision that challenges the Court's reading of the Constitution. Presidents, in general, maintain that they are committed to the original constitutional order, so when their interpretations are challenged, they assert the authority to settle political disagreements. In resolving these divided political disputes, the president sometimes makes broad claims that place the executive branch outside the rule of law. Consequently, the Court becomes more prominent as it intervenes. As principled interpreters, members of the judiciary harvest the authority from those opposed to address the ambiguous prerogatives and, at times, the apathy of the executive to enunciate and maintain the pledges of the regime.[42]

Even in the context of normal politics, the Supreme Court is necessary. The judiciary stands as a check on institutions that attempt to impose their view of the Constitution on the people at large, which is particularly relevant when the people are the ones subjected to that interpretation. As such, the Court's greatest strength may be in acting as a countermajoritarian institution as it imposes its will in determining a balance between individual and polity principles. The Court's autonomy and authority in interpreting constitutional meaning is paramount to defining constitutional flexibility to changing times.

The Constitution gives no universal guidance to a changing world. As such, when the Court evaluates foreign-affairs cases, it constitutionally weighs competing claims: individual rights vis-à-vis the weighty concerns of national security. What might have been regarded as adequate emergency gauges in the past—assessed against normal situations—may not be considered adequate for the present crises. As the nature of crises evolves over time, the Court reevaluates its constitutional foreign-affairs jurisprudence as it rebalances geopolitical concerns with government action and subversion of civil rights and liberties. To understand the Court's authority in these cases, it is important to contextualize the Court's decisions by analyzing the historical context within which cases are appealed. Equally central to understanding judicial decision making are the political maneuverings of key political actors. Contextualizing in this way creates the political space in which the Court takes judicial notice of external forces when it assesses competing rights claims.

For example, in the internment cases, the Court sided with FDR, asserting that the president had statutory and constitutional authority to act during an emergency. Ultimately, the Court relied on "the good faith of executive officials"[43] and reasoned that FDR's authority superseded individual rights, given the constraining external factors of the tenuous political climate and the fear, as assessed by the Court, of an immediate attack on U.S. soil.

Korematsu was largely viewed as testimony to the continued viability of Cicero's maxim: *inter arma silent leges* (during wartime the law is silent).[44] In fact, "to an overwhelming majority, the Court's jurisprudence in times of" emergency has been more "in line with the dictates of *Korematsu*";[45] the Court has acted to suppress rights and liberties under conditions of threat. What *Korematsu* taught future Courts, however, was to be more vigilant as they weigh the assertions of inherent power made by executives when they move to constrain or deny individual rights.

During the Vietnam War, the courts rejected national-security claims by the executive,[46] and more recently, the Court rebuked the Bush administration's assertions of unilateral authority. While the Court has favored policies in an ongoing war or state of emergency, it also has a significant record of satisfying its constitutional responsibility to defend individual liberties (even in wartime).

The Bush administration mounted an unprecedented unilateral claim to conduct an offensive war, and as the war efforts got underway, the president's authority was under scrutiny. To protect its bid for exclusive and plenary power, the administration willingly ridiculed judicial supremacy. In fact, the administration maintained that a coordinate branch could not check it. In addition, Bush asserted that the president was granted broad, inherent war-making powers (echoing *Curtiss-Wright*) when acting in the constitutional capacity as commander-in-chief to conduct a successful campaign. The administration never suggested that it needed congressional approval for the policies it implemented, but if there was any doubt, Bush maintained, it was granted statutory authorization via the Authorization for Use of Military Force against Iraq Resolution (AUMF), which yielded considerable latitude.

Taking into account changing external factors and doctrinal posturing, the Court concluded that although discretionary latitude was afforded the president during wartime (evident, given the federal courts' response), the Bush administration did not have a claim to unfettered and unreviewable decision making. In this instance, rights claims trumped the administration's assertion that ordinary laws must be set aside in an effort to secure the nation. Despite the administration's broad claims, *Rasul* and *Hamdi* placed some statutory limits on executive authority and at the same time affirmed the president's single-most-important prerogative: the unilateral authority to categorize individuals, including U.S. citizens, as "enemy combatants." *Rasul*, *Hamdi*, and *Padilla* did not, however, threaten the foundations of the imperial presidency.

The amalgamation of these three cases demonstrated that the Court could provide a definitive statement of what powers the president was afforded during wartime. The Court was flexing; *Boumediene* postured a demonstrable challenge to presidential powers. In balancing legal norms and external factors (polity principles, individual rights claims, and a changing political landscape),[47] the Court had the authority to determine that despite extenuating circumstances, individuals have rights. What was evident was the Court's sensitivity to how far it should intervene. For example, the *Hamdan* Court did not clarify what that procedure for guaranteeing rights should be. The newly formed Roberts Court was left to extrapolate what that process might include when it decided *Boumediene*.

The detainee cases illustrated the Court's prowess in mounting a more systematic reproach to the Bush administration than it had ever done before. These cases also showed the Court's determination to speak to the necessary and practical role of the legislature—special military tribunals (Combatant Status Review Tribunals [CSRTs]) must either be established by statute or, if created by presidential order, follow rules and procedures consistent with the Uniform Code of Military Justice (UCMJ) and the Geneva Conventions. The Court's directive (*Hamdan*) also illustrated how it acted as a mediator between the two branches, endorsing polity principles. Insisting that Congress play a more prominent role showed the Court's authority to direct another institution to act, because the president had sought and Congress had approved statutory authorization.

When balancing polity principles, the Court evaluated the interaction of the two branches in light of Justice Robert Jackson's counsel. The Court was unencumbered to determine that even if the branches cooperated, their actions could still be found unconstitutional; the Military Commissions Act (MCA) was an unconstitutional suspension of the federal courts' jurisdiction to hear habeas applications from detainees whom the administration had labeled "enemy combatants."[48] After 1936, Congress had largely been left out of the conversation. Now the Court required explicit statutory authorization (a contrary finding to *Dames*, which relied on tacit authority). Given the geopolitical concerns of the war on terror, coupled with Republicans' having congressional majorities at the time, Congress was unlikely to have refused President Bush's request. And even with "their rhetorical bluster, congressional Democrats had" shown themselves to be entirely eager to grant the Bush administration "all the national security powers that he had asked for in the Protect America Act."[49] Only a countermajoritarian Court could stand up to the strong majorities supporting unilateral authority.

The Court's sharp reproach to the administration's contention that it could offer an alternative constitutional understanding[50] showcased the Court's institutional positioning to assert that it was not the "regime" that had the authority to "say what the law is," because that role belonged to the Court. Through the lens of legal time—its doctrinal posturing—the Court could flex its institutional muscle and define the executive's reach as it formulated the nation's foreign affairs. Institutionally, the Court was unwilling to back down in the face of an executive attempting to commandeer the primary function of the judiciary; its duty to elucidate constitutional principles included the metes and bounds of executive authority. The Court has long held that it has the authority to interpret the Constitution. In fact, it is "respected by this Court and the country [that judicial supremacy] is a permanent and indispensable feature of our constitutional system."[51] It is clear that judicial supremacy is so well settled that no modern executive can justifiably defy that formal principle. When challenged on the supremacy over constitutional interpretation, the Court will oppose the principal commitments of the majority alliance and reestablish its institutional legitimacy.

The war on terror saw national-security powers unavoidably encroaching on domestic issues. When the line between foreign and domestic policy becomes distorted, as it did in *Youngstown*, the president's expanding pool of foreign-policy powers takes on greater domestic prominence. This invasion can yield protests and political inconveniences that confront a president's monopoly over foreign policy making. The cacophony of the Korean War and the war on terror illustrated the Court's serving as a guardian by interpreting constitutional principles to erect barriers to presidential encroachment. In balancing competing claims, the Court will challenge the executive branch irrespective of the president's place in political time, and it will provide a restatement of constitutional foreign-affairs principles.

The Court can be a reactionary rival to increasing executive power. The Bush administration's extralegal counterterrorism program was "the most dramatic, sustained, and radical challenge to the rule of law in American history."[52] Under the authority of its own rules, the Bush administration created an alternative legal system, which the Court scaled back when it ruled in the detainee cases.

The Bush administration "borrowed against the power of future presidencies" more than any other president, including Richard Nixon. Consequently, it is believed that executives "will be viewed by Congress and the courts . . . with a harmful suspicion and mistrust."[53] But the ensuing mistrust fades quickly as foreign policy making remains front and center in any executive's national agenda. Future presidents of either party "may make symbolic gestures" toward a sharing of powers, yet it is highly unlikely "that the next President will actually cede most of the new powers that the Bush Administration grabbed for itself."[54] The Bush administration repeatedly challenged the nation's laws and constitutional principles, and Obama did little to roll back Bush's prerogatives.

In fact, Obama's criticism of the Bush-Cheney presidency made him look vulnerable: "[W]e are at war[,] and when President Obama pretends we aren't, it makes us less safe."[55] But as Karl Rove noted, "people suspended judgment" so they could let Obama "play his hand."[56] Despite the scrutiny, the Obama administration felt compelled to forge ahead. In mid-2013, leaked top-secret files illustrated the Obama administration's entrenchment of "the post-9/11 surveillance state bequeathed to him" by the Bush administration. This entrenchment contradicted Attorney General Eric Holder's letter to senators on January 5, 2010, which "informed them that there was no appetite inside the executive branch for any declassification of the secret interpretation of the Patriot Act. . . . Congress [responded by] extending the expiring Patriot Act provisions."[57]

And when Umar Farouk Abdulmutallab pled guilty to the attempted bombing of Flight 253 on Christmas Day 2009 and was sentenced to life in prison,[58] the Obama administration "saw the ruling as confirmation that its new legal policy was constitutional." With this ruling and the triumphs of the "Warsame policy, and the sense that killing [Osama] bin Laden was a shield against accusations that it was soft on terrorism, the Obama administration began to display restored confidence in its legal policy about captives."[59] It is clear that presidents will continue to forge new ground, but constitutional fluidity is dependent on the Court's jurisprudence.

NOT A FIXED PRINCIPLE

The Court's doctrinal posturing is alterable and not linear. Even though it found in favor of the broad prerogatives of FDR, it just as quickly determined that Truman had reached too far when he asserted the unilateral authority to conduct the Korean War. *Youngstown* posed, in stark terms, the question of whether there were any constitutional limits to the president's authority to assert broad powers to safeguard the nation against foreign threats. The constitutional pendulum shifted as the Court reevaluated the extent to which the executive could claim inherent authority. Even during times of war, the Court has used judicial review to check presidential assertions of power. In Truman's case, the threat of seizing private steel mills created a political and constitutional crisis that solicited a reformulation of the role of the executive and the very nature of presidential power. While affiliated presidents, such as Truman and Bush, are stewards of a mature coalition and use the courts to achieve concrete policy results to maintain party cohesion, in the conduct of foreign affairs, the Court does not simply align with these presidents as it ordinarily would in domestic cases. In light of almost twenty years of unparalleled exploitation of executive authority, the Court reassessed and redefined the scope of presidential power to the point of immobilizing the accumulation of executive power. And judicial supremacy in demarcating executive power did not retreat in significance.

The Court might refute unilateral power in one case, yet it is not averse to increasing presidential prerogatives in another if it determines the necessity of doing so (e.g., *Dames, Regan,* and *Zivotofsky*). Jackson's practical approach to presidential power offered to future courts a flexible schema. As he stated, difficult constitutional questions "have given rise to some of the most persistent controversies in our constitutional history." For Jackson, the Court needed to take a broad view of the executive's powers in international discourse: "We should not use this occasion to circumscribe, much less to contract, the lawful role of the President as Commander-in-Chief." However, as justices remain legally cognizant of the practical capacity and desire to keep the nation safe, the Court remains committed to balancing individual rights with unfettered presidential decision making. As such, it continues to recognize that "presidential powers are not fixed."[60] Acknowledging that executive powers oscillate, the Court will challenge claims of independent authority.

A BRANCHING POINT: REENGINEERING LEGISLATION

While the *Youngstown* Court determined that the executive had no independent authority to make domestic law—that squarely fell to the legislative—justices noted that legislation could be passed to support or enable executive decision making in the formulation of foreign affairs. The Court took this exception to another level, however. Relying explicitly on Jackson's concurrence—absence of congressional disapproval of the president's actions could be construed as approval—we may conclude that if the Court feels compelled to grant more authority where none exists, the Court will manufacture it, as it did with *Curtiss-Wright*, *Dames*, and *Regan*. The *Dames* Court made available to other courts and the executive branch the principle of tacit statutory authority. Congressional silence was now synonymous with the sanctioning of presidential initiatives.

Dames was a clear illustration of the Court's capacity to exalt presidential control over the nation's foreign affairs as it engineered a shift in authority from Congress to the president. In this instance, it was clear that the external circumstances constrained the Court. It determined that the president needed the flexibility to act, and freezing assets was a reasonable way for the executive to bargain in delicate negotiations when responding to international emergencies.[61] In balancing the rights of the claimants, the plurality agreed that the executive had a tenuous claim to use bargaining chips with other nation-states. And if individual rights were denied, then the Court unequivocally decided that it was a necessary forfeiture, given the nature of the case and the president's authority to conduct foreign affairs.

As the executive and Congress vie for power, the Court is institutionally positioned to act as an agent of change. Congress can create inducements and coercive measures on the president to concur, and (if it can muster the political will) it can also exercise an effective veto on most (although not all) executive policies. But even when Congress attempts to rein in the president, as many argue that the War Powers Resolution (WPR) was intended to do,[62] it remains the Court's duty to determine whether those measures have undermined the power and authority of the president, which is what we find with *Regan* and cases interpreting the WPR.[63]

The Court can find exceptions to justify and sanction broad discretionary authority to the president when restricting individual rights (e.g., limiting travel to Cuba because of national-security concerns during the Cold War, which the Donald Trump administration is currently renegotiating). Being hemmed in legislatively will not prevent the Court from assigning broader power to the executive branch. Granting broad presidential prerogatives essentially strips the authority of the legislative branch to statutorily determine what checks and limits should be placed on the president. "Judicial authority waxes"[64] as it alters American political development and aids in reconstituting which responsibilities are best reserved for the executive branch. This kind of judicial posturing suspends the checks and balances of Congress, stripping it of the responsibility and burdens of leadership.[65] Consequently, it appears in most circumstances that the judiciary and the executive "can have a working and mutually beneficial relationship."[66]

REGIMES AND DEVELOPMENTAL NARRATIVES

This view of judicial supremacy shapes the development of constitutional jurisprudence and constitutional politics in international affairs. This deliberative process can benefit and constrain an incumbent president and legislatures intent on seeing the international agenda to successful completion.

Karen Orren and Stephen Skowronek define American political development as the analysis of durable shifts in governing authority,[67] where "political construction of constitutional meaning" is key to that examination.[68] The placement, affiliation, and degree of governing authority consume much of politics, which is largely resolved in practice.[69] Routinely, resolution is seen through political action, but at key moments, judicial interpretation extends constitutional jurisprudence to the political sphere.

Continued political skirmishes over interpretive authority resolved judicially reconstitute the Constitution and future contestations. As such, "authority is not fixed."[70] Judicial supremacy reshapes the authority to interpret the Constitution and places the Supreme Court at the center of politics—and at the core of American political development.

Analyzing the interactions between the president and the Court in foreign affairs sheds new light on the developmental narrative of the imperial president. Those intent on realizing the political foundations of executive authority and unilateral power must acknowledge the Court's role. Rather than "generally swim[ming] with the political current,"[71] in international affairs, the Court's justices swim where they choose. The result is that the judiciary "has been a resource, a stimulus, and a constraint on the President."[72] The Court's authority is therefore a recurring theme in the developmental narrative of the imperial presidency.

Interpretative review can thus sustain a path, provide a branching point, or forge new paths by closing off one path[73] and opening another. New paths are reinforced over developmental time with succeeding decisions and redefinitions advanced by the Court as it weighs exigent circumstances with internal legal norms. The Court not only shapes path development but, by "shifting constitutional debates into the courts[,] also alters the relative influence of different participants in the process to affect outcomes."[74]

During constitutional moments, when cleavages between old and new regimes exist, the Court directly and noticeably influences political orders by creating or maintaining the present regime. In foreign affairs, when a cleavage between the old and new regimes is distinct, the Court can make legal the construction and stabilization of a new political order, as was the case in *Curtiss-Wright*. And over time, the Court has maintained a distinct constitutional jurisprudence as it has continued to determine presidential prerogatives in foreign policy making and war making.

Political actors can aid in enunciating a "constitutional vision [that] affiliated justices are [more] likely to share [in] that constitutional vision and help implement it directly."[75] Consequently, affiliated political actors might find refuge from a Court that is willing to arbitrate "on their behalf."[76] In "transitional periods," political actors articulating a constitutional vision "can have politically destabilizing effects." It is therefore argued that "judicial authority is strong at these moments precisely because regime authority is weak." The Court is positioned to yield "controversial decisions that the elected officials cannot make, or at least would prefer to avoid making."[77]

In the politics of opposition and affiliation, the Court has decided a number of foreign-affairs cases that have backed and challenged the assertions made by reconstructive and affiliated presidents. Reconstructive presidents are more inclined to challenge the interpretive turn of the judiciary and "express that substantive disagreement by seeking to subvert . . . judicial authority,"[78] but in foreign policy making and war making, the Court is more prominent in pursuing its own agenda.

Analyzing the presidency in isolation and studying the Court in purely doctrinal terms severely limit our understanding of the developmental narrative of the executive in the formulation of international relations. Judges play a significant role in driving doctrinal shifts, but the evolution of doctrine significantly affects the trajectory of a path; judicial decisions in one time period that influence the trajectory of decision making in later time periods have profound consequences.

The Court alone governs constitutional accommodations. A revisionist constitutional foreign-affairs jurisprudence is (re)formulated only at the hands of the justices. The theoretical framework advanced here clearly indicates that the Court is not a passive and constrained institution. Rather, it profoundly influences the path of the other two institutions by altering our understanding of the executive's role and authority in foreign affairs (generally) and war making (specifically) through the legal doctrine it crafts. The precedent set by the Court in the newly created constitutional order of 1936 shaped and constrained normal decision making as the sequential development of a new path evolved over time. The *Curtiss-Wright* Court strategically positioned itself to alter the developmental narrative of the executive branch. Initially laying the foundation in *Curtiss-Wright* with a new constitutional order, the Court provided the legal justifications for redefining the executive's role in later cases.

CLOSING

At the onset of military exigencies, Congress and the public at large give presidents enormous freedom to formulate and act in foreign and security policy. Depending on how the federal courts define the appropriate balance between security and liberty, and individual rights claims, their determinations can potentially result in a major foreign-policy incident if they err in judgment. Consequently, adjudicating competing national-security concerns vis-à-vis the liberty of the individual presents a significantly greater challenge for the courts than merely determining a violation of some law. As such, courts struggle over the constitutional bounds of the executive and legislature sharing powers. In their pronouncements, the courts have generally been regarded as supporting a president's Hamiltonian assertion of power in this area.

The conventional notion is that during times when the executive is energetic, well liked, and politically proficient; or when the country is at war or when there is a perceived foreign threat, the president is dominant in pursuing a foreign-policy agenda. And in times of politically vulnerable administrations, or when domestic worries lead debate, Congress is more persuasive. There have also been times when legislative and public attention on issues at home have produced political moments for executives to chase their preferred foreign agenda without much interference from the legislature.[79] Reading the Court into this narrative illustrates that this development is one of intercession. At times it is accommodating, which is sometimes incompatible with the demands of the administration; at other times, it is a narrative of rearticulation, where the role of the executive during tenuous times is reconfigured. Ultimately, it is the Court's responsibility, in times of emergency, to ensure that the government branches' use of their war powers follows constitutional principles.

A notable pattern to emerge in constitutional politics and jurisprudence in foreign policy and war making is the Court's shift from the outmoded standard of the original constitutional order, which balanced power between the two political branches, to a new constitutional order, which provides for the practical realities of a changing world that is besieged with continued and heightened levels of national-security concerns. The presidency, with the Court's assistance, has been significantly transformed. The power and authority wielded by the executive today are a far cry from those in the presidency of yesterday. With the demands of ever-pervasive emergency situations, the decision making of the Court is serviceable, contemporaneously acceptable, and marketable for future cases. As evolutionary discourse or judicial principles become embedded, constitutional change can be instigated outside the legalized Constitution.

APPENDIX

Tables

TABLE 1. SELECT PRESIDENTIAL ORDERS ISSUED DURING WARTIME AND EMERGENCIES, 1934–2007

President	EO/ Proclamation	Date	Description
FDR	Proclamation 2087	May 28, 1934	Forbade the shipment of arms to combatants in the Chaco region
	Proclamation 2147	November 14, 1935	Revoked the arms embargo at the termination of hostilities in the Chaco region
	EO 8953	November 27, 1941	Established Los Angeles–Long Beach Harbor Naval Defensive Sea Area in California
	EO 9066	February 19, 1942	Authorized the secretary of war to prescribe military areas
	EO 9102	March 18, 1942	Established the War Relocation Authority
	Public Law 77-503	March 21, 1942	Made it a federal offense for any person to refuse to leave a military area authorized by a military commander
TRUMAN	EO 10340	April 8, 1952	Directed the secretary of commerce to take possession of and operate the plants and facilities of certain steel companies
JFK	Proclamation 3447	February 3, 1962	Imposed an embargo on all trade with Cuba
CARTER	EO 12170	November 17, 1979	Blocked Iranian Government Property
	EO 12276 and 12285	January 19, 1981	Established the U.S.-Iran agreement on releasing the American hostages

(continued on next page)

TABLE 1. SELECT PRESIDENTIAL ORDERS ISSUED DURING WARTIME AND
EMERGENCIES, 1934–2007 (continued)

President	EO/ Proclamation	Date	Description
REAGAN	EO 12294	February 24, 1981	Suspended litigation against Iran
G. W. BUSH	EO 13234	November 9, 2001	Established a presidential task force on citizen preparedness in the war on terrorism
	EO 13321	December 17, 2003	Gave emergency appointment authority to the secretary of defense
	EO 13356	August 27, 2004	Strengthened terrorism information dissemination
	EO 13376	April 13, 2005	Made amendments to EO 12863 relating to the Foreign Intelligence Advisory Board
	EO 13382	June 28, 2005	Blocked property of proliferators of weapons of mass destruction and their supporters
	EO 13388	October 25, 2005	Strengthened terrorism information dissemination
	EO 13425	February 14, 2007	Established trial by military commission for alien unlawful enemy combatants

Source: The American Presidency Project, http://www.presidency.ucsb.edu/sou.php.

TABLE 2. AUTHORIZED FOREIGN WARS OF THE UNITED STATES, 1798–2003	
War	**Acts**
Naval war with France, 1798	Act of May 28, 1798, ch. 48, 1 Stat. 561 Act of July 9, 1798, ch. 68, 1 Stat. 578
War with Barbary States, 1802 and 1815	Act of February 6, 1802, ch. 4, 2 Stat. 129 Act of March 3, 1815, ch. 90, 3 Stat. 230
War with Great Britain, 1812	Act of June 18, 1812, ch. 102, 2 Stat. 755
Mexican War, 1846	Act of May 13, 1846, ch. 16, 9 Stat. 9
War with Spain, 1898	Act of April 25, 1898, ch. 189, 30 Stat. 364
World War I, 1917 (Germany and Austria-Hungary)	Act of April 6, 1917, ch. 1, 40 Stat. 1 Act of December 7, 1917, ch. 1, 40 Stat. 429
World War II, 1941 (Japan and Germany)	Act of December 8, 1941, ch. 561, 55 Stat. 795 Act of December 11, 1941, ch. 564, 55 Stat. 796
Korean War, 1950	Nonauthorized
Vietnam War, 1964	Gulf of Tonkin Resolution, P.L. 88-408, 78 Stat. 384, August 10, 1964
Persian Gulf War, 1991	P.L. 102-1, 105 Stat. 3, January 14, 1991
War in response to terrorist attacks of September 11, 2001 (Operation Enduring Freedom)	P.L. 107-40, 115 Stat. 224, September 18, 2001
Iraq War, 2003 (Operation Iraqi Freedom)	P.L. 107-243, 116 Stat. 1498, October 16, 2002

Sources: "Official Declarations of War by Congress," *United States Senate*, https://www.senate.gov/pagelayout/history/h_multi_sections_and_teasers/WarDeclarationsbyCongress.htm; Richard Grimmett, "Instances of Use of United States Armed Forces Abroad, 1789–2007," *Congressional Research Service Report 7-5700, RL32170*, Library of Congress, January 14, 2008, www.crs.gov.

NOTES

CHAPTER 1

1. *See* Appendix Table 1 for a select list of presidential orders issued. This trend was more evident during the Lyndon Johnson and Richard Nixon years (Gordon Silverstein, *Imbalance of Powers* [New York: Oxford University Press, 1997], 66).

2. *See generally* David G. Adler, "Court, Constitution, and Foreign Affairs," in *The Constitution and the Conduct of American Foreign Policy*, ed. David G. Adler and Larry N. George (Lawrence: University of Kansas Press, 1996); *see also* Louis Fisher, *Constitutional Conflicts between Congress and the President*, 5th ed. (Lawrence: University Press of Kansas, 2007); and Nancy Kassop, "Expansion and Contraction: Clinton's Impact on the Scope of Presidential Power," in *The Presidency and the Law: The Clinton Legacy*, ed. David Gray Adler and Michael A. Genovese (Lawrence: University Press of Kansas, 2002).

3. Harold Hongju Koh asserts that this trend has been evident since at least World War II and most markedly since the Vietnam War (Harold Hongju Koh, *The National Security Constitution: Sharing Power after the Iran-Contra Affair* [New Haven, Conn.: Yale University Press, 1990]).

4. Alexander M. Bickel, *The Least Dangerous Branch*, 2d ed. (New Haven, Conn.: Yale University Press, 1986).

5. Silverstein, *supra* note 1, at 6.

6. *See generally* Lori F. Damrosch, "Covert Operations," in *Foreign Affairs and the U.S. Constitution*, ed. Louis Henkin, Michael J. Glennon, and William D. Rogers (Ardsley-on-Hudson, N.Y.: Transnational Publishers, 1990).

7. Adler, *supra* note 2, at 23.

8. *United States v. Curtiss-Wright Export Corp.*, 299 U.S. 304, 320 (1936); *see* Eric A. Posner and Adrian Vermeule, "Accommodating Emergencies," in *The Constitution in Wartime*, ed. Mark Tushnet (Durham, N.C.: Duke University Press, 2005). Posner and Vermeule maintain that there are two views when assessing the proper role of the Constitution during

times of emergency: "the accommodation view is that the Constitution should be relaxed or suspended during an emergency," whereas the strict view "is that constitutional rules are not, and should not be, relaxed during an emergency" (55, 56–58).

9. Norman Dorsen, "Foreign Affairs and Civil Liberties," *American Journal International Law* 83 (1989): 840.

10. *See* Richard A. Posner, *Not a Suicide Pact: The Constitution in a Time of National Emergency* (New York: Oxford University Press, 2006); John Yoo, *Crisis and Command: A History of Executive Power from George Washington to George W. Bush* (New York: Kaplan Publishing, 2009); John C. Eastman, "Listening to the Enemy: The President's Power to Conduct Surveillance of Enemy Communications during Time of War," *ILSA Journal of International and Comparative Law* 13 (2006): 1; *see also* Stephen G. Calabresi, *The Unitary Executive: Presidential Power from Washington to Bush* (New Haven, Conn.: Yale University Press, 2008).

11. Edward S. Corwin holds an inconsistent opinion on executive prerogatives. He insists that the Framers' notion of balanced government included the view "of a *divided initiative in the matter of legislation and a broad range of autonomous executive power or 'prerogative'*" (Edward S. Corwin, *The President: Office and Powers, 1787–1957*, 4th rev. ed. [New York: New York University Press, 1957], 14, emphasis in original). For a detailed discussion of the meaning of "executive power," *see* 3–30.

12. *See* John Yoo, *War by Other Means: An Insider's Account of the War on Terrorism* (New York: Atlantic Monthly Press, 2006), 19; John Yoo, "The Terrorist Surveillance Program," *George Mason Law Review* 14, no.3 (2007): 569–70.

13. Yoo, *supra* note 10, at 73.

14. John Yoo, "The Continuation of Politics by Other Means: The Original Understanding of War Powers," *California Law Review* 84 (1996): 167, 294. Yoo even rejects the role of the Court in early judicial decision making and these prior cases' significance: "[T]he precedent set by [*Bas, Talbot*, and *Barreme*] remains quite modest. All three revolved around the question of how much of the value of a ship and its cargo, seized by an American commander during the naval operations against France, flowed to the commander instead of to the ship's owner" (*id.* at 293). But even Yoo concedes that the three cases supported the conclusion that Congress could make limited declarations of war (*id.* at 294) and acknowledges that the "Court held [that] Congress has sole authority to decide on the legal nature of hostilities" (*id.* at 167).

15. *See* David Barron and Martin Lederman, "The Commander in Chief at the Lowest Ebb—Framing the Problem, Doctrine, and Original Understanding," *Harvard Law Review* 121 (2008): 689, 696. Barron and Lederman reconfirm that Congress was given an active and leading role in foreign affairs and that in most cases, Congress has not been idle in this duty (*id.* at 941).

16. This is a term used by Stephen Griffin. But Griffin asserts that the constitutional order of the early Republic was replaced after World War II with executives' initiating war (Stephen Griffin, *Long Wars and the Constitution* [Cambridge, Mass.: Harvard University Press, 2013]).

17. Arthur Schlesinger, *Imperial President* (New York: Houghton Mifflin Harcourt, 1973).

18. Oren Gross, "Chaos and Rules: Should Responses to Violent Crises Always Be Constitutional?" *Yale Law Journal* 112 (2003): 1011, 1090.

19. Kimberley L. Fletcher, "Truman's Rhetoric Entrenches Unilateral Authority and Fashions a Trend for Future Executive Use," *Presidential Studies Quarterly* 47, no. 4 (2017): 720–51. Kimberley L. Fletcher, "Unilateral Executive Power Enshrined in Law," *Northern Illinois Law Review* 37, no. 2 (2017).

20. *See* David G. Adler, "The Judiciary and Presidential Power in Foreign Affairs: A Critique," *Richmond Journal of Law and the Public Interest* 1, no. 1 (1996).

21. This principle may be better explained as a system of shared powers. Collective decision making implies a kind of contemporaneous collaboration that the Constitution's structure does not necessarily impose.

22. Louis Fisher, *Presidential War Powers*, 2d ed. (Lawrence: University Press of Kansas, 2004), 1.

23. In the first Congress, Roger Sherman, who had been a delegate in Philadelphia, argued in defense of the shared-power arrangement in foreign affairs, stating, "The more wisdom there is employed, the greater security there is that the public business will be well done" (*Annals of Congress* [1789], 1:1085); James Wilson, whose contributions to the drafting of the Constitution were second only to those of James Madison, asserted that the shared-powers approach provided a "security to the people" (Jonathan Elliot, ed., *The Debates in the Several State Conventions on the Adoption of the Federal Constitution*, 5 vols. [New York: Burt Franklin, 1974]. First published by J. P. Lippincott in 1861.).

24. No. 75, in Edward Meade Earle, *The Federalist Papers* (New York: Modern Library, 1937), 487.

25. Madison to Thomas Jefferson, May 13, 1789, quoted in Leonard D. White, *The Federalists* (New York: Macmillan, 1948), 65.

26. *See* Joseph Story for an explanation of the essential republican principle of entrusting the representative branch with the decision to go to war: it is the "highest sovereign prerogative; . . . it is in its own nature and effects so critical and calamitous, that it requires the utmost deliberation. . . . War . . . never fails to impose upon the people the most burdensome taxes, and personal sufferings. . . . [I]t should therefore be difficult in a republic to declare war; but not to make peace. . . . The cooperation of all the branches of the legislative power ought, upon principle, to be required in this the highest act of legislation" (Joseph Story, *Commentaries on the Constitution of the United States*, vol. 3 [Boston: Hilliard, Gray and Cambridge, 1833], 60–61). At the time of the founding, the understanding of the phrase "declare war" was settled and enjoyed a reputable practice, but it was the sole authority of the legislature: it "give[s] notice by the proper authority of intent to convert a state of peace into a state of war" (*id.*). For a discussion of republicanism, *see* Gordon S. Wood, *The Creation of the American Republic, 1776–1787* (New York: W. W. Norton, 1969), 1–124.

27. *See* John Rutledge, in *The Record of the Federal Convention of 1787*, ed. Max Farrand (New Haven, Conn.: Yale University Press, 1937), 1:65. James Wilson preferred a single president but "did not consider the Prerogatives of the British Monarch as a proper guide in defining the executive powers. Some of these prerogatives were of a Legislature nature. Among others that of war & peace & c" (*id.* at 1:64–66).

28. Edwin B. Firmage, "War, Declaration of," in *Encyclopedia of the American Presidency*, ed. Leonard W. Levy and Louise Fisher, vol. 4 (New York: Simon and Schuster, 1994), 1573. *See* James Madison, the chief architect of the Constitution, in *Federalist* No. 48: "[T]he founders of our republics . . . seem never for a moment to have turned their eyes from the danger to liberty from the overgrown and all-grasping prerogative of an hereditary magistrate" (in Earle, *supra* note 24, at 321–22). The Framers vested in Congress many of John Locke's federative powers and William Blackstone's royal prerogatives (John Locke, *Second Treatise on Civil Government*, 1690; Sir William Blackstone, *Commentaries* 2 Blackstone, Commentaries on the Laws of England, 1908, 238).

29. Elliot, *supra* note 23, at 2:507. Roger Sherman's justification of the sharing of powers in foreign affairs reiterated Benjamin Franklin's appeal to the delegates to set aside their remaining differences in favor of the collective judgment (*Annals of Congress* [1789], 1:1085; Farrand, *supra* note 27, at 2:641–43).

30. Elliot, *supra* note 23, at 2:528.

31. Adler, *supra* note 2, at 23.

32. Farrand, *supra* note 27, at 1:65–66, 70, 73–74.

33. Adler, *supra* note 2, at 23.

34. Executive discretion was reserved for defensive actions during an emergency and not for general war making or offensive military actions. And when a defensive war moved to offensive in character, the president needed to seek congressional authorization (for example, the Barbary Wars [1801–1815]).

35. In Clinton Rossiter, *The Federalist Papers* (New York: Penguin, 1961), 415–23. *See* Griffin, *supra* note 16, for a discussion of Alexander Hamilton's "broader vision of presidential power" (25). The Supreme Court upheld this line of thinking in *Fleming*: "[T]he President as commander-in-chief is authorized to direct the movements of the naval and military forces placed by law at his command, and to employ them in the manner he may deem most effectual to . . . subdue the enemy (*Fleming v. Page*, 50 U.S. 603, at 603, 614 (1850)).

36. Adler, *supra* note 2, at 21. As Louis Henkin states, "The evidence is that in the Framers' contemplation, the armed forces would be under the command of the President but at the disposition of Congress" (Louis Henkin, *Constitutionalism, Democracy, and Foreign Affairs* [New York: Columbia University Press, 1990], 25).

37. Hamilton, *Federalist* No. 69, in Rossiter, *supra* note 35, at 415–23.

38. *See* Adler for a discussion of the clerklike function of the recognition clause and its subsequent abuse (David G. Adler, "The President's Recognition Power: Ministerial or Discretionary?" *Presidential Studies Quarterly* 25, no. 2 (1995): 267–87).

39. *See generally Federalist* No. 75, in Earle, *supra* note 24.

40. *Bas v. Tingy*, 4 U.S. 37 (1800); *Talbot v. Seeman*, 5 U.S. 1 (1801); *Little v. Barreme*, 6 U.S. 2 Cranch 170 (1804); *United States v. Smith*, 27 F. Cas. 1192, 1229 (No. 16342) (C.C.D.N.Y. 1806); *Prize Cases*, 67 U.S. 635, 668 (1863); *see* Saikrishna Prakash, "Unleashing the Dogs of War," *Cornell Law Review* 93 (2007): 45, 60–61; Michael D. Ramsey, "Textualism and War Powers," *University of Chicago Law Review* 69 (2002): 1543, 1620.

41. The Quasi-War was an undeclared war fought mainly at sea between the French Republic and the United States (1798–1800).

42. For a discussion of an imperfect war, *see* the opinion of William Paterson, delegate to the Constitutional Convention from New Jersey (Farrand, *supra* note 27, at 45–46); *see also Miller v. The Ship Resolution*, 2 U.S. 19 (1781). According to the Federal Court of Appeals, a "perfect war is that which destroys the national peace and tranquility, and lays the foundation of every possible act of hostility," and an imperfect war "does not entirely destroy the public tranquility, but interrupts it only in some particulars, as in the case of reprisals" (*id.* at 20). The conflict with France was the first limited war, but it was certainly not the last. Other examples of limited war included the First Barbary War, the Spanish-American War, and the First Gulf War. In the case of the First Gulf War, Congress limited the authorization of the use of military force "to achieve implementation of Security Council Resolutions" (Authorization for Use of Military Force against Iraq Resolution, Public Law 1021-1, Section 2(a), 105 Stat. 3, 3 (1991)).

43. *Talbot*, at 31–32. For a more current endorsement of this proposition, *see Holtzman v. Schlesinger*, 414 U.S. 1304 (1973): "[T]he President is constitutionally disabled in nonemergency situations from exercising the war-making power in the absence of some affirmative action by Congress" (*id.* at 1304, 1308). Chief Justice Thurgood Marshall, writing for a unanimous Court, added that "it is not denied . . . that Congress may authorize general hostilities, in which case the general laws of war apply to our situation; or partial hostilities, in which case the laws of war, so far as they actually apply to our situation, must be noticed. In

my judgment, nothing in the 172 years since those words were written alters that fundamental constitutional postulate" (*id.* at 312 [quoting *Talbot*, at 1, 28 (1801) (citation omitted)]).

44. Fisher, *supra* note 22, at 25.

45. *Bas* at 40–42; and *Barreme* at 170, 177–78.

46. When referring to the president/executive, I use the masculine pronoun to reflect historical and contemporary conditions.

47. *Bas* at 40–42.

48. *Id.*

49. *Id.*

50. Norman J. Small, *Some Presidential Interpretations of the Presidency* (Baltimore: Johns Hopkins University Press, 1932), 34; *see also* Special Session Message (July 4, 1861), in James Richardson, ed., *Compilation of the Messages and Papers of the Presidents* (Washington, D.C.: U.S. Government Printing, 1897), 7:3225.

51. Richardson, *supra* note 49, at 7:3224–25, 7:3232.

52. Abraham Lincoln, *Special Message to Congress*, July 4, 1861, www.presidency.ucsb. edu.

53. *See also* 12 Stat. 284, 326 (1861); Corwin, *supra* note 11, at 228–34, 448–53; *see also Ex parte Merryman*, 17 Fed. Case No. 9487, at 153 (1861); *see* 10 Op. Att'y Gen. 74, 81 (1861); *Ex parte Milligan*, 71 U.S. 4 Wall. 2 (1866). In *Milligan*, the Court was regarded as a guardian and not a suppressor during times of war.

54. 2 Blackstone at 668.

55. *Prize Cases*, at 635, 668.

56. *Id.* at 669.

57. *Id.* at 668.

58. *Id.* at 660 (emphasis in original). Unlike President Harry S. Truman and President George W. Bush, Abraham Lincoln never asserted that he had full authority to act; in fact, he admitted that he went beyond the constitutional boundaries set out for the president and therefore required congressional authorization (Richardson, *supra* note 50, at 7:3225). Lincoln used statutory authorization enacted in 1795 and 1807 and upheld by the Supreme Court to justify his actions. The statutes approved presidential use of military force to suppress insurrections (*Prize Cases*, at 660, 668).

59. Retroactive legislation, Lincoln concluded, was necessary, given his actions: acting in the absence of law and at times against it (Cong. Globe, 37th Cong., 1st Sess. 393 (1861) (Senator Howe)).

60. Adler, *supra* note 2, at 21.

61. Fisher, *supra* note 22, at 8. A select group of academics (e.g., Yoo) and several presidents (Harry S. Truman, Lyndon B. Johnson, Richard Nixon, Gerald Ford, Jimmy Carter, Ronald Reagan, and George W. Bush) have asserted that the commander-in-chief clause is a source of independent presidential war-making authority. However, these claims have no merit. No basis for this claim can be found at the Constitutional Conventions or the state ratifying conventions, and the Court has never held that this clause can be used as a basis for presidents to claim unilateral war-making power (*see* David G. Adler, "Constitution and Presidential Warmaking," *Political Science Quarterly* 103, no. 1 [1988]: 8–13, 28–29).

62. *See* Appendix Table 2 for wars, both declared and undeclared. Once delegation has been given to the executive branch, the authority to act remains in the hands of the president, and the courts have generally upheld such legislation's validity (*see United States v. Bethlehem Steel*, 315 U.S. 289 (1942); *Bowles v. Willingham*, 321 U.S. 503 (1944); *Yakus v. United States*, 321 U.S. 414 (1944); and *Lichter v. United States*, 334 U.S. 742 (1948)). Claims of an

"emergency" are a convenient way for any president to attract legislative support, but when unilateral action is asserted in defense of national security, it is imperative to distinguish between genuine emergencies that are pushed on the nation and those that simply arise because of neglect or contrivance. A clear example of the questionable nature of emergencies was evident in the actions taken by President Franklin D. Roosevelt, who proclaimed thirty-nine different emergencies in a six-year period. *See* Congressman Bruce Barton's objections to these declarations (84 Cong. Rec. 2854 (1939)).

63. When there was no standing army, congressional control was at its strongest. Even the naval wars against the Barbary pirates and France were infrequent and fully authorized by Congress. When instances required action, presidents asked Congress for authority. For example, in 1789, John Adams asked for congressional authority with the Quasi-War against France, as did James Madison in 1812 with the war waged against England. Two years after James Polk sent soldiers into the disputed territory along the Texas-Mexico border in 1846, the House of Representatives censured him for "unnecessarily and unconstitutionally" starting a war (Cong. Globe, 30th Cong., 1st Sess. 95 (1848); Fisher, *supra* note 22, at 39–44). And William McKinley had to defend his intervention in Cuba in 1898 by describing the conflict as "right at our door" (Richardson, *supra* note 50, at 13:6289).

64. *Durand v. Hollins*, 4 Blatch, 451 (1860).

65. *Id.*, 454. In 1914, Woodrow Wilson relied on *Durand* to legally justify the occupation of Veracruz, Mexico, by American forces. When addressing a joint session of Congress, Wilson stressed the necessity for immediate action. He asserted that he would not exceed the constitutional powers granted to him as president and that the actions he would take would include conferencing and cooperating with both chambers of Congress (Richardson, *supra* note 50, at 16:7936). Wilson proceeded without authority, but two days later, Congress passed a joint resolution justifying the president's use of force ordered the previous day.

66. *See* Griffin, *supra* note 16; Silverstein, *supra* note 1; and Mariah Zeisberg, *War Powers: The Politics of Constitutional Authority* (Princeton, N.J.: Princeton University Press, 2013).

67. It should be noted that the United States was always active in a military sense. In fact, the Spanish-American War (1898) was the first significant U.S. intervention.

68. *See* Margaret MacMillan, *Paris 1919: Six Months That Changed the World* (New York: Random House, 2001).

69. *See generally* Ronald Kahn and Kenneth Kersch, eds., *The Supreme Court and American Political Development* (Lawrence: University Press of Kansas, 2006); *see also* Ronald Kahn, "Social Constructions, Supreme Court Reversals, and American Political Development," in *The Supreme Court and American Political Development*, ed. Ronald Kahn and Ken Kersch (Lawrence: University Press of Kansas, 2006), 100. The institutional costs of changing paths may be too high for the executive branch to shoulder alone, but with the assistance of a collaborative court, these costs may be minimized (Paul Pierson, "Increasing Returns, Path Dependence, and the Study of Politics," *American Politics Science Review* 94, no. 2 [2000]: 251–67, 257).

70. *See* Adler, *supra* note 2; *see* Fisher, *supra* note 2.

71. *See generally* Griffin, *supra* note 16.

72. *See generally* Jeffrey A. Segal and Harold J. Spaeth, *The Supreme Court and the Attitudinal Model* (New York: Cambridge University Press, 2002).

73. *See* Karl Llewellyn, *Jurisprudence: Realism in Theory and Practice* (Chicago: University of Chicago Press, 1962).

74. Cases dealing with foreign policy making can, at times, deal with political rather than strictly legal questions. In these instances, the Court is in a position to refuse to

hear cases on the basis of the political-question doctrine (i.e., *Baker v. Carr*, 369 U.S. 186 (1962)). I am not drawing a firm distinction between political and legal questions, however. I am merely noting the realm of possible and likely outcomes that the Court may choose to take.

75. Marc Galanter suggests that courts do more than simply resolve disputes; they also "prevent them[,] . . . [m]obilize them, displace them, and transform them" (Marc Galanter, "The Radiating Effects of Courts," in *Empirical Theories of Courts*, ed. Keith D. Boyum and Lynn Mather [New York: Longman, 1983], 123).

76. Lee Epstein and Jack Knight, *The Choices Justices Make* (CQ Press, 1998); *see also* Forrest Maltzman, James F. Spriggs II, and Paul J. Wahlbeck, *Crafting Law on the Supreme Court: The Collegial Game* (New York: Cambridge University Press, 1998).

77. *See generally* Kahn and Kersch, *supra* note 69.

78. *See* Clayton Cornell and Howard Gillman, eds., *The Supreme Court and American Politics* (Chicago: University of Chicago Press, 1999), 67–68.

79. Martin Shapiro, "Law and Politics: The Problem of Boundaries," in *Oxford Handbook of Law* (Oxford, UK: Oxford University Press, 1989), 99.

80. *See* Bruce Ackerman, *We the People* (Cambridge, Mass.: Belknap Press of Harvard University Press, 1998).

81. *See* Kahn and Kersch, *supra* note 69.

82. *See* Pamela Brandwein, "The *Civil Rights Cases* and the Lost Language of State Neglect," in *The Supreme Court and American Political Development*, ed. Ronald Kahn and Ken Kersch (Lawrence: University Press of Kansas, 2006); *see also* Kahn, *supra* note 69.

83. *See* Mark A. Graber, "Legal, Strategic or Legal Strategy: Deciding to Decide during the Civil War and Reconstruction," in *The Supreme Court and American Political Development*, ed. Ronald Kahn and Ken Kersch (Lawrence: University Press of Kansas, 2006).

84. Zeisberg, *supra* note 66. Mariah Zeisberg argues for the politics of constitutional authority, which leaves out a discussion of the judiciary.

85. Ackerman, *supra* note 80.

86. Rogers Smith, "Political Jurisprudence, the 'New Institutionalism,' and the Future of Public Law," *American Political Science Review* 82, no. 1 (1988): 48, 94–96; *see also* Howard Gillman, *The Constitution Besieged* (Durham, N.C.: Duke University Press, 1993), 15–18; Elizabeth Bussiere, *(Dis)Entitling the Poor* (University Park: Pennsylvania State University Press, 1997), 11–22; and Cornell and Gillman, *supra* note 78, at 3–5.

87. Kahn, *supra* note 69.

88. Howard Gillman, "Party Politics and Constitutional Change: The Political Origins of Liberal Judicial Activism," in *The Supreme Court and American Political Development*, ed. Ronald Kahn and Kenneth Kersch (Lawrence: University Press of Kansas, 2006), 141.

89. *See* Graber, *supra* note 83; and Kahn and Kersch, *supra* note 69.

90. *See* Mark Graber, "The Non-majoritarian Difficulty: Legislative Deference to the Judiciary," *Studies in American Political Development* 7 (1993): 35–73; *see also* Keith E. Whittington, "Interpose Your Friendly Hand: Political Supports for the Exercise of Judicial Review by the U.S. Supreme Court," *American Political Science Review* 99 no. 4 (2005): 583–96.

91. *See* Howard Gillman, "How Political Parties Can Use the Courts to Advance Their Agendas: Federal Courts in the United States, 1875–1891," *American Political Science Review* 96 (2002): 3.

92. *See* Mark Tushnet, "The Supreme Court and the National Political Order: Collaboration and Confrontation," in *The Supreme Court and American Political Development*, ed. Ronald Kahn and Kenneth Kersch (Lawrence: University Press of Kansas, 2006).

93. *See id.*

94. *See generally* Kahn and Kersch, *supra* note 69.

95. Stephen Skowronek, *The Politics Presidents Make: Leadership from John Adams to George Bush* (Cambridge, Mass.: Belknap Press of Harvard University Press, 2008).

96. *Id.* at 30.

97. *See generally* David Collier and Ruth Berins Collier, *Shaping the Political Arena: Critical Junctures, the Labor Movement, and Regime Dynamics in Latin America* (Princeton, N.J.: Princeton University Press, 1991); *see also* Thomas Ertman, *Birth of the Leviathan: Building States and Regimes in Medieval and Early Modern Europe* (New York: Cambridge University Press, 1997). Scholars examine how shocks may have a marked effect that is conditioned on when in the chain of events they occur. Historical institutionalism evaluates outcomes as being dependent on the timing of exogenous factors in relation to particular institutional configurations. It is difficult, however, to categorize exogenous and endogenous factors when examining two institutions. I argue against isolating these factors, because we underestimate the interplay between them, how intertwined they are, and their constraint on judicial decision making.

98. Segal and Spaeth, *supra* note 72.

99. *See* Terry M. Moe, "Political Institutions: The Neglected Side of the Story," *Journal of Law, Economics, and Organization* 6 (1990).

100. *Id.* Increasing returns can be understood in two distinct ways. First, the costs of switching from one path to another, in some circumstances, increase over time. Second, timing and sequence matter. *See generally* Collier and Collier, *supra* note 97, at 31; and Skowronek, *supra* note 95.

101. Pierson, *supra* note 69; *see* Karen Orren and Stephen Skowronek, *The Search for American Political Development* (New York: Cambridge University Press, 2004). It should be noted that Paul Pierson is fundamentally at odds with Karen Orren and Stephen Skowronek.

102. *See* Richard Rose, "Inheritance before Choice in Public Policy," *Journal of Theoretical Politics* 2 (1990): 263–91.

103. Pierson, *supra* note 69. Pamela Brandwein offers a critique of path dependence. Path dependence is complicated when we include a discussion of judicial decision making (Pamela Brandwein, *Rethinking the Judicial Settlement of Reconstruction* [New York: Cambridge University Press, 2011]).

104. Pierson, *supra* note 69.

105. *Id.* at 261.

106. *Id.*

107. Margaret Levi, "A Model, a Method, and a Map: Rational Choice in Comparative and Historical Analysis," in *Comparative Politics: Rationality, Culture, and Structure*, ed. Mark I. Lichbach and Alan S. Zuckerman (New York: Cambridge University Press, 1997), 28, 19–41.

108. Pierson, *supra* note 69, at 265.

109. Orren and Skowronek, *supra* note 101, at 103. If exogenous shocks are "informed by structures, identities, cleavages, [and] programs, agendas present in the prior period," then we need to analyze those "structures, identities, cleavages, [and] programs" to identify which occurrences reinforce established patterns of governance and which are "redirecting" (*id.*; *see also* Smith, *supra* note 85, at 51).

110. Ronald Kahn calls this process the social construction process. Employing this frame, he examines when a path is expected to switch or end completely (*supra* note 69).

111. *See* Kahn and Kersch, *supra* note 69, at 3; *see also* Tushnet, *supra* note 92.

112. *See* Kahn and Kersch, *supra* note 69, at 19.

113. *See generally id.*

114. *See* Graber, *supra* note 83.

115. In fact, history is not linear. Historical institutionalism rarely "conforms to simple linear models of causation or neatly schematized understandings of political order"; rather, "it is assumed that institutional politics . . . comprise[s] . . . multiple orders and patterns of intercurrence that often create unintended consequences, paradoxes[,] and disjunctures" (Gillman, *supra* note 88, at 141).

116. Kahn asserts that if *Plessy* and *Lochner* had not been overturned, they "would have added illegitimacy of not only the Court but also the rule of law, which in part gets its moral support from having the Constitution engage in what Lawrence Lessig calls 'translation with fidelity.'" Change is therefore grounded on the "constitutive decision-making process" (Kahn, *supra* note 69, at 101; Lawrence Lessig, "Understanding Changed Readings: Fidelity and Theory," *Stanford Law Review* 47, no. 3 [February 1995]).

117. *See generally* Keith Whittington, *Political Foundations of Judicial Supremacy: The Presidency, the Supreme Court, and Constitutional Leadership in the U.S. History* (Princeton, N.J.: Princeton University Press, 2007).

118. *See* Kahn, *supra* note 69, at 85.

119. A case in point, Kahn argues, is evident in the higher-education segregation cases in the 1940s and 1950s before *Brown*, which overturned *Plessy* (*supra* note 69). *See also* Thomas M. Keck, who asserts that the interaction of the internal and external forces is fluid ("From *Bakke* to *Grutter*: The Rise of Rights-Based Conservatism," in *The Supreme Court and American Political Development*, ed. Ronald Kahn and Kenneth Kersch [Lawrence: University Press of Kansas, 2006]).

120. *See* the work of Julie Novkov (state courts) ("*Pace v. Alabama*: Interracial Love, the Marriage Contract, and Postbellum Foundations of the Family," in *The Supreme Court and American Political Development*, ed. Ronald Kahn and Kenneth Kersch [Lawrence: University Press of Kansas, 2006]); Brandwein (state neglect), *supra* note 82; and Wayne D. Moore (Congress) ("[Re]Construction of Constitutional Authority and Meaning: The Fourteenth Amendment and *Slaughter-House Cases*," in *The Supreme Court and American Political Development*, ed. Ronald Kahn and Kenneth Kersch [Lawrence: University Press of Kansas, 2006]). These scholars demonstrate that concessions exist in the political sphere with respect to constitutional meanings in view of politics and societal norms that result in change over developmental time.

121. Kahn, *supra* note 69, at 101. External features include those that are social and economic and not simply political.

122. *Id.*, at 85.

123. *See generally id.*

124. Kahn argues that landmark cases often entrench the incremental process of negotiations between political, social, and economic concepts that have raged for long periods (*id.*). Mark Graber contends that the meaning of a case as part of a path can change as the path evolves: "[P]recedent shapes and constrains normal decision-making, not that stare decisis never encompasses policy preferences and strategic considerations" (Graber, *supra* note 83, at 48). He adds that the decisions "between available alternatives made at one point in time typically limit or change the alternatives that may be selected at later points in time" (*id.* at 41–42).

125. Kahn, *supra* note 69, at 99–102.

126. Theda Skocpol and Paul Pierson, eds., *The Transformation of American Politics: Activist Government and the Rise of Conservatism* (Princeton, N.J.: Princeton University Press, 2007).

127. Kahn, *supra* note 69, at 99–102.

128. Paul Pierson and Theda Skocpol, "Historical Institutionalism in Contemporary Political Science," in *Political Science: The State of the Discipline*, ed. H. Milner and I. Katznelson (New York: W. W. Norton, 2002).

129. *Id.* at 699; *see also* Kahn, *supra* note 69.

130. *See generally* Sven Steinmo, Kathleen Thelen, and Frank Longstreth, *Structuring Politics* (New York: Cambridge University Press, 1992).

131. As Mark Tushnet argues, law does not simply follow politics (*supra* note 92).

132. Moore, *supra* note 120.

133. Orren and Skowronek, *supra* note 101, at 123–31.

134. Epstein and Knight, *supra* note 76; Maltzman, Spriggs, and Wahlbeck, *supra* note 76; *see generally* Keck's discussion of fluidity between internal and external forces and the inherent feedback loop (*supra* note 119).

135. Mark J. Richards and Herbert M. Kritzer, "Jurisprudential Regimes in Supreme Court Decision Making," *American Political Science Review* 96, no. 2 (2002): 305–20; *see* Cass R. Sunstein, *Legal Reasoning and Political Conflict* (New York: Oxford University Press, 1998).

136. Carol Nackenoff ("Constitutionalizing Terms of Inclusion: Friends of the Indian and Citizenship for Native Americans, 1880s–1930s," in *The Supreme Court and American Political Development*, ed. Ronald Kahn and Kenneth Kersch [Lawrence: University Press of Kansas, 2006]), 10.

137. Kahn, *supra* note 69, at 87.

138. Tushnet, *supra* note 92; *see also* Kahn, *supra* note 69.

139. *See generally* Graber, *supra* note 83; Novkov, *supra* note 120; and Brandwein, *supra* note 82, for a full discussion of when and why the Court might decide to change a path.

140. Whittington, *supra* note 117; *see also* George I. Lovell and Scott E. Lemieux, "Assessing Juristocracy," *Maryland Law Review* 65 (2006): 100; and George I. Lovell, *Legislative Deferrals* (Cambridge, UK: Cambridge University Press, 2003).

141. Whittington, *supra* note 117, at xi.

142. *Id.* at 53.

143. *See* Kahn, *supra* note 69, at 73–74.

144. *Id.*, at 74.

145. Brandwein (*supra* note 82) suggests that this open-ended quality means that judicial decision making appears not to have the thickening quality of political time; *see also* Kahn, *supra* note 69.

146. Kahn, *supra* note 69, at 102.

147. Kim Scheppele, "Small Emergencies," *Georgia Law Review* 40 (2006): 835–62.

148. Kahn, *supra* note 69, at 101.

149. *Id.*

150. Kahn, *supra* note 69, at 102–3.

151. Mark Tushnet, *The Constitution in Wartime* (Durham, N.C.: Duke University Press, 2005), 22.

152. This power is also evident with rights of privacy for women and homosexuals (Kahn, *supra* note 69).

153. *See* Jonathan Casper's discussion of the Court's reshaping politics (Jonathan Casper, "The Supreme Court and National Policy Making," *American Political Science Review* 70 [1976]: 50–63).

154. *See* Graber, *supra* note 90.

155. Kahn, *supra* note 69, at 93–95.

156. James G. March and Johan P. Olsen, *Rediscovering Institutions* (New York: Free Press, 1989), 128; and Smith, *supra* note 86, at 48.

157. Keith Whittington draws this theory from Skowronek's framework of the cyclical president (*supra* note 117, at 54).

158. *Id.*

159. *Id.*

160. Skowronek, *supra* note 95.

161. Whittington, *supra* note 117.

162. *See* Skowronek, *supra* note 95; *see also* Whittington, *supra* note 117.

163. James G. March and Johan P. Olsen, quoted in Rogers Smith, *Liberalism and American Constitutional Law*, 2d ed. (Cambridge, Mass.: Harvard University Press, 1990), 95.

164. Richard Funston, "The Supreme Court and Critical Elections," *American Political Science Review* 69 (1975): 795–811; and Ackerman, *supra* note 80.

165. *See* Novkov, *supra* note 120.

166. Orren and Skowronek, *supra* note 101, at 170. *See* Brandwein's discussion of critical junctures (*supra* note 82); *see also* Gerry Berk, *Alternative Tracks: The Constitution of American Industrial Order, 1865–1917* (Baltimore: Johns Hopkins University Press, 1997).

167. This case selection does not account for the certiorari process.

168. *See* Graber, *supra* note 83. Graber asserts that the Court is a strategic player, having a larger role to play in the developmental path of those affected by its decision. And the impact of a case may not be fully realized until time has elapsed; as more time elapses, the meanings of cases may continue to evolve.

169. *Zivotofsky v. Kerry*, 576 U.S. ___ (2015).

170. Sunstein, *supra* note 135.

CHAPTER 2

1. Robert H. Jackson, *The Struggle for Judicial Supremacy* (New York: Vintage, 1941), 314–15.

2. *See generally* Segal and Spaeth, *supra* chap. 1, note 72.

3. Kahn and Kersch, *supra* chap. 1, note 69.

4. Walter Dean Burnham, *Critical Elections and the Mainsprings of American Politics* (New York: W. W. Norton, 1970).

5. Kahn and Kersch, *supra* chap. 1, note 69.

6. Skowronek, *supra* chap. 1, note 95, at 299.

7. James T. Patterson, *Congressional Conservatism and the New Deal* (Lexington: University of Kentucky Press, 1967), chaps 1–3.

8. George Wolfskill, *The Revolt of the Conservatives: A History of the American Liberty League, 1934–1940* (Boston: Houghton Mifflin, 1962), 21–36.

9. Skowronek, *supra* chap. 1, note 95.

10. Joseph Alsop and Turner Catledge, *168 Days* (Garden City, N.Y.: Doubleday, Doran, 1938), 138–45; and Ackerman, *supra* chap. 1, note 80, at 266–94.

11. Franklin D. Roosevelt, January 6, 1937, "Annual Message to Congress," *Public Papers and Addresses* (www.presidency.ucsb.edu). In fact, in this address, FDR challenged the Court and defended his own reading of the Constitution.

12. *Id.*

13. Skowronek, *supra* chap. 1, note 95.

14. *See* Whittington, *supra* chap. 1, note 117.

15. *Id.* at 23.

16. Arthur M. Schlesinger, *Politics of Upheaval: The Age of Roosevelt* (Boston: Houghton Mifflin, 1960), 468–96; and Peter Irons, *The New Deal Lawyers* (Princeton, N.J.: Princeton University Press, 1982), 17–199.

17. See *NLRB v. Jones and Laughlin Steel Corp.*, 301 U.S. 1 (1937). These reversals, however, came after the Court's decision in *Curtiss-Wright*. Essentially, the Supreme Court left FDR unconstrained from the burden of trying to unify incompatible interests; see Barry Cushman, "The Man on the Flying Trapeze," *Journal of Constitutional Law* 15, no. 1 (2010): 183–263. Cushman demonstrates that the Court's shift was in response to better drafting by Congress and not a fear of facing a united Congress and president.

18. *See* Skowronek, *supra* chap. 1, note 95.

19. *See* Fletcher, *supra* chap. 1, note 19 ("Truman's Rhetoric").

20. Joint Resolution, May 28, 1934, H.J. Res. 347.

21. Proclamation No. 2087, 44 Stat. 1744 (1934).

22. *A.L.A. Schechter Brothers Poultry Corp. v. United States*, 295 U.S. 495 (1935).

23. *Panama Refining Co. v. Ryan*, 293 U.S. 388 (1935).

24. *See* H. Jefferson Powell, "The Story of Curtiss-Wright Export Corporation," in *Presidential Power Stories*, ed. Christopher H. Schroeder and Curtis Bradley (New York: Foundation Press, 2009), 196.

25. David H. Zook Jr., *The Conduct of the Chaco War* (New York: Bookman Associates, 1960), 69–72; and Brice W. Farcau, *The Chaco War: Bolivia and Paraguay, 1932–1935* (Westport, Conn.: Greenwood Publishing Group, 1996).

26. *See generally* Farcau, *supra* note 25.

27. Theodore Roosevelt, December 6, 1904, "State of the Union Address," Teaching AmericanHistory.org.

28. Robert Dallek, *Franklin D. Roosevelt and American Foreign Policy, 1932–1945* (New York: Oxford University Press, 1979), 11–20.

29. *Id.*

30. *See generally* Griffin, *supra* chap. 1, note 16.

31. Announced on Inauguration Day, March 4, 1933 (TeachingAmericanHistory.org).

32. FDR, *Annual Message to Congress*, January 3, 1936, www.presidency.ucsb.edu.

33. Dallek, *supra* note 28, at 47–48.

34. Congressman Hamilton Fish III argued that presidential discretionary authority to decide which side is the aggressor in a conflict is tantamount to "an act of war and not an act of peace. . . . You might as well take all the constitutional powers away from Congress and give them to the President" (78 Cong. Rec. 9374 (1934)).

35. Dallek, *supra* note 28, at 71–72.

36. *Id.*

37. Robert A. Divine notes that it is "the greatest and most profitable international secret of our time" (Robert A. Divine, "The Case of the Smuggled Bombers," in *Quarrels That Have Shaped the Constitution*, ed. John A. Garraty [New York: Harper and Row, 1964], 214); *see also* George Seldes, *Iron, Blood and Profits: An Exposure of the World-Wide Munitions Racket* (New York: Harper and Brothers, 1934).

38. Dallek, *supra* note 28, at 102.

39. Despite the skepticism in the press ("Chaco Arms Ban Pressed in House; Hull Spurs Action," *New York Times*, May 23, 1934, at 1) and the British assessment of the gravity and urgency of action, a committee of the League of Nations called for the administration to set in place an embargo similar to the League's embargo (Sec'y Cordell Hull to Rep. Samuel McReynolds, May 22, 1934, in "Chaco Arms Ban Pressed in House," 15).

40. *See generally* Farcau, *supra* note 25; Zook, *supra* note 25.

41. Congress enacted the draft without making any changes to it. *See* H.R.J. Res. 347, 73d Cong., ch. 365, 48 Stat. 811 (1934). *See* 78 Cong. Rec. 9373–75, 9432–33 (1934) for an account of the brief discussions that took place in both chambers of Congress and the lack of questions raised concerning the apparent ambiguity in Section 1 of the Resolution.

42. Powell, *supra* note 24, at 195–231. This point is discussed at length by Powell, who finds the same ambiguity.

43. Proclamation No. 2087, 44 Stat. 1744 (1934).

44. A second proclamation revoked the first, holding that the Joint Resolution was not an unconstitutional delegation of legislative power. External affairs are very different; Congress must therefore afford the executive a degree of discretion that would not be granted in the domestic arena (Proclamation No. 2147, 49 Stat. 3480 (1935)). Joint Resolution 347 appeared to be an anomaly in the struggle between the executive branch and Congress. A year later, critics of FDR effectively left the executive no discretionary power (*see* Neutrality Act of 1935). The footing he had gained with the Chaco Joint Resolution was all but lost as a result of the Neutrality Acts (Neutrality Act of 1935, ch. 837, 49 Stat. 1081, *amended by* Neutrality Act of 1937, ch. 146, 50 Stat. 121).

45. *See* Divine, *supra* note 37.

46. *Id.*

47. Brief for Appellees, Curtiss-Wright Export Corporation and Curtiss Aeroplane and Motor Company, Inc., 18–19 (*Curtiss-Wright*, 299 U.S. 304 (No. 98)); *see also* Brief for Appellees, John S. Allard, Clarence W. Webster, and Samuel J. Abelow, 10–21 (*Curtiss-Wright*, 299 U.S. 304 (No. 98)).

48. *United States v. Curtiss-Wright Exp. Corp.*, 14 F. Supp. 230 (S.D.N.Y. 1936), reported the original decision by the court and the supplementary opinion rendered after reargument.

49. The *Aurora* Court acceded to redelegation but noted that the 1810 act under consideration simply looked at whether the president could determine whether a certain event had occurred (*Cargo of the Brig Aurora v. United States*, 11 U.S. 382, 388 (1813)).

50. *See J. W. Hampton, Jr. and Co. v. United States*, 276 U.S. 394 (1928); *see also* Keith E. Whittington and Jason Iuliano, "The Myth of the Nondelegation Doctrine," *University of Pennsylvania Law Review* 165 (2017). Whittington and Iuliano contend that "during the nineteenth and early twentieth centuries, the nondelegation doctrine served as a meaningful check on the unbridled expansion of the administrative state. Then[,] during the New Deal, the Supreme Court dismantled the doctrine and paved the way for Congress to delegate away any powers it deemed appropriate" (380); *see also* Gary Lawson, "The Rise and Rise of the Administrative State," *Harvard Law Review* 107 (1994): 1231, 1237–41.

51. The Court held that the president had "unlimited authority to determine the policy and to lay down the prohibition, or not to lay it down, as he may see fit." Moreover, "Congress left the matter to the President without standard or rule, to be dealt with as he pleased" (*Panama Refining Co. v. Ryan*, 293 U.S. 388, at 415–18 (1935)).

52. *Curtiss-Wright*, 14 F. Supp. at 239.

53. Franklin D. Roosevelt, *F.D.R.: His Personal Letters 1905–1928* (New York: Duell Sloan and Pearce, 1948), 237–40.

54. Frank Freidel, *Franklin D. Roosevelt: A Rendezvous with Destiny* (Boston: Little Brown, 1990), 1:253, 1:260. The Spanish Civil War (1936–1939) was a perfect example of FDR's assertions that an embargo should be flexible and discretionary. As the dynamics of any war changed, he needed to be able to adapt (Roosevelt, *supra* note 53, at 500–1).

55. Dallek, *supra* note 28, at 108.

56. *See generally* George McJimsey, *The Presidency of Franklin Delano Roosevelt* (Lawrence: University Press of Kansas, 2000), 293–96.

57. *See* brief for the United States and *Curtiss-Wright,* 299 U.S. 304 (1936) (No. 98).

58. Brief for Appellees, Allard et al., at 20 (*Curtiss-Wright,* 299 U.S. 304 (No. 98)).

59. *Id.*; *see also* Brief for Appellees, Curtiss-Wright Export Corp., and Curtiss Aeroplane and Motor Company, Inc., at 16–26 (*Curtiss-Wright,* 299 U.S. 304 (No. 98)).

60. Brief for Appellees, Curtiss-Wright Export Corporation, and Curtiss Aeroplane and Motor Company, Inc., at 18–19 (*Curtiss-Wright,* 299 U.S. 304 (No. 98)); *see also* Brief for Appellees, John S. Allard, Clarence W. Webster, and Samuel J. Abelow, 10–21 (*Curtiss-Wright,* 299 U.S. 304 (No. 98)).

61. R. Walton Moore, "Memorandum on Neutrality" (August 27, 1935), in Justus D. Doenecke and Mark A. Stoler, *Debating Franklin D. Roosevelt's Foreign Policies 1933–1945* (Lanham, Md.: Rowman and Littlefield, 2005), 97, 98–99.

62. *See* brief for the United States at 8, *Curtiss-Wright,* 299 U.S. 304 (No. 98) (quoting *Panama Ref. Co. v. Ryan,* 293 U.S. 388, at 422–25 (1935)).

63. Gordon Silverstein, "Judicial Enhancement of Executive Power," in *The President, the Congress and the Making of Foreign Policy,* ed. Paul Peterson (Norman: University of Oklahoma Press, 1994), 28–29.

64. Joel F. Paschal, *Mr. Justice Sutherland* (Princeton, N.J.: Princeton University Press, 1951).

65. 44 Cong. Rec. 2506 (1909); George Sutherland, "The Internal and External Powers of the National Government," *North American Review* 191 (1910): 373, 388.

66. Sutherland, *supra* note 65, at 48–49.

67. *Id.* at 50.

68. 45 Cong. Rec., 2616.

69. Powell, *supra* note 24.

70. George Sutherland, *Constitutional Power and World Affairs* (New York: Columbia University Press, 1919), 43–44.

71. *Id.*

72. Thomas Jefferson asserted that James Madison's handiwork prevented the nation from becoming entangled in conflicts: "[O]ne effectual check to the Dog of war [is] by transferring the power of letting him loose from those who are to spend to those who are to pay" (Julian C. Boyd, ed., *The Papers of Thomas Jefferson* [Princeton, N.J.: Princeton University Press, 1950], xv, 397).

73. Fletcher, *supra* chap. 1, note 19 ("Unilateral Executive Power"), at 320; *see* Alexander Hamilton, *Pacificus No. 1,* in Earle, *supra* chap. 1, note 24. Hamilton famously asserted executive energy.

74. *McCulloch v. Maryland,* 17 U.S. 316 (1819); and *Reid v. Covert,* 354 U.S. 1 (1957).

75. James McReynolds dissented without opinion, and Harlan Stone did not participate (*Curtiss-Wright,* at 333).

76. Edward Purcell, "Understanding *Curtiss-Wright,*" *Law and History Review* 31, no. 4 (2013).

77. *See Curtiss-Wright,* at 317. However, the historical context makes this unlikely.

78. *Id.*

79. *Id.,* at 55; *see also* David M. Golove, "Treaty-Making and the Nation: The Historical Foundations of the Nationalist Conception of the Treaty Power," *Michigan Law Review* 98 (2000): 1075.

80. For example, *Fong Yue Ting v. United States*, 149 U.S. 698 (1893): "The United States are vested by the [C]onstitution with the entire control of international relations, and with all the powers of government necessary to maintain that control" (*id.* at 711). In contrast, *see Cunningham v. Neagle*, 135 U.S. 1 (1890), where the powers of the executive included the power "to enforce the rights, duties, and obligations growing out of the [C]onstitution itself, our international relations, and all the protection implied by the nature of the government under the [C]onstitution" (*id.* at 64); *see Missouri v. Holland*, 252 U.S. 416 (1920); *see* Sutherland, *supra* note 70, at 154–55.

81. Sutherland, *supra* note 70, at 122–28.

82. *Id.* at 71–76 and 110–11.

83. *Id.* at 75–76.

84. *Id.* at 94–97.

85. *Id.*

86. For example, in 1919 and 1920, the Court decided several cases—*Schenck v. United States*, 249 U.S. 47 (1919); *Frohwerk v. United States*, 249 U.S. 204 (1919); *Debs v. United States*, 249 U.S. 211 (1919); *Abrams v. United States*, 250 U.S. 616 (1919); *Gilbert v. Minnesota*, 254 U.S. 325 (1920); *Pierce v. United States*, 252 U.S. 239 (1920); and *Schaefer v. United States*, 251 U.S. 466 (1920)—dealing with First Amendment rights of individuals, the press, and political figures disapproving of America's involvement in World War I. The Court repeatedly upheld criminal convictions carrying prison sentences for individuals who used political speech to challenge the war effort. The Court embraced the principle that when assessing civil liberties and "[w]hen a nation is at war[,] many things that might be said in time of peace are such a hindrance to its effort that their utterance will not be endured so long as men fight and that no Court could regard them as protected by any constitutional right" (*Schenck*, at 52); *see also Gitlow v. New York*, 268 U.S. 652 (1925). The *Gitlow* Court reasoned that Benjamin Gitlow's conviction was lawful, because the government could suppress or even punish speech that directly promoted the unlawful overthrow of the government.

87. In *United States v. O'Brien* (391 U.S. 367 (1968)), the Court upheld the conviction of an activist who had burned his draft card to protest the Vietnam War. While the law in place limited free speech, the Court argued, the law served an important government interest—managing a draft during wartime. In *New York Times Co. v. United States* (403 U.S. 713 (1971)), the government, citing national security, got a temporary restraining order to stop the publication of the Pentagon Papers. The Court, however, determined that the First Amendment protected the right of the *New York Times* to print the materials.

88. Walter LaFeber, "The Constitution and United States Foreign Policy," *Journal of American History* 74, no. 3 (1987): 51.

89. Michael J. Gerhardt, "The Limited Path Dependency of Precedent," *College of William and Mary Law School Faculty Publications*, Paper 974.

90. Edward Purcell discusses at length the reasoning behind Charles Evans Hughes's decision to assign Sutherland the majority opinion (*supra* note 76).

91. *See generally* Fletcher, *supra* chap. 1, note 19 ("Unilateral Executive Power"); and Louis Fisher, "The Staying Power of Erroneous Dicta: From *Curtiss-Wright* to *Zivotofsky*," *Constitutional Commentary* 31, no. 2 (2016).

92. Kevin T. McGuire and Barbara Palmer, "Issue Fluidity on the U.S. Supreme Court," *American Political Science Review* 89, no. 3 (1995).

93. *Curtiss-Wright* at 315.

94. Fletcher, *supra* chap. 1, note 19 ("Unilateral Executive Power"), at 317; and *Curtiss-Wright* at 319–20.

95. Adler, *supra* chap. 1, note 2, at 40; *see also* Fisher, *supra* chap. 1, note 2.

96. Fletcher, *supra* chap. 1, note 19 ("Unilateral Executive Power"), at 317; and Annals of Congress, 6th Cong., 613 (1800). Sutherland's reference would be powerful evidence, given John Marshall's elevation, a year later, to chief justice. However, Marshall intended only that the executive should convey to other nations U.S. foreign policy *after* it had been accepted. Marshall undoubtedly meant that the executive was the "sole organ" in *implementing*—that is, merely announcing, not formulating—American foreign policy. As chief justice, Marshall never invoked the "sole-organ" doctrine in defense of unilateral executive power, even though he had opportunity to do so; *see* Louis Fisher, "The Law: Presidential Inherent Power: The 'Sole Organ' Doctrine," *Presidential Studies Quarterly* 37 (2007): 139 (clarifying Marshall's "sole-organ" speech; emphasis added).

97. Powell, *supra* note 24, at 223.

98. *Curtiss-Wright* at 320.

99. *Id.* at 321–22.

100. *Id.* at 327–29.

101. *Panama Refining* at 421–22.

102. *Carter v. Carter Coal Co.*, 298 U.S. 238, at 295 (1936).

103. Public Law 402, 74th Cong., 1st Sess. (August 30, 1935).

104. *See generally* Graber, *supra* chap. 1, note 83. Case precedent evolves over time and is not necessarily immediately significant (Louis Henkin, *Foreign Affairs and the Constitution* [Mineola, N.Y.: Foundation Press, 1972], 25–26). Critics of broad independent executive authority dismiss Justice Sutherland's language as radically incorrect. Sutherland's reference to the "sole-organ" doctrine is argued as misquoting and misrepresenting Marshall's position.

105. Law reviews were quiet at first but noted, "[O]n the face of it the case is a long step toward executive autonomy in the field of foreign relations" (James Wm. Moore, "Recent Decisions," *Georgetown Law Journal* 25 [1937]: 738, 740). The first academic review of Sutherland's opinion was extremely critical but was also printed ten years after the decision (David M. Levitan, "The Foreign Relations Power: An Analysis of Mr. Justice Sutherland's Theory," *Yale Law Journal* 55, no. 467 [1946]).

106. Graber, *supra* chap. 1, note 83.

107. *Zivotofsky v. Kerry*, 725 F. 3d 197 D.C. Cir. (2013); *see* Fletcher, *supra* chap. 1, note 19 ("Truman's Rhetoric").

108. Fisher, *supra* note 91.

109. Adapted from Fletcher, *supra* chap. 1, note 19 ("Truman's Rhetoric").

110. *See* House Select Committee to Investigate Covert Arms Transactions with Iran, 100th Cong., 1st Sess., Vol. 100–7 (part II) 37 (1987).

111. Silverstein, *supra* chap. 1, note 1, at 147.

112. *Id.* at 26.

113. *United States v. Belmont*, 301 U.S. 324, 330 (1937).

114. *United States v. Pink*, 315 U.S. 203 (1942).

115. *Dames and Moore v. Regan*, 453 U.S. 654 (1981).

116. *Regan v. Wald*, 468 U.S. 243 (1984).

117. *United States v. Belmont*, 331, 332.

118. Justice Douglas expressly quoted from *Curtiss-Wright*'s explanation of the executive's role as "sole organ" in *Pink*, which Sutherland did not do in *Belmont* (*see Pink*, at 229).

119. After the noticeable reference to *Curtiss-Wright* in *Pink*, *Curtiss-Wright* was infrequently cited and rather trivial until *Johnson v. Eisentrager*, 339 U.S. 763 (1950). The *Eisentrager* Court determined that U.S. courts had no jurisdiction over German war criminals detained in a U.S.-managed prison in Germany.

120. *Curtiss-Wright* at 322.

121. Acquisition of Naval and Air Bases in Exchange for Over-Age Destroyers, 39 Op. Att'y Gen. 484, at 486–88 (1940).

122. This assertion is contrary to Joseph Lockhart's position that the executive has the discretion to determine national-security concerns (Office of the Press Secretary, *White House Press Briefing*, April 13, 1999, www.presidency.ucsb.edu).

123. Silverstein, *supra* chap. 1, note 1, at 10; adapted from Fletcher, *supra* chap. 1, note 19 ("Truman's Rhetoric").

124. Fisher, *supra* chap. 1, note 22, at 73; *see Mistretta v. United States*, 488 U.S. 361 (1989). The *Mistretta* Court confirmed that with an ever-changing world that yielded technical concerns, Congress could not perform its necessary duties without delegating some of its power. The Court thus found this delegation "constitutionally sufficient"—*see also Chevron U.S.A., Inc. v. Natural Resources Defense Council, Inc.*, 467 U.S. 837 (1984); and *Whitman v. American Trucking Associations, Inc.*, 531 U.S. 457 (2001)—and rarely has the Court found the nondelegation doctrine unconstitutional. For example, in *Clinton v. City of New York*, 524 U.S. 417 (1998), the Court determined that the Line Item Veto Act of 1996 violated the Presentment Clause.

125. *See generally* Fletcher, *supra* chap. 1, note 19 ("Truman's Rhetoric").

126. *Public Papers*, February 3, 1949, www.presidency.ucsb.edu.

127. Adapted from Fletcher, *supra* chap. 1, note 19 ("Truman's Rhetoric").

128. *Public Papers*, Harry S. Truman, 1943–1950. September 29, 1952, *Rear Platform and Other Informal Remarks in MN, ND, and MT*, www.presidency.ucsb.edu.

129. Fletcher, *supra* chap. 1, note 19 ("Truman's Rhetoric").

130. Kassop, *supra* chap. 1, note 2.

131. Walter Dellinger, "Deployment of United States Armed Forces into Haiti," *Opinions of the Office of Legal Council* 18, no. 34 (September 27, 1994): 572–73.

132. Kassop, *supra* chap. 1, note 2, at 5.

133. *Curtiss-Wright* at 320.

134. Koh, *supra* chap. 1, note 3, at 94.

135. U.S. Department of State, "The Legality of United States Participation in the Defense of VietNam," *Department of State Bulletin* 54 (1966): 474.

136. U.S. Department of Justice, Office of Legal Counsel, *Access to Classified Information*, by Christopher H. Schroeder, Acting Assistant Attorney General, November 26, 1996.

137. *Id.* at 4 (citing a Justice Department brief).

138. *The President's Constitutional Authority to Conduct Military Operations against Terrorists and Nations Supporting Them*, WL 34726560, at 86 (Office of Legal Counsel, September 25, 2001) (quoting *Curtiss-Wright*).

139. U.S. Department of Justice, Office of Legal Counsel, 2006, 1.

140. *See generally* Charlie Savage, *Takeover: The Return of the Imperial Presidency and the Subversion of American Democracy* (New York: Little, Brown, 2008); *see generally* Fletcher, *supra* chap. 1, note 19 ("Truman's Rhetoric").

141. Anthony Simones, "The Reality of *Curtiss-Wright*," *Northern Illinois University Law Review* 16 (1995): 411, 415; adapted from Fletcher, *supra* chap. 1, note 19 ("Truman's Rhetoric").

142. This analysis is contrary to the views of Robert Dahl ("Decision Making in a Democracy: The Supreme Court as a National Policy-Maker," *Journal of Public Law* 6 [1957]: 279–95) and Gerald Rosenberg (*The Hollow Hope*, 2d ed. [Chicago: University of Chicago Press, 1993]).

143. *A.L.A. Schechter Brothers Poultry Corp. v. United States*, 295 U.S. 495 (1935).

144. *Humphrey's Executor v. United States*, 295 U.S. 602 (1935).

145. *See* Graber, *supra* chap. 1, note 83. Mark Graber asserts that when we examine the mutual-construction process, it facilitates an interpretive turn where the Court can overturn precedent; *see generally* Kahn and Kersch, *supra* chap. 1, note 69.

CHAPTER 3

1. *Strauder v. West Virginia*, 100 U.S. 303 (1880); *see also Batson v. Kentucky*, 476 U.S. 79 (1986).

2. *Smith v. Allwright*, 321 U.S. 649 (1944); *see also Gomillion v. Lightfoot*, 364 U.S. 339 (1960).

3. *Morgan v. Virginia*, 328 U.S. 373 (1946).

4. *Brown v. Board of Education*, 347 U.S. 483 (1954); *Plessy v. Ferguson*, 163 U.S. 537 (1896); *see generally* cases involving school segregation and busing—e.g., *Bolling v. Sharpe*, 347 U.S. 497 (1954); and *Browder v. Gayle*, 142 F. Supp. 707 (M.D. Ala. 1956).

5. For example, on December 15, 1941, Congressman John Rankin (D-MS) stated, "I'm for catching every Japanese in America, Alaska, and Hawaii now and putting them in concentration camps. . . . Damn them! Let's get rid of them now!" (Congressman John Rankin, Address to the House, *Congressional Record*, February 19, 1942, quoted in John Howard, *Concentration Camps on the Home Front* [Chicago: University of Chicago Press, 2009], 15).

6. "Authorizing the Secretary of War to Prescribe Military Areas," February 19, 1942, www.presidency.ucsb.edu.

7. *Yasui v. United States*, 320 U.S. 115 (1943); *Hirayabashi v. United States*, 320 U.S. 81 (1943); *Ex parte Mitsuye Endo*, 323 U.S. 283 (1944); and *Korematsu v. United States*, 323 U.S. 214 (1944).

8. *See* Greg Robinson, *By Order of the President: FDR and the Internment of Japanese Americans* (Cambridge, Mass.: Harvard University Press, 2001), 14.

9. Henry Stimson Diary, January 9, 1933, HLSP, quoted in *id.* at 47.

10. Robinson, *supra* note 8, at 48.

11. Franklin Roosevelt (FDR) indicated that the United States would associate itself "with world disarmament efforts[,] by stating that America would abide by any multilateral pact, thus signaling to Japan his desire to avoid war." In December 1933, he then declared that "he had no intention of isolating [the Japanese] diplomatically," and as a show of good faith, he "withdrew most of the American fleet from the Pacific to the Atlantic, as the Japanese had repeatedly requested" (*id.* at 48).

12. *Id.* at 51.

13. *Id.*

14. This speech gives some insight into how FDR framed the impact of the ensuing war and the impetus for issuing orders to intern Japanese Americans (FDR, "Day of Infamy" speech to Congress, December 8, 1941, *National Archives* 33, no. 4 [Winter 2001], www.archives.gov).

15. *See* Halford Ross Ryan, *American Rhetoric from Roosevelt to Reagan*, 2d ed. (Prospect Heights, Ill.: Waveland Press, 1987), 24–25.

16. Some of these stories were true (the Philippines was going to be invaded by Japan), and others were false (California was vulnerable and would be attacked by Japan). Ronald F. Reid and James F. Klumpp, *American Rhetorical Discourse*, 3d ed. (Long Grove, Ill.: Waveland Press, 2005).

17. *Id.* at 24–25.

18. "Day of Infamy" speech, *supra* note 14 ("I speak the will of the Congress and of the people when I assert [that] . . . this form of treachery shall never endanger us again. . . .

[O]ur people, our territory and our interests are in grave danger. . . . [S]ince the unprovoked and dastardly attack by Japan[,] . . . a state of war has existed between the United States and the Japanese Empire" [*id.*]).

19. *Id.*

20. The Axis powers' attack of Yugoslavia and Greece, their domination of the Balkans, Hitler's invasion of Russia (1941), the attacks of Malaya and Thailand, and now the United States all occurred without warning (*id.*).

21. *Id.*

22. *Id.*

23. *Id.*

24. Robinson, *supra* note 8, at 74.

25. *See generally id.*

26. The "FDR Memo" was a secret memorandum he sent to his chief of naval operations (cited in *id.* at 57): This "control" was limited, however, to Hawaii, because the Japanese posed "an inherent and undifferentiated threat to national security" (*id.*).

27. *Id.* at 57.

28. *Id.* at 59.

29. FDR and General Walter Short—a local army commander at Pearl Harbor—were both cautious of this potential threat (*id.* at 74).

30. Executive Order 8953, "Establishing Los Angeles–Long Beach Harbor Naval Defensive Sea Area California," November 27, 1941, www.presidency.ucsb.edu.

31. General Short met with John Poindexter (territorial governor) on the afternoon of December 7, 1941, and spoke of a "massive campaign of sabotage by Japanese Hawaiians." Following this meeting, Poindexter agreed to sign a proclamation authorizing unlimited martial law in the territory. This policy remained in effect for most of the war (Governor Poindexter's Martial Law, *Pacific Citizen*, October 16, 1948, 2).

32. *See generally* Robinson, *supra* note 8, at 60.

33. Initially, Japanese Americans were not the only group singled out. German and Italian aliens were also taken into custody—620 and 98, respectively (President's Official File 10-B, Justice Department, FBI Reports, 1941, Box 15).

34. Robinson, *supra* note 8, at 75.

35. This early analysis, while unfounded, was sustained in Robert Jackson's dissenting *Korematsu* (1944) opinion issued two years later (*Korematsu* at 245, 248).

36. Robinson, *supra* note 8, at 80.

37. *Id.* at 84.

38. *Id.* at 84; *see also* Roger Daniels, *Concentration Camps USA: Japanese Americans and World War II* (New York: Holt, Rinehart, and Winston, 1971); and Peter Irons, *Justice at War* (New York: Oxford University Press, 1983).

39. Robinson, *supra* note 8, at 87.

40. *Id.*

41. Irons, *supra* note 38, at 38.

42. Robinson, *supra* note 8, at 92.

43. Francis Biddle to Leland Ford, January 24, 1942, and Francis Biddle to Leland Ford, January 27, 1942, reprinted in Commission on Wartime Relocation and Internment of Civilians (CWRIC) Papers, pp. 5739–40 (reel 5, pp. 417–18).

44. Robinson, *supra* note 8, at 92. Greg Robinson suggests that the implication of this letter was that Leland Ford would have to lobby the Justice Department to have the authority transferred from the Enemy Alien Control Program to the army.

45. *Id.*

46. *See id.* at 96–97. The War Relocation Authority (WRA) divided individuals of Japanese descent into four groups: Issei (immigrant Japanese who were born in Japan; around forty thousand), Nisei (American-born and American-educated children of Issei parents; around sixty-three thousand), Kibei (American-born individuals who were educated in Japan [in whole or in part]; around nine thousand), and Sansei (second-generation, American-born children of Nisei; around forty-five hundred) (*id.*).

47. *State of the Union Address*, January 6, 1942, www.presidency.ucsb.edu.

48. *Id.*

49. Richard N. Current, "How Stimson Meant to 'Maneuver' the Japanese," *Mississippi Valley Historical Review* 40, no. 1 (1953): 67–69.

50. *Id.* at 67–79.

51. Robinson, *supra* note 8, at 116.

52. February 11, 1942 (*id.* at 69).

53. In fact, these members of Congress sent FDR a unified letter recommending the "immediate evacuation of all persons of Japanese lineage"—aliens and citizens alike—from the entire strategic area of California, Washington, and Oregon (*see generally* Robinson, *supra* note 8, at 204).

54. "The Fifth Column," *Los Angeles Times*, February 13, 1942: "[T]he Pacific Coast is in imminent danger of a combined attack from within and from without. . . . [C]ommunication takes place between the enemy at sea and enemy agents on land. . . . The Pacific Coast is officially a combat zone; some part of it may at any moment be a battlefield. Nobody's constitutional rights include the right to reside and do business on a battlefield." Walter Lippmann relied on false reports from Earl Warren and other sources on the West Coast.

55. Harry S. Truman: Library and Museum. Ca. February 10, 1942, www.trumanlibrary.org/whistlestop/study.

56. February 19, 1942, www.presidency.ucsb.edu. Any concerns of FDR's over the necessity of internment were laid to rest when he received a memorandum shortly before signing the order: "In time of national peril, any reasonable doubt must be resolved in favor of action to preserve the national safety, not for the purpose of punishing those whose liberty may be temporarily affected by such action, but for the purpose of protecting the freedom of the nation, which may be long impaired, if not permanently lost, by nonaction" (Document 6, Budget Director Harold D. Smith to the President, February 19, 1942, President's Official File 4805: Military Areas, 1941–1942). James H. Rowe Jr., assistant to the attorney general, was the most ardent critic of the proposed policy to relocate and intern. He denounced the proposal as unconstitutional and asserted that as a result of public hysteria, the president's hand had been forced. Rowe warned the president of mounting public pressure and the constitutional issues surrounding the policy (James H. Rowe Jr. Papers, Assistant to the Attorney General Files, Alien Enemy Control Unit, Box 33). Attorney General Francis Biddle sent a last-ditch memo on February 17, 1942, advising the president not to launch a massive, immediate evacuation and internment of Japanese Americans (President's Official File 18, Navy Department, March–April 1942, Box 7).

57. EO 9066, "Authorizing the Secretary of War to Prescribe Military Areas," www.presidency.ucsb.edu.

58. William Rehnquist, *All the Laws but One: Civil Liberties in Wartime* (New York: Vintage, 1998), 224.

59. March 18, 1942, www.presidency.ucsb.edu.

60. *See* www.presidency.ucsb.edu. FDR also signed Public Law 77-503 (56 Stat 173) ("to provide a penalty for violation of restrictions or orders with respect to persons entering,

remaining in, leaving, or committing any act in military areas or zones"), which made it a federal offense for any person refusing to leave a military area authorized by EO 9066.

61. Quoted in Milton S. Eisenhower, *The President Is Calling* (New York: Doubleday, 1974), 118; *see also* Eric L. Muller, "Apologies or Apologists? Remembering the Japanese American Internment in Wyoming," *Wyoming Law Review* 1 (2001): 473. In the spring of 1943, Director Dillon S. Myer (WRA) sent a letter to the secretary of war advising him to relax the exclusion order effective immediately, but the secretary said he would not consider the recommendation until the "vicious, well-organized, pro-Japanese minority group[s]" were removed from the relocation centers (May 10, 1943; *see generally* Robinson, *supra* note 8).

62. For example, Proclamation No. 1, "Military Areas 1 and 2" (March 2, 1942). This proclamation allocated the Pacific Coast line of California, Oregon, and Washington and the southern portion of Arizona as military areas and pronounced that all persons of Japanese descent were to be removed (www.encyclopedia.denshow.org).

63. Second Quarterly Report, Papers of Philleo Nash, July 1 to September 30, 1942, War Relocation Authority, circa late 1942.

64. Robinson, *supra* note 8.

65. One alternative policy path might have been the limited local martial law that FDR was contemplating if the Court ruled adversely. Alternatively, the Court could have determined that the president did not have the authority to intern, relocate, and exclude.

66. Public Proclamation No. 3 extended travel restrictions, curfew, and contraband regulations to Japanese Americans (*U.S. National Archives*, www.archives.gov).

67. Glen Kitayama, "*Yasui v. United States*," in *Encyclopedia of Japanese American History*, ed. Brian Niiya, Facts On File, www.fofweb.com.

68. *Id.*

69. Irons, *supra* note 38.

70. *See* Roger Daniels, "The Japanese American Cases, 1942–2004: A Social History," *Law and Contemporary Problems* 68 (2004): 159.

71. By the time *Hirabayashi* and *Korematsu* reached the Court, Charles Fahy had learned of the Ringle Report, which clearly undermined the rationale behind the policy of internment. Contrary to the report, Fahy argued before the Court, it was impossible to segregate loyal Japanese Americans from disloyal ones (*see* Robinson, *supra* note 8, at chap. 5).

72. *Id.*, at chap. 5.

73. *Yasui* at 63.

74. Morris L. Ernst to FDR, April 15, 1943, OF 197 (Japan), quoted in Robinson, *supra* note 8, at 299. Ernst, a Roosevelt crony, frequently sent FDR updates on political news and gossip.

75. Morris Ernst to Hon. Harlan F. Stone, March 6, 1943, Harlan Stone Papers, LC, reprinted in CWRIC Papers, pp. 6772–75 (reel 6, pp. 358–61), quoted in Robinson, *supra* note 8, at 190.

76. Robinson, *supra* note 8, at 190 (Hon. Harlan F. Stone to Morris Ernst, March 17, 1943, Harlan Stone Papers, LC, reprinted in CWRIC Papers, pp. 6772–6775 [reel 6, pp. 358–61]).

77. FDR, Memorandum for Morris Ernst, April 24, 1943, OF 197 (Japan).

78. Robinson, *supra* note 8, at 191.

79. *Hirabayashi* at 81.

80. *Id.* at 91.

81. *Id.* at 92. Harlan Stone also cited the precedent of *Ex parte Quirin*, 317 U.S. 1, at 25–26 (1942).

82. *Hirabayashi* at 93.

83. *Id.*

84. *Id.*

85. *Id.* at 93–98.

86. *Id.* at 102.

87. *Id.* at 98.

88. *Id.*

89. *Id.* at 100. And it was not the Court's job to scrutinize the details that contributed to John DeWitt's findings (*id.* at 102).

90. *See* Morton Grodzins, *Americans Betrayed* (Chicago: University of Chicago Press, 1949), 353.

91. *See* Alpheus Thomas Mason, *The Supreme Court from Taft to Warren* (Baton Rouge: Louisiana State University Press, 1968), 167. Regarding the role of the Court, Stone said, "The only check upon our own exercise of power is our own sense of self-restraint": *United States v. Butler*, 297 U.S. 1, 79 (1936). Eugene Rostow adds that this "is rooted in a respect for the dignity and high purpose of the other branches of government, and a sympathetic understanding of the problems they must try to resolve" (Eugene V. Rostow, "The Democratic Character of Judicial Review," *Yale Law School Faculty Scholarship Series* 66, no. 2 [1952]: 213).

92. Rostow, *supra* note 91, at 106.

93. *Id.* at 112.

94. Sidney Fine, "Mr. Justice Murphy and the *Hirabayashi* Case," *Pacific Historical Review* 32, no. 2 (1964): 255; *see also* Irons, *supra* note 38, at 245–47.

95. Rostow, *supra* note 91, at 210.

96. Fine, *supra* note 94, at 201.

97. Mason, *supra* note 91, at 135. Alpheus Mason regards Stone's support of FDR's New Deal objectives as powerful evidence.

98. Alan F. Westin, *The Supreme Court* (New York: W. W. Norton, 1961), 158.

99. *Id.* at 170.

100. Mason, *supra* note 91, at 167. Stone wrote to his former law student William O. Douglas, who was serving alongside him: "I am anxious to go as far as I reasonably can to meet the views of my associates. . . . [I]t would be wiser for me to stand by the substance of my opinion and for you to express your views . . . as you have already done" (H.F.S. to William O. Douglas, June 4, 1943, cited in Alpheus T. Mason, *Harlan Fiske Stone* [New York: Viking Press, 1956], 675). This brief note reflected Stone's effort to preserve the appearance of Court unanimity and to address Douglas's concern with respect to the forthcoming *Korematsu* opinion; *see also* Maltzman et al., *supra* chap. 1, note 76.

101. Segal and Spaeth, *supra* chap. 1, note 72, at 57.

102. Helen Thomas, *Felix Frankfurter, Scholar on the Bench* (Baltimore: Johns Hopkins Press, 1960), 249.

103. *Home Building and Loan Association v. Blaisdell*, 290 U.S. 398 (1934), 426; *see also* Thomas, *supra* note 102, at 249.

104. Fine, *supra* note 94, at 201.

105. Cited in *id.* at 206.

106. Stanley F. Reed to H.F.S., June 3, 1943, cited in Mason, *supra* note 100, at 676.

107. *Hirabayashi* at 93.

108. *See* Daniels, *supra* note 38, at 134–35.

109. *Hirabayashi* (*id.* at 106).

110. *Id.* at 107.

111. *See generally* J. Woodford Howard Jr., *Mr. Justice Murphy* (Princeton, N.J.: Princeton University Press, 1968), 343.

112. *Hirabayashi* at 110.

113. *Id.*

114. Howard, *supra* note 111, at 307–9.

115. *Id.* at 307–9; *Hirabayashi* at 235.

116. F.F. to F.M., June 10, 1943, No. 870, Box 132, cited in Howard, *supra* note 111, at 307–8.

117. *Hirabayashi* at 114.

118. *Id.* at 113.

119. *Id.* at 114.

120. EO 9423, February 16, 1944, "Transfer of the War Relocation Authority to the Department of the Interior," 9 FR 1903, February 18, 1944, *National Archives*, www.archives.gov.

121. *See* William Dudley, ed., *Japanese American Internment Camps* (Farmington Hills, Mich.: Greenhaven Press, 2002), 19–20, 62, 117, and 131.

122. *Korematsu* at 261.

123. Robinson, *supra* note 8, at 209.

124. *Ex parte Endo* at 283.

125. *Id.* at 302–3.

126. Posner and Vermeule, *supra* chap. 1, note 8, at 55.

127. *Korematsu* at 216.

128. The "rally effect" (John E. Mueller, *War, Presidents, and Public Opinion* [New York: Wiley, 1973]) gave FDR a twelve-point increase after the Japanese attacked Pearl Harbor, John Kennedy a thirteen-point boost during the Cuban Missile Crisis (1962), George H. W. Bush a fourteen-point lift when Iraq invaded Kuwait (1990), and George W. Bush a thirty-five-point jump following the attacks of September 11 (2011). *See generally* gallup.com.

129. Grodzins, *supra* note 90, at 358.

130. *Korematsu* at 216; and Eugene V. Rostow, "The Japanese American Cases," *Yale Law School Faculty Scholarship Series* 54, no. 489 (1945): 509.

131. Milton R. Konvitz, *The Alien and the Asiatic in American Law* (Ithaca, N.Y.: Cornell University Press, 1946), 258.

132. *Korematsu* at 216–19.

133. *Id.* at 323.

134. *Id.*

135. *See* Charlotte Williams, *Hugo Black: A Study in the Judicial Process* (Baltimore: Johns Hopkins Press, 1950), 165.

136. *Id.* at 166.

137. *Id.*

138. *Id.*

139. *Adarand Constructors, Inc. v. Peña*, 515 U.S. 200 (1995).

140. Harlan F. Stone to Harry Black, November 9, 1944, cited in Mason, *supra* note 100, at 677–78.

141. *Id.*; *see also* Konvitz, *supra* note 131, at 259–60.

142. *Korematsu* at 224.

143. *Id.* at 224–25.

144. *See* Thomas, *supra* note 102, at 248.

145. *Id.* at 244.

146. Frank Murphy to Eugene Gressman, undated, Box 183, Murphy Papers, cited in Fine, *supra* note 94, at 208.

147. *Korematsu* at 233.

148. *Id.* at 235–37.

149. *Id.* at 240.

150. *Id.* at 233.

151. *Id.*

152. *Id.* After *Korematsu*, Frank Murphy became convinced that it was time to impose judicial checks on the growth of military power (Howard, *supra* note 111, at 367).

153. *Endo* at 307–8.

154. In fact, he stated that there was no conceivable way for him to determine the reasonableness (Daniels, *supra* note 38, at 139–40).

155. *Korematsu* at 244, 248.

156. *Id.*

157. *Id.* at 247.

158. In the end, Jackson withdrew his draft opinion in *Quirin*, probably because of Felix Frankfurter's famous memorandum to the Court, which "urged the Justices not to splinter over relatively unimportant procedural matters in the midst of a total war" (*see* Edward G. White, Felix Frankfurter's "Soliloquy," in *Ex parte Quirin*: Nazi Sabotages Constitutional Conundrums, 5 Green Bag 2d 423); *see generally* Dennis J. Hutchinson, "'The Achilles Heel' of the Constitution: Justice Jackson and the Japanese Exclusion Cases," *Supreme Court Review* 2002 (2002): 455–94.

159. Hutchinson, 2002, *supra* note 158, at 455, 488.

160. Jackson's draft opinion, 10, in White, *supra* note 158, at 241.

161. *See* Tushnet, *supra* chap. 1, note 92, at 124.

162. Robinson, *supra* note 8, at 229. The new Western Defense commander, General Henry Pratt, issued a proclamation that permitted all Japanese Americans except those found to have "pro-Japanese attitude" to return home. And in July 1945, the WRA proclaimed that all relocation centers except Tule would be closed between October 15 and December 15, 1945 (*id.* at 230).

163. Anne E. Marimow and Robert Barnes, "Federal Appeals Court Maintains Freeze of Trump's Travel Ban. Attorney General Vows Supreme Court Appeal," *Washington Post*, May 25, 2017.

CHAPTER 4

1. *Youngstown Sheet and Tube Co. v. Sawyer*, 343 U.S. 579 (1952).

2. For example, Powell, *supra* chap. 2, note 24, at 226–27: "Youngstown . . . marks an appropriate end-point for an examination of Curtiss-Wright's immediate impact" (*id.*). The Pentagon Papers case was a clear example of the Court's acceptance of congressional delegations of power to the executive (*New York Times Co. v. United States*, 403 U.S. 713 (1971)).

3. Fletcher, *supra* chap. 1, note 19 ("Unilateral Executive Power").

4. 80 H.R. 3020, Public Law 80-101, 61 Stat. 136, enacted June 23, 1947.

5. Whittington, *supra* chap. 1, note 117, at xii.

6. *See generally* the decisions rendered in the aftermath of *Curtiss-Wright* (1936). Chapters 2 and 3 show how the Court institutionalized the dominant role of the executive in foreign policy making.

7. *See generally* Stephen Skowronek (*supra* chap. 1, note 95), who coined the term "affili-

ated president"; *see also* Keith Whittington (*supra* chap. 1, note 117), who evaluates the role of an affiliated president and judicial supremacy.

8. October 11, 1952, in *Public Papers, 1952–1953*, cited in Whittington, *supra* chap. 1, note 117, at 798; *see also* Mary Dudziak, *Cold War Civil Rights* (Princeton, N.J.: Princeton University Press, 2011), 91–102. Justice Tom Clark was appointed by President Harry Truman because of "faithful service by political intimates" (Whittington, *supra* chap. 1, note 117, at 90).

9. Whittington, *supra* chap. 1, note 117, at 23.

10. *See* Skowronek's discussion of leadership and political time (*supra* chap. 1, note 95, at 18, 35).

11. Harry S. Truman, *Memoirs* (Garden City, N.Y.: Doubleday, 1995), 2:393.

12. Glenn D. Paige, *The Korean Decision* (New York: Free Press, 1968), 187.

13. The President's New Conference of June 29, 1950, *Public Papers of the Presidents of the United States, Harry S. Truman, 1950* (Washington, D.C.: U.S. Government Printing Office, 1965), 503.

14. *Id.* at 504.

15. Statement of Rep. Harold Cooley, Democrat of North Carolina, in U.S. House, 81st Cong., 2d sess., August 10, 1950, Cong. Rec. 96:12201.

16. For a discussion of the decision not to seek congressional authorization, *see* Paige, *supra* 12, at 187, 305–6; Ronald J. Caridi, *The Korean War and American Politics* (Philadelphia: University of Pennsylvania Press, 1968), 44–48; and David Rees, *Korea: The Limited War* (Baltimore: Penguin Books, 1970), 21–35.

17. Cooley, June 28, 1950, *supra* note 15, at 9320.

18. Wilfred E. Binkley, *The Man in the White House* (Baltimore: Johns Hopkins University Press, 1959), 91; and Cabell Phillips, *The Truman Presidency* (New York: Macmillan, 1966), 399.

19. *See, e.g.,* the statements of Rep. Graham Barden (D-NC), August 2, 1950, Cong. Rec. 96:11626; and Republican Senator Kenneth Wherry of Nebraska, August 11, 1950 (*id.* at 12277).

20. Proclamation, *Public Papers of the Presidents of the United States, 1950*, 746–47.

21. Truman, *supra* note 11, 2:476–85. Clinton Rossiter notes that "almost all of the President's lengthy catalogue of emergency powers go into operation upon the declaration of an emergency ascertained and proclaimed by himself alone" (Clinton Rossiter, *Constitutional Dictatorship* [Princeton, N.J.: Princeton University Press, 2007], 299).

22. Richard Neustadt, "Congress and the Fair Deal: A Legislative Balance Sheet," *Public Policy* 5 (1954): 373.

23. Debate in the House of Representatives, August 1, 1950, Cong. Rec. 96:11506–41, and the remarks in the Senate, August 2 and August 4, 1950 (*id.* at 11558, 11581, 11824–27). "[I]n its wisdom [Congress believed] it would be proper to grant stand-by controls" (Senator Burnet Maybank, Democrat of South Carolina, chairman of the Committee on Banking and Currency [*id.* at 12154]). Truman made it clear that if Congress found it necessary to grant standby authority, it should be granted at the discretion of the president. Ultimately, he should be able to decide where, when, and how price and wage controls would be instituted (Letter to Committee Chairman on the Defense Production Bill, August 1, 1950, *Public Papers of the Presidents of the United States, 1950*, 567). Testimony by Bernard Baruch (an authority figure on economic controls) in August 1950 and subsequent Senate hearings resonated with Congress and the public.

24. *U.S. Statutes at Large 1950*, "Defense Production Act," September 8, 1950, 64:798.

25. *Id.* at 799.

26. *See* U.S. Senate, Committee on Banking and Currency, *Defense Production Act of 1950,* 21.

27. Sec. 501, *U.S. Statutes at Large 1950,* 64:812.

28. Senate Report, 1950, 2250, 7–8.

29. *U.S. Statutes at Large 1950,* 64:812. The only limitation specified by Congress was Section 503: required measures could not be taken by the president that were inconsistent with either the Taft-Hartley Act of 1947 or any other federal labor standards (Cong. Rec. 96:12905–6).

30. Robert Rogers, *An Economic History of the American Steel Industry* (New York: Routledge, 2009), 123–24.

31. "Delegating Certain Functions of the President under the Defense Production Act of 1950," www.presidency.ucsb.edu.

32. Public Law 81-774, 50 U.S.C. Appx Sec. 2061 et seq.

33. *See generally* Maeva Marcus, *Truman and the Steel Seizure Case: The Limits of Presidential Power* (New York: Columbia University Press, 1977).

34. Radio and Television Report to the American People on the National Emergency, December 15, 1950, *Public Papers of the Presidents of the United States, 1950,* 744.

35. *See* testimony of Eric Johnston in U.S. Senate, Committee on Banking and Currency, *Defense Production Act Amendments of 1951, Hearings,* 519.

36. Wage Stabilization Program, 1950–1953, 1:4; Johnston, *supra* note 35, at 519; *see also* Alonzo Hamby, *Beyond the New Deal* (New York: Columbia University Press, 1973), 446–48; and Cyrus Ching, *Review and Reflection* (New York: B. C. Forbes, 1953), 92–93.

37. Johnston, *supra* note 35, at 519; and Joseph Rayback, *A History of American Labor* (New York: Free Press, 1966), 412.

38. Arthur R. McClure, *The Truman Administration and the Problems of Postwar Labor, 1945–1948* (Rutherford, N.J.: Fairleigh Dickinson University Press, 1969), 36, 81; and Phillips, *supra* note 18, at 31–32.

39. 29 U.S.C. Sec. 141–97, 80 H.R. 3020, Public Law 80–101, 61 Stat. 136, enacted June 23, 1947.

40. McClure, *supra* note 38, at 159; and Susan Hartmann, *Truman and the 80th Congress* (Columbia: University of Missouri Press, 1971), 5.

41. Harry Millis and Emily Brown, *From the Wagner Act to Taft-Hartley* (Chicago: University of Chicago Press, 1950), 398, 489–96.

42. *Id.* at 363.

43. R. Alton Lee, *Truman and Taft-Hartley: A Question of Mandate* (Lexington, Ky.: Greenwood Press, 1980), 80–105. In fact, Truman's 1948 campaign made effective use of the pro-labor veto message and won him labor's support for his candidacy.

44. Wage Stabilization Program, 1950–1953, 2:3, www.archives.gov.

45. Cong. Rec. 96:9537; *see* Marcus, *supra* note 33, at 32.

46. John M. Fenton, *In Your Opinion* (Boston: Little, Brown, 1960), 91; *see also* Elmo Roper, *You and Your Leaders* (New York: William Morrow, 1957), 145.

47. Fenton, *supra* note 46, at 90.

48. Neustadt, *supra* note 22, at 373; *see also* Samuel Lubell, *The Future of American Politics* (Westport, Conn.: Greenwood Press, 1952), 230–31. *See* the polls in *Public Opinion Quarterly* 15:386–87; and Athan Theoharis, "The Rhetoric of Politics: Foreign Policy, Internal Security, and Domestic Politics in the Truman Era, 1945–1950," in Barton J. Bernstein, *Politics and Policies of the Truman Administration* (Chicago, Ill.: Quadrangle Books, 1970), 217.

49. Fenton, *supra* note 46, at 73, 92. A mere 23 percent of the electorate approved of Truman's actions (*id.*).

50. *See* Cabell Phillips, "Congress Falls Behind in Election-Year Lag," *New York Times*, June 1, 1952, E7.

51. Robert Hirschfield, *The Power of the Presidency: Concepts and Controversy*, 3d ed. (New York: Routledge, 2012), 17–18.

52. Statement by the President on the Labor Dispute in the Steel Industry, December 22, 1951, *Public Papers of the Presidents of the United States, 1951*, 651.

53. Memorandum and Draft of April 3, 1952, Gardner Ackley to Arnall, April 7, 1952, Steel, Decentralized Files of Various Directors of OPS, RG 295, NA.

54. Note from Ben Moreell to Roger L. Putman, July 14, 1952, Wage Stabilization Steel Industry, General Subject Files 1951–1953, Records of the Office of the Administrator, ESA, RG 296, NA, quoted in Marcus, *supra* note 33, at 56.

55. *See Steel* 130 (January 1952): 492, discussed in Marcus, *supra* note 33, at 58.

56. Statement by the President on the Labor Dispute in the Steel Industry, December 22, 1951, *Public Papers of the Presidents of the United States, 1951*, 651; *see* Truman, *supra* note 11, at 2:528–30, cited in Marcus, *supra* note 33, at 60.

57. Statement by the President on the Labor Dispute in the Steel Industry, December 22, 1951, *Public Papers of the Presidents of the United States, 1951*, 652.

58. *See* Grant McConnell, *Steel Seizure of 1952* (Indianapolis: Bobbs-Merrill, 1960), 31; *see also* Memorandum to Assistant Attorney General Baldridge Re: President's Power to Seize the Steel Industry, p. 5, Lloyd Files, Box 6, Truman Papers, TL.

59. *See* Memorandum Re: Steel Developments, Enarson Riles, April 7, 1952, Box 5, Enarson Papers, TL.

60. Griffin, *supra* chap. 1, note 16, at chap. 2. Stephen Griffin argues that Truman led the way in a new constitutional order by taking unilateral steps in the Korean War.

61. Cases involving the invocation of presidential inherent powers never actually ruled on the legality of seizures. The first case (1941) involved the North American Aviation plant, which was seized by Executive Order 8773 (Fed. Reg. 6:2777). The second case (1941) involved the Federal Shipbuilding and Drydock Company, which was seized by Executive Order 8868 (Fed. Reg. 6:4349). And the last case (1941) involved Air Associates, Inc., which was seized by Executive Order 8938 (Fed. Reg. 6:5599).

62. Memorandum from Kayle to Stowe, April 1, 1952, *Stowe Papers*, TL, pp. 1–2, discussed in Marcus, *supra* note 33, at 77.

63. Memorandum to Assistant Attorney General Baldridge: President's Power to Seize the Steel Industry, p. 7. David Lloyd, one of Truman's administrative assistants, asserted in a memorandum to the Justice Department, "Although each of the statutes considered above is of at least arguable applicability, it is not desirable to rely on them. . . . Basing the seizure solely upon the inherent powers—while it does not assure freedom from this principle—at least leaves some leeway for maneuver" (*id.* at 7, discussed in Marcus, *supra* note 33, at 77).

64. Marcus, *supra* note 33, at 77.

65. Radio and Television address to the American People on the Need for Government Operation of the Steel Mills, April 8, 1952, *Public Papers of the Presidents of the United States, 1952–1953*, 246–50; Fed. Reg., EO 10340 "Directing the Secretary of Commerce to Take Possession of and Operate the Plants and Facilities of Certain Steel Companies" (*id.* at 17:3139). The order gave Charles Sawyer the discretionary power to determine the terms and conditions of employment while the government operated the mills. The order also asserted that the president's authority to issue such a directive rested on the Constitution, specifically the commander-in-chief clause (*id.*).

66. Radio and Television address, *Public Papers*, April 8, 1952, 247, www.presidency.ucsb.edu.

67. Marcus, *supra* note 33, at 81–84.

68. *Public Papers*, April 26, 1952, 393, www.presidency.ucsb.edu. The history books are replete with examples of charges of incompetence, treason, and even conspiracy, and they were all directed at the executive branch, albeit by irresponsible members of Congress. Robert Beisner notes that those opposing the administration "unleashed the most vicious campaign of abuse and slander against political leaders in American history" (Robert Beisner, *Dean Acheson: A Life in the Cold War* [New York: Oxford University Press, 2009], 319). Because Republicans could not defeat Truman in 1948, they criticized him in a number of areas, including his use of nuclear weapons, the influence of Communism in the U.S. government, the loss of China, and the U.S. failure in Korea (Patterson, *supra* chap. 2, note 7, at 169–205).

69. Polls showed that 51 percent approved of the president's action, while 43 percent opposed it. And in Congress, the divide was along party lines for the most part: Republicans disapproved of the action, while Democrats favored the seizure. A larger majority, 55 percent, believed that Truman had the power as president to seize the mills (Public Opinion Index for Industry, Special Report, enclosed in a note, Claude Robinson to Senator Robert A. Taft, April 30, 1952, Box 720, Taft Papers, LC, *The Gallup Poll*). Another poll reported that 35 percent approved of the seizure, and 43 percent censured it (Gallup, *The Gallup Poll, 1935–1971*, 2:1065). Maeva Marcus suggests that given the volume of correspondence from the public to the White House, to Congress, to the Justice Department, and to editors of various newspapers, it was clear that the general public was split (*supra* note 33, at 91).

70. Special Message to the Congress, *Public Papers*, April 9, 1952, 251. Truman noted that he was more than willing to follow Congress's lead if it decided to pass a bill, but in the event that it did not, he said, "I would naturally have to take the responsibility myself." But Truman also noted that he did not believe that legislation was necessary (Truman, *supra* note 11, at 2:535).

71. A bill that had reached the Judiciary Committee on referral was halted, because Judge David Pine's decision had been handed down, and Senator Pat McCarran wanted to see what course the case would take (Note from McCarran to Hon. Hugh Butler, May 13, 1952, Files on S. 3106, NA).

72. Special Message to Congress, *Public Papers*, April 9, 1952, 251.

73. Truman, *supra* note 11, at 2:535.

74. U.S. House of Representatives, *The Steel Seizure Case*, H. Doc. 534, 82d Cong., 2d sess. (Washington, D.C.: U.S. Government Printing Office, 1952), 253.

75. If it was found that the seizure was illegal, the steel companies could file a suit for damages under the Federal Tort Claims Act (U.S. House, *supra* note 74, at 253–54). Holmes Baldridge was unable to adequately explain exactly what he meant by a legal taking that is subject to just compensation under the Fifth Amendment.

76. *Id.* at 257–58.

77. *Id.* at 265–66. Alexander Holtzoff, quoting Chief Justice Salmon Chase, commented, "Congress is the legislative department of the Government. The President is the executive department. Neither can be restrained in its action by the judicial department, though the acts of both when performed are in proper cases subject to its cognizance" (*Mississippi v. Johnson*, 4 Wall. 475 (1867)). U.S. House, *supra* note 74, at 265.

78. U.S. House, *supra* note 74, at 363 (*see also* discussion, *id.*, at 366).

79. *Youngstown*, 103 F. Supp. 569 (D.D.C. 1952); U.S. House, *supra* note 74, at 66.

80. U.S. House, *supra* note 74, at 75–76; *see* William Howard Taft, *Our Chief Magistrate and His Powers* (New York: Columbia University Press, 1916), 139–40.

81. Pine therefore gave U.S. Steel the option to withdraw its modified injunction and reinstate its original application (U.S. House, *supra* note 74, at 76).

82. No. 745—*Charles Sawyer, Secretary of Commerce, Petitioner v. The Youngstown Sheet and Tube Co. et al.*, Petition for a Writ of Certiorari to the U.S. Court of Appeals for the District of Columbia Circuit and Application for Stay, U.S. House, *supra* note 74, at 513.

83. The day the Court granted cert, the union and the industry were at the White House discussing terms of an agreement, and a settlement was certain until the industry heard that the Court was taking the case (noted in Marcus, *supra* note 33, at 336, interview with Arthur Goldberg, September 11, 1972).

84. Sawyer was ordered to "take no action to change any term or condition of employment while this stay is in effect unless such change is mutually agreed upon by the steel companies . . . and the bargaining representatives of the employees" (U.S. House, *supra* note 74, at 457).

85. Memorandum, "Future Action in the Steel Case," Harold Enarson and Milton Kayle to John R. Steelman, May 23, 1952, Box 4, Stowe Papers, TL.

86. No. 745—Brief for Petitioner, U.S. House, *supra* note 74, at 810.

87. *Id.* at 810–11. Examples included the Revolutionary War of 1812 and the actions of Abraham Lincoln, Woodrow Wilson, and FDR.

88. "The President's News Conference," May 22, 1952, *Public Papers of the Presidents of the United States, 1952–1953*, 362 (emphasis added).

89. *Id.*

90. Whittington, *supra* chap. 1, note 117.

91. *New York Times*, May 23, 1952, 1, 14; *see also* Arthur Krok's comment in *New York Times*, May 23, 1952, 20.

92. *See also* Clinton Rossiter, *The Supreme Court and the Commander in Chief* (Ithaca, N.Y.: Cornell University, 1951). Rossiter maintains that the Court has been extremely careful in its declarations of the president as commander-in-chief: "It has been respectful, complimentary, on occasion properly awed" (4). C. Herman Pritchett agrees with the Corwin-Rossiter position that the Court has enlarged presidential power and would do little to interfere with its development (C. Herman Pritchett, "The President and the Supreme Court," *Journal of Politics* 11, no. 1 [1949]: 91–92).

93. For example, Emanuel Celler, chairman of the House Judiciary Committee, asserted that the Court was more than likely to conclude that it had no power to pass judgment on the president's action (Cong. Rec. 98:A3278).

94. The Supreme Court, in 1946, was split into two blocks—the Black-Douglas-Murphy-Rutledge block and the Frankfurter-Jackson faction, with the remaining justices swinging between the two to form a majority in cases (*see* Harvey G. Hudspeth, "A Court Divided: Harlan Fiske Stone, Judicial Review, and Administrative Regulation of the Economy, 1941–1946," *Essays in Economic and Business History* 18 [2000]: 18).

95. Dahl, *supra* chap. 2, note 142; Funston, *supra* chap. 1, note 164.

96. Marcus, *supra* note 33, at 182.

97. William E. Leuchtenburg, "A Klansman Joins the Court," *Crosskey Lectures: University of Chicago Law School*, no. 2 (1973): 1–31.

98. C. Herman Pritchett, "Stanley Reed," in *The Justices of the United States Supreme Court*, ed. Leon Friedman and Fred L. Israel (New York: Chelsea House in association with Bowker, 1969), 3:2372–89; *see also* C. Herman Pritchett, *The Roosevelt Court* (New York: Macmillan, 2014), 208, 260; and Fred Rodell, *Nine Men* (New York: Vintage Books, 1955), 262, 268.

99. It is interesting to note, after Justice Owen Roberts's "switch in time," that Frankfurter wrote to FDR, "And now, with the shift by Roberts, even a blind man ought to see that the Court is in politics, and understand how the Constitution is 'judicially' construed. It is a deep object lesson—a lurid demonstration—of the relation of men to the

'meaning' of the Constitution" (Felix Frankfurter, March 30, 1937, Box 243, Frankfurter Papers, L.C).

100. *Korematsu* at 224. Similarly, Frankfurter believed that the Court could not determine whether Hawaii was a battlefield at the time of the challenged trial. That judgment was the president's, and the president's alone (*Duncan v. Kahanamoku*, 327 U.S. 304, at 313, 335–37, 344–45 (1946)).

101. *See* John P. Frank, "William O. Douglas," in *The Justices of the United States Supreme Court: 1789–1969*, ed. Leon Friedman and Fred L. Israel (Broomall, Pa.: Chelsea House), 4:2454; and William Douglas, *Go East, Young Man* (New York: Random House, 1974), 452–53.

102. *See* Rodell, *supra* note 98, at 76; *see also Duncan v. Kahanamoku* (1946). Although the Court ruled against the government (Douglas sided with the majority), this case was decided after the war had ended.

103. *See* Warner W. Gardner, "Robert H. Jackson, 1892–1954: Government Attorney," *Columbia Law Review* 55 (1955): 442. Jackson promulgated the legal justification for FDR's seizure of the North American Aviation plant and engineered the "legal underpinnings of the destroyers for bases" pact with Great Britain. Jackson's expansive construction of the executive's authority sanctioned FDR's deal without gaining specific congressional legislation (U.S. Department of Justice, *Official Opinions of the Attorneys General*, 39:484–96); *see also* Philip Kurland, "Robert H. Jackson," in *The Justices of the United States Supreme Court: 1789–1969*, ed. Leon Friedman and Fred L. Israel (Broomall, Pa.: Chelsea House), 4:2560–61.

104. Rodell, *supra* note 98, at 262.

105. Richard Kirkendall, "Fred M. Vinson," in *The Justices of the United States Supreme Court: 1789–1969*, ed. Leon Friedman and Fred L. Israel (Broomall, Pa.: Chelsea House), 4:2640–41, 2649. Vinson's move to the Supreme Court was based on Truman's belief that, given Vinson's record as a successful mediator largely between Congress and the executive branch, he could employ these skills and appease the badly divided Court. Even though Vinson had been elevated to the Court, he remained an adviser to Truman (*id.* at 2641–42, 2648); Robert Scigliano, *The Supreme Court and the Presidency* (New York: Free Press, 1971), 76.

106. Richard Kirkendall, "Harold Burton," in *The Justices of the United States Supreme Court: 1789–1969*, ed. Leon Friedman and Fred L. Israel (Broomall, Pa.: Chelsea House), 4:2617–18; and Alan F. Westin, *Anatomy of a Constitutional Law Case* (New York: Columbia University Press, 1990), 132.

107. Richard Kirkendall, "Tom C. Clark," in *The Justices of the United States Supreme Court: 1789–1969*, ed. Leon Friedman and Fred L. Israel (Broomall, Pa.: Chelsea House), 4:2665–77. Justice Jackson (concurring opinion) took notice of Clark's well-known endorsement of the inherent powers of the president (*Youngstown* at 649n17).

108. Leuchtenburg, *supra* note 97, at 29.

109. Richard Kirkendall, "Sherman Minton," in *The Justices of the United States Supreme Court: 1789–1969*, ed. Leon Friedman and Fred L. Israel (Broomall, Pa.: Chelsea House), 4:2699–708; Westin, *supra* note 106, at 132; and Fred Rodell, "Our Not So Supreme Supreme Court," *Look*, July 31, 1951, 64.

110. Marcus, *supra* note 33, at 191.

111. *Goldwater v. Carter*, 444 U.S. 996 (1979).

112. Senate, *Constitution of the United States, Analysis and Interpretation*, 546–49; Westin, *supra* note 106, at 23; *see also* Bickel, *supra* chap. 1, note 4, at 184. Alexander Bickel suggests that the foundation for this doctrine is "[t]he Court's sense of lack of capacity, compounded

in unequal parts of (a) the strangeness of the issue and its intractability to principles resolution; (b) the sheer momentousness of it, which tends to unbalance judicial judgment; (c) the anxiety, not so much that the judicial judgment will be ignored, as that perhaps it should but will not be; [and] (d) finally ('in a mature democracy'), the inner vulnerability, the self-doubt of an institution which is electorally irresponsible and has no earth to draw strength from."

113. *Youngstown* at 589.

114. William H. Rehnquist, *The Supreme Court: How It Was, How It Is* (New York: William Morrow, 1987), 94–95.

115. There is a parallel here with FDR's Court-packing plan of 1937. Faced with strong opposition from both parties in Congress, FDR was unsuccessful in packing the Court with justices who were not hostile to his New Deal (Rehnquist, *supra* note 114; *see also* Charles Sawyer, *Concerns of a Conservative Democrat* [Carbondale: Southern Illinois University Press, 1968]).

116. Rehnquist, *supra* note 114, at 95; *see also* Marcus, *supra* note 33. Marcus makes a similar observation. On examination, District Judge Pine's decision, which held against Truman, used a similar logic, "apparently influenced [by] public opinion, for the Gallup Poll taken after the announcement of the ruling showed less support for the seizure than had been evidenced in previous polls. This popular reaction, which theoretically should not have had an effect on the outcome of the steel seizure as it traveled through the higher courts, as a practical matter became an important element in the legal decision-making process" (130).

117. Sawyer, *supra* note 115, at 268–69.

118. *Youngstown* at 585.

119. Patricia L. Bellia, "Executive Power in *Youngstown*'s Shadows," *Constitutional Commentary* 19, no. 1 (2002): 98–106.

120. *Loving v. United States*, 517 U.S. 748 (1996).

121. *Youngstown* at 585–86.

122. *Id.* at 587.

123. *Id.* at 589.

124. *Id.* at 639.

125. *Id.* at 610.

126. Frankfurter noted that this was the opposite of what the public expected from the Court in constitutional cases. He pointed out, "This eagerness to settle—preferably forever—a specific problem on the basis of the broadest possible constitutional pronouncements may not unfairly be called one of our minor national traits" (*id.* at 594).

127. *Id.* at 598–602.

128. *Id.* at 653.

129. *Id.* at 635.

130. James Risen and Eric Lichtblau, "Bush Lets U.S. Spy on Callers without Courts," *New York Times*, December 16, 2005.

131. *See* Robert Bloom and William J. Dunn, "The Constitutional Infirmity of Warrantless NSA Surveillance: The Abuse of Presidential Power and the Injury to the Fourth Amendment," *William and Mary Bill of Rights Journal* 15, no. 1 (2006).

132. *Padilla v. Rumsfeld*, 352 F.3d 695 (2003).

133. *Youngstown* at 636.

134. *Id.*

135. As Louis Fisher notes, rarely has the Court extended "so far with so little evidence to support its [*Curtiss-Wright*] conclusion" (*supra* chap. 1, note 22, at 69); *see also* H. Jefferson Powell, *The President's Authority over Foreign Affairs* (Durham, N.C.: Carolina Academic Press, 2002), 11–23.

136. *Youngstown* at 635.

137. *Id.* at 637.

138. *Id.*

139. *Id.*

140. *Id.* at 640.

141. *Id.* at 644.

142. *Id.*

143. *Id.* at 645.

144. *Id.* at 655–57.

145. *Id.* at 655.

146. *Id.*

147. *Id.* at 635.

148. *Youngstown* at 660. It is worth mentioning that Harold Burton's draft opinions revealed a greater concern about the current emergency and about the prospect of a strike resulting from the Court's ruling: "The immediate crisis . . . is the threatened occur[r]ence of a nationwide strike affecting the entire steel industry. I accept the Government's conclusion that its occur[r]ence would imperil the national safety with particular relation to our national defense and to our military responsibilities in Korea and elsewhere" (*see* case #744–45, Notes and Memos, Box 242, Burton Papers, LC).

149. *Youngstown* at 662.

150. Because three statutes existed—the Taft-Hartley Act, the Selective Service Act, and the Defense Production Act—Truman had exceeded his constitutional powers when he ordered the seizure of the steel mills on his own authority (*Youngstown* at 664–66). For Justice Clark, the *Barreme* precedent (1804; *see* Chapter 1) was conclusive. When Congress legislates an identifiable formula, the executive must follow it and not use his own discretion to enlarge the procedure to deal with the current situation.

151. Graber, *supra* chap. 1, note 83; Orren and Skowronek, *supra* chap. 1, note 101.

152. John P. Roche, "Executive Power and Domestic Emergency," *Western Political Quarterly* 5, no. 4 (1952): 617.

153. *Youngstown* at 707.

154. *Id.* at 710.

155. Willard Hurst notes, "The general approval of the Steel Seizure decision of 1952 expressed a different judgment, from that expressed in 1934–36, of the balance between the need for action and the desirability of restraint" (Willard Hurst, "Review and the Distribution of National Powers," in *Supreme Court and Supreme Law*, ed. Edmond Cahn [New York: Greenwood Press, 1954], 157).

156. Arthur Krock, *New York Times*, June 3, 1952, 28; *see also* Chicago *Tribune*, June 4, 1952, 20; *Cincinnati Enquirer*, June 3, 1952, 4; and *New York Times*, June 3, 1952, 1.

157. *Chicago Sun-Times*, June 3, 1952, 21; *see also* Krock, *supra* note 156. Krock points out that he had heard frequent comments in Washington that it was better to endure a strike than to inflate the president's emergency powers during a time of peace.

158. *New York Post*, June 3, 1952, 29.

159. The Court was aware that Truman was perturbed by its ruling. So Hugo Black, apprehensive that Truman would take the ruling personally, decided to invite Truman and the justices of the Court to a party at his house. Douglas recalled, "Truman was gracious though a bit testy at the beginning of the evening. But after the bourbon and canapés were passed, he turned to Hugo and said, 'Hugo, I don't much care for your law but, by golly, this bourbon is good'" (Douglas, *supra* note 101, at 450).

160. Truman noted, "I think Chief Justice Vinson's dissenting opinion hit the nail right on the head, and I am sure that someday his view will come to be recognized as the correct one" (Truman, *supra* note 11, at 2:539).

161. *See generally* Graber, *supra* chap. 1, note 83.

162. *Youngstown* at 635–38.

163. *Goldwater v. Cater*, 444 U.S. 996, 998 (1979).

164. *Dames and Moore v. Regan*, 453 U.S. 654, 678–79 (1981) (*see* Chapter 5).

165. For example, *Crockett v. Reagan*, 558 F. Supp. 893, 899 (D.D.C. 1982), aff'd, 720 F. 2d 1355 (D.C. Cir. 1983), cert. denied, 467 U.S. 1251 (1984) (El Salvador); and *Sanchez-Espinoza v. Reagan*, 568 F. Supp. 596 (D.D.C. 1983), aff'd, 770 F. 2d 202 (D.C. Cir. 1985) (Nicaragua).

166. *Sanchez-Espinoza v. Reagan*, 770 F. 2d 202, 211 (D.C. Cir. 1985).

167. "Iran-Contra Investigation," joint hearings before the Senate Select Committee on Secret Military Assistance to Iran and the Nicaraguan Opposition and the House Select Committee to Investigate Covert Arms Transactions with Iran, 100th Cong., 1st Sess., Vol. 100–7 (part II) 37 (1987).

168. *Id.* at 38.

169. *Curtiss-Wright* at 320.

170. "Iran-Contra Investigation," *supra* note 167, at 39.

171. In this instance, President Ronald Reagan's Executive Order 12333 stated that covert operations could be conducted only by the Central Intelligence Agency (CIA) unless another agency was expressly designated by the president. But no express designation was given to the National Security Council (NSC) (*id.*, remarks by Senator George Mitchell).

172. *Youngstown* at 645.

173. Koh, *supra* chap. 1, note 3, at 71; and Michael J. Glennon, *Constitutional Diplomacy* (Princeton, N.J.: Princeton University Press, 1990), 20–21.

174. Koh, *supra* chap. 1, note 3, at 71, emphasis in original; and Fisher, *supra* chap. 2, note 91.

175. Koh, *supra* chap. 1, note 3, at 112–13.

176. Marcus, *supra* note 33.

177. Philip Perlman, present during a conversation between Truman and James McGranery, the new attorney general, informed the president that evidence was before the Court, mentioning the affidavits filed by government officials and that his own testimony before the Court had indicated sufficient evidence of the emergency facing the nation (Sawyer, *supra* note 115, at 271); *see also* Sue Davis, *Corwin and Peltason's Understanding the Constitution*, 7th ed. (Belmont, Calif.: Thomas Wadsworth Publishing, 2007), 72; and Malcolm Smith and Cornelius P. Cotter, *Powers of the President during Crisis* (New York: Da Capo Press, 1972), 139.

178. Schlesinger, *supra* chap. 1, note 17, at 148; *see* Roche, *supra* note 152, at 617–18; *see also* Jay Murphy, "Some Observations on the Steel Decision," *Alabama Law Review* 4 (1951–1952): 230.

179. *See* Corwin, *supra* chap. 1, note 11, at 156; *see also* Edward Corwin, "The Steel Seizure Case: A Judicial Brick without Straw" *Columbia Law Review* 53, no. 1 (1953): 65.

180. *Youngstown* at 662.

181. Corwin, *supra* note 179, at 65.

182. *See, e.g., United States v. Am. Tel. and Tel. Co.*, 551 F. 2d 384, 392 (D.C. Cir. 1976); and *Olegario v. United States*, 629 F. 2d 204, 224 (2d Cir. 1980). Presumably, because the lower courts had been applying the framework correctly, there was no need for the Supreme Court to take up a case addressing the scope of executive authority until 1981.

183. Paul A. Freund, "Supreme Court, 1951 Term," *Harvard Law Review* 66 (1952): 103–4.

184. Glendon Schubert, *Presidency in the Courts* (Minneapolis: University of Minnesota Press, 1957), 250, www.muse.jhu.edu.

185. *Id.*; *see generally* C. Herman Pritchett, *The American Constitution*, 2d ed. (New York: McGraw Hill, 1968). *See, e.g.,* Chapter 1 for a full discussion of the Supreme Court as a political institution.

186. Mason, *supra* chap. 3, note 91, at 186–87.

187. *Youngstown* at 642.

188. Whittington, *supra* chap. 1, note 117, at 24.

189. *Id.*

190. *Id.*

CHAPTER 5

1. *See* Stephen Skowronek's cyclical theory of presidents (*supra* chap. 1, note 95).

2. Silverstein, *supra* chap. 1, note 1, at 10.

3. *Id.*

4. *New York Times Co. v. United States*, 403 U.S. 713 1971; Silverstein, *supra* chap. 1, note 1, at 11.

5. Silverstein, *supra* chap. 1, note 1, at 10.

6. *Dames* at 669.

7. Skowronek, *supra* chap. 1, note 95, at 362.

8. *See* "Iranian Situation and United States Energy Conservation: Remarks at the White House Briefing for State Governors," November 16, 1979, *Public Papers*, 2132–35.

9. Executive Order 12170, "Blocking Iranian Government Property," 44 U.S. Fed. Reg. 65, 729 (1979).

10. Executive Order 12276, "Direction Relating to Establishment of Escrow Accounts," January 19, 1981, appears at 46 Fed. Reg. 7, 913 C.F.R. 1981; Executive Order 12277, "Direction to Transfer Iranian Government Assets," 46 Fed. Reg. 7, 915. Over the course of 1981, several executive orders were issued to address the Iranian government and the assets in question. There are no references to executive agreements in the Constitutional Convention, *The Federalist Papers*, or (more importantly) the text of the Constitution, but since *Curtiss-Wright*, presidents have used executive agreements as their primary means of dominating the conduct of foreign policy. And *Dames* was no different. A unilateral executive agreement, by its very nature, excludes participation by the Senate. Presidents have asserted the power to use executive agreements on the grounds of independent constitutional powers (*see* Adler for a full discussion of this issue [*supra* chap. 1, note 2, at 28]).

11. *See* Declaration of the Government of the Democratic and Popular Republic of Algeria *and* Declaration of the Government of the Democratic and Popular Republic of Algeria concerning the Settlement of Claims by the Government of the United States of America and the Government of the Islamic Republic of Iran (hereinafter, Algerian Accords), reprinted in Robert M. McGreevey, "The Iranian Crisis and U.S. Law," *Northwestern Journal of International Law and Business* 2 (1980): 384, 447–54. For details on the hostage crisis, *see Dames* at 662–68.

12. The Algerian Accords stated that "the United States will act to bring about the transfer to the Central Bank [of Iran], within six months from [the] date [of the Accords], of all Iranian deposits and securities in U.S. banking institutions in the United States" (Algerian Accords, reprinted in McGreevey, 1980, *supra* note 11, at 449).

13. 50 U.S.C. Sec. 1701–06 (Supp. IV 1980).

14. *Dames* at 675.

15. *Id.* at 688.

16. *Id.* at 677–78.

17. *Id.* at 660 (quoting *Youngstown* at 643) (Jackson, R., concurring).

18. The Iranian Crisis and U.S. Law (IEEPA) acknowledges the executive's broad authority to respond to foreign threats "if the President declares a national emergency with respect to such threat" (50 U.S.C. Sec. 1701(a) (Supp. IV 1980)).

19. This occurs when the inflation rate is high, the economic growth rate slows down, and unemployment remains steadily high.

20. Lawrence Shoup notes, "What Carter had that his opponents did not was the acceptance and support of elite sectors of the mass communications media. . . . [T]heir favorable coverage. . . . propell[ed] him . . . to the top of the opinion polls. . . . [He won] key primary election victories, enabling him to rise from an obscure public figure to President-elect in the short space of 9 months" (Lawrence Shoup, *The Carter Presidency and Beyond* [Palo Alto, Calif.: Rampart Press, 1980], 10).

21. "Election of 1976," *The American Presidency Project*, www.presidency.ucsb.edu; *see* Jules Witcover, *Marathon: The Pursuit of the Presidency 1972–1976* (New York: Viking Press, 1977).

22. Skowronek, *supra* chap. 1, note 95, at 400.

23. *See* Hamilton Jordan, *Crisis: The Last Year of the Carter Presidency* (New York: G. P. Putnam's Sons, 1982), 55, for an account of the private conversation Jimmy Carter had with his advisers. He believed that he must be firm in his resolve.

24. Skowronek, *supra* chap. 1, note 95, at 401. Carter's national-security adviser, Zbigniew Brzezinski, asserted, "It is a crisis for sure but it is also an opportunity, a chance for the President to show the world that he is capable of handling a crisis of international implications. A chance to show America's resolve" (Jordan, *supra* note 23, at 53, 252–54).

25. Skowronek notes that Carter set aside the "administration's record on the labor front" to focus on the crisis at hand (*supra* chap. 1, note 95, at 401).

26. "American Federation of Labor and Congress of Industrial Organization: Remarks," November 15, 1979, *Public Papers*, 2122–26.

27. "Interview with the President," January 15, 1980, *Public Papers*, www.presidency. ucsb.edu.

28. Skowronek, *supra* chap. 1, note 95, at 402.

29. "Crisis management," Skowronek asserts, "became a kind of campaign in itself. As the White House announced doctrines, embargos, freezes, boycotts, immigration regulations, and draft registration, political leaders were invited up to pledge their support and bear witness to Carter's toughness and competence under pressure." Skowronek points out, "As the hostage crisis vindicated the President's effort to place energy security over social reform in domestic politics, the Soviet invasion vindicated his drift back to a Cold War defense policy" (*id.* at 402).

30. *Id.* at 400–4.

31. The Gallup Poll, *Public Opinion* 1979, 187–88, and *Public Opinion 1980*, 5.

32. Carter turned "a reconstruction from within . . . to something of a crap shoot," something unparalleled in presidential history (Skowronek, *supra* chap. 1, note 95, at 402).

33. The IEEPA stipulates that once the president has declared a national emergency, he can "investigate, regulate, direct and compel, nullify, void, prevent[,] or prohibit, any acquisition, holding, withholding, use, transfer, withdrawal, transportation, importation[,] or

exportation of, or dealing in, or exercising [of] any right, power, or privilege with respect to, or transactions involving, any property in which any foreign country or a national thereof has any interest" (50 U.S.C. Sec. 1702 (a)(1)(B) (Supp. IV 1980)).

34. Executive Order 12170, 44 Fed. Reg. 65, 729 (1979).

35. *See* McGreevey, *supra* note 11, at 386. President Carter issued this order after Iran announced it was planning to withdraw all the funds it had deposited in U.S. banks.

36. Treas. Reg. Sec. 535.203(e), 31 C.F.R. 667 (1980).

37. Treas. Reg. Sec. 535.805, 31 C.F.R. 684 (1980).

38. *Dames* at 663–64. Dames and Moore sued for approximately $3.5 million for services it asserted it had performed before the contract was unilaterally terminated (*id.* at 664).

39. *Id.* To secure judgment, property of certain Iranian banks was attached (*id.*).

40. *Id.* at 664–65; *see* "General Principles" of the first Algerian Accords, reprinted in McGreevey, *supra* note 11, at 447, para. 4–9 and 448–50.

41. Executive Order 12276 and Executive Order 12285, 46 Fed. Reg. 7913–32 (1981). The *Dames* Court asserted that the president's action in these executive orders was also taken pursuant to Treas. Reg. Sec. 535.805, 31 C.F.R. 684 (1980), which "made the license to attach expressly revocable" (*Dames* at 673).

42. Executive Order 12294, 46 Fed. Reg. 14111–12 (1981).

43. *Dames* at 666.

44. *Id.* at 666–67.

45. *Id.* at 667.

46. *Id.* at 654.

47. Rex E. Lee, oral argument, *Dames and Moore*. The Oyez Project at IIT Chicago-Kent College of Law, May 5, 2013, http://www.oyez.org/cases/1980-1989/1980/1980_80_2078.

48. *Id.*

49. *Id.*

50. *Id.*

51. *See Dames* at 661, 669. The Court noted, "Justice Jackson's classification of executive actions . . . [is] analytically useful" (*id.*).

52. Lee, *supra* note 47. Lee also noted that the *Pink* Court made reference to scholars and members of Congress who had given the claims-settlement authority significant attention (*id.*).

53. *Id.*

54. *Dames* at 635–38 (citing *Youngstown*).

55. *Id.*

56. *Id.* at 679 (quoting Henkin, *supra* chap. 2, note 104, at 262).

57. *Id.* at 679 (footnote omitted).

58. *Id.* at 680.

59. *Id.* at 675–80. The Court rested on two circuit court of appeals decisions that provided an interpretation of the IEEPA: *Chas. T. Main Int'l, Inc. v. Khuzestan Water and Power Auth.*, 651 F. 2d 800 (1st Cir. 1981); and *American Int'l Group, Inc., et al. v. Islamic Republic of Iran, et al.*, 657 F. 2d 430 (D.C. Cir. 1981).

60. *Id.* at 673–74.

61. *Id.* at 674.

62. 22 U.S.C. Sec. 1732 (1976).

63. *Dames* at 677.

64. *Id.* at 679–82.

65. *Haig v. Agee*, 453 U.S. 280 (1981).

66. *Dames* at 678 (quoting *Haig* at 291). The *Haig* Court upheld the right of the secretary of state to rescind passports regardless of the lack of explicit statutory authority. One thing to note is that Congress could not have consolidated its approval or even its disapproval in the three days between the decisions on *Haig* and *Dames*.

67. 22 U.S.C. Sec. 1621–44m (1976).

68. *Dames* at 682.

69. *Id.* at 686 (quoting *Youngstown* at 610) (Frankfurter, F., concurring).

70. IEEPA, 50 U.S.C. Sec. 1702 (a)(1)(B) (Supp. IV 1980).

71. 50 U.S.C. Sec. 1702 (a)(1)(B) of the IEEPA is indistinguishable in language from 50 U.S.C. app. Sec. 5(b)(1)(B)(1976). However, the Trading with the Enemy Act (TWEA) was passed in 1917 to deal only with war—H.R. Rep. No. 459, 95th Cong., 1st Sess. 4 (1977), available on CIS microfiche: No. H. 463-14 (hereinafter cited as H.R. Rep. No. 459)—and stated that it "did not include a provision permitting use of the act during a national emergency." Franklin D. Roosevelt used it to proclaim a bank holiday to avert the hoarding of gold (*id.*; *see also* Comment, "Presidential Emergency Powers Related to International Economic Transactions: Congressional Recognition of Customary Authority," *Vanderbilt Journal of Transnational Law* 11 [1978]: 515, 518). Following this usage, the TWEA was used for a variety of reasons (1941–1971), including to establish foreign direct-investment controls on American investors and to levy a surcharge on imports (*see* H.R. Rep. No. 459, at 15).

72. *Dames* at 672–74.

73. *Orvis v. Brownell*, 345 U.S. 183 (1953).

74. *Dames* at 672–73.

75. 50 U.S.C. Sec. 1702(a)(1)(B) (Supp. IV 1980). A similar line of reasoning was reached by a court in the First Circuit (*Chas. T. Main International, Inc. v. Khuzestan Water and Power Authority*, 651 F. 2d 800 (1st Cir. 1981)).

76. *Dames* at 672.

77. *Youngstown* at 673 (Jackson, R., concurring).

78. H.R. Rep. No. 459, *supra* note 71, at 1; *see also* S. Rep. No. 466, 95th Cong., 1st Sess. 2 (1977).

79. 123 Cong. Rec. H6872 (daily ed., July 12, 1977) (remarks of Rep. Leggett).

80. *Id.*

81. 50 U.S.C. app. Sec. 5(b)(1)(1976).

82. H.R. Rep. No. 459, *supra* note 71, at 15.

83. 50 U.S.C. Sec. 1702(a)(1)(B) (Supp. IV 1980).

84. *Youngstown* at 603. In *Youngstown*, the issue before the Court was Congress's refusal to grant the president the authority to seize domestic property, but *Dames* reinforced the notion that express power to attach foreign assets was given by Congress.

85. *Orvis v. Brownell*, 345 U.S. 183, 184–85 (1953).

86. *Id.* at 185.

87. *Id.* at 189.

88. *Id.* at 186.

89. *Id.* at 186–87.

90. *Dames* at 672–73n5 (citing *Orvis* at 186).

91. *Id.*

92. H.R. Rep. No. 459, *supra* note 71, at 15.

93. One change in the IEEPA warrants a brief discussion. In the original House version, the legislative branch could veto any regulation taken by the executive under the IEEPA (*see* H.R. Rep. No. 459, *supra* note 71, at 16), but the Senate version removed this power from

Congress (S. Rep. No. 466, *supra* note 78, at 2). A case could be made that the deletion of this provision indicated that Congress believed that the president should have ultimate unilateral power to act under the IEEPA. However, upon further examination of the Senate record, it becomes clear that the Senate rejected the proposal not because it believed that it should not have the power to veto executive declarations under the IEEPA but because it believed that it already had the power, under the National Emergencies Act, to veto a president's declaration of an emergency: 123 Cong. Rec. H12559 (daily ed. November 30, 1977) (remarks of Rep. Bingham). It should also be noted that these were the remarks of the major sponsor of the bill as he attempted to gain his colleagues' approval after the Senate rejected a portion of the bill.

94. *Dames* at 660.

95. *Id.*

96. *Id.* at 686 (quoting *Youngstown* at 610–11) (Frankfurter, F., concurring).

97. The Court has interpreted the Constitution liberally to identify the presence of inherent powers, and as Justice Robert Jackson's cautionary note in *Youngstown* pointed out, "'Inherent' powers, 'implied' powers, 'incidental' powers, 'plenary' powers, 'war' powers[,] and 'emergency' powers are used, often interchangeably and without fixed or ascertainable meanings" (*Youngstown* at 646–47).

98. *See* Raoul Berger, "The Presidential Monopoly of Foreign Relations," *Michigan Law Review* 71, no. 1 (1972): 33.

99. Laurence Tribe understands that *Myers v. United States* (272 U.S. 52 (1926)) asserts that "the federal executive, unlike the Congress, could exercise power from sources not enumerated, so long as not forbidden by the constitutional text" (Laurence H. Tribe, *American Constitutional Law* [New York: Foundation Press, 1978], 159). Tribe cites Henkin (*supra* chap. 2, note 104, at 68) to anchor the proposal that "Congress shares in the 'unenumerated foreign affairs power'" (166).

100. Berger, *supra* note 98, at 22 (quoting Farrand, *supra* chap. 1, note 27, at 1:66–67); *see also Federalist Paper* No. 45 (James Madison, in Earle, *supra* chap. 1, note 24, at 237).

101. Henkin, *supra* chap. 2, note 104, at 31; *see also* Arthur W. Rovine, "Separation of Powers and International Executive Agreements," *Indiana Law Journal* 52, no. 2 (1977): 397, 412.

102. Tribe, *supra* note 99.

103. *Gibbons v. Ogden*, 22 U.S. (9 Wheat.) 1 (1824); *see United States v. E. C. Knight Co.*, 156 U.S. 1 (1895). The *E. C. Knight* Court began to place limits on congressional power and did so for about forty years. However, during the 1930s, the Court changed direction and began granting more power to the federal government under the Commerce Clause.

104. U.S. Constitution, Art. II, Sec. 2, cl. 2; U.S. Constitution, Art II, Sec. 2, cl. 1. The Commander-in-Chief Clause is available at least in time of war, and under the Court's logic of *Hirabayashi*, the national government of the war power can view executive agreements as a legitimate exercise, including every action that is related to war and that affects its development (*Hirabayashi* at 93). The situation in *Dames* did not involve a declared war, so there was only a weak case supporting the use of the Commander-in-Chief Clause under the facts of that case.

105. U.S. Constitution, Art. II, Sec. 3. This section also provides, "[H]e shall take Care that the Laws be faithfully executed." *See also* Tribe, who argues that any effort to control this power, "based on the separation of powers and delegation of powers doctrines," has been less than successful and demonstrates that "it is only by an extraordinary triumph of constitutional imagination that the Commander in Chief is conceived as commanded by law" (*supra* note 99, at 157).

106. *Federalist Papers*, No. 69, 354 (A. Hamilton) (London: J. M. Dent, 1911); *see also* Henkin, *supra* chap. 2, note 104, at 41. This power was believed to be more "a function . . .

than a 'power,' a ceremony which in many countries is performed by a figurehead" (*id.*).

107. Rovine, *supra* note 101, at 415.

108. In 1933, People's Commissar for Foreign Affairs Maxim Litvinov gave the U.S. government all rights to pursue claims for property resulting from the nationalization of all Russian insurance companies in 1918 and 1919 (*Pink* at 210–12).

109. *See* U.S. Constitution, Art. VI, cl. 2. The *Pink* Court held, "A treaty is a 'Law of the Land' under the supremacy clause. . . . Such international compacts and agreements as the Litvinov Assignment have a similar dignity" (*Pink* at 230).

110. Rovine, *supra* note 101, at 415.

111. *Dames* at 682.

112. *See* Henkin, *supra* chap. 1, note 36, at 185.

113. *Id.* at 331.

114. *Dames* at 682–83.

115. *Pink* at 229 (quoting *Curtiss-Wright* at 320); *see also Dames* at 682–83, for the Supreme Court's analysis of *Pink*, and at 661, for the Court's discussion of *Curtiss-Wright*. One reason the *Dames* Court interpreted *Pink* in broad terms was that at the time *Pink* was decided (1942), it served as an opportunity for the Court to communicate emphatically to the states their absolute incapacity in the area of foreign affairs. *Dames* did not, however, involve any issue relating to state law or federal preemption, thereby necessitating the *Dames* Court to reread *Pink* in its broadest terms. As McGreevey asserts, "[T]he recognition power was not used during the Iranian crisis" (*supra* note 11, at 436), because the Islamic Republic of Iran succeeded the shah's government without the need for a formal declaration (*id.* at 346 [footnote omitted]). All cases cited by McGreevey (*id.* at 388nn14–22) and *Dames* itself were initially filed in federal court. In none of these instances was there an argument of federal preemption of a state law.

116. *Dames* at 678. McGreevey restricts further the extent to which *Pink* and *Belmont* can be applied—only to circumstances including "alien claimants" and rejection by state courts "to apply the act of state doctrine to foreign decrees." But McGreevey cites no language from either case to support this assertion (*supra* note 11, at 436–37).

117. "[T]he IEEPA constitutes specific congressional authorization to the President to nullify the attachments and order the transfer of Iranian assets" (*Dames* at 675).

118. "Crucial to our decision today is the conclusion that Congress has implicitly approved the practice of claim settlement by executive agreement" (*id.* at 680).

119. *Id.* at 688.

120. 22 U.S.C. Sec. 1621–44m (1976).

121. *Dames* at 680.

122. Before a new country could be added, congressional action was required (*id.* at 680–81). Congress thus did not want to leave this issue fully in the hands of the president, which suggests that legislatures refute the argument of implied congressional acquiescence.

123. The *Dames* Court noted, "By creating a procedure to implement future settlement agreements, Congress placed its stamp of approval on such agreements" (*id.* at 680).

124. *Id.* at 681.

125. S. Rep. No. 800, 81st Cong., 1st Sess. 5 (1949). The House version was altered by the Senate "[t]o provide that the members of the Commission be appointed by the President with the advice and consent of the Senate." This modification, which was eventually adopted, the Court asserted, demonstrated that Congress was not submissively acquiescing a unilateral executive role in the claims-settlement process. The Court's reliance on this statute may well be inappropriate to show "the history of acquiescence in executive claims settlement." In fact, the legislative history has substantiated the act's objective; *see Dames*

at 686. In fact, the actual text of the International Claims Settlement Act (ICSA) clearly showed that it was intended to apply to circumstances far different from those in *Dames* (22 U.S.C. Sec. 1623(a) (1976)).

126. 95 Cong. Rec. 8837 (1949). The legislative majority accepted the power of the president to settle claims against foreign countries (*id.* at 8840); *see also* 96 Cong. Rec. 2969 (1950), where one member of Congress referenced the long-standing position of the Courts to find agreements of this kind within the president's wheelhouse.

127. *See Youngstown* at 637 (Jackson, R., concurring) for a fuller discussion of Justice Jackson's discussion of the zone of twilight.

128. *Id.* at 637; *see also Dames* at 678.

129. *Dames* at 686 (quoting *United States v. Midwest Oil Co.*, 236 U.S. 459, 469 (1915)).

130. *Dames* at 680.

131. *See* Henkin, *supra* chap. 2, note 104, at 32.

132. *See* Rovine, *supra* note 101, at 423; *see also* Henkin, *supra* chap. 2, note 104, at 174; and Tribe, *supra* note 99, at 285.

133. *See Principality of Monaco v. Mississippi*, 292 U.S. 313, at 331 (1934).

134. *See Youngstown* at 603–4 (Frankfurter, F., concurring); *see also* D. Christopher Ohly, "Advice and Consent: International Claims Settlement Agreements," *California Western International Law Journal* 5 (1975): 271: "The [*Curtiss-Wright*] Court properly noted that if such 'inherent power' exists[,] . . . it was 'vested in the federal government' and not in any individual branch thereof" (285).

135. *Dames* at 661–62.

136. *See* Thomas A. O'Donnell, "Illuminating or Eliminating the Zone of Twilight: Congressional Acquiescence and Presidential Authority in Foreign Affairs," *University of Cincinnati Law Review* 95 (1982): 99, which points out that the Court had long "ignored" Jackson's taxonomy until the decision of *Dames.*

137. The same issues presented in *Youngstown* are extremely likely to result if *Dames* is applied to emergency situations arising in the future.

138. *Youngstown* at 586. By virtue of the changes from the TWEA adopted in the IEEPA, the president was not seizing property and placing it under the executive branch's control; he was simply "disposing" of it (*id.* at 672n5).

139. *Id.* at 587.

140. *Dames* at 669 (Rehnquist quoting Black's majority opinion in *Youngstown* at 585).

141. *Id.*

142. *Id.*

143. *Id.* at 603–4.

144. *Id.* at 610–11.

145. *Id.* at 640.

146. *Id.* at 652.

147. *Id.*

148. *Id.*

149. *Id.*

150. *Id.* at 674 (quoting *Youngstown* at 637) (Jackson, R., concurring).

151. *Id.* at 675.

152. *Pink* at 230; *see also* Berger, *supra* note 98. Raoul Berger notes, however, "It would require a constitutional amendment . . . to make an executive agreement, concluded by the President alone, equally binding" (*id.* at 48).

153. Henkin, *supra* chap. 2, note 104, at 57; *see generally* Fisher and Adler (*supra* chap. 1, note 2), who both assert that this power is unreservedly Congress's duty alone.

154. Ohly, *supra* note 134, at 286.

155. Morris D. Forkosch, "The United States Constitution and International Relations: Some Powers and Limitations Explored," *California Western International Law Journal* 5, no. 2 (1975): 246n138.

156. See *Dames* at 678; *see also* Rovine, *supra* note 101, at 397.

157. *Dames* at 687–88.

158. *See* Rovine's discussion of Senate objections to executive use of unilaterally conducting international agreements (*supra* note 101, at 397); *see also* Henkin, *supra* chap. 2, note 104, at 179.

159. *Dames* at 686.

160. *Id.* (citing *Youngstown* at 637) (Jackson, R., concurring).

161. *Id.* at 680.

162. *Youngstown* at 609 (Frankfurter, F., concurring).

163. *Id.* at 638–39 (Jackson, R., concurring).

164. *Id.* at 635 (Jackson, R., concurring).

165. *See* Forkosch, *supra* note 155, at 229 (quoting Corwin, *supra* chap. 1, note 11, at 308, emphasis in original): "In the field of foreign relations . . . 'the power to determine the substantive content of American foreign policy is a *divided* power, with the lion's share falling usually to the President, though by no means always.'"

166. *Curtiss-Wright* at 319.

167. *Pink* at 229.

168. *Youngstown* at 650 (Jackson, R., concurring).

169. *Dames* at 688.

170. *Id.* at 622.

171. *Id.* at 669.

172. *Id.* at 673–74; *see also* H.R. Rep. No. 915, 96th Cong., 2d Sess. 3 (1980), which accepted the practice of the government to block foreign assets to offset expected claims against the foreign country.

173. *See* Rovine, *supra* note 101, at 419.

174. *Dames* at 667 (citing the district court).

175. *Id.* at 688.

176. Carter made it clear that he would speak to the frustrations of the nation: "I've got to give expression to the anger of the American people. If they perceive me as firm and tough in voicing their rage, maybe we'll be able to control this thing" (cited in Jordan, *supra* note 23, at 55).

177. President Ronald Reagan ratified the Algerian Accords with Executive Order 12294, even though he was unhappy with some of the provisions of the agreement (EO 12294, 46 Fed. Reg. 14111–12 (1981)); *see also* the president's message to Congress, "Suspension of Litigation against Iran," 17 Weekly Comp. Pres. Doc. 189 (February 24, 1981).

178. Mark P. Sullivan, "Cuba: U.S. Restrictions on Travel and Remittances," *CRS Report for Congress*, Order Code RL31139 (2007): 1.

179. Proclamation 3447, "The Embargo on All Trade with Cuba." February 3, 1962, 27 Fed. Reg. 1085 (1962).

180. 28 Fed. Reg. 6974 (1963) (codified as amended at 31 C.F.R. Sec. 515.101 to .809 (9184)).

181. Proclamation 3447, 1962, *supra* note 179, at 2.

182. *Id.*

183. *See* C.F.R. Sec. 515560(a)(3)(1984). However, specific licenses may be granted for humanitarian, cultural, or athletic purposes and events (*id.* at Sec. 515560(a)(1)).

184. Memorandum of September 8, 1978, 45 Fed. Reg. 40695; Memorandum of September 12, 1979, 2 Public Papers 1655–56; Presidential Determination of September 8, 1980, 45 Fed. Reg. 59549; Memorandum of September 10, 1981, 46 Fed. Reg. 45321; Memorandum of September 8, 1982, 47 Fed. Reg. 39797; Memorandum of September 7, 1983, 48 Fed. Reg. 40695; and Memorandum of September 11, 1984, 49 Fed. Reg. 35927.

185. *See* C.F.R. Sec. 515560 (1982) (current version at 31 C.F.R. Sec. 515560 (1984)). Regulation 560 was promulgated in response to Cuba's efforts to destabilize democratic governments in Central America: Joint Appendix at 171–72, *Regan* (No. 83-436) (declaration of Thomas O. Enders) (hereinafter Joint Appendix). The Reagan administration amended the 1977 general license pursuant to Section 805 (*id.* at Sec. 515805) of the Cuban Assets Control Regulations (CACRs), which were in effect on July 1, 1977.

186. *See* Joint Appendix, *supra* note 185, at 172.

187. *Id.* at 174–75. It had not been a significant source of revenue for Fidel Castro's government in Cuba, but tourism was a major source of revenue prior to 1958 (*see* Sullivan, *supra* note 178).

188. Trading with the Enemy Act of 1917, ch. 106, 40 Stat. 411 (current version at 50 U.S.C. app. Sec. 5(b)(1982)).

189. For a brief history of the TWEA, *see generally Revision of Trading with the Enemy Act, Markup before the House Committee on International Relations*, 95th Cong., 1st Sess. 5, 8–9 (1977) (hereinafter cited as *Revision of TWEA*).

190. Act of March 9, 1933, ch. 1, 48 Stat. 1 (current version at 50 U.S.C. app. Sec. 5(b) (1982)); *see also Revision of TWEA*, *supra* note 189.

191. *Revision of TWEA*, *supra* note 189, at 8; *see also* S. Rep. No. 1170, 93d Cong., 2d Sess. 7 91974.

192. *Revision of TWEA*, *supra* note 189, at 212, and 2, 5, 8–9. Before 1977, there were four declarations of national emergency under the TWEA: FDR's 1933 bank-holiday declaration (Proclamation No. 2040, *reprinted* in 48 Stat. 1691 (1933)), Harry Truman's declaration of national emergency in response to the Korean conflict (Proclamation No. 2914, reprinted in Fed. Reg. 9029 (1950)), Richard Nixon's 1970 declaration vis-à-vis a Post Office strike (Proclamation No. 3972, reprinted in 3 C.F.R. 473 (1966—1970)), and Nixon's 1970 declaration regarding the nation's balance-of-payments crisis (Proclamation No. 4074, reprinted in 36 Fed. Reg. 15724 (1971)).

193. Public Law 94-412, 90 State. 1255 (1976) (codified as amended at 50 U.S.C. Sec. 1601–51 (1982)).

194. *Id.*

195. H.R. Rep. No. 459, *supra* note 71, at 6–7.

196. Act of December 28, 1977, Public Law 95-223, Sec. 101(b), 91 Stat. 1625, 1625, *reprinted* in 50 U.S.C. app. Sec. 5(b) note (1982).

197. 28 Fed. Reg. 6974, *supra* note 180.

198. *Wald v. Regan*, 708 F. 2d 794 (1st Cir. 1983), *revised* 104 S. Ct. 3026 (1984).

199. *Wald v. Regan*, No. 82-1690-T (D. Mass. July 16, 1982), reprinted in Petitioner's Brief for Writ of Cert. at 24a, *Wald* (No. 83-436).

200. *Id.*

201. *Id.* at 35a (*Wald* (No. 83-436)).

202. *Id.*

203. *Wald*, 708 F. 2d 794, at 801.

204. *Id.* The First Circuit did not discuss the constitutional argument, because it found that the challenged regulation lacked the statutory authority (*id.* at 795).

205. *Id.* at 796–800.

206. *Id.* at 800–1.

207. *See id.* at 796–97.

208. *Id.* at 798 (construing Act of December 28, 1977, Public Law 95-223, Sec. 101(b), 91 Stat. 1625, 1625). The Court also concluded that Congress had passed the grandfather clause to shield "existing trade embargoes [and] to mitigate the adverse effect that automatic repeal would have had on the President's negotiating position with respect to other countries" (*see Wald*, 708 F. 2d 794, at 798).

209. *Wald*, 708 F. 2d 794, at 799 (interpreting *Emergency Controls on International Economic Transactions: Hearings before the Subcommittee. On International Economic Policy and Trade of the House Comm. On International Relations*, 95th Cong., 1st Sess. 19 (1977) (hereinafter cited as *Emergency Controls Hearings*) at 167. The court highlighted House and Senate committee hearings to reveal that every time legislators had talked about the term "authorities" in the grandfather clause, they had referred to "existing uses" of TWEA authority; *see* Mary Keenan Harrington, *"Regan v. Wald* and the Grandfather Clause of Trading with the Enemy Act: A Lesson in Explicit Vagueness," *Pace Law Review* 5, no. 3 (1985). Harrington notes that administrative spokesmen for the IEEPA understood the grandfather clause as being narrowly construed. Only existing exercise of Section 5(b) authority would be preserved. Testimony from the Department of the Treasury and the Department of State listed the uses of 5(b) that they wanted grandfathered. Travel to Cuba was not included in that list: *id.* (citing *Emergency Controls Hearings* at 3036n20).

210. *Id.* (quoting *Kent v. Dulles*, 357 U.S. 116, 129 (1958)).

211. *Wald*, 708 F. 2d 794, at 800.

212. *Regan v. Wald*, 104 S. Ct. 3026 (1984).

213. *Id.* at 3035. Because the First Circuit struck down the regulation on statutory grounds, it did not have to determine whether the regulation also violated the constitutional right to travel.

214. *Zemel v. Rusk*, 381 U.S. 1 (1965).

215. The *Zemel* Court cited *Kent* (1958); *Aptheker v. Secretary of State*, 378 U.S. 500 (1964); Art. 13 (quoted in S. Doc. No. 123, 81st Cong., 1st Sess., p. 1157); and *Korematsu* (1944).

216. *Zemel* at 15–16.

217. *Aptheker* (1964) was the first case in which the Court considered the constitutionality of personal restrictions on the right to travel abroad. Justice Arthur Goldberg maintained that the right to travel was not absolute, but the language of the Internal Security Act of 1950—also known as the McCarran Act—was too broad. Less than a year later, restrictions on travel to particular countries or specific areas were subsequently upheld in *Zemel* (1965).

218. *Regan* at 3037–39.

219. In reintroducing the Reagan administration's restraints on travel-related matters between the United States and Cuba, the Court found that the Treasury Department had acted with statutory authority when it placed currency-control regulations intended to deny Cuba U.S. currency (*Regan* at 3037–39).

220. *Regan* at 3033–34. The Supreme Court pointed out that Section 5(b) of the TWEA covered far-reaching language authorizing the executive to control any transactions involving property (*id.* at n16). In addition, the language of Section 203(a) of the IEEPA, outlining the process to follow after a declaration of a national emergency, simply shadowed the language of Section 5(b) of the TWEA. This shared language, the Court concluded, was

evidence that Congress did not distinguish between travel-related transactions and other transactions in property (*id.* at n17).

221. *See id.* at 3034–35. Section 201(b) specifically banned all transactions involving property in which Cuba or its nationals had an interest except when expressly authorized by a license (31 C.F.R. Sec. 515.501(b)(1984)).

222. *Id.* at 3035.

223. *Id.* at 3035–36. The Court concurred with the court of appeals that C. Fred Bergsten's assistant secretary of the treasury testimony, given before Representative James Cavanaugh and the House Committee on International Relations, advocated a narrow reading of the grandfather clause (*Revision of TWEA, supra* note 189, at 21–22).

224. *Regan* at 3036.

225. *Id.* at 3036–37.

226. *Id.* at 3037.

227. *Id.*

228. *Id.*

229. *Youngstown* at 635 (Jackson, R., concurring).

230. *See* Act of December 28, 1977, Public Law 95-223, Sec. 201–8, 91 Stat. 1625, 1626–29 (1977) (codified at 50 U.S.C. Sec. 1701–6 (1982)).

231. *Emergency Controls Hearings, supra* note 209, at 13–14, 16.

232. *See* H.R. Rep. No. 459, *supra* note 71, at 7.

233. *See Emergency Controls Hearings, supra* note 209, at 13–14.

234. *Dames* at 656.

235. *Id.* at 672–74.

236. *Id.* at 673.

237. *Curtiss-Wright* at 320.

238. *Id.*

239. *Regan* at 3039.

240. William Brennan and Thurgood Marshall's dissent suggested that the precedent set by the Court in *Zemel* and *Kent* was overturned in *Haig,* but *Regan* established how the Court would rethink travel in light of Congress's enacted provisions.

241. Justices Marshall, Brennan, and Lewis Powell joined Harry Blackmun's dissent, and Justice Powell's separate dissent reached the same conclusion as Blackmun's (*Regan* at 3049 (Powell, L., dissenting)). The dissenters identified compelling language in the *Congressional Record,* which led them to conclude that there was uncertainty in the legislative record of the statute (Harrington, *supra* note 209, at 719; *Regan* at 3044–45 (Blackmun, H., dissenting)). However, the majority found convincing support that the legislature had intended a broad reading of the grandfather clause (*Regan* at 3034). But the mere presence of uncertainty induced the expansive interpretation adopted by the majority.

242. *Regan* at 3040 (Blackmun, H., dissenting).

243. Act of December 28, 1977, Public Law 95-223, 91 Stat. 1625.

244. *Regan* at 3042.

245. *Id.* at 3045.

246. *Id.* at 3045–46.

247. *Id.* at 3045.

248. *Id.*

249. *Id.* at 3046.

250. *Id.*

251. *Id.*

252. *Id.* at 3046–47.

253. *Id.* at 3047.

254. *Dames* at 671–72.

255. *Regan* at 3034–35; *see also* 50 U.S. C. app Sec. 5(b)(1982).

256. *Youngstown* at 635 (Jackson, R., concurring).

257. *See id.* at 635.

258. *Id.* at 688 and 669. This point echoed the functionalist approach of Jackson and Frankfurter in *Youngstown*.

259. *Dames* at 688n13.

260. *Crockett v. Reagan*, 720 F. 2d 1355 (1983); *see also Lowry v. Reagan* (676 F. Supp. 333 (1987)); and *Dellums v. Bush* (752 F. Supp. 1141 (1990)).

261. 50 U.S.C. 1541–48 (1973).

262. *Crockett*, 720 F. 2d 1355, at 1355.

263. *Dames* at 671.

264. Whittington, *supra* chap. 1, note 117, at 169.

265. *See id.*, at chap. 2.

266. *Id.* at 13.

267. Skowronek, *supra* chap. 1, note 95, at 404.

268. However, in the area of domestic affairs, Carter used the judiciary to resolve those issues that were not being settled in the political arena (e.g., abortion). Taking such issues as abortion to the courts, Carter moved the policy concern from the political sphere to legal time. He maintained that his hands were tied and that the courts had the sole authority to interpret the law. However, he was one of the most resourceful in pushing "institutional independence to its outer limits" (*id.* at 368, 403–4).

269. *Id.* at 404.

270. *See generally* Whittington, *supra* chap. 1, note 117.

271. Although Reagan opposed the dominant regime in domestic policy, in the area of foreign affairs, he willfully invoked an order sanctioning Carter's action and thus extended executive reach by unilaterally restricting travel.

CHAPTER 6

1. Jeanne Cummings, "Gonzales Rewrites Law of War; White House Counsel's Methods Outrage Military Legal Experts," *Wall Street Journal*, November 26, 2002, A4.

2. Karen J. Greenberg, Joshua L. Dratel, and Jeffrey S. Grossman, eds., *The Enemy Combatant Papers: American Justices, the Courts and the War on Terror* (New York: Cambridge University Press, 2008), ix.

3. *Id.*

4. *Id.* at ix.

5. *Id.*

6. *Id.* at xii.

7. *Id.* at x.

8. "South Lawn Speech," *Public Papers*, September 16, 2001.

9. Greenberg et al., *supra* note 2, at x.

10. *See Kucinich v. Bush*, 236 F. Supp. 2d 1 (D.D.C. 2002). The court rejected Dennis Kucinich's appeal to block President George W. Bush's withdrawal from the Antiballistic Missile Defense treaty. Drawing on *Goldwater* (1979), the court determined that the president had the unilateral authority to terminate treaties without the advice and consent of the Senate.

11. Greenberg et al., *supra* note 2, at xiii.

12. *Rasul v. Bush*, 542 U.S. 466 (2004).

13. *Hamdi v. Rumsfeld*, 542 U.S. 507 (2004).

14. *Rumsfeld v. Padilla*, 542 U.S. 426 (2004).

15. *Hamdan v. Rumsfeld*, 126 S. Ct. 2749 (2006); *Hamdan v. Rumsfeld*, 548 U.S. 557 (2006).

16. *Boumediene v. Bush*, 553 U.S. 723 (2008); *Boumediene v. Bush*, 128 S. Ct. 2229 (2008).

17. Germany and the European Union (2008) had accused the government of violating internationally accepted standards for humane treatment and due process (Jane Mayer, *The Dark Side: The Inside Story of How the War on Terror Turned into a War on American Ideals* [New York: First Anchor Books, 2009], 332).

18. *ABC News*, "Timeline of Supreme Court rulings on Guantanamo," June 12, 2008 (hereinafter Timeline).

19. *See generally* Robert A. Levy and William Mellor, *The Dirty Dozen: How Twelve Supreme Court Cases Radically Expanded Government and Eroded Freedom* (Washington, D.C.: Cato Institute, 2008), 131.

20. Executive Order (EO) 13224 declared formally that the nation was on high alert and that subsequent attacks were conceivable ("Blocking Property and Prohibiting Transactions with Persons Who Commit, Threaten to Commit, or Support Terrorism," September 23, 2001, www.presidency.ucsb.edu); *see also* EO 13372: "Clarification of Certain Executive Orders Blocking Property and Prohibiting Certain Transactions," February 16, 2005 (Fed. Reg. 70, 28).

21. *See* Savage, *supra* chap. 2, note 140.

22. George W. Bush, "Address to Joint Session of Congress following September 11 Attacks," September 20, 2001, americanrhetoric.com.

23. President Bush had an approval rating of 51 percent (September 7–19, 2001). Following the attacks, Bush hit an approval rating of 90 percent (September 21–22, 2001) and stayed in the high 80s and 70s until around July 2002 (gallup.com); *see* Pew for similar polling data (Pew Research Center for the People and the Press).

24. "Remarks by the President from Speech Unveiling 'Most Wanted Terrorist List,'" FBI Headquarters, Washington, D.C., October 10, 2001, in George W. Bush, *We Will Prevail* (New York: Bloomsbury Academic, 2001), 38.

25. Ronald Brownstein, "Finally Face to Face, Candidates Deepen Their Division on Iraq," *Los Angeles Times*, October 1, 2004, 25.

26. Skowronek, *supra* chap. 1, note 95, at 18–21.

27. Whittington, *supra* chap. 1, note 117, at 23–25.

28. Skowronek, *supra* chap. 1, note 95, at 36–39; Whittington, *supra* chap. 1, note 117, at 23–24.

29. Whittington, *supra* chap. 1, note 117, at 16–17.

30. This duality is akin to Max Weber's "traditional" and "charismatic" leadership. The two are not compatible and will inevitably undermine the party system (quoted in Gary Wills, *Certain Trumpets: The Nature of Leadership* [New York: Touchstone, 1994], 102–3).

31. Public Law 107-243, 116 Stat. 1498, enacted October 16, 2002, H.J. Res. 114.

32. 50 U.S.C. 1541–48.

33. Authorization for Use of Military Force against Iraq Resolution (AUMF), Public Law 107-243, 116 Stat. 1498, enacted on October 16, 2002.

34. Memorandum from John Yoo, deputy assistant attorney general (*see also* Robert J. Delahunty, Special Counsel, to William J. Haynes II, General Counsel of the Department of Defense, January 9, 2002, http://lawofwar.org/Yoo_Delahunty_Memo.htm).

35. *Id.*

36. Louis Fisher and David Gray Adler, "The War Powers Resolution: Time to Say Goodbye," *Presidential Studies Quarterly* 113, no. 1 (1998): 3–4; War Powers Resolution, 1973 (50 U.S.C. 1541–48). This act represented an abject surrender of the war power. Ultimately, "Congress cannot delegate to a subunit the constitutional power to decide war" (Fisher and Adler, at 3–4). It is a predicate of the Separations of Powers doctrine that Congress may not redelegate its constitutional power, a principle that dates to John Locke's writings (*supra* chap. 1, note 28). Essentially, a power could not be transferred from the hands of one branch into the hands of another, because the people, who are sovereign, delegated the authority. The AUMF therefore unconstitutionally delegated the war power to the president.

37. Greenberg et al., *supra* note 2, at xvii; *see* Robert J. Delahunty and John C. Yoo, "The President's Constitutional Authority to Conduct Military Operations against Terrorist Organizations and the Nations That Harbor or Support Them," *Harvard Journal of Law and Public Policy* 25 (2002): 487.

38. Bush solicited Congress for statutory authority in September 2001. This act signaled that he was willing to work with the legislative branch, but it was merely symbolic. Bush signed the USA PATRIOT Act (2001) into law on October 26, 2001, which significantly expanded the power of government agencies to engage in domestic-surveillance activities and restrict judicial review of such efforts. More importantly, this legislation gave the attorney general expanded power to detain and deport aliens suspected of having terrorist affiliations; *see* Michael T. McCarty, "Recent Developments: USA Patriot Act," *Harvard Journal on Legislation* 39 (2002).

39. "The President's Radio Address," September 29, 2001, *Public Papers*, www.presidency.ucsb.edu.

40. Greenberg et al., *supra* note 2, at xi.

41. For example, the domestic-surveillance program was rationalized by Bush's assertion that his war powers naturally undermined any limitation legislated before the attacks (John Yoo, "The Terrorist Surveillance Program and the Constitution," *George Mason Law Review* 14, no. 3 [2007]: 565–604).

42. Cited in Karen Greenberg, *Rogue Justice: The Making of the Security State* (New York: Crown, 2016), 263.

43. Cited in Greenberg et al., *supra* note 2, at xi.

44. David Cole, *Engines of Liberty: The Power of Citizen Activism* (New York: Basic Books, 2016), 190.

45. *Id.*

46. On the evening of the arguments given in *Hamdi* and *Padilla*, CBS broadcast photographs on *60 Minutes II* showing U.S. Army personnel engaged in physical and sexual abuse of prisoners at Abu Ghraib prison. The photographs, which immediately became symbols of the war, helped fuel protests over the conduct of the war. It was later revealed that CBS executives had withheld the report for almost two weeks at the request of Defense Department officials. They finally broadcast the photographs when they got wind that the *New Yorker* was working on a report by Seymour Hersh on the same subject (*see generally* Dan Rather, *60 Minutes: Abuse at Abu Ghraib*, May 5, 2004, cbs.com).

47. Joseph Margulies, *Guantanamo and the Abuse of Presidential Power* (New York: Simon and Schuster, 2007), 152.

48. Jonathan Mahler, "Why This Court Keeps Rebuking This President," *New York Times*, June 15, 2008, WK3.

49. Military Order, "Detention, Treatment, and Trial of Certain Non-citizens in the War against Terrorism," November 13, 2001, Fed. Reg. 66, 222.

50. This was a created category (*Ex parte Quirin* (1942)). The *Ex parte Quirin* Court used the term "enemy combatant" as a way to distinguish between the historical meanings of unlawful and lawful combatants: "unlawful combatants [we]re . . . subject to capture and detention[,] . . . to trial and punishment by military tribunals," and an unlawful combatant was defined as a "spy who secretly and without uniform passes the military lines of a belligerent in time of war, seeking to gather military information and communicate it to the enemy, or an enemy combatant who without uniform comes secretly through the lines for the purpose of waging war by destruction of life or property" (*id.* at 30–31).

51. Greenberg et al., *supra* note 2, at x.

52. *Id.*

53. *Id.*

54. Such protections as shelter, food, soap, and clothes ("Fact Sheet: Status of Detainees at Guantanamo," February 7, 2002, www.presidency.ucsb).

55. Military Order, *supra* note 49.

56. Cole, *supra* note 44, at 157.

57. Ty S. W. Twibell, "The Road to Internment: Special Registration and Other Human Rights Violations of Arabs and Muslims in the U.S.," *Vermont Law Review* 29, no. 407 (2005): 549.

58. *See generally* Jennifer Harper, "Journalists Prepare to See War from the Battlefield," *Washington Times*, March 4, 2003, A5.

59. *See generally* Robin Wagner-Pacifici, "The Innocuousness of State Lethality in an Age of National Security," in *States of Violence: War, Capital Punishment, and Letting Die*, ed. Austin Sarat and Jennifer Culbert (Baltimore: John Hopkins University, 2009).

60. *See* "Victory in Iraq or Victory in the Polls," *Editor and Publisher*, December 3, 2005, 1.

61. *See* Koh, *supra* chap. 1, note 3, at 137.

62. Cole, *supra* note 44, at 153

63. *Id.*

64. *Quirin* upheld military commission trials and executions during World War II. In fact, Bush's military tribunal order was shaped by FDR's order upheld in *Quirin* (*see* Jack L. Goldman and Cass R. Sunstein, "Military Tribunals and Legal Culture: What a Difference Sixty Years Makes," *Constitutional Commentary* 19 (2002).

65. Cole, *supra* note 44, at 163.

66. *See* Donald D. Rotunda, "The Detainee Cases of 2004 and 2006 and Their Aftermath Generally," *Syracuse Law Review* 57, no. 1 (2006–2007).

67. Cole, *supra* note 44, at 170. In fact, Fred Korematsu had submitted an amicus brief in support of *Rasul* noting that "history teaches that we tend to sacrifice civil liberties too quickly based on claims of military necessity and national security" (Brief for Rasul as Amici Curiae Supporting Petitioner, *Rasul v. Bush*, 542 U.S. 466 (2004) (Nos. 03-334, 03-343), 2004 WL 103832, at *3). John Paul Stevens was fully aware of the Court's historical case history and seemed intent on not retracing it (Jeffrey Toobin, "After Stevens: What Will the Supreme Court Be Like without Its Liberal Leader?" *New Yorker*, March 22, 2010).

68. Cole, *supra* note 44, at 191.

69. *Id.*

70. *Hirabayashi* at 93.

71. *New York Times Co.* at 722 (1971) (Douglas, W., joined by Black, H., concurring).

72. *Hamdi v. Rumsfeld*, 542 U.S. 507 (2004) at 521 (emphasis added).

73. Draft memorandum 2004, cited in Margulies, *supra* note 47, at 145.

74. 2004 WL 1432134.

75. Cole, *supra* note 44, at 160; *see also* Ava Gruber, "Raising the Red Flag: The Continued Relevance of the Japanese Internment in the Post-Hamdi World," *University of Kansas Law Review* 54, no. 307 (2006): 310.

76. *Eisentrager* at 768, 779.

77. *Id.* at 779.

78. Cliff Sloan, a clerk for Stevens in the mid-eighties, noted that "[t]he Second World War was the defining experience of his life." He went on to say that "[n]o one can challenge his patriotism, and that's why he was the right guy to take on the Bush Administration's position at that time in that way" (*see* Toobin, *supra* note 67, at 1437). When justices on the Court defer too much to the purported expertise of the executive on matters of national security, it results in questionable decision making (*id.*). This was the case during and after World War I, when the Court upheld several questionable prosecutions of political dissenters on the ground that their advocacy put the nation in danger. Interestingly, in a memo to Justice Wiley B. Rutledge, when Stevens served as his clerk, he wrote, "I should think that even an alien enemy ought to be entitled to a fair hearing on the question [of] whether he is in fact dangerous" (Joseph T. Thai, "The Law Clerk Who Wrote *Rasul v. Bush*," *Virginia Law Review* 92 [2006]: 501). While a 6–3 majority in *Ahrens v. Clark* (335 U.S. 188 (1948)) saw it the other way, Stevens collaborated with Rutledge, writing a rather long dissent. In 1973, Stevens and Rutledge were vindicated when the Court essentially overruled the precedent set in *Ahrens*. The dissent in *Ahrens*, Stevens said, was applicable in the detainee case (*see* Toobin, *supra* note 67). In fact, Stevens cited Rutledge's dissent in the *Ahrens* case. Joseph Thai, a law clerk for Stevens, concluded that "Stevens' work on *Ahrens* as a law clerk exerted a remarkable influence over the *Rasul* decision" (*see* Thai, 501).

79. *Rasul* at 478–81.

80. Petitioners' brief at 31–32, *Rasul v. Bush*, 542 U.S. 466 (2004) (No. 03-334), 2004 WL 96762.

81. *Rasul* at 485.

82. *Id.* at 484.

83. *Braden v. 30th Judicial Circuit Court of Kentucky*, 410 U.S. 484 (1973).

84. Rotunda, *supra* note 66, at 13.

85. *Rasul* at 485.

86. *United States v. Nixon*, 418 U.S. 683 (1974).

87. *Rasul* at 506.

88. *Id.* at 481. Antonin Scalia noted that the Court's ruling allowed Guantanamo Bay detainees to file petitions in any one of the ninety-four federal judicial districts, essentially allowing them to "forum shop," which was strictly prohibited by statute (*id.* at 482).

89. *Id.* at 476.

90. *Id.* at 480.

91. *Id.*

92. Cole, *supra* note 44, at 161.

93. *Id.*; *Hamdi* at 532–33.

94. *Hamdi* at 509.

95. *Hamdi v. Rumsfeld*, 296 F. 3d 278 (4th Cir. 2002).

96. No. 02-439 E.D. Va.; *Hamdi II*, 296 F. 3d 278, 279, 283 (2002).

97. *Hamdi II.*

98. *Id.* The Fourth Circuit cited *Curtiss-Wright* (1936), *Dames* (1981), and the *Prize Cases* (1863).

99. *Hamdi II* at 283–84.

100. *Id.* at 113–16, 283, 284.

101. Rotunda, *supra* note 66, at 15.

102. *Hamdi* at 553 (Souter, D., joined by Ginsburg, R., concurring in part, dissenting in part, and concurring in the judgment).

103. *Id.* at 579.

104. *Id.* at 516.

105. *Id.*

106. *Id.* at 518.

107. *Id.* at 515.

108. *Id.*

109. *Id.* at 512; AUMF, Public Law 107-40, Sec. 1–2, 115 Stat. 224 (2001).

110. *Hamdi* at 541 (Souter, D., dissenting).

111. *Id.* at 533.

112. *Id.* at 509.

113. *Id.* at 554–55.

114. *Id.* at 536 (emphasis in original).

115. *Id.* at 538.

116. *Id.* at 533–34.

117. *Id.* at 533.

118. *Id.* at 533–36.

119. *Id.* at 534 (emphasis in original).

120. *Id.* at 534–35 (citation omitted).

121. *Id.* at 540.

122. *Id.* at 579. This reasoning was similar to Hugo Black's majority opinion in *Korematsu.*

123. *Id.*

124. *Id.* at 592.

125. *Id.* at 581 (quoting Hamilton, *Federalist Papers* No. 74, in Earle, *supra* chap. 1, note 24).

126. Just as George Sutherland exaggerated John Marshall's "sole-organ" doctrine, Clarence Thomas committed the same error in *Hamdi.* He stated, "The president is the sole organ of the nation in its external relations, and its sole representative with foreign nations," adding that "the Constitution vests in the President executive power, which provides that the president is commander-in-chief of the armed forces" (*id.* at 581).

127. *Id.* at 584 (citing *Dames* at 668, quoting *Youngstown* at 637) (Jackson, R., concurring); *see generally* David Adler's discussion on inherent power (David Gray Adler, "The Steel Seizure Case and Inherent Presidential Power," *Constitutional Commentary* 19 [2002]: 163–95).

128. *Hamdi* at 595 (citing *Haig v. Agee*, 453 U.S. 280 [1981]).

129. *Id.* at 509.

130. *Id.* at 533, 535.

131. *Padilla v. Hanft*, 2005 WL 2175946, C.A. 4 (S.C.).

132. *Id.* at 446.

133. *Id.* at 426.

134. *Id.* at 451.

135. *Id.* at 430.

136. *Hamdi* at 518.

137. *Ex parte Quirin* at 37.

138. Powell, *supra* chap. 4, note 135, at xiv.

139. *Padilla* at 545 (Kennedy, A., concurring).

140. *Ex parte Quirin* (1942).

141. Greenberg et al., *supra* note 2, at xiii.

142. *Id.*

143. Linda Hirshman, *Sisters in Law* (New York: HarperCollins, 2015). Sandra Day O'Connor's final year on the Court was her last opportunity to vigorously advocate for a system that would keep the government bound to the core conservative values of the Constitution.

144. Bush desired an individual with judicial experience and a proven ideological track record. He also wanted to avoid what he regarded as the mistakes of his predecessors. David Souter was a nominee whose views turned out to be a surprise, at least to conservatives.

145. *See generally* Lisa Tucker McElroy, *John G. Roberts, Jr.: Chief Justice* (Minneapolis, Minn.: Lerner Publications, 2007).

146. *Hamdan v. Rumsfeld*, 415 F. 3d 33 (D.C. Circuit) (2005).

147. *Id.*

148. John Burns, "The Iraqi Election: The Process; The Vote, and Democracy Itself, Leave Anxious Iraqis Divided," *New York Times*, January 30, 2005.

149. Dexter Filkins, "844 in U.S. Military Killed in Iraq in 2005," *New York Times*, January 1, 2006.

150. *See* "Presidential Approval Ratings—George W. Bush," http://www.gallup.com/poll/116500/presidential-approval-ratings-george-bush.aspx, accessed April 10, 2017.

151. Bush initially considered Harriet Miers. There was no one more devoted to him or his agenda than Miers. Unfortunately, her nomination quickly became a political joke, and within twenty-three days, she dropped out (*see* "Why Miers Withdrew as Supreme Court Nominee," *NPR*, October 27, 2005; and "Q&A: Miers Withdraws; What's Next?" *NPR*, October 27, 2005).

152. For example, Samuel Alito had an opportunity to usher *Roe v. Wade* (410 U.S. 113 (1973)) to its demise. Writing his own opinion in *Planned Parenthood of Southeastern Pennsylvania v. Casey* (505 U.S. 833 (1992)), Alito stated that he would have approved the Pennsylvania law in full, giving states a road map to restrict abortions as much as possible without outlawing the practice altogether. However, the following year, O'Connor, Kennedy, and Souter saved *Roe* in their joint opinion. Interestingly, John Roberts, then the deputy solicitor general, signed a brief urging the justices of the Court to overrule *Roe* once and for all. Now, the very judge who had wanted *Roe* overturned was being nominated to replace O'Connor.

153. "The President's News Conference," *Public Papers*, December 19, 2005. The committee vote went along party lines, 10–8. When the vote went to the Senate floor (January 31), Alito's opponents found forty-two votes against him, which was more than the forty needed for a filibuster. But many of the senators voting against Alito made it clear that they would not support a filibuster; consequently, the fifty-eight votes in favor amounted to a comfortable margin of victory for Alito's confirmation (David Stout, "Alito Is Sworn In as Justice after 58–42 Vote to Confirm Him," *New York Times*, January 31, 2006).

154. Cited in Greenberg, *supra* note 42, at 130.

155. *Hamdi* at 507, 519–20, 521–22.

156. *Hamdan* at 577–60.

157. Emily Hartz, *From the American Civil War to the War on Terror: Three Models of Emergency Law in the U.S. Supreme Court* (Berlin: Springer-Verlag, 2013), 10.

158. *Id.* at 10.

159. William Winthrop, *Military Law and Precedents* (Washington, D.C.: U.S. Government Printing Office, 1920), 831.

160. Emily Hartz, "From *Milligan* to *Boumediene*: Three Models of Emergency Ju-

risprudence in the American Supreme Court," *Baltic Journal of Law and Politics* 3, no. 2 (2010): 92.

161. Emily Hartz and Dimitrios Kyritsis, "*Boumediene* and the Meaning of Separation of Powers in Emergency Law," *Review of Constitutional Studies* 15, no. 1 (2010): 179

162. Public Law 109-148 of December 20, 2007, Title X; 119 Stat. 2739.

163. Hartz, *supra* note 157, at 104; *see Boumediene v. Bush*, 553 U.S. 723 at 792, 765.

164. Order Establishing Combatant Status Review Tribunals (CSRTs) established by Deputy Secretary of Defense, June 7, 2004, www.dod.gov/news/Sep2004/d2004091ad minreview.pdf.

165. Also known as HR-6166. Public Law 109-366, 120 Stat. 2600 (October 17, 2006), enacting Chapter 47A of title 10 of the U.S. Code (as well as amending Section 2241 of Title 28).

166. *Id.* at Sec. 3(a)(1)(IV)(949a)(b)(E)(ii) and evidence obtained through coercion (*id.* at Sec. 3(a)(1)(III)(948t)(d)).

167. Greenberg et al., *supra* note 2, at xiii.

168. *Hamdan v. Rumsfeld*, 415 F. 3d 33 (2005) (Circuit Judge Randolph, majority opinion).

169. *Id.*

170. *Hamdan* at 2750.

171. *Id.* at 2751.

172. *Id.* at 2800 (Kennedy, A., concurring) (*see also id.* at 2799 (Breyer, S., concurring)).

173. *Id.* at 2775 (citing *Hamdi* (2004)).

174. *Id.* at 2775 (citing *Hamdi* at 518, *Quirin* at 28–29, and In re *Yamashita*, 327 U.S. 1 (1946) at 11)).

175. *Id.* at 2775.

176. *Id.* at 2796–97.

177. *Id.* (emphasis added).

178. *Id.* at 2750.

179. *Id.* at 2797–98.

180. *Id.* at 2788.

181. *Id.* at 2792.

182. *Id.* at 2804.

183. *Id.* at 2797.

184. *Id.* at 2765–66 (Breyer, S., concurring).

185. *Id.* at 2762 (quoting 28 U.S.C. Sec. 2241(e)).

186. 28 U.S.C.A. Sec. 2241(e) (Supp. 2007).

187. *Hamdan* at 2799.

188. *Id.* at 666.

189. *Id.* at 653.

190. App. to Pet. for Cert. 64a.

191. *Id.* at 65a–67a; *Hamdan* at 2828.

192. *See Prize Cases* at 670.

193. *Hamdan* at 2760.

194. Savage, *supra* chap. 2, note 140, at 208.

195. *Id.* at 333; Public Law 110–55, 121 Stat. 552.

196. Savage, *supra* chap. 2, note 140, at 205–8.

197. The Suspension Clause allowed for habeas to be suspended only "when in Cases of Rebellion or Invasion the public safety may require it" (*Boumediene* at 3).

198. *Boumediene* at 8, 52.

199. *Id.* at 48.

200. *Id.* at 6.

201. Antiterrorism and Effective Death Penalty Act of 1996, Public Law 104-132, 110 Stat. 1214 (also known as AEDPA).

202. *Boumediene* at 52–70.

203. *Id.* at 67.

204. *Id.* at 68.

205. *Id.* at 70.

206. Alito and Roberts vindicated their appointments when they dissented in favor of the administration in *Boumediene* (*see generally* Dahl, *supra* chap. 2, note 142).

207. *Boumediene* at 83.

208. *Id.* at 82.

209. *Id.* at 68, 76–80.

210. *Id.* at 90.

211. *Id.* at 92.

212. *Id.* at 93.

213. *Id.* at 95.

214. *Hamdi* at 532; *Boumediene* at 95.

215. Fritz Synder, "Overreaction Then (*Korematsu*) and Now (the Detainee Cases)," *The Critique: A Critical Studies Journal* 2, no. 1 (2009): 105.

216. *Boumediene* at 2249 (Scalia, A., dissenting).

217. *Boumediene* at 2307 (Scalia, A., dissenting). It should be noted that there are two concerns with Scalia's findings. First, Iraq had nothing to do with the September attacks (Snyder, *supra* note 215, at 105). Second, according to Mark Denbeaux et al., the release of thirty prisoners did not return them to the battlefield (Mark Denbeaux et al., *Justice Scalia, the Department of Defense, and the Perpetuation of an Urban Legend: The Truth about Recidivism of Released Guantanamo Detainees*, Center for Policy and Research, Guantanamo Report, June 2008, 2–3).

218. Even without this decision, the Bush election was the epitome of Stephen Skowronek's definition of the election of a leader who was more concerned with adapting existing commitments than rejecting them. Bush not only noted in his 2000 campaign book (*A Charge to Keep*) his loyalty to completing the work of the Reagan Revolution (Skowronek, *supra* chap. 1, note 95, at 130) but also, through a wide range of domestic concerns, banked on the support of the judiciary to confirm his priorities as an affiliated leader. *See, e.g., Zelman v. Simmons-Harris*, 536 U.S. 639 (2002). In this instance, when Republicans could not get school-choice vouchers passed as part of "No Child Left Behind" (2001), Bush efficaciously admonished the Court to eliminate federal constitutional obstacles in similar state programs. This directive enabled the vouchers to find tolerable political ground.

219. *Cheney v. U.S. District Court of the District of Columbia*, 124 S. Ct. 1391 (2004). To shield White House deliberations from public view, President Bush invoked executive privilege. Presidents often justify closed-door deliberations to ensure that their advisers can speak freely, but this confidentiality often extends from the deliberations to the ensuing decisions. Congress, the deliberative body, is often excluded from this decision-making process and hears presidential policy choices, oftentimes, when the public does. In fact, many perceived national-security directives issued by presidents have been used to initiate secret missions by intelligence and defense agencies (*see* Christopher Simpson, *National Security Directives of the Reagan and Bush Administrations* [Boulder, Colo.: Westview Press, 1995]).

220. Maltzman et al., *supra* chap. 1, note 76.

221. McGuire and Palmer, *supra* chap. 2, note 92, at 691–702.

222. *See* Damrosch, *supra* chap. 1, note 6, at 87–97.

223. *See* Louis Fisher, "Judicial Review of the War Power," *Presidential Studies Quarterly* 35 (2005): 466, 484–88; *see also* Neal Devins, "Congress, the Supreme Court, and Enemy Combatants: How Lawmakers Buoyed Judicial Supremacy by Placing Limits on Federal Court Jurisdiction," *College of William and Mary Law School Faculty Publications*, Paper 345, 2007.

224. Corwin, *supra* chap. 1, note 11, at 16.

225. John Yoo, *The Powers of War and Peace: The Constitution and Foreign Affairs after 9/11* (Chicago: University of Chicago Press, 2006), 574–75.

226. *See* Mark Graber, "Forward: From the Countermajoritarian Difficulty to Juristocracy and the Political Construction of Judicial Power," *Maryland Law Review* 69, no. 1 (2006): 7. An affiliated president can accomplish policy objectives that split the party base by getting the courts involved and having them take the majority of the blame; *see also* Whittington's discussion of *Shelley v. Kraemer*, 334 U.S. 1 (1948) and *Baker* (1962) (*supra* chap. 1, note 117, at 126–34).

227. *See* Jack Balkin and Sandford Levinson, "The Process of Constitutional Change: From Partisan Entrenchment to the National Surveillance State," *Fordham Law Review* 75, no. 2 (2006): 489–535.

228. *See generally* Tushnet, *supra* chap. 1, note 8.

229. *See* Kim Lane Scheppele, "Law in a Time of Emergency: States of Exception and the Temptations of 9/11," *University of Pennsylvania Journal of Constitutional Law* 6 (2004): 1001.

230. Greenberg, *supra* note 42, at 248.

231. *Id.* at 249.

CONCLUSION

1. *See* Tushnet, *supra* chap. 1, note 92, at 117–37.

2. Whittington, *supra* chap. 1, note 117, at 75.

3. Lee Epstein et al., "The Supreme Court during Crisis," *New York University Law Review* 80, no. 1 (2005): 1

4. Whittington, *supra* chap. 1, note 117, at 292–93.

5. *Id.* at 166.

6. *Id.* at 158.

7. Charlie Savage, *Power Wars: Inside Obama's Post-9/11 Presidency* (New York: Little, Brown, 2015), 37.

8. *Id.* at 39.

9. *Id.* at 37.

10. Savage, *supra* chap. 2, note 140, at 37.

11. Corwin, *supra* chap. 1, note 11, at 29.

12. Griffin, *supra* chap. 1, note 16.

13. Corwin, *supra* chap. 1, note 11, at 29, 26, 93, 304–5, 199, 200.

14. James Buchanan attempted this when he explained in his inaugural address that he would "cheerfully submit" to the *Dred Scott v. Sandford*, 60 U.S. 393 (1857), ruling, "whatever this may be" (Mark Graber, *Dred Scott and the Problem of Constitutional Evil* [New York: Cambridge University Press, 2006], 33–34; and James D. Richardson, ed., *A Compilation of the Messages and Papers of the Presidents*, vol. 5 [Washington, D.C.: U.S. Government Printing Office, 1899], 431).

15. Orren and Skowronek, *supra* chap. 1, note 101.

16. Edward G. White, *The Constitution and the New Deal* (Cambridge, Mass.: Harvard University Press, 2000), 200.

17. *Id.*

18. *Id.*

19. *See* Wayne D. Moore, "(Re)Construction of Constitutional Authority and Meaning: The Fourteenth Amendment and Slaughter-House Cases," in Kahn and Kersch, *supra* chap. 1, note 120, at 229–74; *see also* Graber, *supra* chap. 1, note 83, at 33–66.

20. Savage, *supra* chap. 2, note 140, at 347.

21. Savage, *supra* note 7, at 557.

22. *Id.*

23. *Id.*

24. White, *supra* note 16, at 77.

25. *Id.* at 80.

26. *Belmont* at 331, 334, 336.

27. For example, Bruce Ackerman (*supra* chap. 1, note 80) asserts that the modern Constitution started in 1937, whereas Stephen Skowronek maintains that Franklin D. Roosevelt's reconstruction of a new political regime began with his first term (1933).

28. I recognize that this point is controversial. It is arguable that presidents began to assert unilateral authority in foreign affairs well before the *Curtiss-Wright* Court defined the sole-organ doctrine. For example, Theodore Roosevelt repeatedly ignored or defied Congress (e.g., Panama Canal, treaty with Santo Domingo, the Great White Fleet). I am not suggesting that presidents have not ignored or defied Congress over the years. However, this book shows that the Court is instrumental in carving out the constitutional jurisprudence and constitutional politics for an executive's unilateral authority in foreign affairs.

29. White, *supra* note 16, at 42; *see also* Quincy Wright, *The Control of American Foreign Relations* (New York: Macmillan, 1922).

30. *Youngstown* at 632.

31. *See* White, *supra* note 16, at 52.

32. For example, the political-question doctrine, grounds of nonjusticiability, and the silence and inaction of Congress (*see* Adler, *supra* chap. 1, note 2).

33. *Youngstown* at 585, 587.

34. Damrosch, *supra* chap. 1, note 6, at 87–97.

35. As with so many briefs before, the Justice Department relied on *Curtiss-Wright* as a precedent to claim exclusive and plenary powers for the Barack Obama administration (U.S. Justice Department, "Brief for the Respondent," *Zivotofsky v. Kerry*, U.S. Supreme Court, No. 13-628, September 2014).

36. *Zivotofsky* at 10.

37. *Id.* at 15.

38. Fisher, *supra* chap. 2, note 91.

39. Fletcher, *supra* chap. 1, note 19 ("Truman's Rhetoric").

40. *See* Graber, *supra* chap. 1, note 83, at 12.

41. Whittington, *supra* chap. 1, note 117, at 294.

42. *Id.*

43. Tushnet, *supra* chap. 1, note 92, at 124.

44. Epstein et al., *supra* note 3, at 3.

45. Lee Epstein et al., "The Effect of War on the Supreme Court," in *Principles and Practice in American Politics: Classic and Contemporary Readings*, ed. Samuel Kernell and Steven S. Smith, 3d ed. (Thousand Oaks, Calif.: Congressional Quarterly Press, 2006), 2.

46. For example, *United States v. United States District Court (Keith)*, 407 U.S. 297 (1972); *New York Times Co.* (1971); *see also Tinker v. Des Moines*, 393 U.S. 503 (1969); and Sanford J. Ungar, *The Papers and the Papers: An Account of the Legal and Political Battle over the Pentagon Papers*, vol. 14 (New York: E. P. Dutton, 1972).

47. *See* Ronald Kahn and his discussion of the mutual-construction process (*supra* chap. 1, note 69).

48. *Boumediene* at 8, 52 (Kennedy, A., majority opinion).

49. Savage, *supra* chap. 2, note 140, at 349.

50. *See generally* Whittington, *supra* chap. 1, note 117. Keith Whittington notes that at times, various political actors—in this instance, the executive—seek to supplant other potential constitutional interpreters (the Court, in this case) and assert their own authority to define the powers or "content of contested constitutional principles" (*id.* at 15).

51. *Cooper v. Aaron*, 358 U.S. 1, 17 (1958).

52. Mayer, *supra* chap. 6, note 17, at 8 (quoting Arthur Schlesinger Jr.).

53. Savage, *supra* chap. 2, note 140, at 349.

54. *Id.*

55. Cited in Savage, *supra* note 7, at 75 (Dick Cheney, December 30, 2009, quoted in Devin Dwyer, "Cheney Rips Obama: President 'Trying to Pretend' U.S. Is Not at War," *ABC News*, December 30, 2009).

56. *Id.*

57. *Id.* at 223.

58. "Umar Farouk Abbdulmutallab Sentenced to Life in Prison for Attempted Bombing of Flight 253 on Christmas Day 2009," *The United States Department of Justice: Justice News*, February 16, 2012, https://www.justice.gov/opa/pr/umar-farouk-abdulmutallab-sentenced-life-prison-attempted-bombing-flight-253-christmas-day.

59. Savage, *supra* note 7, at 348.

60. *Youngstown* at 635.

61. *Dames* at 673–74.

62. *See generally* Fisher, *supra* chap. 1, note 2, at 270–77.

63. For example, *Immigration and Naturalization Service v. Chadha*, 462 U.S. 919 (1983); *Crockett v. Reagan*, 558 F. Supp. 893 (D.D.C. 1982), *affirmed per curiam*, 720 F. 2d 1355 (D.C. Cir. 1983), *cert. denied*, 467 U.S. 1251 (1984); *Sanchez-Espinoza v. Reagan*, 568 F. Supp. 596 (D.D.C. 1983), *affirmed*, 770 F. 2d 202 (D.C. Cir. 1985); *Conyers v. Reagan*, 578 F. Supp. 324 (D.D.C. 1984), *affirmed*, 765 F. 2d 1124 (D.C. Cir. 1985); *Lowry v. Reagan*, 676 F. Supp. 333 (D.D.C. 1987), *affirmed*, No. 87-5426 (D.C. Cir. 1988); *Dellums v. Bush*, 752 F. Supp. 1141 (D.D.C. 1990); *Campbell v. Clinton*, 203 F. 3d 19 (D.C. Cir. 2000); *Doe v. Bush*, 323 F. 3d 133 (1st Cir. 2003); and *Kucinich v. Obama*, 2011 U.S. Dist. LEXIS 121349.

64. Whittington, *supra* chap. 1, note 117, at 289.

65. *Id.* at 295

66. *Id.* at 287.

67. Orren and Skowronek, *supra* chap. 1, note 101, at 123.

68. Whittington, *supra* chap. 1, note 117, at 291.

69. *Id.*

70. *Id.*

71. *Id.* at 160.

72. *Id.* at 292.

73. Kahn, *supra* chap. 1, note 69; *see also* Gretchen Ritter, who also adheres to this assertion (Gretchen Ritter, *The Constitution as Social Design: Gender and Civic Membership in the American Constitutional Order* [Stanford, Calif.: Stanford University Press, 2006]).

74. Whittington, *supra* chap. 1, note 117, at 295.
75. *Id.* at 73.
76. Graber, *supra* chap. 1, note 90, at 37–61.
77. Whittington, *supra* chap. 1, note 117, at 73.
78. *Id.* at 161.
79. *See generally* Powell, *supra* chap. 4, note 135.

SELECTED CASES CITED

Cases included are those involving foreign affairs, national-security concerns, discretionary and unreviewable executive authority, and the Supreme Court's use of precedent.

Abrams v. United States, 250 U.S. 616 (1919)
Ahrens v. Clark, 335 U.S. 188 (1948)
A.L.A. Schechter Brothers Poultry Corp. v. United States, 295 U.S. 495 (1935)
American Int'l Group, Inc., et al. v. Islamic Republic of Iran, et al., 657 F. 2d 430 (D.C. Cir. 1981)
Aptheker v. Secretary of State, 378 U.S. 500 (1964)
Baker v. Carr, 369 U.S. 186 (1962)
Bas v. Tingy, 4 U.S. 37 (1800)
Boumediene v. Bush, 553 U.S. 723 (2008); 128 S. Ct. 2229 (2008)
Bowles v. Willingham, 321 U.S. 503 (1944)
Bush v. Gore, 531 U.S. 98 (2000)
Cargo of the Brig Aurora v. United States, 11 U.S. 382, 388 (1813)
Carter v. Carter Coal Co., 298 U.S. 238 (1936)
Chas. T. Main Int'l, Inc. v. Khuzestan Water and Power Auth., 651 F. 2d 800 (1st Cir. 1981)
Cheney v. U.S. District Court of the District of Columbia, 124 S. Ct. 1391 (2004)
Chevron U.S.A., Inc. v. Natural Resources Defense Council, Inc., 467 U.S. 837 (1984)
Crockett v. Reagan, 558 F. Supp. 893, 899 (D.D.C. 1982), aff'd, 720 F. 2d 1355 (D.C. Cir. 1983)
Cunningham v. Neagle, 135 U.S. 1 (1890)
Dames and Moore v. Regan, 453 U.S. 654 (1981)
Debs v. United States, 249 U.S. 211 (1919)
Dellums v. Bush, 752 F. Supp. 1141 (1990)
Duncan v. Kahanamoku, 327 U.S. 304 (1946)
Durand v. Hollins, 4 Blatch. 451 (1860)

Ex parte Mitsuye Endo, 323 U.S. 283 (1944)

Ex parte Quirin, 317 U.S. 1 (1942)

Fleming v. Page, 50 U.S. 603 (1850)

Fong Yue Ting v. United States, 149 U.S. 698 (1893)

Frohwerk v. United States, 249 U.S. 204 (1919)

Gilbert v. Minnesota, 254 U.S. 325 (1920)

Goldwater v. Carter, 444 U.S. 996 (1979)

Haig v. Agee, 453 U.S. 280 (1981)

Hamdan v. Rumsfeld, 415 F. 3d 33 (2005), 548 U.S. 557 (2006), 126 S. Ct. 2749 (2006)

Hamdi v. Rumsfeld, 542 U.S. 507 (2004)

Hirabayashi v. United States, 320 U.S. 81 (1943)

Holtzman v. Schlesinger, 414 U.S. 1316 (1973)

Home Building and Loan Association v. Blaisdell, 290 U.S. 398 (1934)

Humphrey's Executor v. United States, 295 U.S. 602 (1935)

Johnson v. Eisentrager, 339 U.S. 763 (1950)

J. W. Hampton, Jr. and Co. v. United States, 276 U.S. 394 (1928)

Kent v. Dulles, 357 U.S. 116 (1958)

Korematsu v. United States, 323 U.S. 214 (1944)

Kucinich v. Bush, 236 F. Supp. 2d 1 (D.D.C. 2002)

Lichter v. United States, 334 U.S. 742 (1948)

Little v. Barreme, 6 U.S. 170 (1804)

Lowry v. Reagan, 676 F. Supp. 333 (D.D.C. 1987)

McCulloch v. Maryland, 17 U.S. 316 (1819)

Miller v. The Ship Resolution, 2 U.S. 19 (1782)

Missouri v. Holland, 252 U.S. 416 (1920)

Myers v. United States, 272 U.S. 52 (1926)

New York Times Co. v. United States, 403 U.S. 713 (1971)

NLRB v. Jones and Laughlin Steel Corp., 301 U.S. 1 (1937)

Orvis v. Brownell, 345 U.S. 183 (1953)

Panama Refining Co. v. Ryan, 293 U.S. 388 (1935)

Pierce v. United States, 252 U.S. 239 (1920)

Planned Parenthood of Southern Pennsylvania v. Casey, 505 U.S. 833 (1992)

Prize Cases, 67 U.S. 635 (1863)

Rasul v. Bush, 542 U.S. 466 (2004)

Regan v. Wald, 468 U.S. 222 (1984)

Reid v. Covert, 354 U.S. 1 (1957)

Rumsfeld v. Padilla, 542 U.S. 426 (2004)

Sanchez-Espinoza v. Reagan, 568 F. Supp. 596 (D.D.C. 1983), 770 F. 2d 202 (D.C. Cir. 1985)

Schaefer v. United States, 251 U.S. 466 (1920)

Schenck v. United States, 249 U.S. 47 (1919)

Talbot v. Seeman, 5 U.S. 1 (1801)

United States v. Belmont, 301 U.S. 324 (1937)

United States v. Bethlehem Steel Corp., 315 U.S. 289 (1942)

United States v. Curtiss-Wright Exp. Corp., 14 F. Supp. 230 (S.D.N.Y. 1936), 299 U.S. 304 (1936)

United States v. E. C. Knight Co., 156 U.S. 1 (1895)

United States v. Nixon, 418 U.S. 683 (1974)

United States v. O'Brien, 391 U.S. 367 (1968)

United States v. Pink, 315 U.S. 203 (1942)
United States v. Smith, 27 F. Cas. 1192 (C.C.D.N.Y. 1806) (No. 16342)
Yakus v. United States, 321 U.S. 414 (1944)
Yasui v. United States, 320 U.S. 115 (1943)
Youngstown Sheet and Tube Co. v. Sawyer, 343 U.S. 579 (1952)
Zemel v. Rusk, 381 U.S. 1 (1965)
Zivotofsky v. Kerry, 576 U.S. ___ (2015)

INDEX

KIMBERLEY L. FLETCHER is an Assistant Professor of Political Science at San Diego State University.